T0291211

Corporate Governance in China:
An Empirical Investigation

Chen Yinghui

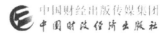

Preface

This study empirically investigates corporate governance issues in China. Chapter 1 examines the effects of the cumulative voting (CV) reform in corporate China on firm – level governance. Evidence based on a sub – sample indicates that CV adoption rebalances the power structure of corporate board. CV implementation also generates positive changes in the personal characteristics of directors. Additional evidence demonstrates that firm – level and province – level governance in China are substitutes. Province – level governance environments also have an important effect on the validity of CV adoption. Chapter 2 explores whether the use of CV produces substantial effects on firm value and corporate policies. However, no consistent evidence indicates that CV adoption has a significant effect on firm performance. No evidence demonstrates that CV adoption can effectively curb tunneling activities from large shareholders, although CV adoption encourages potentially beneficial related party transactions. Chapter 3 probes whether investors from different institutional and legal environments pay different attentions to the quality of corporate governance based on A – and H – shares framework. Though, based on a sub – sample, evidence shows that H – share investors pay more attention to corporate governance than A – share investors, this effect is not persistent in the long run. In sum, no strong and consistent evidence indicates that salient differences exist in attitudes towards corporate governance between H – and A – share investors.

Acknowledgments

I would never been able to complete this work without the help and support of the kind people around me, to only some of whom it is possible to give particular mention here.

I would like to express my deepest gratitude to my principal supervisor, Professor Julan Du. This work would not have been possible without his excellent guidance, caring, support and patience, not to mention his advice and unsurpassed knowledge of financial economics. The good advice, support and friendship of my second supervisor, Professor Duozhe Li, has been invaluable on both academic and personal level, for which I am extremely grateful. I would also like to thank Professor Chi – Chur Chao, who gave me great help and best suggestions. I would also like to thank Professor Travis Ng, whose instructive discussion with me on this study enlightened me a lot and made this study a great improvement. I would also like to thank the other members of my committee for their beneficial suggestions.

I would like to thank Wu Sun, my fellow postgraduate, who as a good friend, was always willing to help me and give me good suggestions.

Finally, and more importantly, I would like to thank my wife Bingjie. Her support, encouragement, quiet patience and unwavering love were undeniably the bedrock upon which the past twelve years of my life have been built. Her tolerance of my occasional vulgar moods is a testament in itself of her unyielding devotion and love. She was always there cheering me up and stood by me through the good times and bad. My parents, brother have given me their unequivocal support throughout, as always, for which my mere expression of thanks likewise does not suffice.

I also acknowledge the financial support of the National Scieace Foundation of China (No. 71772179).

Contents

Chapter 1　Regulatory Reform of Cumulative Voting in Corporate China: Who Were Elected

1.1　Introduction

In emerging markets, the expropriation of minority shareholders by controlling shareholders is the primary concern in corporate governance. Regulatory authorities in such economies have recently introduced various Western corporate governance mechanisms to protect the interests of minority shareholders and help develop capital markets. For instance, the Mexican regulatory authority formulated the Code of "Best" Corporate Practices with the purpose of increasing the transparency of corporate information release to increase transparency in corporate information release and the regularity of corporate dividend payout. The China Securities Regulatory Commission (CSRC), the Chinese security market regulatory authority, has been attempting to strengthen its supervision of listed firms since the early 2000s. One prominent corporate governance mechanism is the cumulative voting (CV) scheme for board directors, which is designed to be an improvement over straight voting. CV makes possible for the minority shareholders, especially large minority shareholders or noncontrolling substantial shareholders, to be fairly represented in the board of directors by allowing them to use all of their voting power at one time. Under straight voting in board election, the vote entitlement of each shareholder is equal to the number of shares he/she holds, and each shareholder votes separately on each director nominee. By contrast, under the CV system, the vote entitlement of each shareholder is equal to the number of shares he/she holds times the number of directors to be elected. The shareholder may either cast all votes to a single candidate or distribute the votes to several candidates. Theoretically, the CV mechanism allows minority shareholders to elect their favored directors and increase their representation in the board; in effect, the possibility of a single majority shareholder controlling the entire board is avoided. Thus, the CV mechanism is widely regarded as a means of enhancing the protection of minority shareholder interests. La Porta et al. (1998) regard CV as one component of the anti – director rights (minority shareholder rights) index, which indicates the importance of CV in upholding minority shareholder interests. In 2002, the CSRC stipulated that firms with more than 30% of their outstanding shares in the hands of controlling shareholders were mandated to adopt the CV scheme in the election of two or more directors; other firms were encouraged to adopt the CV but could decide on the adoption on a voluntary basis.

The cumulative voting is a long – standing corporate governance mechanism. In the United States, CV emerged in the late 19th century, reached its peak in the first half of the 20th century, and started declining in 1950. In most states and counties, adopting the scheme is optional. At the turn of the century, a series of corporate scandals has prompted several major U. S. companies to implement CV when electing directors, including Sears – Roebuck and Company, Hewlett – Packard, and Toys "R" Us. The ups and downs that CV has experienced in the United States are probably related to its merits and demerits. On the positive side, CV may enhance corporate governance by facilitating the representation of minority shareholders in the board, involving corporate raiders and dissidents in firm decisions, and electing more outside directors. On the negative side, CV may cause troubles to the firm because the elected dissidents could lower the efficiency of corporate operations by possibly creating a stalemate in the boardroom; it may also facilitate hostile takeovers. Clearly, CV typically gains popularity when the primary concern is enhancing corporate governance and protecting minority investors.

The United States and emerging market economies stand at different stages of market economy development. In emerging economies such as China, upholding minority shareholder interests is important because of the inadequate legal institutions and weak investor protection. Ownership is highly concentrated and largely different from the relatively dispersed ownership structure in the United States. However, the risk of hostile takeovers is relatively limited in China and other emerging markets; thus, CV might be particularly potent in upholding minority shareholder interests. Very few studies have analyzed the effects of CV on corporate policy and firm performance, and whether CV has enhanced the representation of minority shareholders in the boardroom. Therefore, this study addresses such issues based on the CV reform experience in China, which was implemented in a large scale and provides a good setting for examining the effects of CV adoption.

This study raises one basic but fundamental question: Can CV adoption enhance the representation of minority shareholders on the board? We attempt to answer this question along several lines. First, we explicitly investigate whether CV has increased the proportion of the representatives of non – controlling shareholders in the board; if so, such stakeholders are likely to elect their representatives into the board under CV. Second, we analyze whether CV has enhanced the supposed "independence" of the elected non – executive independent directors; if minority shareholders play a larger role in the election of independent directors under CV, the elected independent directors should have less close relations with corporate executives than those under straight voting. Third, we examine whether CV has enhanced the professionalism and qualifications of the elected directors; if CV has reduced the dominance of controlling shareholders in picking directors, the criteria for selecting directors may shift from loyalty and conformity to professionalism and qualifications.

In dealing with the "endogeneity" or "self – selection" problem in the firm – level study of corporate governance reform schemes, we construct a control group to match the treatment group (firms that adopted CV in practice) by applying two different matching approaches. One matching method is called BL matching, a variant of the approach in Barber and Lyon (1996) and Huson et al. (2004); it searches for control-group firms based on firm size (book value of total assets), operating performance [operating income/assets (ROA)], industry, and the largest shareholder ownership share of all of the other listed companies without adopting CV. The other matching method is the "coarsened exact matching" (CEM) developed by Iacus et al. (2011, 2012). After deriving the treatment and control groups, we apply the difference – indifferences (DID) style analysis to compare the changes in the individual characteristics of directors in CV – using firms with those in non – CV – using firms.

Using a sub – sample of firms in which the top 10 largest shareholders are not related, we find that the percentage of executive directors representing the second largest shareholder is significantly higher in the CV – using firms than that in non – CV – using firms. This finding suggests that CV adoption helps reduce the dominance of the controlling shareholder in the boardroom and enhances the balance of power distribution in the boardroom.

We also find that the percentage of independent directors with close relations with firm executives, such as former colleagues or college alumni/alumnae, is smaller in CV – using firms than in non – CV – using firms. In addition, CV – using firms possess a larger proportion of independent directors with advanced professional titles, such as accountants, lawyers, engineers, and economists, compared with non – CV – using firms.

The cumulative voting is found to have raised the degree of professionalism of board directors. The percentage of executive directors who have previously worked as chief executive officers (CEOs) or chairmen and who have previously worked in the same industry has increased the CV implementation. The educational qualifications of executive directors were higher in CV – using firms than in non – CV – using firms. In addition, a small number of the CV – elected executive directors had political background, such as working for the central government, being deputies to the National People's Congress, and membership in the CPPCC. These findings are robust in the sense that the regression results from the two samples generated by the BL and CEM matching methods are consistent with each other.

We also attempt to determine the types of CV – using firms that are more likely to generate better directors using the CV rule in terms of personal characteristics. In addition, we examine the interactions between firm – level and province – level governance to verify whether improved province – level institutional and legal environments engender positive changes in director characteristics. We find CV firms located in provinces featured with relatively weak outer governance environments are more likely to elect directors with better personal characteristics.

In general, we find that province – and firm – level governance are substitutes because CV firms in provinces exhibit weak governance settings but have high probability to generate better CV – elected directors. In addition, firms with only one person acting as CEO and chairman form a barrier to the positive changes in firm – level governance. Firm age is negatively related to the changes in director characteristics, and the ratio of the share ownership of the largest shareholders to that of the second one increases the probability that the proportion of directors as representatives of the second shareholders increases after CV adoption by 0. 05. Moreover, the sum of shareholdings among the second to the tenth shareholders exhibits a positive effect on the increase of professional directors. Firms with bad performance are likewise strongly motivated to enhance firm – level governance and change existing bad situations.

This study contributes to the literature on shareholder voting mechanisms. Several studies (Bhagat and Brickley, 1984; Harris and Raviv, 1988; Grossman and Hart, 1988; DeAngelo and DeAngelo, 1985; Klapper and Love, 2004; Zingales, 1994, 1995; Bethel and Gillan, 2002; Klapper et al. , 2006; Bebchuk et al. , 2009; Iliev et al. , 2011) have previously investigated the effects of different shareholder voting mechanisms on corporate governance. None of them, however, has directly examined and compared the individual characteristics of elected directors under different corporate voting schemes. To our best knowledge, our work is the first study that directly compares director characteristics under different shareholder voting mechanisms. This research addresses the issue of whether CV has elevated the representation of minority shareholders on the board. Several earlier studies have indicated that CV positively affects corporate valuation, but these studies have failed to identify the channels through which CV influences firm performance. Thus, the results of previous studies might have been affected by confounding factors. This paper fills the void by investigating the differences in the personal characteristics of elected directors under different voting mechanisms.

This book is also related to the growing body of literature on board of directors. A substantial literature focuses on the three – way relationship among shareholders, boards, and top management (e. g. Hermalin and Weisbach, 1988, 2003; Hallock, 1997; Agrawal and Knoeber, 2001; Gompers et al. , 2003; Brick et al. , 2006; Adams et al. , 2010). For instance, Masulis et al. (2012) find that firms with foreign independent directors exhibit significantly poorer performance. Ni and Purda (2012) argue that an increase in the proportion of independent directors on a firm's board induces more conservative operating decisions, and that the cumulative effect of these decisions reduces the stock – based measures of company risk. By contrast, this paper examines the differences in the personal characteristics of directors under different shareholder voting mechanisms and focuses on whether the relations between CEO/chairman and independent directors in CV – using firms are less close than those in non – CV – using firms. Our findings indicate that the CV – using firms might enhance the "independence" of independent directors, thus implying that the implementation of the CV rule could enhance the effectiveness of independent directors in monitoring and advising.

This book is also related to a large body of literature on law and finance. For example, La Porta et al. (1998) investigate the legal rules and investor protection measures in 47 countries and reveal that only 27% of the sample countries have laws for CV or proportional representation, with German – legal – origin countries demonstrating the highest percentage (33%). Klapper and Love (2004) report a wide variation in firm – level governance and lower average firm – level governance in countries with weaker legal systems based on data on firm – level corporate governance rankings across 14 emerging markets. They also provide evidence that provisions in firm – level corporate governance matter more in countries with weaker legal environments. In addition, Price et al. (2011) examine the relationship between the efforts of Mexico to improve corporate governance and firm performance and transparency. They demonstrate that a single reform on corporate governance launched by regulators alone is insufficient to fundamentally change economic behavior. This paper attempts to determine whether provisions in firm – level corporate governance, such as CV, matter in China, a country with a weak legal environment.

This study is also related to the literature on international corporate governance. In particular, this book is closely related to the literature on the interaction between country – level and firm – level governance. Klapper and Love (2004) argue that the relationship between the two levels of governance is evident. In addition, they contend that country – level and firm – level governance are complements based on a sample of 495 firms and 25 countries. Using the Corporate Governance Quotient (CGQ) dataset provided by the Institutional Shareholder Services, Aggarwal et al. (2009) conclude that country – level and firm – level governance are positively related. Based on the same dataset but using different variable definitions and governance measures, Chhaochharia and Laeven (2009) reveal that many firms adopt governance provisions beyond those adopted by all of the firms in the country.

Francis et al. (2012) combine data used by Klapper and Love (2004) with the Dealscan database and find that firm – level and country – level corporate governance are substitutes in writing and enforcing financial contracts. Bruno and Claessens (2010) also use the CGQ data for firm – level governance; they construct a corporate governance index to measure country – level governance and find that country – level and firm – level governance are neither complements nor substitutes. The present research is different from the above – mentioned studies and is concerned with the interaction between firm – level governance and outer governance settings at the province level. Large disparities in economic development are notable among different provinces of China, and the differences in province – level governance may induce different behaviors of firms from various provinces. Therefore, focusing on this relatively micro view to explore the interaction between province – level and firm – level governance is a new and interesting contribution to the previous literature.

Owing to data unavailability, our study has several limitations, that is, we rely only on apparent "visible" connections that cannot capture hidden connections in other forms. By investigating these visible connections, we can still gauge the significant differences between CV – elected and non – CV – elected directors.

The rest of the chapter proceeds as follows. Section 1.2 presents the institutional setting and conceptual framework of this study. Section 1.3 discusses the empirical methods used in this study. Section 1.4 describes the variables and the data employed. Section 1.5 presents the findings on the relationship between CV adoption and the individual characteristics of board directors. Section 1.6 investigates factors that may induce changes in director characteristics before and after CV adoption for CV – using firms. Section 1.7 discusses the findings, and Section 1.8 concludes.

1. 2   Institutional Setting and Conceptual Framework

In emerging market economies, the concentration of corporate ownership is prevalent, and the expropriation of minority shareholder interests is a primary concern in corporate governance. At the end of 2001, the mean (median) proportion of shares owned by the controlling shareholders was 44. 2% (43. 7%) for 1129 listed firms. [1]In our sample matched by the BL method, the corresponding value is 45. 5% (44. 4%) for 1290 listed firms, and in the sample matched by the CEM process, the value is 45. 3% (44. 6%) for 1106 listed firms. On average, the proportion of shares held by the second to the tenth largest shareholders was approximately 16. 7%. In the sample matched by the BL method, the corresponding number is roughly 16. 6% for 1287 listed firms, and in the sample matched by the CEM approach, it is 16. 5% for 1105 listed firms. Thus, a high degree of ownership concentration is a salient feature of listed companies in China. Moreover, the majority of listed firms in China have parent companies that typically control multiple subsidiaries. This aspect results in the complicated listing of firm ownership structures and reduces the transparency in business operations and corporate governance. Both characteristics indicate that the conflict of interests between the controlling shareholders and the minority and other stakeholders can be potentially severe; this phenomenon is common in emerging markets, including several Asian economies (Claessens et al. , 2002).

In January 2002, the Ministry of Commerce and the CSRC jointly issued the Code of Corporate Governance for Listed Companies in China to elevate the corporate governance standards for listed firms. The content of the Code is largely similar to that of corporate governance standards implemented in developed economies, such as the OECD Principle of Corporate Governance 1999. The Code addresses a host of issues in corpo-

---

[1]   The values are obtained by own calculation according to the data provided by CSMAR, one of data sources of this paper that will be discussed later.

rate governance to enhance investor protection. Article 31 states that, "The election of directors shall fully reflect the opinions of minority shareholders. A cumulative voting system shall be earnestly advanced in shareholders' meetings for the election of directors. Listed companies that are more than 30% owned by controlling shareholders shall adopt a cumulative voting system, and the companies that do adopt such a system shall stipulate the implementing rules for such cumulative voting system in their articles of association. "[1] Regulatory authorities in China have put forward the CV rule for the first time in this Code.

We find only two CV – using firms in 2001 through our hand – collected data on director elections. [2]The Code follows the "comply – or – explain" rule, which encourages a company to report its actual corporate governance status, disclose the difference between its actual status and the status required by the Code, and provide the reasons for the existence of such a difference. Thus, many firms that should have adopted CV did not use it in practice; thus, a relative large pool of potential control group firms is created and can be useful in comparing the differences between the CV – elected directors and the non – CV – elected directors. For instance, the Code stipulates that firms whose controlling shareholders with 30% or more of the outstanding shares are mandated to adopt CV in electing two or more directors, whereas other firms are encouraged to adopt CV but they can decide on the adoption on a voluntary basis. However, in our basic sample from 2002 to 2005, many firms whose controlling shareholders have more than 30% of the outstanding shares did not adopt CV. This implementation problem is particularly relevant for emerging markets where formal institutions are generally underdeveloped (Qian and Zhao, 2011). Lu and Shi (2012) focus on the relationship between the entire Code and firm performance. The present study, however, primarily focuses on whether the characteristics of CV – elected directors differ from those of the non – CV – elected directors.

Typically, a voting scheme consists of two stages—nomination stage and election stage. CV is largely about how votes are counted for each shareholder in the stage of election. One may put serious concern on the stage of nomination. Nomination can be

---

[1] For more information, see http: //www. ecgi. org/codes/documents/code_en. pdf.
[2] Qian and Zhao (2011) report 5 firms that adopted CV in practice before 2002.

important. For independent director elections, the "Establishment of Independent Director Systems by Listed Companies Guiding Opinion" issued by CSRC on 16 August 2001 states that "A listed company's board of directors, supervisory board and shareholders who individually or together hold not less than 1% of the shares in the listed company may nominate candidates for Independent Director. Such directors will be decided through election by the shareholders' general meeting. " (Article 4). For the elections of executive directors, an implicit stipulation in Company Law of China states that "Shareholders individually or jointly holding three percent (3%) of the shares of the company may, ten days prior to the general meeting of shareholders, submit a temporary written proposal to the board of directors. " (Article 103). This implies that shareholders could nominate directly their favored director candidates to the shareholder meeting circumventing the corporate board in the form of temporary proposal. But, on the whole, an explicit and standard norm for director nomination does not exist in corporates of China. A successful case on this concern is the board election in 2012 of Gree Electric Appliances Inc. In that case, institutional investors successfully jointly nominated and casted their votes to their favored candidate to the corporate board. [1] In what follows, like previous empirical literature on CV, we focus on the election stage of the voting scheme.

Under the CV rule in the election of directors, the total votes a stockholder can cast for a candidate is the number of stock shares he/she owns multiplied by the number of directors to be elected. Thus, minority shareholders can cast all of their voting rights for one or several of their favored candidates who are likely to be elected into the board. Compared with straight voting, the CV rule provides minority shareholders with the opportunity to elect at least one director whom they favor. Under CV, large minority shareholders or non – controlling substantial shareholders can elect at least one preferred candidate into the board as long as the stake of those substantial shareholders is not excessively small relative to that of the controlling largest shareholder.

We can illustrate this point with an example. Assume that a company has 1,000 shares outstanding owned by 10 stockholders, and five directors will be elected to the

---

① For some comments on this, see http: //finance. sina. com. cn/stock/t/20120601/003112195558. shtml.

board. Suppose that the largest shareholder holds 510 shares, accounting for 51% of total shares, whereas the other nine shareholders hold 490 shares together, accounting for 49% of total shares. Under straight voting with the one – share – one – vote rule, 1000 votes can be cast for each candidate. The controlling shareholder can rest assured that all of the five elected directors are his/her favored candidates, thus completely dominating the preferences of the other nine shareholders. Under CV, however, 5000 (1000 × 5) votes can be cast. Holding 51% of stock shares, the controlling shareholder holds 2550 votes, whereas the remaining 2450 votes are held by the other nine stockholders. The CV rule allows shareholders to cast all of their votes for one or several candidates. Theoretically, the other nine shareholders can coordinate and ensure that at least two candidates of their choice get elected, whereas the controlling shareholder can elect at most three preferred candidates into the board. Thus, the primary advantage of the CV mechanism is to allow candidates favored by large minority shareholders to be elected into the board.

The central objective of this study is to examine whether the implementation of CV has changed the power structure of the board and the personal characteristics of executive directors and independent directors. We assess the effects of CV along three major lines. First, we analyze whether CV has reduced the dominance of the controlling shareholder in the board and raised the influence of the large minority shareholders. Theoretically, CV allows some representatives of large minority shareholders (non – controlling substantial shareholders) to be elected into the board as executive directors; this provision will result in a balanced power structure in the boardroom. Therefore, we examine whether the proportion of executive directors representing the controlling largest shareholder (large minority shareholders or non – controlling substantial shareholders) in the boardroom of the CV – using firms is smaller (larger) than that in the non – CV – using firms.

Second, we examine whether the independent directors in CV – using firms have less visible close relations with corporate executives (CEO and board chairperson). Independent directors are widely expected to play a vital role in corporate monitoring and advising. Thus, a high degree of "independence" is a precondition to the efficacy of independent directors in monitoring corporate management. Under straight voting, the controlling shareholder and the management team that he/she picks can dominate in selecting independent directors. Consequently, the selected independent directors might have close personal relations with the controlling shareholder and the corporate executives; thus, they can possibly serve as puppets of the board and cannot actively exercise their monitoring duty. Under CV, minority shareholders (especially non – controlling substantial shareholders) can affect the decision – making process in the firm. Thus, the selected independent directors are less likely to have close personal relationships with the controlling shareholder and the corporate executives. Considering data limitations, we focus on examining the visible and observable relationships between independent directors and corporate executives, that is, whether the selected independent directors and the CEO or board chairperson are former colleagues and/or college alumni/alumnae. CV is expected to raise the degree of "independence" of the independent directors to introduce into the boardroom more directors without visible close relations.

Finally, we examine whether the CV – elected executive and non – executive independent directors are more professional, better educated, and less bureaucratic than the non – CV – elected directors. Under straight voting, the election of board directors is dominated by the controlling shareholder and corporate executives; thus, the elected board directors are often puppets who succumb to the will of the controlling shareholder and corporate executives, and such situation weakens corporate governance (Yeh and Woidtke, 2005). Loyalty and compliance are the likely primary considerations of the controlling shareholder in selecting directors under straight voting. Consequently, the directors elected under straight voting might be weaker in terms of professional knowledge, professional experience, and educational qualifications, which would negatively influence the role they play in corporate advising and monitoring. Under CV, the dominance of the controlling shareholder is decreased as long as the large minority shareholders hold sufficiently large ownership shares. Non – controlling substantial shareholders may nominate and elect into the board directors who are professional, experienced, and knowledgeable to constrain the power of the controlling shareholder and strengthen corporate monitoring and advising. Other small minority shareholders may likewise support this move because it will help improve the capability of board directors in corporate governance.

In our analysis, we investigate whether CV election has changed the personal characteristics of directors, which include the CEO work experience, the board chairman work experience, work experience in the same industry, professional background, educational qualifications, central and local government work experience, and membership of national – or local – level People's Congress and People's Political Consultative Conference.

After examining the changes in the characteristics of executive and non – executive independent directors, we attempt to explore the types of CV – adopting firms that are more likely to select directors different from those elected through straight voting in terms of personal characteristics. One finding is that firms from provinces featured with relatively weak outer governance settings elected different directors with a higher probability. This result suggests that outer governance environments and firm – level governance are substitutes.

1.3 Methodology

Our study faces the typical difficulties encountered in corporate governance research. For example, the adoption of CV is not a random event but an endogenous firm decision. Numerous firms with controlling shareholders owning 30% or more of the stocks did not implement CV by following the CSRC requirement. This implementation problem is especially relevant for emerging markets where formal institutions are generally underdeveloped (Qian and Zhao, 2011). Thus, we apply two different nonparametric matching methods to control for the confounding influence of pretreatment (before CV adoption) control variables in our setting. The vital goal of matching is to prune observations from the dataset so that the remaining data exhibit a better balance between the treatment and control groups and less model dependence, which is expected to reduce statistical bias compared with the case without matching. For the purpose of robustness, we initially employ the BL matching method, followed by the CEM matching process, thereby generating two different control group samples used in the empirical analysis. Throughout the two matching methods, we match firms year by year. After completing the matching process, we run the DID – style regressions to further address the "self – selection" problem. For convenience, we focus on the BL method in our main text and illustrate the CEM approach in detail in Appendix A.

1.3.1　Control Group Method

The BL matching method (Barber and Lyon, 1996) is extensively used in finance literature. We adopt this matching method to construct a control group, which can control for the industrial and pre – performance effects on cumulative voting that may endogenously affect the nomination and election of directors.

In our basic sample, we identify a firm as a CV user if it adopted CV in any year between 2002 and 2005. All CV – using firms in our sample are considered as potential treatment group firms. The remaining listed companies in the universe of corporations in China (non – CV users) are regarded as potential control group firms. The BL method tries to match each CV – using firm with one non – CV – using firm based on the designated rules. Following Barber and Lyon (1996), we match firms on the basis of similarity in industry (one digit SIC code released by CSRC), Firm size (logarithm of book value of total assets), and firm performance (one year lagged industry – adjusted ROA). In our setting, we add the dimension of the degree of corporate ownership concentration, which is also vital to the CV adoption decision of the firm. Klapper et al. (2006) reveal that firms with larger minority block shareholders are more likely to allow CV. Moreover, the Code points out that listed companies with 30% or more of outstanding shares owned by their controlling shareholder should adopt the CV system. We divide both CV users and non – CV users into two groups. One group consists of firms in which the controlling shareholders hold less than 30% of stock shares; this group is called the voluntary group. The other group consists of firms in which the controlling shareholders hold 30% or more of stock shares; this group is called the regulatory group. In the next step, we apply the BL method to these two sub – samples and consider the similarity in industry, Firm size, and firm performance, as well as the own-

ership share of the controlling shareholder when we construct the matching – CV user control groups. Results in Table 1 – 1 suggest that Firm size and firm performance are
important factors that affect firm CV adoption decisions, thus supporting our selection of
criteria for constructing the BL control group. [1]

Table 1 –1   **The Factors Affecting CV Adoption**

Model	(1)	(2)
	CV (*Shrcr*1 <30%)	CV (*Shrcr*1 ⩾30%)
Intercept	– 1. 105 *	0. 274
	(0. 60)	(0. 46)
ROA_t – 1	– 0. 002 *	– 0. 001 *
	(0. 00)	(0. 00)
*Shrcr*1	0. 010	0. 001
	(0. 01)	(0. 01)
Firm size	0. 005	– 0. 042 **
	(0. 03)	(0. 02)
Firm age	– 0. 141 **	– 0. 042
	(0. 07)	(0. 04)
Leverage	– 0. 008	– 0. 006
	(0. 01)	(0. 01)
Duality	0. 109	0. 001
	(0. 07)	(0. 06)
Board size	– 0. 005	0. 008
	(0. 02)	(0. 01)
Board_ind	0. 135	– 0. 658 *
	(0. 57)	(0. 36)
*shrhfd*5	– 0. 000	0. 000
	(0. 00)	(0. 00)
bshare	0. 001	– 0. 004
	(0. 01)	(0. 01)

---

[1]   Table 1 – 1 also shows that firm age is also an important dimension on firm CV adoption decisions. In Appendix A,
we also incorporate this factor into CEM control group constructing.

continued

Model	(1)	(2)
	CV (*Shrcr*1 < 30%)	CV (*Shrcr*1 ≥ 30%)
mshare	− 0. 001	0. 000
	(0. 01)	(0. 01)
Industry	Controlled	Controlled
Year	Controlled	Controlled
Observations	4606	7076
PseudoR^2	0. 101	0. 089

Note: This table reports the probit regression results on the factors that may affect firms' CV adoption decisions. Variable $ROA\_t - 1$ denotes industry adjusted ROA lagged once; variable *shrhfd5* represents the sum of squares of the percentage points of shareholdings by the first to the fifth largest shareholders; variables *bshare* stands for the logarithm of shares (plus 1) held by corporate board; and variable *mshare* presents the logarithm of shares (plus 1) held by management. Column (1) presents the estimates using a sub – sample in which the percentage of shares held by the largest shareholders is less than 30% , and column (2) reports the estimates based on a sub – sample in which the percentage of shareholdings of the largest shareholders is more than or equal to 30%. Robust standard errors are in parentheses. *** , ** , and * denote significance at the 1% , 5% , and 10% levels, respectively.

Specifically, we adopt the following matching procedure: (1) match a CV user to a non – CV user with the nearest proportion of shares held by the controlling shareholder and with the same SIC code, (2) the Firm size (year – end total assets) of the non – CV user is 1/2 – 2 times that of the CV user, and (3) the pre – performance of the non – CV user is within ± 10% that of the CV user. If no such non – CV user exists, we select the one with the nearest percentage of shares held by the controlling largest shareholder to match the CV user with the same SIC code and with performance within ± 10% that of the sample company, regardless of firm size. Nevertheless, if no such non – CV user exists, we subsequently relax the industry code condition and select a non – CV user with the closest percentage of shares held by the controlling largest shareholder.

1. 3. 2   Regression Design

To further reduce the "self – selection" bias, we employ the DID – style regression analysis. Our identification strategy follows the principles of DID, in that we primarily compare the changes in the treatment group firms before and after the CV implementation, and compare the changes of the treatment group firms with those of the control group firms. The DID – style regressions can remove biases in the comparisons between CV users and non – CV users in the post – CV period that could result from the permanent differences between these two groups. Such regressions can also preclude the biases in comparison over time in the CV – using firms as a result of the time trends.

Our baseline regression model that is based on firm – level data is as follows:

$$Y_{it} = \beta_0 + \beta_1 CV + \delta_0 t + \delta_1 CV \times t + \gamma X_{it} + \varepsilon_{it} \qquad (1-1)$$

where Y_{it} is the outcome variable of interest for firm i in period t, t is a dummy variable taking the value of 1 for the post – CV time period, X_{it} is a vector of control variables, and ε_{it} is an error term. The dummy variable CV takes the value of 1 if firm i has adopted CV, which captures the possible differences between the treatment and the control groups prior to the change in the shareholder voting mechanism. Including the time period dummy, t, as a separate explanatory variable, allows us to capture the aggregate factors that would change Y_{it} even in the absence of change in voting mechanism. The interaction term, $CV * t$, is the central explanatory variable, which takes the value of 1 for those observations in the treatment group in the post – CV period. δ_1 captures the treatment effect in this DID style regression model.

We also investigate the differences in the personal characteristics of directors between CV – using firms and non – CV – using firms based on director – level data. In this scenario, given that all of the outcome variables of interest are either a dummy variable indicating whether a director possesses several characteristics of interest or not, or a categorical variable indicating, for example, the level of educational qualifications, we apply the non – linear DID method (Puhani, 2012) to avoid or reduce the "endogeneity" or "self – selection" problem. The regression model is specified as follows:

$$Y_{it} = \Phi(\beta_0 + \beta_1 CV + \delta_0 t + \delta_1 CV \times t + \gamma X_{it} + \varepsilon_{it}) \qquad (1-2)$$

where all variables are as defined earlier, and $\Phi(\cdot)$ denotes the cumulative normal distribution function. The sign of the treatment effect in this DID probit model is equal to the sign of δ_1 owing to the strict monotonicity of $\Phi(\ \cdot\ )$. [1]

For the empirical analysis of the types of CV firms that are likely to elect better directors though CV adoption, we adopt simple probit models.

1.4 Data and Variables

We identify the CV – adopting firms and the CV – elected directors from the information on shareholder meetings contained in The Disclosure by Listed Companies available from SHSE and SZSE. The central part of our analysis is the examination of the personal characteristics of executive and independent directors. The detailed information is hand collected from the résumés of directors included in the company annual reports disclosed by SHSE and SZSE or released by SINA Finance, a Chinese stock website run by SINA Corporation, a listed company in NASDAQ. [2] We read and check all of the files provided by both data sources to extract information for constructing the indicators of the personal characteristics of directors. In addition, firm – level accounting, financial, corporate ownership, and corporate governance data are obtained from the China Stock Market and Accounting Research (CSMAR) database.

A total of 408 CV – using firms are listed in the A – share market for the period 2002 – 2005, among which 55 firms elected only one director or only supervisors through the CV rule in their elections and thus are excluded. Therefore, the sample that is used to compare director characteristics includes 353 CV – using firms. Table 1 – 2 describes the distribution of CV adoption over years. The table clearly demonstrates that the peak of CV adoption occurs in 2005 in which 253 CV firms clustered

---

① Unlike linear DID model, where we can directly estimate the magnitude of the treatment effect, we cannot directly identify the magnitude of the treatment effect in the DID probit model here, as shown in Puhani (2012). However, we can still identify the sign of the treatment effect.

② Although, we read all firm annual reports released by SHSE and SZSE to obtain personal information of directors, almost all firm annual reports before 2004 exclude director résumés. To fill this gap, we fall back on SINA Finance. If there are still some director résumés that cannot be found, then we try to search them via Baidu, a famous Chinese search engine (a listed company in NASDAQ).

and accounted for 71. 67% of all of the CV firms in the sample period. Based on Table 1 − 2, the number of firms with the largest shareholders owning less than 30% that adopted the CV rule is less than that of firms with the largest shareholders owning 30% or more proportion of shares held by the largest shareholders more than or equal to 30% , although both assume an increasing trend in the sample period.

Table 1 − 2   Distribution of CV Firms over the Years

Year	No. of CV Firms	$Shrcr1 < 30\%$	$Shrcr1 \geqslant 30\%$
2002	30	7	23
2003	35	6	29
2004	35	6	29
2005	253	52	201
Total	353	71	282

Note: This table reports the distribution of the number of firms adopting the CV rule over the years in the period 2002 − 2005.

We use the BL method to match the CV firms with 353 non − CV control firms, among which 57 matches correspond to 114 CV firms, that is, each of the 57 non − CV firms matches two different CV firms. [①] After BL matching, we obtain 296 non − CV control firms in the CV period (treatment period). We initially collect the data on director characteristics in the post − CV period (treatment period $t = 1$) , and then move back to collect the personal characteristics of board directors in the pre − CV period (pre − treatment period $t = 0$) ; 5 CV − using firms and 2 matching non − CV control firms have no available data in the pre − CV period. Therefore, under the BL matching procedure, the constructed sample consists of 1291 firm − year observations, of which 701 firm − year observations (348 observations in the pre − treatment period and 353 observations in the treatment period) adopted the CV rule and 590 firm − year observations (294 observations in the pre − treatment period and 296 observations in the treatment period) did not. Table 1 − 3 lists the basic summary statistics of the three key control variables used to construct the control group. Panels A, B, C, and D of Table 1 − 3 show that the differences in the means of $ROA\_t − 1$ between CV and non −

① For example, non − CV firm A not only matches CV firm B, but also matches CV firm C in the same year.

CV firms for the four different cases are all highly significant at least at 5% level before BL matching process, but the statistical significance of the differences no longer exists after BL matching process, as shown in Panels E, F, G, and H of the same table. Also the differences in the means of *Firm size* (where *Firm size* refers to firm yearend total assets) between CV and non – CV firms for the cases shown in Panels B, C, and D are all significantly different at the 1% level before BL matching, but the statistical significance of the differences disappears after the BL matching process. Similarly, the differences in the means of *Shrcr1* are significant at least at the 5% level for the cases in Panels B, C, and D before the BL matching, but the significance of the differences no longer holds after BL matching.

The Code states that listed companies with 30% or more of their stocks owned by controlling shareholders shall adopt the CV rule. In line with this provision, firm characteristics in terms of firm pre – performance and *firm size* around the 30% threshold. Panels C and G of Table 1 – 3 present the basic comparison in terms of these three variables between CV and non – CV firms. Panel C of the table shows that the differences in the means of all three variables between non – CV and CV firms are all statistically significant at least at the 1% level before the BL matching process, but the significance of the differences vanishes after the BL matching process from Panel G.

Table 1 – 3   Descriptive Statistics of the Three Key Control Variables

Panel A: Before BL Matching with *Shrcr1* < 30

Variable	Mean		Diff	*t*Value
	Non – CV Firms	CV Firms		
ROA_t-1	-2.190 (20.84)	-0.267 (11.34)	-1.924**	-2.06
Firm size	5.85×10^9 (4.42×10^{10})	5.17×10^9 (2.61×10^{10})	6.73×10^8	0.33
Shrcr1	23.691 (5.65)	24.298 (5.45)	-0.607	-1.56

Panel B: Before BL Matching with $Shrcr1 \geqslant 30$

Variable	Mean		Diff	tValue
	Non – CV Firms	CV Firms		
$ROA\_t - 1$	0. 809 (8. 59)	1. 401 (7. 06)	– 0. 592 **	– 2. 10
Firm size	4.12×10^{9} (1.99×10^{10})	2.66×10^{9} (3.22×10^{9})	1.46×10^{9} ***	3. 40
Shrcr1	50. 024 (12. 43)	52. 120 (12. 78)	– 1. 096 **	– 2. 39

Panel C: Before BL Matching with $Shrcr1$ in (25, 35)

$ROA\_t\ 1$	1. 856 (19. 34)	0. 556 (7. 99)	– 2. 422 ***	– 3. 06
Firm size	1.72×10^{9} (2.70×10^{9})	2.20×10^{9} (2.37×10^{9})	-4.81×10^{8} ***	– 2. 84
Shrcr1	29. 212 (2. 38)	30. 392 (2. 56)	– 1. 181 ***	– 6. 73

Panel D: Before BL Matching with $Shrcr1$ in [0, 100]

$ROA\_t - 1$	– 0. 420 (14. 95)	1. 125 (7. 95)	– 1. 546 ***	– 4. 67
Firm size	4.82×10^{9} (3.20×10^{10})	3.08×10^{9} (1.10×10^{10})	1.74×109 ***	2. 91
Shrcr1	40. 013 (16. 88)	47. 530 (15. 75)	– 7. 517 ***	– 14. 90

Panel E: After BL Matching with $Shrcr1 < 30$

$ROA\_t - 1$	0. 866 (5. 48)	– 1. 802 (14. 44)	2. 667	1. 51
Firm size	6.53×10^{9} (4.07×10^{10})	4.87×10^{9} (2.62×10^{10})	1.66×10^{9}	0. 30
Shrcr1	24. 419 (16. 88)	24. 101 (15. 75)	0. 318	0. 38

Panel F: After BL Matching with $Shrcr1 \geqslant 30$

Variable	Mean		Diff	tValue
	Non – CV Firms	CV Firms		
ROA_t-1	1. 339 (7. 96)	0. 844 (9. 20)	0. 495	0. 73
Firm size	$3. 27 \times 10^9$ ($4. 12 \times 10^9$)	$2. 93 \times 10^9$ ($3. 78 \times 10^9$)	$3. 40 \times 10^8$	1. 11
Shrcr1	50. 464 (11. 91)	51. 096 (12. 83)	0. 633	– 0. 65

Panel G: After BL Matching with $Shrcr1$ in (25, 35)

ROA_t-1	– 0. 592 (10. 13)	0. 448 (7. 08)	1. 040	– 0. 74
Firm size	$2. 16 \times 10^9$ ($2. 31 \times 10^9$)	$2. 47 \times 10^9$ ($2. 95 \times 10^9$)	– 3. 10 $\times 10^8$	– 0. 73
Shrcr1	30. 390 (2. 54)	30. 583 (2. 62)	– 0. 192	– 0. 47

Panel H: After BL Matching with $Shrcr1$ in [0, 100]

ROA_t-1	1. 248 (10. 42)	0. 344 (7. 54)	0. 904	1. 40
Firm size	$3. 87 \times 10^9$ ($1. 79 \times 10^{10}$)	$3. 29 \times 10^9$ ($1. 18 \times 10^{10}$)	$5. 80 \times 10^8$	0. 55
Shrcr1	45. 465 (14. 00)	46. 067 (15. 80)	0. 602	0. 55

Note: This table reports the t test results on the means of the three key variables (standard deviations in parentheses) as criteria of the BL matching method before and after matching process, respectively. Here variable *Firm size* stands for firm year – end total assets in RMB. The units of variables *ROA_t1* and *Shrcr1* are percentage, where $t-1$ denotes lag 1 period. column *Diffs* presents the difference between columns (2) and (3). ***, **, and * denote significance at the 1%, 5%, and 10% levels, respectively.

We use the above sample to analyze the differences in characteristics between CV directors and non – CV directors. The definitions of the main variables used in the empirical analysis are listed in TableA1 in Appendix A.

Table A1 briefly defines the main variables used in the empirical analysis, and Table A2 reports the summary statistics from the sample constructed through the BL method for main variables. Panel A in Table A2 focuses on the main outcome variables on director attributes. The means of the main outcome variables for both the treatment and control groups in the pretreatment period are nearly the same. For example, the means of *CEO_exp* in the two groups differ by 1. 2% , and the mean age in the two groups differs by only 0. 24% , nearly identical. None of the differences between the treatment and control groups are significant. The differences in the means of almost all main outcome variables of the two groups during the pretreatment period are insignificant. Panel B of Table A2 presents the summary statistics on the main control variables defined in Table A1. Similarly, the mean differences of almost all of the control variables of the two groups in the pretreatment period are insignificant.

The use of CV may manifest substantial effects on director characteristics. We use *Share*1 as a regressand to test for a significant decrease in the percentage of executive directors as representatives of the controlling shareholders under CV and examine whether the boards generated by the CV rule include more directors as representatives of minority shareholders. Using *Share*2 and *Share*2_5 as dependent variables, we also investigate whether a significant increase exists in the percentage of executive directors as representatives of other shareholders. According to Klapper et al. (2006), firms with larger minority block shareholders are more likely to allow CV because the shares held by the minority shareholders are sufficiently large to secure seats in the board for their representatives. Given the high concentration of ownership in China, *Share*2 therefore is a key indicator to directly show whether the CV rule works among CV users. Additionally, *Share*2_5 measures the percentage of executive directors from the second to the fifth shareholders and indicates whether CV can bring to the board more executive directors as representatives of minority shareholders. We incorporate *Boardsize*, *Board_ind*, *Dualilty*, *Related*, *Shrcr*1, *Shrcr*5, *Sd*, *Fd*, and *Regulatory* as governance covariates, as well as *Firm size*, *Leverage*, *Firm age*, and *ROA* as financial control variables.

1. 5 CV and the Characteristics of Elected Directors

1. 5. 1 CV and Power Distribution in the Board

One potential consequence of the implementation of CV is providing non – controlling substantial shareholders with the opportunity to elect their representatives into the boardroom, which is expected to induce a relatively balanced power distribution in the board. We examine the proportions of executive directors as representatives of the largest controlling shareholder, the second largest shareholder, the second to the fifth largest shareholders, and the second to the tenth largest shareholders in the board. We attempt to test whether CV raised the proportion of the executive directors as representatives of the non – controlling substantial shareholders in the boardroom.

Panel A of Table 1 – 4 provides the basic descriptive statistics of the power distribution in the board in terms of the means of the percentages of the directors representing the top 10 shareholders during the pretreatment and treatment periods based on the BL sample. Panel B of Table 1 – 4 presents the univariate analysis results of the DID – style comparison between the CV – using firms and their control group firms before and after the implementation of CV. The comparison focuses on the differences in the proportion of representatives of the controlling largest shareholder and the proportion of those of the second largest shareholder (the proportion of those of the second to the fifth largest shareholders, and the proportion of those of the second to the tenth largest shareholders). We initially subtract the proportion of directors as representatives of the non – controlling substantial shareholders (the second, the second to the fifth, and the second to the tenth, respectively) from the proportion of the controlling largest shareholder in the pretreatment and treatment periods for treatment and control groups, respectively. We subsequently examine whether significant discrepancies exist in the mean differences between the two periods for each group. Finally, we subtract the differences of control group between the two periods from those of treatment group between the two periods, and test whether the results are significantly different from 0.

In Panel B, the results based on the full sample do not demonstrate any statistically significant changes in the proportion of the representative of the controlling largest shareholder relative to that of the non – controlling substantial shareholders. This outcome implies the lack of statistically significant changes in the power distribution between the largest shareholder and the non – controlling substantial shareholders after the implementation of CV.

Considering that the controlling largest shareholder and substantial shareholders might be related in that they are related parties[1] (individuals or entities capable of benefiting from significant influence or control rights over the financial and operational activities of a listed firm), we then focus on a sub – sample that contains only firms without parties related to the top 10 shareholders. Based on the sub – sample, we do find that the power of the second largest shareholder has increased, although the result is not significant.

Panel C of Table 1 – 4 reports the main results of DID – type regressions that whether more executive directors are elected into the board as representatives of non – controlling substantial shareholders under CV. Columns (1), (2) and (3) list the full sample regression results in which the dependent variable is the proportion of representatives of the largest controlling shareholder, the second largest shareholder, and the second to the fifth largest shareholder in the board, respectively. Clearly, the full sample analysis does not produce any significant results. The use of CV could not decrease the percentage of executive directors representing the controlling shareholder in the board of directors; at the same time, the CV adoption could not increase the percentage of directors as representatives of non – controlling substantial shareholders in the

---

[1]   China's Ministry of Finance issued "Accounting Criteria of Corporations—Related Parties and Related Party Transactions Disclosure," in 1997. It defines "related parties" as individuals or entities capable of benefiting from significant influence or control rights over a listed firm's financial and operational activities. Related parties of a public company may include its parent company or subsidiaries, other companies that share its parent, its large and influential investors, its joint ventures or joint operating partners, the principal individual investors or key management personnel and their family members, and other companies controlled or heavily influenced by its principal individual investor or family members.

boardroom.

The result based on the sub – sample indicates that the use of CV significantly increased the percentage of directors representing the second largest shareholder in the board of directors, although the size of the sub – sample (approximately 70 firms and 150 observations in total) is considerably smaller than that of the full sample. This evidence suggests that the CV adoption might have changed the composition of corporate boards to some extent. In particular, the relative power of the second largest shareholder has increased to some degree. Nonetheless, no sign shows that the CV adoption weakened the control power of the controlling largest shareholders.

Table 1 – 4 **The Power Distribution in the Board**

Panel A: Descriptive Statistics of the Power Distribution in the Board

Variable	Mean			
	Treatment Group		Control Group	
	Pretreatment period	Treatment period	Pretreatment period	Treatment period
Share1	55. 726 (28. 97)	57. 084 (31. 78)	55. 393 (25. 40)	55. 300 (25. 57)
Share2	7. 688 (12. 74)	9. 380 (16. 75)	6. 849 (11. 41)	7. 331 (12. 05)
Share2_5	13. 952 (19. 15)	15. 009 (21. 92)	13. 934 (17. 01)	14. 281 (17. 63)
Share2_10	15. 519 (20. 34)	15. 857 (22. 53)	15. 337 (17. 96)	15. 505 (18. 36)

Panel B: Univariate Analysis on Power Distribution in the Board

(1)	(2)	(3)	(4)
Pretreatment Period	Treatment Period	Diff	t Value
Full Sample Case: Controlling Shareholders V. S. the Second Shareholders			
Treatment Group			
48. 038 (1. 91)	47. 623 (2. 24)	0. 415 (2. 94)	0. 14

continued

(1)	(2)	(3)	(4)
Pretreatment Period	Treatment Period	Diff	t Value
Control Group			
48. 544	47. 969	0. 576	0. 22
(1. 80)	(1. 83)	(2. 56)	
Difference – in – Differences Between Treatment and Control Groups			
		– 0. 160	0. 04
		(3. 98)	
Full Sample Case: Controlling Shareholders V. S. the Second to the Fifth Shareholders			
Treatment Group			
41. 774	41. 946	– 0. 172	– 0. 05
(2. 24)	(2. 52)	(3. 38)	
Control Group			
41. 460	41. 018	0. 441	0. 15
(2. 13)	(2. 14)	(3. 02)	
Difference – in – Differences Between Treatment and Control Groups			
		– 0. 613	0. 13
		(4. 61)	
Full Sample Case: Controlling Shareholders V. S. the Second to the tenth Shareholders			
Treatment Group			
40. 207	41. 091	– 0. 884	– 0. 26
(2. 30)	(2. 56)	(3. 44)	
Control Group			
40. 056	39. 794	0. 262	0. 08
(2. 19)	(2. 19)	(3. 10)	
Difference – in – Differences Between Treatment and Control Group			
		– 1. 146	0. 24
		(4. 71)	
Subsample Case: Controlling Shareholders V. S. the Second Shareholders			
Treatment Group			
48. 853	39. 192	9. 662	0. 84
(5. 86)	(9. 91)	(11. 51)	

continued

(1)	(2)	(3)	(4)
Pretreatment Period	Treatment Period	Diff	t Value
Control Group			
48. 268 (4. 16)	40. 654 (5. 76)	7. 613 (7. 11)	1. 07
Difference – in – Differences Between Treatment and Control Groups			
		2. 048 (12. 39)	– 0. 17
Subsample Case: Controlling Shareholders V. S. the Second to the Fifth Shareholders			
Treatment Group			
41. 546 (7. 11)	34. 033 (10. 89)	7. 513 (13. 01)	0. 58
Control Group			
42. 216 (4. 78)	32. 298 (7. 10)	9. 918 (8. 56)	1. 16
Difference – in – Differences Between Treatment and Control Groups			
		– 2. 404 (14. 45)	0. 17
Subsample Case: Controlling Shareholders V. S. the Second to the Tenth Shareholders			
Treatment Group			
38. 823 (7. 41)	32. 181 (11. 37)	6. 641 (13. 57)	0. 49
Control Group			
41. 012 (4. 86)	31. 259 (7. 23)	9. 753 (8. 72)	1. 12
Difference – in – Differences Between Treatment and Control Groups			
		– 3. 112 (14. 92)	0. 21

Panel C: Multivariate Analysis on Power Distribution in the Board

Model	(1)	(2)	(3)	(4)	(5)	(6)
	Share1	Share2	Share2_5	Share1	Share2	Share2_5
Intercept	−27.896 (21.55)	26.571** (10.68)	47.464*** (14.03)	−31.738 (55.47)	31.089 (24.46)	50.832 (31.08)
CV	−2.425 (2.22)	1.733* (1.02)	1.840 (1.36)	1.072 (6.02)	−1.435 (2.66)	2.832 (3.37)
t	0.824 (0.95)	0.496 (0.50)	0.406 (0.66)	−5.077 (6.40)	−0.179 (2.82)	1.804 (3.59)
CV × t	1.249 (1.60)	1.161 (0.87)	0.818 (1.07)	2.461 (9.35)	8.180** (4.12)	3.082 (5.24)
Regulatory	1.010 (3.17)	0.476 (1.92)	−0.743 (2.31)	2.229 (7.68)	−0.550 (3.38)	−4.250 (4.30)
Board size	−0.568 (0.51)	0.342* (0.20)	0.827*** (0.27)	−0.182 (1.23)	1.023** (0.54)	1.147* (0.69)
Board_ind	5.895 (10.78)	3.394 (4.87)	8.332 (6.34)	13.533 (21.48)	2.955 (9.48)	11.428 (12.04)
Duality	−3.308 (2.87)	1.614 (1.46)	1.722 (2.19)	1.604 (7.40)	−0.154 (3.26)	3.500 (4.14)
Related	−1.711 (1.19)	−0.471 (0.59)	−1.404** (0.71)			
Shrcr1	0.655*** (0.10)	−0.100** (0.04)	−0.171*** (0.06)	0.733*** (0.27)	−0.088 (0.10)	−0.127 (0.13)
Shrcr2_10	−0.167 (0.11)	0.307*** (0.06)	0.577*** (0.08)	−0.325 (0.26)	0.341** (0.11)	0.770*** (0.14)
Sd	−1.542 (2.69)	−0.288 (1.24)	−0.332 (1.64)	3.449 (6.66)	6.931 (2.94)	1.145 (3.73)
Fd	−14.704 (11.56)	19.902 (16.61)	21.655 (13.82)	−15.518 (30.10)	0.711 (13.28)	2.314 (16.87)
Firm size	2.759*** (1.04)	−1.073** (0.54)	−1.782*** (0.68)	2.504 (2.60)	−1.250 (1.14)	−2.261 (1.45)

continued

Model	(1)	(2)	(3)	(4)	(5)	(6)
	Share1	Share2	Share2_5	Share1	Share2	Share2_5
Leverage	−7.380*	2.722	2.951	−9.469	−6.995*	−4.519
	(4.11)	(2.35)	(2.91)	(8.31)	(3.66)	(4.65)
Firm age	5.099***	−1.591	−3.622***	4.304	−3.114	−3.012
	(1.96)	(1.01)	(1.37)	(5.08)	(2.24)	(2.84)
ROA	6.923	−5.332	−0.828	52.655	4.110	21.866*
	(8.80)	(3.34)	(4.75)	(29.85)	(13.16)	(16.73)
Observations	1227	1230	1230	154	154	154
Adj. R^2	0.203	0.173	0.309	0.182	0.244	0.408

Note: This table reports the summary statistics and the DID – style analysis on power distribution in the board, using the sample constructed by the BL method. Panel A describes the means and standard deviations (in parentheses) of the proportion of the top 10 shareholders in the pretreatment and the treatment periods, respectively. Panel B presents the univariate analysis results of the DID – style comparison between the CV – using firms and their control firms before and after the implementation of CV. The comparison focuses on the differences in the proportion of representatives of the controlling largest shareholder and the proportion of those of the second largest shareholder (the proportion of those of the second to the fifth largest shareholders, and the proportion of those of the second to the tenth largest shareholders). We initially subtract the proportion of directors as representatives of the non – controlling substantial shareholders (the second, the second to the fifth, and the second to the tenth, respectively) from the proportion of the controlling largest shareholder in the pretreatment and treatment periods for treatment and control groups, respectively. Then we examine whether significant discrepancies exist in the means of differences between the two periods for each group. Finally, we subtract the differences of control group between the two periods from those of treatment group between the two periods, and test whether the results are significantly different from 0. Panel C presents the DID regression estimates [columns (1), (2), (3), (4), (5), and (6)] for testing whether minority shareholders can elect their representatives into the board of directors. columns (1), (2) and (3) use all the sample, while columns (4), (5), and (6) include only firms without related parties among the top 10 shareholders. Standard errors (in parentheses) are heteroskedasticity consistent and clustered at the firm level. ***, **, and * denote significance at the 1%, 5%, and 10% levels, respectively.

1.5.2　CV and the Personal Characteristics of Executive Directors

Next, we examine whether CV adoption changes the personal characteristics of executive directors.

Panel A of Table 1 – 5 reports the results of the DID – style regressions that test for the existence of differences in educational qualifications between CV and non – CV executive directors. The percentage of executive directors with a master's degree or a higher degree who were elected into in the board of directors increases following the implementation of CV. At the same time, the percentage of executive directors with poor educational qualifications, such as junior college or below, significantly declines after the CV adoption.

Panel B of Table 1 – 5 presents the empirical results on the differences in managerial and professional experiences between CV and non – CV executive directors. Several statistically significant findings emerge, such as the larger proportion of executive directors elected through the CV rule having work experience as CEO, as chairman of the board of directors, or in the same industry. Another statistically significant finding is that CV – elected executive directors are younger than non – CV elected ones. Nevertheless, no evidence shows that CV elections could increase the fraction of executive directors who are professionals, such as accountants, lawyers, engineers, and economists.

Panel C of Table 1 – 5 presents the empirical results of DID regressions that explore for differences in political connections between CV – elected and non – CV – elected executive directors. The results indicate that a smaller fraction of the CV executive directors, compared with the non – CV directors, comprises former central government officials and/or delegates to the National People's Congress.

Table 1 – 5   CV and the Personal Characteristics

of Executive Directors

Panel A: Educational Qualifications of Executive Directors

Model	(1)	(2)	(3)	(4)	(5)	(6)	(7)
	$Edu1$	$Edu2$	$Edu3$	$Edu4$	$Edu5$	$Edu6$	$Edu7$
Intercept	15.962 **	66.986 ***	82.948 ***	76.573 ***	– 48.475 **	– 11.046	– 59.521 ***
	(8.09)	(16.39)	(18.74)	(21.01)	(20.99)	(10.10)	(22.99)
CV	0.728	4.145 **	4.873 **	– 2.998	– 1.148	– 0.727	– 1.875
	(0.99)	(1.78)	(2.07)	(2.06)	(1.98)	(0.85)	(2.16)
t	0.129	– 1.166	– 1.037	0.765	0.360	– 0.088	0.272
	(0.41)	(0.71)	(0.82)	(0.92)	(0.80)	(0.42)	(0.85)

continued

Model	(1)	(2)	(3)	(4)	(5)	(6)	(7)
	Edu1	Edu2	Edu3	Edu4	Edu5	Edu6	Edu7
$CV \times t$	−1.051	−4.104***	−5.156***	0.101	4.577***	0.477	5.055***
	(0.71)	(1.19)	(1.36)	(1.43)	(1.37)	(0.60)	(1.38)
Regulatory	−0.940	−1.351	−2.290	1.282	1.184	−0.177	1.008
	(1.59)	(2.57)	(2.94)	(2.97)	(2.91)	(1.38)	(3.19)
Board size	−0.053	0.182	0.129	0.016	−0.104	−0.042	−0.146
	(0.16)	(0.34)	(0.39)	(0.40)	(0.37)	(0.20)	(0.41)
Board_ind	−5.320	−12.254	−17.575*	−17.648*	21.714**	13.509**	35.223***
	(4.03)	(8.92)	(9.89)	(9.13)	(9.16)	(5.68)	(9.73)
Duality	1.092	1.322	2.413	2.159	−2.609	−1.963**	−4.573
	(1.47)	(2.36)	(2.65)	(2.54)	(2.71)	(0.97)	(2.90)
Related	0.515	2.245**	2.760***	−0.703	−0.964	−1.093**	−2.057*
	(0.48)	(0.90)	(1.02)	(1.01)	(1.02)	(0.53)	(1.12)
Shrcr1	−0.054	−0.088	−0.142	0.009	0.178*	−0.045	0.132
	(0.05)	(0.08)	(0.10)	(0.10)	(0.09)	(0.05)	(0.10)
Shrcr2_10	−0.020	−0.129*	−0.150	−0.008	0.223**	−0.066	0.157
	(0.05)	(0.08)	(0.09)	(0.10)	(0.10)	(0.04)	(0.11)
Sd	−0.650	−2.538	−3.188	−2.612	5.998	−0.198	5.800**
	(0.99)	(1.94)	(2.17)	(2.39)	(2.38)	(1.01)	(2.52)
Fd	−5.387***	−1.634	−7.021	−11.258	−0.703	18.982**	18.279***
	(1.75)	(9.49)	(9.99)	(8.49)	(9.50)	(8.15)	(4.78)
Firm size	−0.318	−2.110***	−2.428***	−1.235	2.752***	0.911*	3.663***
	(0.41)	(0.81)	(0.92)	(1.02)	(0.99)	(0.48)	(1.10)
Leverage	1.870	1.734	3.604	5.829	−8.383**	−1.051	−9.433**
	(2.13)	(3.22)	(3.68)	(4.27)	(3.43)	(1.34)	(3.76)
Firm age	−0.512	−0.251	−0.764	−3.847**	4.718***	−0.107	4.611**
	(0.77)	(1.58)	(1.77)	(1.95)	(1.81)	(0.82)	(1.96)
ROA	−2.057	1.248	−0.809	3.057	−2.933	0.684	−2.248
	(3.21)	(5.78)	(6.02)	(13.22)	(9.41)	(3.03)	(10.83)
Observations	1227	1227	1227	1227	1227	1227	1227
Adj. R^2	0.006	0.027	0.016	0.057	0.033	0.071	0.039

Panel B: Professional Experiences of Executive Directors

Model	(1) CEO_exp .	(2) Chair_exp	(3) Exe_exp	(4) Ind_exp	(5) Pro_exp	(6) Dir_age
Intercept	6. 897 (15. 71)	40. 815 ** (15. 90)	31. 763 * (16. 71)	76. 357 *** (10. 38)	− 31. 970 (23. 91)	21. 903 *** (3. 36)
CV	1. 547 (1. 69)	− 1. 293 (1. 62)	0. 931 (1. 79)	0. 041 (1. 06)	0. 019 (2. 46)	0. 332 (0. 39)
t	− 0. 379 (0. 74)	0. 516 (0. 64)	0. 264 (0. 76)	0. 627 (0. 46)	− 1. 619 * (0. 93)	0. 433 *** (0. 15)
CV × t	2. 436 * (1. 39)	2. 125 * (1. 16)	3. 402 ** (1. 48)	3. 467 *** (0. 86)	1. 387 (1. 49)	− 1. 078 *** (0. 25)
Regulatory	− 3. 995 (2. 50)	1. 763 (2. 58)	− 1. 556 (2. 65)	0. 725 (1. 37)	6. 586 * (3. 60)	1. 171 ** (0. 56)
Board size	− 1. 210 *** (0. 32)	− 1. 278 *** (0. 33)	− 1. 603 *** (0. 34)	− 0. 262 (0. 20)	1. 848 *** (0. 46)	0. 159 ** (0. 07)
Board_ind	15. 320 ** (7. 64)	24. 063 *** (6. 57)	25. 620 *** (8. 24)	4. 295 (4. 27)	14. 621 (10. 32)	− 2. 853 * (1. 70)
Duality	− 3. 610 (2. 38)	1. 676 (2. 39)	− 3. 056 (2. 82)	0. 481 (1. 06)	− 5. 991 * (3. 23)	− 0. 110 (0. 60)
Related	− 0. 854 (0. 93)	0. 067 (0. 78)	− 0. 958 (0. 96)	0. 844 * (0. 48)	− 1. 806 (1. 22)	− 0. 148 (0. 19)
Shrcr1	− 0. 173 ** (0. 08)	− 0. 160 ** (0. 08)	− 0. 260 *** (0. 09)	0. 023 (0. 04)	0. 216 * (0. 11)	− 0. 001 (0. 02)
Shrcr2_10	0. 044 (0. 08)	0. 037 (0. 08)	0. 044 (0. 08)	− 0. 027 (0. 04)	− 0. 230 * (0. 12)	− 0. 023 (0. 02)
Sd	1. 409 (1. 91)	1. 187 (1. 98)	2. 328 (2. 05)	− 3. 499 *** (1. 32)	0. 966 (2. 64)	− 0. 234 (0. 40)
Fd	− 22. 634 *** (3. 58)	1. 507 (7. 71)	− 12. 099 * (7. 31)	1. 234 (3. 72)	− 24. 840 (18. 04)	− 2. 675 ** (1. 08)
Firm size	2. 273 *** (0. 78)	− 0. 122 (0. 76)	1. 888 ** (0. 81)	0. 974 * (0. 53)	3. 649 *** (1. 17)	1. 081 *** (0. 17)

continued

Model	(1)	(2)	(3)	(4)	(5)	(6)
	CEO_exp	*Chair_exp*	*Exe_exp*	*Ind_exp*	*Pro_exp*	*Dir_age*
Leverage	0.458	2.756	−0.093	−1.668	−3.087	−1.123*
	(2.95)	(2.79)	(2.92)	(1.86)	(3.91)	(0.62)
Firm age	−0.969	−2.596*	−3.520**	−1.630*	−1.371	0.640**
	(1.57)	(1.45)	(1.68)	(0.92)	(2.07)	(0.31)
ROA	15.684**	19.760**	16.449**	−1.115	−15.278**	3.956***
	(7.50)	(8.06)	(6.49)	(2.34)	(7.42)	(1.15)
Observations	1227	1227	1227	1227	1227	1227
Adj. R^2	0.075	0.055	0.092	0.065	0.127	0.129

Panel C: Political Connections of Executive Directors

Model	(1)	(2)	(3)	(4)	(5)	(6)	(7)
	Pol1	*Pol2*	*Pol3*	*Pol4*	*Pol5*	*Pol6*	*Pol7*
Intercept	−10.604*	4.644	−5.529*	1.731	−10.375**	6.840	−0.076
	(6.41)	(17.64)	(2.89)	(4.58)	(4.74)	(4.37)	(20.05)
CV	1.186*	−1.894	0.106	0.388	−0.140	0.318	0.138
	(0.63)	(1.70)	(0.26)	(0.48)	(0.50)	(0.52)	(1.88)
t	−0.031	−0.666	0.069	−0.036	0.233	0.064	−0.338
	(0.22)	(0.72)	(0.12)	(0.18)	(0.26)	(0.19)	(0.77)
CV × t	−0.968**	0.507	−0.176	0.014	−0.590*	0.178	−0.669
	(0.40)	(1.09)	(0.20)	(0.32)	(0.32)	(0.31)	(1.23)
Regulatory	1.201	−0.578	0.020	0.773	0.226	−0.035	1.495
	(0.88)	(2.39)	(0.41)	(0.75)	(0.68)	(0.75)	(2.78)
Board size	−0.090	−0.590**	−0.146*	−0.008	−0.116	0.050	−0.830**
	(0.11)	(0.30)	(0.08)	(0.13)	(0.11)	(0.13)	(0.37)
Board_ind	2.575	−15.067*	1.612	6.345***	3.772	1.902	−4.175
	(2.75)	(8.60)	(1.70)	(2.21)	(2.45)	(2.24)	(9.87)
Duality	−1.047	2.853	0.302	−0.189	1.204	1.987*	5.500**
	(0.66)	(2.26)	(0.42)	(0.64)	(0.88)	(1.04)	(2.61)

continued

Model	(1)	(2)	(3)	(4)	(5)	(6)	(7)
	*Pol*1	*Pol*2	*Pol*3	*Pol*4	*Pol*5	*Pol*6	*Pol*7
Related	-0.226	-0.068	-0.260*	-0.034	0.040	0.158	-0.009
	(0.32)	(0.89)	(0.15)	(0.22)	(0.25)	(0.26)	(1.00)
Shrcr1	0.018	-0.040	-0.014	-0.045	-0.014	-0.047*	-0.116
	(0.02)	(0.07)	(0.02)	(0.03)	(0.02)	(0.02)	(0.09)
Shrcr2_10	0.095***	0.027	-0.003	-0.019	-0.028	-0.045*	0.043
	(0.03)	(0.08)	(0.01)	(0.03)	(0.03)	(0.03)	(0.10)
Sd	0.107	-2.287	-0.411*	-0.350	-0.420	-0.813	-3.002
	(0.69)	(1.79)	(0.22)	(0.44)	(0.53)	(0.62)	(2.09)
Fd	0.444	11.218	-1.016	0.888	-2.754***	-3.385**	7.013
	(1.39)	(19.28)	(0.78)	(1.96)	(1.05)	(1.32)	(18.27)
Firm size	0.485	0.808	0.393**	0.027	0.729***	-0.099	1.530
	(0.32)	(0.87)	(0.18)	(0.25)	(0.23)	(0.21)	(0.99)
Leverage	-1.345	1.284	-0.047	0.114	-1.401**	-0.049	-0.568
	(0.92)	(3.21)	(0.33)	(0.57)	(0.71)	(0.81)	(3.74)
Firm age	0.142	2.665*	-0.055	-0.627	-0.938*	-0.836*	1.105
	(0.54)	(1.60)	(0.17)	(0.38)	(0.49)	(0.51)	(1.76)
ROA	1.894	3.390	0.022	-0.637	-0.904	-0.706	0.664
	(2.94)	(6.01)	(0.65)	(1.00)	(1.18)	(1.58)	(6.36)
Observations	1227	1227	1227	1227	1227	1227	1227
Adj. R^2	0.022	0.012	0.013	0.005	0.022	0.013	0.013

Note: This table reports the DID – style regressions to examine whether CV changes the personal characteristics of executive directors, using the sample constructed through the BL method. Panel A presents the DID regression estimates [columns (1), (2), (3), (4), (5), (6), and (7)] for examining whether the educational background of CV – elected executive directors is different from those of non – CV – elected ones. Panel B presents the DID regression estimates [columns (1), (2), (3), (4), (5), and (6)] for testing whether the managerial and professional experiences of CV – elected executive directors is different from those of non – CV – elected ones, and whether difference in average age of directors exists under the two different voting rules. Panel C presents the DID regression estimates [columns (1), (2), (3), (4), (5), (6), and (7)] for exploring whether the political connections of CV – elected directors are different from those of non – CV – elected ones. Standard errors (in parentheses) are heteroskedasticity consistent and clustered at the firm level. ***, **, and * denote significance at the 1%, 5%, and 10% levels, respectively.

In sum, we find that the CV – elected executive directors typically had richer Managerial and industry experience, better education, and less political capital than the non – CV – elected directors, thereby suggesting that CV might have enhanced the professionalism of executive directors in the boardroom.

Considering the positive effects of implementing CV, the next logical step in exploring the effects of CV adoption on corporate governance is deciphering whether or not the significant changes in personal characteristics of executive directors come from executive directors as representatives of shareholders other than the largest ones. If CV – elected executive directors representing shareholders other than the largest ones have better professional experience, such as being CEO or chairman, and having worked in the same industry that the firms belong to, shareholders other than the largest ones did elect into corporate boards better directors through the CV rule. By contrast, if CV – elected executive directors representing the largest shareholders have better educational qualifications, then the largest shareholders elected directors who serve as window dressing when CV was adopted. Clearly, general professional experience is more important to firm operations or firm decisions than educational background. This observation is especially relevant in China, allowing for educational qualifications such as master or doctorate degrees of many firm executives or government officials hide too much inflation. An in – depth investigation necessitated examining changes in director characteristics for directors representing shareholders other than the largest ones and for those representing the largest shareholders. We separately run similar regressions as before based on these two classes of directors. Table 1 – 6 presents regression results based on elected executive directors on behalf of shareholders other than the largest ones. From panel A of Table 1 – 6, clearly, CV – elected executive directors not representing the largest shareholders do not have significant positive changes in educational qualifications. Similarly, Panel C of Table 1 – 6 shows no significant change in the political connections of CV – elected executive directors not representing the largest shareholders. By contrast, Panel B of Table 1 – 6 shows that CV adoption generates more executive directors with CEO or chairman experience and with previous work experience in the same industry as the firm.

Table 1 − 6　CV and the Personal Characteristics of Executive Directors Not Representing the Largest Shareholders

Panel A: Educational Qualifications of Executive Directors

Model	(1)	(2)	(3)	(4)	(5)	(6)	(7)
	Edu1	Edu2	Edu3	Edu4	Edu5	Edu6	Edu7
Intercept	− 0.015	0.749 ***	0.735 ***	0.295	− 0.269	0.239	− 0.030
	(0.14)	(0.21)	(0.24)	(0.31)	(0.30)	(0.18)	(0.33)
CV	0.001	0.024	0.026	− 0.010	− 0.006	− 0.009	− 0.016
	(0.02)	(0.02)	(0.03)	(0.03)	(0.03)	(0.02)	(0.03)
t	0.010	− 0.026 **	− 0.016	0.003	0.011	0.002	0.013
	(0.01)	(0.01)	(0.01)	(0.01)	(0.01)	(0.01)	(0.01)
CV × t	− 0.018	− 0.007	− 0.024	− 0.004	0.031	− 0.002	0.029
	(0.01)	(0.02)	(0.02)	(0.02)	(0.02)	(0.01)	(0.02)
Regulatory	− 0.006	0.005	− 0.001	0.007	− 0.007	0.001	− 0.006
	(0.02)	(0.03)	(0.04)	(0.04)	(0.04)	(0.02)	(0.04)
Board size	− 0.001	0.008 *	0.007	− 0.002	− 0.005	0.001	− 0.004
	(0.00)	(0.00)	(0.00)	(0.01)	(0.01)	(0.00)	(0.01)
Board_ind	− 0.074	− 0.160	− 0.234 *	− 0.202	0.291 **	0.145	0.436 ***
	(0.07)	(0.11)	(0.12)	(0.13)	(0.13)	(0.09)	(0.14)
Duality	0.005	0.014	0.019	0.029	− 0.026	− 0.023	− 0.048
	(0.02)	(0.03)	(0.03)	(0.04)	(0.04)	(0.01)	(0.04)
Related	0.003	0.031 **	0.035 **	0.009	− 0.026 *	− 0.017 *	− 0.043 ***
	(0.01)	(0.01)	(0.01)	(0.02)	(0.02)	(0.01)	(0.02)
Shrcr1	− 0.001	− 0.001	− 0.001	0.000	0.001	− 0.000	0.001
	(0.00)	(0.00)	(0.00)	(0.00)	(0.00)	(0.00)	(0.00)
Shrcr2_10	− 0.000	− 0.001	− 0.001	− 0.000	0.002	− 0.001 *	0.001
	(0.00)	(0.00)	(0.00)	(0.00)	(0.00)	(0.00)	(0.00)
Sd	− 0.006	− 0.006	− 0.012	− 0.009	0.029	− 0.007	0.021
	(0.02)	(0.03)	(0.03)	(0.03)	(0.03)	(0.01)	(0.04)
Fd	− 0.079 ***	− 0.036	− 0.115	− 0.125	0.034	0.207	0.240 ***
	(0.03)	(0.11)	(0.12)	(0.13)	(0.12)	(0.13)	(0.08)

continued

Model	(1)	(2)	(3)	(4)	(5)	(6)	(7)
	Edu1	Edu2	Edu3	Edu4	Edu5	Edu6	Edu7
Firm size	0.006	-0.031 ***	-0.024 **	0.011	0.020	-0.007	0.013
	(0.01)	(0.01)	(0.01)	(0.01)	(0.01)	(0.01)	(0.02)
Leverage	0.002	0.021	0.022	-0.040	-0.019	0.037	0.018
	(0.03)	(0.05)	(0.05)	(0.05)	(0.05)	(0.03)	(0.06)
Firm age	-0.001	0.008	0.007	-0.036	0.048 *	-0.019	0.029
	(0.01)	(0.02)	(0.02)	(0.03)	(0.03)	(0.01)	(0.03)
ROA	-0.032	0.035	0.002	-0.371 **	0.251 *	0.117	0.369 **
	(0.07)	(0.11)	(0.12)	(0.15)	(0.14)	(0.09)	(0.15)
Observations	1074	1074	1074	1074	1074	1074	1074
Adj. R^2	0.008	0.015	0.012	0.002	0.020	0.014	0.026

Panel B: Professional Experiences of Executive Directors

Model	(1)	(2)	(3)	(4)	(5)
	CEO_exp	Chair_exp	Exe_exp	Ind_exp	Pro – exp
Intercept	0.252	0.118	0.369	0.771 ***	-0.062
	(0.29)	(0.24)	(0.41)	(0.21)	(0.32)
CV	0.035	-0.012	0.023	0.030	0.050
	(0.03)	(0.03)	(0.05)	(0.02)	(0.03)
t	-0.025 **	-0.010	-0.035 *	-0.004	-0.010
	(0.01)	(0.01)	(0.02)	(0.01)	(0.01)
CV × t	0.045 *	0.047 **	0.092 ***	0.063 ***	0.011
	(0.02)	(0.02)	(0.04)	(0.02)	(0.02)
Regulatory	-0.033	0.022	-0.011	0.005	0.035
	(0.04)	(0.03)	(0.06)	(0.03)	(0.05)
Board size	-0.013 **	-0.008 *	-0.021 **	-0.004	0.015 **
	(0.01)	(0.00)	(0.01)	(0.00)	(0.01)
Board_ind	0.238	0.112	0.351 *	0.130	0.106
	(0.12)	(0.10)	(0.18)	(0.09)	(0.14)
Duality	-0.040	0.004	-0.036	-0.003	-0.045
	(0.04)	(0.03)	(0.05)	(0.02)	(0.04)

continued

Model	(1)	(2)	(3)	(4)	(5)
	CEO_exp	Chair_exp	Exe_exp	Ind_exp	Pro – exp
Related	−0.008	0.021	0.012	0.013	−0.013
	(0.02)	(0.01)	(0.02)	(0.01)	(0.02)
Shrcr1	−0.001	−0.001	−0.003	−0.000	0.001
	(0.00)	(0.00)	(0.00)	(0.00)	(0.00)
Shrcr2_10	0.002	0.002	0.004*	0.001	−0.003*
	(0.00)	(0.00)	(0.00)	(0.00)	(0.00)
Sd	−0.029	−0.044*	−0.073	−0.047*	0.013
	(0.04)	(0.02)	(0.05)	(0.03)	(0.04)
Fd	−0.192***	0.055	−0.136	0.036	0.004
	(0.06)	(0.10)	(0.12)	(0.08)	(0.24)
Firm size	0.008	0.006	0.014	0.006	0.026
	(0.01)	(0.01)	(0.02)	(0.01)	(0.02)
Leverage	0.077	0.084	0.161**	−0.024	−0.012
	(0.05)	(0.04)	(0.07)	(0.03)	(0.06)
Firm age	−0.009	−0.041	−0.050	−0.016	−0.009
	(0.03)	(0.02)	(0.04)	(0.02)	(0.03)
ROA	0.250*	0.136	0.386*	0.005	−0.139
	(0.14)	(0.11)	(0.20)	(0.08)	(0.16)
Observations	1074	1074	1074	1074	1074
Adj. R^2	0.034	0.025	0.044	0.038	0.043

Panel C: Political Connections of Executive Directors

Model	(1)	(2)	(3)	(4)	(5)	(6)	(7)
	Pol1	Pol2	Pol3	Pol4	Pol5	Pol6	Pol7
Intercept	−0.068	−0.112	−0.043	−0.054	−0.015	0.049	−0.104
	(0.10)	(0.22)	(0.03)	(0.04)	(0.07)	(0.05)	(0.26)
CV	−0.005	−0.015	0.000	0.000	0.016***	0.007	0.009
	(0.01)	(0.02)	(0.01)	(0.01)	(0.01)	(0.01)	(0.02)

continued

Model	(1)	(2)	(3)	(4)	(5)	(6)	(7)
	Pol1	Pol2	Pol3	Pol4	Pol5	Pol6	Pol7
t	−0.003 (0.00)	0.000 (0.01)	0.004 (0.00)	0.003 (0.00)	0.001 (0.00)	0.001 (0.00)	0.001 (0.01)
$CV \times t$	0.004 (0.01)	0.001 (0.02)	−0.005 (0.00)	−0.002 (0.00)	−0.004 (0.00)	0.000 (0.00)	0.002 (0.02)
Regulatory	0.029 ** (0.01)	−0.013 (0.03)	0.001 (0.00)	0.004 (0.01)	−0.003 (0.01)	−0.005 (0.01)	0.018 (0.03)
Board size	−0.001 (0.00)	−0.002 (0.00)	−0.000 (0.00)	0.002 (0.00)	−0.000 (0.00)	0.001 (0.00)	−0.003 (0.00)
Board_ind	0.019 (0.04)	−0.271 *** (0.10)	0.006 (0.01)	0.025 * (0.01)	−0.002 (0.02)	−0.046 (0.04)	−0.232 * (0.12)
Duality	0.005 (0.01)	0.012 (0.02)	0.001 (0.01)	0.005 (0.01)	0.011 (0.01)	0.006 (0.01)	0.032 (0.03)
Related	−0.004 (0.00)	0.011 (0.01)	−0.005 (0.01)	−0.002 (0.01)	−0.001 (0.00)	0.003 (0.00)	0.000 (0.01)
Shrcr1	−0.000 (0.00)	−0.001 (0.00)	0.000 (0.00)	−0.000 (0.00)	−0.000 (0.00)	−0.000 (0.00)	−0.002 (0.00)
Shrcr2_10	0.001 *** (0.00)	0.001 (0.00)	0.000 (0.00)	−0.000 (0.00)	−0.000 (0.00)	−0.000 (0.00)	0.001 (0.00)
Sd	0.009 (0.01)	−0.045 ** (0.02)	−0.007 * (0.00)	0.006 (0.01)	−0.009 ** (0.00)	−0.008 (0.01)	−0.046 * (0.02)
Fd	0.026 (0.04)	0.163 (0.18)	−0.007 (0.01)	0.023 (0.04)	−0.017 (0.01)	−0.018 (0.01)	0.186 (0.17)
Firm size	0.003 (0.01)	0.015 (0.01)	0.002 (0.00)	0.002 (0.00)	0.003 (0.00)	−0.001 (0.00)	0.019 (0.01)
Leverage	−0.003 (0.02)	0.022 (0.04)	0.004 (0.01)	0.003 (0.01)	−0.023 ** (0.01)	0.001 (0.01)	−0.010 (0.05)

continued

Model	(1)	(2)	(3)	(4)	(5)	(6)	(7)
	*Pol*1	*Pol*2	*Pol*3	*Pol*4	*Pol*5	*Pol*6	*Pol*7
Firm age	− 0.003	0.019	0.000	0.001	− 0.005	− 0.002	0.011
	(0.01)	(0.02)	(0.00)	(0.00)	(0.00)	(0.01)	(0.02)
ROA	0.030	0.036	0.009	− 0.011	− 0.021	− 0.004	− 0.046
	(0.05)	(0.10)	(0.01)	(0.01)	(0.01)	(0.02)	(0.10)
Observations	1074	1074	1074	1074	1074	1074	1074
Adj. R^2	0.024	0.020	− 0.006	− 0.002	0.014	− 0.001	0.019

Note: This table reports the DID – style regressions to examine whether CV brings about changes in the personal characteristics of executive directors not representing the largest shareholders, using the sample constructed through BL method. Panel A presents the DID regression estimates [columns (1), (2), (3), (4), (5), (6), and (7)] to test whether the educational background of executive directors elected via CV is different from those elected via straight voting. Panel B presents the DID regression estimates [columns (1), (2), (3), (4), and (5)] to test whether the managerial and professional experiences of executive directors elected via CV is different from those elected via straight voting. Panel C presents the DID regression estimates [columns (1), (2), (3), (4), (5), (6), and (7)] to test whether the political connections of directors elected via CV are different from those elected via straight voting. Standard errors (in parentheses) are heteroskedasticity consistent and clustered at the firm level. ***, **, and * denote significance at the 1%, 5%, and 10% levels, respectively.

Table 1 – 7 presents the other set of regressions based on elected executive directors representing the largest shareholders. The significant and negative coefficients of the interaction terms in columns (2) and (3) of Panel A of Table 1 – 7 indicate that CV adoption elected less executive directors with relatively poor educational background than those elected through straight voting. Consistent with this finding, the results in columns (5) and (7) of Panel A of Table 1 – 7 similarly show that CV adoption elects more executive directors with better educational qualifications who represent the largest shareholders than those elected through straight voting. The negative and significant coefficient of interaction term in column (1) of Panel C in Table 1 – 7 suggests that CV – elected executive directors representing the largest shareholders have less central government work experience than those non – CV – elected. The results in Panel B of Table 1 – 7 demonstrate no significant changes in professional experience for CV – elected executive directors representing the largest shareholders. This set of regressions suggests that the largest shareholders use CV only to elect executive directors with better educational qualifications as window dressing, whereas shareholders other than the largest ones elect executive directors with more experience in industry and senior management through the CV rule. In other words, CV adoption generates more directors who are expected to have an important and positive effect on the decisions and operations of the firm.

Table 1 –7   CV and the Personal Characteristics of Executive Directors Representing the Largest Shareholders

Panel A: Educational Qualifications of Executive Directors

Model	(1)	(2)	(3)	(4)	(5)	(6)	(7)
	Edu1	Edu2	Edu3	Edu4	Edu5	Edu6	Edu7
Intercept	0. 197 *	0. 495 *	0. 691 **	0. 759	− 0. 501	− 0. 255 *	− 0. 756
	(0. 11)	(0. 25)	(0. 28)	(0. 47)	(0. 49)	(0. 15)	(0. 49)
CV	0. 016	0. 079 **	0. 095 **	0. 021	− 0. 041	− 0. 018	− 0. 059
	(0. 02)	(0. 03)	(0. 04)	(0. 05)	(0. 05)	(0. 01)	(0. 05)
t	0. 004	− 0. 004	0. 000	0. 015	− 0. 001	− 0. 009	− 0. 010
	(0. 01)	(0. 01)	(0. 01)	(0. 02)	(0. 01)	(0. 01)	(0. 01)
$CV \times t$	− 0. 016 *	− 0. 058 ***	− 0. 075 ***	− 0. 004	0. 061 ***	0. 010	0. 071 ***
	(0. 01)	(0. 02)	(0. 02)	(0. 02)	(0. 02)	(0. 01)	(0. 02)
Regulatory	0. 006	0. 006	0. 012	− 0. 046	− 0. 002	0. 002	− 0. 000
	(0. 03)	(0. 04)	(0. 05)	(0. 07)	(0. 06)	(0. 02)	(0. 07)
Board size	− 0. 002	− 0. 005	− 0. 007	− 0. 005	− 0. 001	0. 001	− 0. 000
	(0. 00)	(0. 00)	(0. 01)	(0. 01)	(0. 01)	(0. 00)	(0. 01)
Board_ind	− 0. 022	− 0. 112	− 0. 133	− 0. 161	0. 222	0. 144 **	0. 365 *
	(0. 08)	(0. 14)	(0. 17)	(0. 26)	(0. 21)	(0. 06)	(0. 21)
Duality	0. 025	0. 030	0. 055	0. 040	− 0. 072 *	− 0. 031 ***	− 0. 103 **
	(0. 02)	(0. 03)	(0. 04)	(0. 05)	(0. 04)	(0. 01)	(0. 04)
Related	− 0. 004	0. 027 *	0. 023	− 0. 039	− 0. 006	− 0. 009	− 0. 015
	(0. 01)	(0. 01)	(0. 02)	(0. 03)	(0. 02)	(0. 01)	(0. 02)
Shrcr1	− 0. 001	− 0. 002 **	− 0. 004 **	0. 003 *	0. 003	− 0. 001	0. 002
	(0. 00)	(0. 00)	(0. 00)	(0. 00)	(0. 00)	(0. 00)	(0. 00)

continued

Model	(1)	(2)	(3)	(4)	(5)	(6)	(7)
	Edu1	Edu2	Edu3	Edu4	Edu5	Edu6	Edu7
Shrcr2_10	−0.000	−0.003 **	−0.003 **	0.001	0.004 *	−0.001	0.003
	(0.00)	(0.00)	(0.00)	(0.00)	(0.00)	(0.00)	(0.00)
Sd	−0.013	−0.046	−0.059 *	−0.068	0.037	−0.010	0.027
	(0.01)	(0.03)	(0.03)	(0.04)	(0.04)	(0.01)	(0.05)
Fd	−0.057 **	−0.095	−0.151	0.047	0.051	0.136 ***	0.186 ***
	(0.03)	(0.12)	(0.11)	(0.11)	(0.08)	(0.04)	(0.07)
Firm size	−0.004	−0.008	−0.013	−0.014	0.030	0.015 **	0.045 **
	(0.01)	(0.01)	(0.01)	(0.02)	(0.02)	(0.01)	(0.02)
Leverage	0.003	0.008	0.011	−0.089	−0.147 **	−0.035	−0.182 ***
	(0.03)	(0.07)	(0.07)	(0.11)	(0.06)	(0.02)	(0.06)
Firm age	0.006	0.008	0.014	−0.007	0.034	0.011	0.045
	(0.01)	(0.02)	(0.03)	(0.04)	(0.05)	(0.01)	(0.05)
ROA	−0.030	−0.078	−0.108	−0.219	−0.124	−0.030	−0.154
	(0.04)	(0.09)	(0.10)	(0.32)	(0.11)	(0.05)	(0.11)
Observations	1147	1147	1147	1147	1147	1147	1147
Adj. R^2	0.001	0.022	0.024	−0.000	0.010	0.023	0.021

Panel B: Professional Experiences of Executive Directors

Model	(1)	(2)	(3)	(4)	(5)
	CEO_exp	Chair_exp	Exe_exp	Ind_exp	Pro_exp
Intercept	0.350	1.171 ***	1.521 **	0.615	−0.678
	(0.39)	(0.36)	(0.66)	(0.72)	(0.70)
CV	0.024	0.048	0.072	0.049	−0.003
	(0.05)	(0.05)	(0.09)	(0.09)	(0.08)
t	0.011	0.016	0.027	0.015	−0.021
	(0.01)	(0.01)	(0.02)	(0.02)	(0.02)
$CV \times t$	0.021	0.001	0.022	0.008	0.019
	(0.02)	(0.02)	(0.04)	(0.02)	(0.02)

continued

Model	(1)	(2)	(3)	(4)	(5)
	CEO_exp	Chair_exp	Exe_exp	Ind_exp	Pro_exp
Regulatory	− 0. 051	− 0. 019	− 0. 070	− 0. 026	0. 105
	(0. 07)	(0. 07)	(0. 12)	(0. 12)	(0. 12)
Board size	− 0. 022 ***	− 0. 022 ***	− 0. 044 ***	− 0. 014	0. 007
	(0. 01)	(0. 01)	(0. 01)	(0. 01)	(0. 01)
Board_ind	− 0. 191	0. 183	− 0. 009	0. 028	0. 086
	(0. 25)	(0. 18)	(0. 38)	(0. 39)	(0. 34)
Duality	− 0. 032	0. 037	0. 005	− 0. 009	− 0. 056
	(0. 04)	(0. 05)	(0. 08)	(0. 07)	(0. 07)
Related	− 0. 026	− 0. 015	− 0. 040	− 0. 025	− 0. 034
	(0. 03)	(0. 02)	(0. 04)	(0. 04)	(0. 04)
Shrcr1	− 0. 003	− 0. 003 **	− 0. 006 **	0. 002	0. 001
	(0. 00)	(0. 00)	(0. 00)	(0. 00)	(0. 00)
Shrcr2_10	− 0. 001	− 0. 002	− 0. 003	0. 000	− 0. 003
	(0. 00)	(0. 00)	(0. 00)	(0. 00)	(0. 00)
Sd	− 0. 040	0. 005	− 0. 035	− 0. 113	− 0. 042
	(0. 04)	(0. 04)	(0. 07)	(0. 07)	(0. 06)
Fd	− 0. 242 ***	− 0. 068	− 0. 311 ***	0. 110	− 0. 712
	(0. 07)	(0. 07)	(0. 10)	(0. 10)	(0. 10)
Firm size	0. 027	− 0. 022	0. 005	0. 022	0. 068
	(0. 02)	(0. 02)	(0. 03)	(0. 03)	(0. 03)
Leverage	− 0. 100	− 0. 124	− 0. 224	− 0. 267	− 0. 313 **
	(0. 08)	(0. 10)	(0. 16)	(0. 17)	(0. 15)
Firm age	0. 020	0. 018	0. 038	0. 048	0. 008
	(0. 05)	(0. 03)	(0. 07)	(0. 07)	(0. 07)
ROA	− 0. 021	0. 052	0. 031	− 0. 496	− 0. 495
	(0. 18)	(0. 19)	(0. 34)	(0. 36)	(0. 30)
Observations	1147	1147	1147	1147	1147
Adj. R^2	0. 013	0. 028	0. 024	0. 001	0. 022

Panel C: Political Connections of Executive Directors

Model	(1)	(2)	(3)	(4)	(5)	(6)	(7)
	Pol1	Pol2	Pol3	Pol4	Pol5	Pol6	Pol7
Intercept	-0.238	-0.079	-0.095	0.200*	-0.181**	0.198**	-0.101
	(0.16)	(0.36)	(0.07)	(0.10)	(0.08)	(0.09)	(0.40)
CV	0.020*	0.003	-0.002	0.017	-0.008	-0.010	0.032
	(0.01)	(0.04)	(0.00)	(0.01)	(0.01)	(0.01)	(0.04)
t	0.004	-0.014	0.002	-0.000	0.003	-0.000	-0.005
	(0.00)	(0.01)	(0.00)	(0.00)	(0.00)	(0.00)	(0.01)
CV × t	-0.017***	-0.000	0.001	-0.001	-0.009*	0.004	-0.018
	(0.01)	(0.02)	(0.00)	(0.01)	(0.00)	(0.01)	(0.02)
Regulatory	-0.004	-0.036	-0.010	0.002	0.021	0.002	-0.052
	(0.01)	(0.05)	(0.01)	(0.02)	(0.02)	(0.01)	(0.06)
Board size	0.000	-0.010**	-0.002*	-0.003	-0.003	-0.001	-0.014**
	(0.00)	(0.00)	(0.00)	(0.00)	(0.00)	(0.00)	(0.01)
Board_ind	0.025	-0.138	0.007	0.094*	0.070	0.014	0.000
	(0.04)	(0.22)	(0.02)	(0.05)	(0.06)	(0.07)	(0.23)
Duality	-0.018**	0.039	0.006	-0.018	0.019	0.016	0.080
	(0.01)	(0.04)	(0.01)	(0.01)	(0.02)	(0.02)	(0.05)
Related	-0.000	-0.021	-0.005	-0.007	-0.002	0.000	-0.017
	(0.01)	(0.02)	(0.00)	(0.01)	(0.01)	(0.01)	(0.03)
Shrcr1	0.001*	0.001	-0.000	-0.001	-0.001	-0.001	-0.000
	(0.00)	(0.00)	(0.00)	(0.00)	(0.00)	(0.00)	(0.00)
Shrcr2_10	0.001	0.000	0.000	-0.000	-0.000	-0.001	0.001
	(0.00)	(0.00)	(0.00)	(0.00)	(0.00)	(0.00)	(0.00)
Sd	-0.008	-0.013	0.000	-0.002	0.004	-0.014	-0.017
	(0.01)	(0.03)	(0.01)	(0.01)	(0.01)	(0.01)	(0.04)
Fd	-0.027	-0.187***	-0.018	0.004	-0.042**	-0.034	-0.289***
	(0.03)	(0.05)	(0.02)	(0.02)	(0.02)	(0.02)	(0.06)
Firm size	0.009	0.014	0.007*	-0.004	0.013***	-0.004	0.024
	(0.01)	(0.02)	(0.00)	(0.00)	(0.00)	(0.00)	(0.02)

continued

Model	(1)	(2)	(3)	(4)	(5)	(6)	(7)
	*Pol*1	*Pol*2	*Pol*3	*Pol*4	*Pol*5	*Pol*6	*Pol*7
Leverage	-0.030*	-0.041	-0.001	0.008	-0.013	-0.005	-0.099
	(0.02)	(0.07)	(0.01)	(0.01)	(0.02)	(0.02)	(0.08)
Firm age	0.014	0.067*	-0.001	-0.019	-0.015	-0.007	0.042
	(0.01)	(0.03)	(0.00)	(0.01)	(0.01)	(0.01)	(0.04)
ROA	0.027	-0.239	-0.007	-0.008	0.004	-0.004	-0.259
	(0.05)	(0.22)	(0.02)	(0.02)	(0.02)	(0.03)	(0.22)
Observations	1147	1147	1147	1147	1147	1147	1147
Adj. R^2	0.014	0.009	0.017	0.009	0.005	0.003	0.004

Note: This table reports the DID – style regressions to examine whether CV brings about changes in the personal characteristics of executive directors representing the largest shareholders, using the sample constructed via BL method. Panel A presents the DID regression estimates [columns (1), (2), (3), (4), (5), (6), and (7)] to test whether the educational background of executive directors elected via CV is different from those elected via straight voting. Panel B presents the DID regression estimates [columns (1), (2), (3), (4), and (5)] to test whether the managerial and professional experiences of executive directors elected via CV is different from those elected via straight voting. Panel C presents the DID regression estimates [columns (1), (2), (3), (4), (5), (6), and (7)] to test whether the political connections of directors elected via CV are different from those elected via straight voting. Standard errors (in parentheses) are heteroskedasticity consistent and clustered at the firm level. ***, **, and * denote significance at the 1%, 5%, and 10% levels, respectively.

1.5.3　CV and the "Independence" of Independent Directors

One important criterion for assessing the effectiveness of the CV mechanism is to examine whether the independent directors elected through CV are more independent than those elected through straight voting in the sense that the former are less likely than the latter to be closely related to the CEO or board chairman. A thorough and exhaustive check of how closely independent directors are associated with corporate executives is impossible. Nonetheless, we still attempt to partially address this issue by examining several striking observable characteristics, such as the proportion of independent directors who are former colleagues of the CEO or board chairman (*Exe_rel*1), the fraction of independent directors who are alumni/alumnae of the CEO or board chairman in college (*Exe_rel2*), and the percentage of independent directors who are either former colleagues or alumni of the CEO or board chairman (*Exe_rel3*).

Table 1 – 8 presents the results of DID – style regressions to test whether the CV – elected board contains more "independent" independent directors. The regressions in columns (1) and (2) examine the interrelations between independent directors and corporate executives as former colleagues and as college alumni/alumnae, respectively. No statistically significant association is noted, although the sign of the interaction term is negative as expected. In column (3), the relationship between independent directors and corporate executives covers both former colleagues and college alumni/alumnae. The regression produces statistically significant estimated results, indicating that CV – elected boards have a larger proportion of independent directors who are less closely connected with the CEO or board chairman.

Table 1 – 8   CV and the "Independence" of Independent Directors

Model	(1)	(2)	(3)
	Exe_rel1	*Exe_rel2*	*Exe_rel3*
Intercept	– 2. 314	– 8. 398	– 11. 158
	(13. 19)	(18. 89)	(21. 69)
CV	– 1. 750	– 2. 460	– 3. 961 *
	(1. 36)	(1. 90)	(2. 19)
t	– 0. 036	0. 028	0. 155
	(0. 67)	(0. 84)	(0. 95)
CV × t	– 1. 208	– 1. 565	– 3. 002 **
	(1. 00)	(1. 27)	(1. 52)
Regulatory	0. 484	– 0. 009	0. 843
	(1. 77)	(2. 55)	(2. 96)
Board size	0. 169	– 0. 057	0. 128
	(0. 27)	(0. 36)	(0. 43)
Board_ind	– 6. 531	19. 777 *	13. 566
	(10. 27)	(10. 89)	(13. 57)
Duality	– 0. 902	– 0. 679	– 1. 426
	(1. 46)	(1. 97)	(2. 24)

continued

Model	(1)	(2)	(3)
	*Exe_rel*1	*Exe_rel*2	*Exe_rel*3
Related	-1.171*	0.713	-0.621
	(0.64)	(0.91)	(1.05)
Shrcr1	0.085	0.083	0.164*
	(0.06)	(0.09)	(0.10)
Shrcr2_10	0.072	-0.034	0.033
	(0.06)	(0.09)	(0.09)
Sd	-3.269***	2.292	-0.857
	(0.99)	(1.95)	(2.08)
Fd	17.933	-8.003**	10.049
	(17.91)	(3.55)	(17.62)
Firm size	0.244	0.504	0.777
	(0.66)	(0.98)	(1.11)
Leverage	-2.818	6.378*	3.313
	(1.93)	(3.51)	(3.85)
Firm age	1.568	-2.852*	-1.410
	(1.29)	(1.72)	(1.99)
ROA	-2.882	-1.129	-4.383
	(3.23)	(4.80)	(5.58)
Observations	1167	1167	1167
Adj. R^2	0.022	0.016	0.021

Note: This table reports the DID regressions [columns (1), (2) and (3)] to examine whether CV – elected independent directors with close relationships with firm's CEO or chairman have less likelihood than non – CV – elected ones, based on the sample constructed by the BL method. We measure the relationship by three different variables—*Exe_rel*1, *Exe_rel*2, and *Exe_rel*3, respectively. Standard errors (in parentheses) are heteroskedasticity consistent and clustered at the firm level. ***, **, and * denote significance at the 1%, 5%, and 10% levels, respectively.

This set of regressions provides evidence that the use of CV may help reduce the percentage of closely related independent directors from the perspective of visible social network relations. In this sense, CV adoption enhances the independence of independent directors to some extent.

1.5.4　CV and the Personal Characteristics of Independent Directors

Similarly, we investigate the educational qualifications, professional experiences, and political connections of independent directors. Panel A of Table 1 – 9 presents the regression results on the educational background of independent directors. Clearly, no statistically significant differences in educational qualifications exist between the CV – elected and non – CV – elected independent directors.

Panel B of Table 1 – 9 reports the regression results on the professional experiences of independent directors. A larger proportion of the CV independent directors consist of economists or one type of professionals, such as economists, lawyers, and accountants, compared with the non – CV independent directors. Independent directors with richer professional experiences are expected to be more capable of conducting corporate monitoring and advising in the decision – making processes of firms. However, no evidence shows that CV and non – CV independent directors exhibit significant differences in work experience in the same industry.

Panel C of Table 1 – 9 presents the political connections of independent directors. A large percentage of the CV independent directors have central government work experiences [column (1)] or political connections in general [column (7)]. Nevertheless, whether this finding is good or bad for improving corporate governance remains unclear.

One striking feature of the independent director system in China is the prevalence of academics serving as independent directors. Although academics are presumably knowledgeable and capable in corporate monitoring and advising, the investing public believes that they are not very active in discharging their duties on the board. Panel D of Table 1 – 9 the regression results on the influence of CV election on the academic background of academic independent directors. The proportion of CV – elected independent directors coming from academic institutions is smaller than that of non – CV directors. The proportion of CV independent directors who are lawyers is also less than that of non – CV ones. column (5) shows the difference in the percentage of independent directors whose research fields are highly relevant to the main business line of the firms on whose boards they sit. No statistically significant differences are detected between the CV and non – CV firms.

Table 1 – 9   CV and the Personal Characteristics of Independent Directors

Panel A: Educational Qualifications of Independent Directors

Model	(1)	(2)	(3)	(4)	(5)	(6)	(7)
	Edu1	Edu2	Edu3	Edu4	Edu5	Edu6	Edu7
Intercept	12. 106	4. 812	16. 918	– 5. 806	76. 425 ***	12. 463	88. 888 ***
	(7. 53)	(14. 09)	(17. 02)	(26. 04)	(24. 06)	(25. 56)	(28. 58)
CV	1. 559 *	0. 712	2. 271	0. 727	– 1. 050	– 1. 948	– 2. 998
	(0. 82)	(1. 51)	(1. 72)	(2. 77)	(2. 46)	(2. 70)	(3. 03)
t	0. 673	– 1. 299 *	– 0. 626	– 1. 084	1. 303	0. 407	1. 710
	(0. 47)	(0. 75)	(0. 85)	(1. 14)	(1. 06)	(1. 17)	(1. 16)
CV × t	– 0. 054	0. 936	0. 882	0. 134	– 0. 538	– 0. 478	– 1. 017
	(0. 66)	(1. 15)	(1. 30)	(1. 81)	(1. 73)	(1. 91)	(1. 96)
Regulatory	0. 229	3. 284 *	3. 513	– 7. 046 *	2. 667	0. 866	3. 533
	(1. 33)	(1. 98)	(2. 37)	(4. 02)	(3. 44)	(3. 90)	(4. 39)
Board size	0. 102	0. 038	0. 140	– 0. 514	0. 065	0. 310	0. 374
	(0. 21)	(0. 33)	(0. 39)	(0. 53)	(0. 47)	(0. 55)	(0. 60)
Board_ind	– 0. 209	6. 547	6. 338	– 1. 233	– 19. 460	14. 355	– 5. 105
	(10. 08)	(8. 09)	(12. 47)	(19. 99)	(15. 50)	(18. 66)	(19. 71)
Duality	1. 771	1. 543	3. 314	2. 660	0. 657	– 6. 631 **	– 5. 974
	(1. 50)	(2. 27)	(2. 64)	(4. 04)	(3. 43)	(2. 96)	(4. 06)
Related	– 1. 317 **	0. 410	– 0. 907	4. 211 ***	– 2. 508 *	– 0. 796	– 3. 304 **
	(0. 64)	(0. 78)	(1. 00)	(1. 41)	(1. 32)	(1. 53)	(1. 55)
Shrcr1	– 0. 032	0. 001	– 0. 031	0. 081	0. 021	– 0. 070	– 0. 049
	(0. 04)	(0. 06)	(0. 08)	(0. 12)	(0. 11)	(0. 12)	(0. 13)
Shrcr2_10	– 0. 047	0. 025	– 0. 022	– 0. 047	0. 089	– 0. 021	0. 068
	(0. 04)	(0. 06)	(0. 08)	(0. 12)	(0. 11)	(0. 12)	(0. 14)
Sd	0. 850	– 4. 358 ***	– 3. 508 **	– 2. 332	– 3. 108	8. 948 **	5. 840 *
	(1. 19)	(1. 19)	(1. 64)	(3. 19)	(2. 83)	(3. 58)	(3. 52)
Fd	– 2. 997	2. 711	– 0. 286	– 22. 374 ***	30. 565 ***	– 7. 905	22. 661 ***
	(1. 98)	(6. 76)	(6. 22)	(6. 81)	(4. 54)	(4. 84)	(4. 98)

continued

Model	(1)	(2)	(3)	(4)	(5)	(6)	(7)
	Edu1	Edu2	Edu3	Edu4	Edu5	Edu6	Edu7
Firm size	-0.293	-0.244	-0.537	1.778	-2.071*	0.829	-1.242
	(0.39)	(0.68)	(0.83)	(1.22)	(1.14)	(1.26)	(1.36)
Leverage	0.218	5.001	5.218	-3.920	1.182	-2.481	-1.299
	(1.66)	(3.24)	(3.97)	(4.88)	(4.85)	(5.74)	(5.80)
Firm age	-0.424	-0.735	-1.159	0.719	0.937	-0.497	0.440
	(0.65)	(1.24)	(1.42)	(2.45)	(2.39)	(2.32)	(2.66)
ROA	8.456	2.603	11.059	-9.637	-10.346	8.923	-1.422
	(6.62)	(9.17)	(14.90)	(8.63)	(8.11)	(12.14)	(14.09)
Observations	1167	1167	1167	1167	1167	1167	1167
Adj. R^2	0.014	0.009	0.008	0.010	0.010	0.012	0.008

Panel B: Professional Experience of Independent Directors

Model	(1)	(2)	(3)	(4)	(5)	(6)
	Pro1	Pro2	Pro3	Pro4	Pro5	Ind_exp
Intercept	46.677***	-4.038	-19.358	5.074	36.753	-15.863
	(16.05)	(15.83)	(14.90)	(14.22)	(26.15)	(10.89)
CV	6.006***	1.922	-1.083	-3.116**	5.392*	0.721
	(1.72)	(1.59)	(1.68)	(1.55)	(2.83)	(0.91)
t	1.791*	-0.094	0.172	-1.235**	0.289	-0.736*
	(0.97)	(0.69)	(0.76)	(0.57)	(1.12)	(0.42)
CV×t	1.358	1.217	1.149	1.701*	5.025***	0.159
	(1.50)	(1.15)	(1.18)	(0.98)	(1.81)	(0.71)
Regulatory	2.895	-0.250	-0.617	6.542***	6.495*	0.381
	(2.51)	(2.14)	(2.24)	(2.19)	(3.94)	(1.35)
Board size	-1.456***	0.228	0.673*	0.264	-0.398	0.106
	(0.34)	(0.30)	(0.37)	(0.32)	(0.56)	(0.21)
Board_ind	-24.754*	8.060	-7.873	1.285	-14.766	27.524***
	(12.86)	(11.98)	(12.04)	(11.88)	(19.73)	(4.98)
Duality	-2.290	-0.309	1.289	0.043	0.378	0.703
	(2.24)	(2.32)	(2.28)	(2.01)	(3.68)	(1.18)

continued

Model	(1)	(2)	(3)	(4)	(5)	(6)
	Pro1	Pro2	Pro3	Pro4	Pro5	Ind_exp
Related	1. 359	− 0. 733	0. 107	− 1. 248	− 0. 035	− 0. 022
	(0. 90)	(0. 85)	(0. 87)	(0. 82)	(1. 37)	(0. 51)
Shrcr1	− 0. 023	− 0. 029	0. 060	− 0. 042	− 0. 052	0. 023
	(0. 07)	(0. 08)	(0. 08)	(0. 07)	(0. 12)	(0. 42)
Shrcr2_10	0. 090	− 0. 033	− 0. 078	0. 047	− 0. 016	0. 008
	(0. 07)	(0. 07)	(0. 08)	(0. 07)	(0. 12)	(0. 50)
Sd	− 2. 922	2. 412	− 1. 375	− 2. 931 *	− 3. 899	− 0. 422
	(1. 14)	(2. 06)	(1. 88)	(1. 72)	(2. 98)	(− 0. 37)
Fd	− 0. 792	− 3. 193	− 14. 914 ***	− 2. 995	− 21. 033 **	2. 420
	(3. 86)	(5. 59)	(3. 53)	(8. 86)	(10. 49)	(8. 24)
Firm size	− 0. 476	0. 547	1. 399 *	− 0. 176	0. 683	0. 621
	(0. 79)	(3. 30)	(0. 71)	(0. 71)	(1. 29)	(0. 54)
Leverage	5. 290	2. 631	0. 458	− 2. 299	7. 170	− 3. 576 **
	(3. 59)	(3. 30)	(2. 84)	(2. 31)	(5. 07)	(1. 53)
Firm age	1. 169	− 0. 599	− 2. 684 *	2. 916 **	1. 720	0. 119
	(1. 46)	(1. 34)	(1. 40)	(1. 30)	(2. 44)	(0. 86)
ROA	4. 992	− 5. 683	− 2. 580	6. 482	5. 147	− 0. 889
	(4. 83)	(4. 12)	(5. 10)	(6. 66)	(8. 60)	(3. 13)
Observations	1167	1167	1167	1167	1167	1227
Adj. R^2	0. 067	0. 004	0. 018	0. 027	0. 025	0. 041

Panel C: Political Connections of Independent Directors

Model	(1)	(2)	(3)	(4)	(5)	(6)	(7)
	Pol1	Pol2	Pol3	Pol4	Pol5	Pol6	Pol7
Intercept	− 28. 592	− 5. 208	− 14. 016	− 14. 662	5. 765	− 0. 056	− 23. 306
	(18. 23)	(21. 47)	(12. 31)	(9. 91)	(6. 05)	(5. 99)	(25. 76)
CV	− 3. 515 **	− 1. 991	− 0. 775	− 0. 640	0. 180	0. 021	− 4. 938 *
	(1. 77)	(2. 37)	(0. 77)	(0. 98)	(0. 60)	(0. 59)	(2. 81)
t	− 0. 811	− 1. 066	− 0. 417	0. 612	− 0. 097	− 0. 453 *	− 2. 213 **
	(0. 84)	(0. 93)	(0. 26)	(0. 43)	(0. 12)	(0. 26)	(1. 09)

continued

Model	(1)	(2)	(3)	(4)	(5)	(6)	(7)
	Pol1	*Pol2*	*Pol3*	*Pol4*	*Pol5*	*Pol6*	*Pol7*
$CV \times t$	2. 164 *	0. 097	0. 432	0. 382	− 0. 111	0. 259	3. 010 *
	(1. 15)	(1. 47)	(0. 38)	(0. 62)	(0. 34)	(0. 36)	(1. 75)
Regulatory	2. 182	− 1. 139	− 0. 390	− 1. 086	− 0. 964	− 0. 533	− 0. 871
	(2. 45)	(3. 26)	(0. 61)	(1. 27)	(0. 73)	(0. 82)	(4. 07)
Board size	0. 098	0. 328	− 0. 036	− 0. 051	0. 077	0. 155	0. 424
	(0. 37)	(0. 50)	(0. 10)	(0. 22)	(0. 10)	(0. 12)	(0. 61)
Board_ind	− 14. 880	1. 712	− 3. 749	− 6. 231	2. 349	6. 381 *	− 9. 583
	(12. 20)	(15. 86)	(3. 44)	(9. 62)	(2. 89)	(3. 67)	(17. 29)
Duality	− 2. 523	0. 580	− 0. 430	0. 769	0. 391	− 0. 168	0. 555
	(2. 13)	(3. 12)	(0. 57)	(1. 32)	(0. 75)	(0. 70)	(3. 49)
Related	− 0. 195	0. 008	− 0. 231	− 0. 633	0. 314	0. 197	0. 028
	(0. 84)	(1. 24)	(0. 24)	(0. 50)	(0. 31)	(0. 24)	(1. 53)
Shrcr1	0. 120	0. 090	0. 070 *	0. 093 **	0. 008	− 0. 005	0. 218 *
	(0. 08)	(0. 10)	(0. 04)	(0. 04)	(0. 02)	(0. 02)	(0. 12)
Shrcr2_10	0. 136	− 0. 029	0. 081	0. 046	− 0. 020	− 0. 019	0. 089
	(0. 09)	(0. 09)	(0. 06)	(0. 04)	(0. 02)	(0. 02)	(0. 12)
Sd	− 1. 153	1. 546	− 0. 018	− 0. 047	0. 388	− 0. 714	0. 911
	(1. 70)	(2. 60)	(0. 87)	(1. 07)	(0. 64)	(0. 48)	(3. 48)
Fd	1. 682	− 7. 266	− 1. 082	− 2. 917 *	− 0. 874	− 2. 192 *	− 7. 888
	(9. 09)	(11. 57)	(0. 93)	(1. 71)	(0. 90)	(1. 22)	(5. 93)
Firm size	1. 783 **	0. 641	0. 584	0. 845 *	− 0. 285	− 0. 048	2. 052
	(0. 86)	(1. 04)	(0. 55)	(0. 50)	(0. 27)	(0. 30)	(1. 25)
Leverage	− 1. 826	− 0. 723	− 1. 850	0. 782	− 0. 320	0. 764	− 2. 212
	(2. 73)	(3. 93)	(1. 25)	(1. 70)	(0. 83)	(0. 64)	(4. 65)
Firm age	− 1. 143	2. 672	1. 130 *	− 0. 609	− 0. 093	− 0. 435	0. 828
	(1. 66)	(2. 17)	(0. 64)	(0. 84)	(0. 60)	(0. 47)	(2. 50)
ROA	11. 697 *	0. 926	− 1. 910	7. 142	0. 818	1. 557	14. 874
	(6. 24)	(8. 43)	(1. 45)	(4. 82)	(1. 64)	(1. 30)	(11. 16)
Observations	1167	1167	1167	1167	1167	1167	1167
Adj. R^2	0. 032	0. 004	0. 021	0. 017	0. 006	0. 003	0. 012

Panel D: Academic Independent Directors

Model	(1)	(2)	(3)	(4)	(5)
	Academe	Econ	Acco	Law	Match
Intercept	102. 139 ***	40. 896 *	22. 283	13. 115	11. 609
	(30. 83)	(21. 17)	(16. 87)	(9. 35)	(14. 75)
CV	5. 605 *	1. 401	2. 003	0. 530	1. 295
	(3. 31)	(2. 23)	(1. 70)	(1. 02)	(1. 45)
t	1. 333	− 0. 309	0. 337	0. 878 **	0. 370
	(1. 32)	(0. 90)	(0. 70)	(0. 45)	(0. 61)
CV × t	− 4. 543 **	− 1. 261	− 0. 412	− 1. 499 **	0. 041
	(2. 17)	(1. 50)	(1. 18)	(0. 73)	(1. 02)
Regulatory	4. 047	− 0. 095	5. 975 **	2. 808 *	− 3. 150
	(4. 85)	(3. 33)	(2. 54)	(1. 45)	(2. 37)
Board size	− 0. 152	− 0. 258	− 0. 724	0. 385 **	0. 600 *
	(0. 67)	(0. 47)	(0. 35)	(0. 19)	(0. 34)
Board_ind	− 33. 440	− 10. 982	− 18. 467	0. 583	− 0. 101
	(22. 95)	(16. 36)	(11. 21)	(7. 81)	(11. 16)
Duality	− 4. 494	− 1. 854	− 4. 104 *	0. 397	2. 016
	(4. 10)	(2. 81)	(2. 12)	(1. 28)	(2. 12)
Related	− 1. 041	− 0. 980	0. 037	− 0. 723	0. 064
	(1. 66)	(1. 15)	(0. 96)	(0. 52)	(0. 69)
Shrcr1	− 0. 318 **	− 0. 012	− 0. 161 **	− 0. 078	− 0. 047
	(0. 14)	(0. 10)	(0. 08)	(0. 05)	(0. 07)
Shrcr2_10	− 0. 275 *	− 0. 043	− 0. 104	− 0. 015	− 0. 122 **
	(0. 15)	(0. 10)	(0. 08)	(0. 05)	(0. 06)
Sd	2. 907	0. 491	2. 851	1. 855	− 1. 528
	(3. 78)	(2. 56)	(2. 18)	(1. 62)	(1. 41)
Fd	− 22. 714 ***	− 6. 317	− 4. 997	− 5. 026 *	− 3. 891
	(5. 63)	(7. 91)	(4. 06)	(2. 87)	(4. 73)
Firm size	− 0. 971	− 0. 578	0. 327	− 0. 588	0. 189
	(1. 50)	(1. 01)	(0. 82)	(0. 44)	(0. 68)

continued

Model	(1)	(2)	(3)	(4)	(5)
	Academe	*Econ*	*Acco*	*Law*	*Match*
Leverage	−4. 988	−0. 697	−1. 829	−0. 951	1. 200
	(6. 31)	(3. 83)	(4. 65)	(2. 01)	(2. 52)
Firm age	−2. 155	0. 403	0. 868	1. 096	−4. 803 ***
	(2. 76)	(1. 90)	(1. 61)	(0. 75)	(1. 39)
ROA	−0. 720	−5. 064	4. 085	2. 942	1. 106
	(12. 26)	(5. 99)	(7. 38)	(2. 80)	(4. 09)
Observations	1167	1167	1167	1167	1167
Adj. R^2	0. 010	0. 008	0. 023	0. 016	0. 022

Note: This table reports the DID – style regressions to examine whether CV changes the personal characteristics of independent directors, based on the sample constructed by the BL method. Panel A presents the DID regression estimates [columns (1), (2), (3), (4), (5), (6), and (7)] for testing whether the educational background of CV – elected independent directors is different from those of non – CV – elected ones. Panel B presents the DID regression estimates [columns (1), (2), (3), (4), (5), and (6)] to investigating whether the professional experience of CV – elected directors differs from those of non – CV – elected ones. Variable *Pro*1 denotes the proportion of independent directors who are accountants; variable *Pro*2 denotes the proportion of independent directors who are lawyers; variable *Pro*3 denotes the proportion of independent directors who are engineers; variable *Pro*4 denotes the proportion of independent directors who are economists; variable *Pro*5 denotes the proportion of independent directors who have at least one of titles listed above; and variable *Ind_exp* denotes the proportion of independent directors with work experience in the same industry to which the firms they are working as independent directors belong. Panel C presents the DID regression estimates [columns (1), (2), (3), (4), (5), (6), and (7)] for examining whether the political connections of CV – elected independent directors are different from those of non – CV – elected ones. Panel D presents the DID regression estimates [columns (1), (2), (3), (4), and (5)] for probing whether personal characteristics of CV – elected independent directors from academic institutions differ from those of non – CV – elected ones. Variable *Econ* denotes the percentage of independent directors specializing in economics, finance or management when they come from academic institutions; variable *Acco* denotes the percentage of independent directors specializing in accounting when they come from academic institutions; and variable *Law* denotes the percentage of independent directors specializing in law when they come from academic institutions. Standard errors (in parentheses) are heteroskedasticity consistent and clustered at the firm level. ***, **, and * denote significance at the 1%, 5%, and 10% levels, respectively.

Similar to the analysis on executive directors, we consider CV – elected independent directors with less close relations with corporate executives and attempt to unravel whether independent directors with no close relations with corporate executives, as previously defined, also exhibit differences in other aspects. Toward this end, we define a dummy variable *drel* with a value of 1 when no independent directors have close relations with corporate executives in a firm, and 0 otherwise. We subsequently introduce triple interaction terms $CV \times drel \times t$ into relevant regressions to identify whether the more "independent" of the independent directors also show differences in other personal characteristics. Table 1 – 10 presents our empirical results in this line of analysis. Evidently, most results on the coefficients of the triple interaction terms are insignificant but the one in column (2) of Panel C of Table 1 – 10 indicates the high proportion of independent directors with local government work experience among those with no close relations with corporate executives. Stated simply, no strong evidence shows that independent directors with no visual close relations with corporate executives exhibit differences in other respects in terms of the personal characteristics of directors.

Table 1 – 10   **CV, Personal Characteristics of Independent Directors, and Their "Independence"**

Panel A: Educational Qualifications of Independent Directors

Model	(1)	(2)	(3)	(4)	(5)	(6)	(7)
	*Edu*1	*Edu*2	*Edu*3	*Edu*4	*Edu*5	*Edu*6	*Edu*7
Intercept	9.706	4.427	14.133	-6.028	77.175 ***	14.721	91.895 ***
	(7.44)	(13.77)	(16.83)	(27.03)	(24.50)	(26.19)	(29.66)
CV	-1.293	3.787 *	2.494	-3.527	-6.573	7.605 *	1.033
	(1.03)	(2.28)	(2.60)	(4.37)	(4.17)	(4.46)	(4.80)
drel	-0.724	2.153	1.430	-2.337	-4.818	5.726	0.907
	(1.25)	(2.22)	(2.65)	(4.22)	(3.91)	(4.24)	(4.68)
$CV \times drel$	4.250 ***	-4.785	-0.535	6.527	8.676 *	-14.668 ***	-5.992
	(1.50)	(3.02)	(3.45)	(5.38)	(5.04)	(5.55)	(5.99)
t	0.989	-1.974	-0.985	-1.030	1.679	0.336	2.015
	(0.63)	(1.16)	(1.27)	(1.85)	(1.83)	(1.79)	(2.03)
$CV \times t$	-0.704	0.355	-0.349	3.183	-2.486	-0.349	-2.834
	(0.83)	(2.10)	(2.21)	(3.31)	(3.13)	(3.53)	(3.78)
$drel \times t$	-0.570	1.173	0.603	-0.154	-0.720	0.271	-0.449
	(0.72)	(1.43)	(1.62)	(2.32)	(2.24)	(2.49)	(2.74)

continued

Model	(1) Edu1	(2) Edu2	(3) Edu3	(4) Edu4	(5) Edu5	(6) Edu6	(7) Edu7
$CV \times drel \times t$	0.630 (1.27)	0.781 (2.70)	1.411 (2.99)	-4.400 (4.27)	2.349 (4.09)	0.639 (4.56)	2.989 (4.88)
Regulatory	0.186 (1.33)	3.343* (1.99)	3.529 (2.38)	-7.091* (4.05)	2.517 (3.41)	1.045 (3.89)	3.562 (4.41)
Board size	0.120 (0.20)	0.059 (0.33)	0.179 (0.39)	-0.533 (0.52)	0.046 (0.47)	0.309 (0.55)	0.355 (0.60)
Board_ind	0.866 (10.58)	7.005 (8.23)	7.872 (13.12)	-0.983 (20.51)	-20.325 (15.62)	13.436 (18.27)	-6.889 (19.91)
Duality	1.940 (1.51)	1.425 (2.24)	3.365 (2.62)	2.807 (4.04)	0.909 (3.44)	-7.081** (2.97)	-6.172 (4.08)
Related	-1.371** (0.65)	0.463 (0.79)	-0.908 (1.00)	4.130*** (1.41)	-2.594** (1.32)	-0.627 (1.54)	-3.222** (1.55)
Shrcr1	-0.024 (0.04)	-0.000 (0.06)	-0.024 (0.08)	0.082 (0.12)	0.027 (0.11)	-0.085 (0.12)	-0.058 (0.13)
Shrcr2_10	-0.038 (0.04)	0.020 (0.06)	-0.018 (0.08)	-0.041 (0.12)	0.103 (0.11)	-0.044 (0.12)	0.059 (0.14)
Sd	0.652 (1.19)	-4.080*** (1.18)	-3.428** (1.63)	-2.610 (3.18)	-3.634 (2.80)	9.672*** (3.54)	6.038* (3.50)
Fd	-1.739 (2.38)	1.734 (6.83)	-0.004 (5.65)	-21.469*** (7.03)	33.050*** (4.70)	-11.577** (5.40)	21.473*** (5.21)
Firm size	-0.201 (0.38)	-0.300 (0.68)	-0.501 (0.82)	1.858 (1.24)	-1.963* (1.12)	0.607 (1.27)	-1.356 (1.38)
Leverage	0.117 (1.63)	5.240 (3.22)	5.357 (3.95)	-4.124 (4.87)	0.754 (4.83)	-1.987 (5.72)	-1.233 (5.80)
Firm age	-0.382 (0.63)	-0.869 (1.23)	-1.251 (1.40)	0.852 (2.46)	1.143 (2.42)	-0.743 (2.28)	0.399 (2.67)
ROA	8.451 (6.47)	2.561 (9.27)	11.012 (14.83)	-9.693 (8.66)	-10.157 (8.18)	8.838 (11.77)	-1.319 (14.03)
Observations	1167	1167	1167	1167	1167	1167	1167
Adj. R^2	0.025	0.010	0.007	0.008	0.014	0.022	0.007

Panel B: Professional Experience of Independent Director

Model	(1)	(2)	(3)	(4)	(5)	(6)
	Pro1	Pro2	Pro3	Pro4	Pro5	Ind_exp
Intercept	45.169***	−6.367	−14.257	6.729	38.305	−12.195
	(16.24)	(16.28)	(14.85)	(14.05)	(26.68)	(10.51)
CV	4.505*	2.092	−2.509	−4.601*	0.937	1.184
	(2.57)	(2.43)	(2.69)	(2.48)	(4.16)	(1.61)
drel	−0.939	0.968	−3.346	−2.638	−5.127	−3.214**
	(2.59)	(2.36)	(2.61)	(2.64)	(4.29)	(1.37)
CV × drel	2.284	−0.413	2.550	2.486	7.117	−0.400
	(3.40)	(3.14)	(3.40)	(3.14)	(5.51)	(1.91)
t	1.662	−1.273	0.480	−1.848*	−0.993	−1.181
	(1.40)	(0.92)	(1.08)	(1.04)	(1.72)	(0.75)
CV × t	−1.801	0.519	4.037*	0.018	2.696	−1.467
	(2.26)	(1.98)	(2.25)	(1.83)	(3.26)	(1.39)
drel × t	0.186	1.967	−0.539	0.990	2.054	0.745
	(1.88)	(1.34)	(1.46)	(1.12)	(2.34)	(0.85)
CV × drel × t	4.002	0.463	−3.617	2.041	2.472	2.427
	(3.18)	(2.69)	(2.74)	(2.23)	(4.36)	(1.77)
Regulatory	2.835	−0.235	−0.661	6.468***	6.348	0.292
	(2.50)	(2.14)	(2.23)	(2.22)	(3.92)	(1.33)
Board size	−1.431***	0.269	0.601*	0.255	−0.403	0.102
	(0.35)	(0.31)	(0.36)	(0.31)	(0.55)	(0.21)
Board_ind	−24.215*	9.642	−10.547	0.372	−15.562	29.103***
	(13.10)	(12.05)	(11.95)	(12.13)	(19.80)	(5.14)
Duality	−2.159	−0.269	1.231	0.104	0.577	0.591
	(2.22)	(2.33)	(2.28)	(2.03)	(3.65)	(1.19)
Related	1.338	−0.735	0.090	−1.264	−0.100	0.044
	(0.89)	(0.85)	(0.86)	(0.82)	(1.36)	(0.50)
Shrcr1	−0.014	−0.022	0.048	−0.041	−0.045	0.018
	(0.07)	(0.08)	(0.08)	(0.07)	(0.12)	(0.04)

continued

Model	(1) Pro1	(2) Pro2	(3) Pro3	(4) Pro4	(5) Pro5	(6) Ind_exp
Shrcr2_10	0. 099 (0. 07)	− 0. 031 (0. 07)	− 0. 082 (0. 08)	0. 051 (0. 07)	− 0. 005 (0. 12)	0. 005 (0. 05)
Sd	− 3. 066 (1. 92)	2. 525 (2. 06)	− 1. 575 (1. 92)	− 3. 103 * (1. 77)	− 4. 292 (2. 99)	− 0. 533 (1. 14)
Fd	0. 537 (3. 42)	− 2. 976 (6. 34)	− 15. 173 *** (4. 27)	− 2. 053 (8. 94)	− 18. 785 * (11. 02)	2. 424 (7. 68)
Firm size	− 0. 417 (0. 79)	0. 574 (0. 68)	1. 352 * (0. 71)	− 0. 165 (0. 71)	0. 756 (1. 29)	0. 517 (0. 53)
Leverage	5. 220 (3. 56)	2. 807 (3. 31)	0. 174 (2. 78)	− 2. 452 (2. 29)	6. 872 (4. 99)	− 3. 782 ** (1. 53)
Firm age	1. 171 (1. 46)	− 0. 712 (1. 34)	− 2. 498 * (1. 38)	2. 977 ** (1. 28)	1. 844 (2. 41)	0. 255 (0. 85)
ROA	5. 089 (4. 84)	− 5. 738 (4. 10)	− 2. 504 (5. 00)	6. 621 (6. 50)	5. 353 (8. 33)	− 0. 704 (3. 17)
Observations	1167	1167	1167	1167	1167	1227
Adj. R^2	0. 068	0. 004	0. 023	0. 027	0. 027	0. 051

Panel C: Political Connections of Independent Directors

Model	(1) Pol1	(2) Pol2	(3) Pol3	(4) Pol4	(5) Pol5	(6) Pol6	(7) Pol7
Intercept	− 29. 110 (18. 30)	− 9. 448 (22. 10)	− 15. 711 (12. 29)	− 15. 112 (10. 51)	6. 022 (6. 30)	− 0. 486 (6. 09)	− 30. 334 (26. 72)
CV	− 4. 858 * (2. 91)	2. 804 (3. 63)	− 0. 338 (0. 91)	− 0. 951 (1. 42)	− 0. 157 (0. 97)	− 0. 501 (0. 93)	− 3. 696 (4. 34)
drel	− 1. 081 (2. 88)	5. 803 (3. 83)	1. 303 (0. 86)	− 0. 128 (1. 64)	− 0. 360 (0. 94)	− 0. 069 (0. 92)	4. 612 (4. 51)

continued

Model	(1)	(2)	(3)	(4)	(5)	(6)	(7)
	Pol1	Pol2	Pol3	Pol4	Pol5	Pol6	Pol7
CV × drel	2.065	−7.731	−0.803	0.456	0.536	0.781	−2.424
	(3.57)	(4.74)	(1.14)	(1.89)	(1.19)	(1.22)	(5.56)
t	−2.155*	0.909	0.050	0.009	−0.320	0.176	−1.214
	(1.18)	(1.61)	(0.38)	(0.74)	(0.24)	(0.46)	(1.70)
CV × t	2.365	−4.030	−0.374	0.537	0.412	−0.402	−0.642
	(1.84)	(2.65)	(0.63)	(1.10)	(0.60)	(0.82)	(2.95)
drel × t	2.214	−3.208	−0.770*	0.999	0.367	−1.055	−1.638
	(1.59)	(2.14)	(0.46)	(0.86)	(0.30)	(0.67)	(2.45)
CV × drel × t	−0.811	6.278*	1.169	−0.439	−0.783	1.018	4.929
	(2.53)	(3.51)	(0.71)	(1.45)	(0.76)	(1.17)	(4.14)
Regulatory	2.159	−1.044	−0.373	−1.087	−0.967	−0.547	−0.818
	(2.44)	(3.26)	(0.61)	(1.29)	(0.73)	(0.82)	(4.07)
Board size	0.114	0.379	−0.019	−0.041	0.074	0.154	0.505
	(0.37)	(0.50)	(0.10)	(0.21)	(0.11)	(0.12)	(0.61)
Board_ind	−14.205	3.202	−3.023	−5.795	2.313	6.348*	−6.328
	(12.29)	(16.77)	(3.36)	(10.28)	(2.96)	(3.78)	(17.67)
Duality	−2.458	0.494	−0.412	0.788	0.395	−0.130	0.660
	(2.13)	(3.10)	(0.57)	(1.32)	(0.76)	(0.70)	(3.48)
Related	−0.219	0.086	−0.226	−0.640	0.307	0.188	0.037
	(0.83)	(1.24)	(0.24)	(0.50)	(0.31)	(0.24)	(1.53)
Shrcr1	0.125	0.093	0.073**	0.095**	0.008	−0.003	0.232*
	(0.08)	(0.10)	(0.04)	(0.04)	(0.02)	(0.02)	(0.12)
Shrcr2_10	0.139	−0.031	0.082	0.046	−0.020	−0.016	0.096
	(0.09)	(0.09)	(0.06)	(0.04)	(0.02)	(0.02)	(0.11)
Sd	−1.184	1.868	0.023	−0.030	0.375	−0.788	1.071
	(1.76)	(2.63)	(0.90)	(1.09)	(0.63)	(0.48)	(3.49)

continued

Model	(1)	(2)	(3)	(4)	(5)	(6)	(7)
	*Pol*1	*Pol*2	*Pol*3	*Pol*4	*Pol*5	*Pol*6	*Pol*7
Fd	2.231	− 8.143	− 1.050	− 2.790*	− 0.860	− 1.871	− 7.417
	(8.68)	(12.16)	(0.88)	(1.63)	(0.93)	(1.22)	(6.94)
Firm size	1.814**	0.617	0.601	0.855*	− 0.283	− 0.029	2.134*
	(0.86)	(1.04)	(0.55)	(0.50)	(0.28)	(0.30)	(1.27)
Leverage	− 1.797	− 0.436	− 1.792	0.824	− 0.329	0.700	− 1.952
	(2.75)	(3.95)	(1.24)	(1.77)	(0.84)	(0.65)	(4.64)
Firm age	1.169	2.494	1.093*	0.635	0.085	0.404	0.653
	(1.70)	(2.24)	(0.64)	(0.83)	(0.57)	(0.47)	(2.55)
ROA	11.689*	0.880	− 1.939	7.125	0.811	1.579	14.773
	(6.15)	(8.47)	(1.47)	(4.84)	(1.65)	(1.34)	(11.00)
Observations	1167	1167	1167	1167	1167	1167	1167
Adj. R^2	0.030	0.003	0.021	0.014	0.010	0.003	0.012

Panel D: Academic Independent Directors

Model	(1)	(2)	(3)	(4)	(5)
	Academy	*Econ*	*Acco*	*Law*	*Match*
Intercept	103.336***	38.162*	26.686	14.360	10.083
	(31.21)	(21.60)	(17.18)	(9.63)	(15.10)
CV	10.731**	2.309	2.976	0.473	2.156
	(4.94)	(3.42)	(2.71)	(1.57)	(2.02)
drel	3.579	2.843	− 2.361	− 0.708	2.053
	(5.14)	(3.53)	(2.68)	(1.53)	(1.92)
CV × drel	− 7.894	− 1.670	− 1.115	0.173	− 1.494
	(6.57)	(4.53)	(3.45)	(2.03)	(2.73)
t	3.183	0.543	0.443	0.348	1.338
	(2.14)	(1.62)	(1.00)	(0.76)	(0.90)
CV × t	− 5.027	0.028	− 2.786	− 0.369	0.967
	(3.96)	(2.69)	(2.01)	(1.39)	(1.87)

continued

Model	(1) Academy	(2) Econ	(3) Acco	(4) Law	(5) Match
drel × t	−2.997 (2.92)	−1.396 (2.31)	−0.172 (1.59)	0.880 (0.90)	−1.591 (1.20)
CV × drel × t	1.666 (5.30)	−1.539 (3.72)	3.516 (2.81)	−1.617 (1.64)	−0.957 (2.36)
Regulatory	4.141 (4.85)	−0.026 (3.33)	5.916** (2.53)	2.808* (1.46)	−3.099 (2.36)
Board size	−0.171 (0.66)	−0.240 (0.47)	−0.762** (0.35)	0.373* (0.20)	0.605* (0.35)
Board_ind	−34.556 (23.12)	−9.605 (16.31)	−21.095 (11.28)	0.163 (7.75)	0.545 (11.23)
Duality	−4.729 (4.11)	−1.867 (2.80)	−4.184** (2.11)	0.365 (1.28)	1.990 (2.15)
Related	−0.950 (1.66)	−0.976 (1.15)	0.072 (0.96)	−0.723 (0.52)	0.072 (0.70)
Shrcr1	−0.329** (0.15)	−0.011 (0.10)	−0.168** (0.08)	−0.081 (0.05)	−0.048 (0.07)
Shrcr2_10	−0.286* (0.15)	−0.045 (0.10)	−0.107 (0.08)	−0.018 (0.05)	−0.124** (0.06)
Sd	3.198 (3.80)	0.624 (2.60)	2.762 (2.18)	1.866 (1.67)	−1.443 (1.42)
Fd	−24.667*** (5.90)	−6.940 (7.78)	−4.927 (3.78)	−5.261* (2.73)	−4.447 (4.70)
Firm size	−1.084 (1.50)	−0.562 (1.01)	0.256 (0.83)	−0.608 (0.44)	0.191 (0.69)
Leverage	−4.852 (6.35)	−0.554 (3.78)	−2.009 (4.66)	−0.957 (2.02)	1.273 (2.51)

continued

Model	(1)	(2)	(3)	(4)	(5)
	Academy	*Econ*	*Acco*	*Law*	*Match*
Firm age	-2.210	0.343	0.950	1.108	-4.827 ***
	(2.75)	(1.88)	(1.59)	(0.76)	(1.39)
ROA	-0.739	-5.213	4.303	2.937	1.011
	(12.00)	(5.93)	(7.46)	(2.76)	(4.05)
Observations	1167	1167	1167	1167	1167
Adj. R^2	0.009	0.010	0.023	0.014	0.020

Note: This table reports the DID – style regressions to examine whether CV – elected independent directors with no close relation to corporate executives also exhibit differences in their personal characteristics, using the sample constructed via BL method. Panel A presents the DID regression estimates [columns (1), (2), (3), (4), (5), (6), and (7)] to test whether CV – elected independent directors with no close relation to corporate executives also exhibit difference in educational qualifications. Panel B presents the DID regression estimates [columns (1), (2), (3), (4), (5), and (6)] to test whether CV – elected independent directors with no close relation to corporate executives also exhibit difference in professional experience. Variable *Pro*1 denotes the proportion of independent directors who are accountants; variable *Pro*2 denotes the proportion of independent directors who are lawyers; variable *Pro*3 denotes the proportion of independent directors who are engineers; variable *Pro*4 denotes the proportion of independent directors who are economists; variable *Pro*5 denotes the proportion of independent directors who have at least one of titles listed above; and variable *Ind_exp* denotes the proportion of independent directors who have the same industry work experience as the firms in which they work as independent directors. Panel C presents the DID regression estimates [columns (1), (2), (3), (4), (5), (6), and (7)] to test whether CV – elected independent directors with no close relation to corporate executives also exhibit difference in political connections. Panel D presents the DID regression estimates [columns (1), (2), (3), (4), and (5)] to test whether CV – elected independent directors with no close relation to corporate executives also show difference in academic background. Variable *Econ* denotes the percentage of independent directors specializing in economics, finance or management when they come from academic institutions; variable *Acco* denotes the percentage of independent directors specializing in accounting when they come from academic institutions; and variable Law denotes the percentage of independent directors specializing in law when they come from academic institutions. Standard errors (in parentheses) are heteroskedasticity consistent and clustered at the firm level. *** , ** , and * denote significance at the 1% , 5% , and 10% levels, respectively.

1.5.5   Individual Director – Level Analyses

As a robustness check, we also examine the preceding issues by conducting regressions at the individual director – level. Relevant tables are presented in AppendixA. The results are consistent with those derived from firm – level analysis. Some parts yield even stronger results. For example, Table A6 presents the director – level regression results on the relations between independent directors and corporate executives. Statistically significant evidence shows that CV independent directors are less likely to be former colleagues or related as college alumni/alumnae of CEOs or board chairmen.

1. 6   Determinants of Changes in Director Characteristics before and after CV Adoptions

Section 1. 5 presents several significant changes in director characteristics. One question that can possibly arise from exploring the changes concerns the types of CV – using firms that are likely to elect directors with significantly different personal characteristics before and after CV adoption. This section attempts to address this concern from both firm – level and region – level attributes. For regional factors that may affect this type of change in director characteristics, we adopt several indices for China provinces by Fan et al. (2011) to measure province – level governance settings. Data on these indices are also derived from the Index of Marketization of China's Provinces 2011 Report released by the National Economic Research Institute. [1]We use variable *mktdex* to denote provincial overall marketization progress; *pro_dev* to represent the development of commodity market; *mile* to measure the development of market intermediaries and the legal environment; *in_dev* to denote the development of market intermediaries (numbers of independent accountants, lawyers, consultants, chambers of commerce, and other professionals); and *ipr* to represent protection of intellectual property rights.

Variables *Shrcr2_10*, *shrz*, *shrhfd10*, Board size, *Board_ind*, and *Duality*, are

---

[1]   National Economic Research Institute (NEIR) is a non – government, nonprofit research organization, founded in 1996 and located in Beijing. NERI focuses on the study about economic theory and empirical policy, and its publication "Index of Marketization of China's Provinces" has been widely cited in economic and financial research on China (Chen et al. , 2006; Firth et al. , 2009; Li et al. , 2009).

used as firm – level governance variables. The variable *shrz* pertains to the ratio of the share ownership held by the largest shareholder to the share ownership held by the second shareholder, and variable *shrhfd*10 denotes the Herfindahl – Hirschman Index of the first 10 shareholders, which measures the concentration of shares among these top shareholders. We incorporate *Firm age*, *Firm size*, firm *Leverage*, market – to – book ratio, and return on assets as financial variables. Finally, we control the logarithm of the percentage of shareholdings of firm board of directors (*lnbs*) and the logarithm of proportion of shareholdings of firm management (*lnms*).

Our outcome variables are seven dummy variables *dexp*, *dsh*2, *drel*, *dpro*5, *dac*, *dpol*1 and *dpol*7 that indicate the changes in the individual attributes of directors. Specifically, variables *dexp*, *dsh*2, and *dpro*5 take the value of 1 if the percentage of directors with executive experience, the percentage of the second largest shareholder's representatives, and the proportion of directors with advanced professional titles, respectively, have increased in the board in the post – CV period, and 0 otherwise. Variables *drel*, *dpol*1 and *dpol*7 equal 1 if the percentage of independent directors with closer relations with executives, the proportion of directors with central government work experience and the proportion of directors with government connections or experience in general, respectively, have increased in the post – CV period, and 0 otherwise. Variable *dac* equals 1 if the percentage of academic directors has decreased in the post – CV period, and 0 otherwise. The variable are defined as such owing to significant changes in the personal characteristics of directors after CV adoption, as elaborated in Section 1.5. Table 1 – 11 presents a series of probit estimates following the previous discussion. [1]

The results in Table 1 – 11 demonstrate that CV firms located in provinces with relatively weak outer governance environments (in terms of the five indices defined previously) are likely to elect better directors in terms of personal characteristics. For example, column (5) of Panel A suggests that a one – unit decrease in *mktdex* increases the probability that the proportion of directors with advanced professional titles or profes-

---

[1] That the coefficients of variable *Duality* in column (6) of Table 1 – 11 are missing is because the probit model cannot identify them because of non – concavity of the likelihood function with respect to *Duality*. Also the joint significance of models (6) and (7) in Table 1 – 11 do not hold in some regressions. However, for completeness, we also list the results on them in relevant panels.

sional experiences increases after CV adoption by 0.025. In other words, CV firms located in provinces with lower *mktdex* exhibit a higher probability to elect directors with better professional experiences than those with higher *mktdex*, whereas estimates in Panel D generate more significant results on this aspect. In general, province – level and firm – level governance are substitutes in that CV firms belonging to provinces with weak governance settings exhibit high probability to generate better CV – elected directors in terms of director personal attributes. The results on the effects of CEO/chairman *Duality* in these panels suggest that firms with only one person acting as both CEO and chairman show significant negative effects on the positive changes in director characteristics, thus implying that firms with only one person acting as CEO and chairman form a barrier to the positive changes in firm – level governance. Thus, the controlling or the largest shareholders possess great power to control firms and are reluctant to see the positive changes in director characteristics because of their interests, such as expropriation benefits. The results in Table 1 – 11 also indicate that *Firm age* is generally negatively related to the changes in director characteristics. Firms with relatively old age are typically unwilling to accept changes compared with the young firms. In all panels, a strongly negative relationship exists between variable *shrz* and the increase in the number of representatives of the second shareholders. For instance, the coefficient − 0.005 in column (2) Panel A indicates that a one – unit decrease in the ratio of the share ownership of the largest shareholders to that of the second one increases the probability that the proportion of directors as representatives of the second shareholders increases after CV adoption by 0.005. This result is quite intuitive because this variable is a measure of the relative power of the largest shareholder to the second one. A high value of *shrz* denotes the strong power of the largest shareholder, such that representatives of the second shareholder experience difficulty coming into the corporate board. Similarly, the results on the sum of shareholdings among the second to the tenth shareholders in all panels indicate a positive effect on the increase in the number of professional directors. For example, the result in Panel A suggests that a one – percentage – point increase in the sum of shareholdings among the second to the tenth shareholders increases the probability that the proportion of directors with advanced professional titles or professional experiences increases after CV adoption by 0.004. In addition, the estimates on firm performance variables, such as *MTB* lagged once and *ROA* lagged once with negative signs, generally indicate that firms with bad performance are strongly motivated to enhance firm – level governance and change the existing bad situations. In sum, our results on this line of analysis are highly consistent regardless of any type of province – level governance measures used. The analysis also implies that the preceding results are robust.

Table 1 – 11   The determinants of changes in director attributes in CV Firms

Model	(1)	(2)	(3)	(4)	(5)	(6)	(7)
	dexp	*dsh2*	*drel*	*dac*	*dpro5*	*dpol4*	*dpol7*
Panel A: Province Level Governance Measure: *mktdcx*							
mktdex	− 0.021	− 0.005	− 0.002	− 0.037 ***	− 0.025 **	0.001	− 0.006
	(0.01)	(0.01)	(0.01)	(0.01)	(0.01)	(0.01)	(0.01)
Shrcr2_10	0.001	0.002	0.000	0.001	0.004 **	− 0.002	0.000
	(0.00)	(0.00)	(0.00)	(0.00)	(0.00)	(0.00)	(0.00)
shrz	− 0.000	− 0.005 **	− 0.000	0.000	0.000	− 0.000	− 0.000
	(0.00)	(0.00)	(0.00)	(0.00)	(0.00)	(0.00)	(0.00)
shrhfd10	0.000	0.000	0.000 **	0.000	0.000 **	− 0.000	0.000
	(0.00)	(0.00)	(0.00)	(0.00)	(0.00)	(0.00)	(0.00)
Board size	0.015	0.014	0.005	− 0.007	− 0.003	− 0.001	− 0.001
	(0.01)	(0.01)	(0.01)	(0.01)	(0.01)	(0.01)	(0.01)
Board_ind	− 0.084	− 0.523	− 0.044	0.472	0.247	0.311	0.717 *
	(0.52)	(0.43)	(0.27)	(0.38)	(0.46)	(0.27)	(0.41)
Duality	− 0.152 *	0.033	0.078 **	− 0.005	− 0.152 **		0.032
	(0.08)	(0.05)	(0.04)	(0.06)	(0.07)		(0.06)
MTB_t − 1	− 0.023	− 0.025	0.001	− 0.026 *	0.011	− 0.020	− 0.067 **
	(0.02)	(0.02)	(0.01)	(0.02)	(0.01)	(0.02)	(0.03)
ROA_t − 1	− 0.119	− 0.171	− 0.037	− 0.456	− 0.321	0.206	− 0.095
	(0.41)	(0.26)	(0.24)	(0.29)	(0.32)	(0.21)	(0.26)
Firm size	− 0.078 ***	− 0.054 ***	0.003	− 0.031	− 0.028	0.020	− 0.010
	(0.03)	(0.02)	(0.01)	(0.02)	(0.03)	(0.02)	(0.02)

continued

Model	(1)	(2)	(3)	(4)	(5)	(6)	(7)
	dexp	dsh2	drel	dac	dpro5	dpol4	dpol7
Firm age	−0.194***	−0.075	−0.101***	−0.057	−0.171***	−0.054	0.010
	(0.07)	(0.05)	(0.04)	(0.06)	(0.06)	(0.04)	(0.06)
Leverage	0.093	0.039	−0.005	0.021	0.087	−0.113	0.034
	(0.10)	(0.06)	(0.07)	(0.07)	(0.09)	(0.08)	(0.07)
lnms	0.039	−0.001	0.005	0.041**	0.035*	−0.005	0.021
	(0.02)	(0.02)	(0.01)	(0.02)	(0.02)	(0.01)	(0.02)
lnbs	−7.408	−3.727	−112.111	4.468	1.107	−11.124	−16.372
	(6.41)	(4.28)	(111.09)	(2.75)	(3.48)	(17.55)	(10.71)
Observations	314	314	314	314	314	279	314

Panel B: Province Level Governance Measure: pro_dev

	(1)	(2)	(3)	(4)	(5)	(6)	(7)
pro_dev	−0.018	−0.006	−0.012	−0.035**	−0.052***	−0.015	−0.026**
	(0.02)	(0.01)	(0.01)	(0.01)	(0.01)	(0.01)	(0.01)
Shrcr2_10	0.001	0.002	0.000	0.001	0.004**	−0.001	−0.000
	(0.00)	(0.00)	(0.00)	(0.00)	(0.00)	(0.00)	(0.00)
shrz	−0.000	−0.005**	−0.000	0.000	0.000	−0.000	−0.000
	(0.00)	(0.00)	(0.00)	(0.00)	(0.00)	(0.00)	(0.00)
shrhfd10	0.000	0.000	0.000**	0.000	0.000*	−0.000	0.000
	(0.00)	(0.00)	(0.00)	(0.00)	(0.00)	(0.00)	(0.00)
Board size	0.016	0.015*	0.006	−0.004	−0.001	−0.002	−0.001
	(0.01)	(0.01)	(0.01)	(0.01)	(0.01)	(0.01)	(0.01)
Board_ind	−0.131	−0.544	−0.044	0.383	0.124	0.263	0.675*
	(0.53)	(0.44)	(0.25)	(0.40)	(0.45)	(0.27)	(0.40)
Duality	−0.157*	0.031	0.075**	−0.010	−0.166**		0.022
	(0.08)	(0.05)	(0.03)	(0.07)	(0.07)		(0.06)
MTB_t-1	−0.024	−0.025	0.001	−0.028*	0.008	−0.028	−0.071**
	(0.02)	(0.02)	(0.01)	(0.01)	(0.01)	(0.02)	(0.03)
ROA_t-1	−0.174	−0.187	−0.070	−0.574*	−0.417	0.198	−0.163
	(0.41)	(0.25)	(0.24)	(0.29)	(0.32)	(0.21)	(0.26)

continued

Model	(1)	(2)	(3)	(4)	(5)	(6)	(7)
	dexp	dsh2	drel	dac	dpro5	dpol4	dpol7
Firm size	-0.080^{***}	-0.054^{***}	0.004	-0.033	-0.029	0.022	-0.008
	(0.03)	(0.02)	(0.01)	(0.02)	(0.03)	(0.02)	(0.02)
Firm age	-0.207^{***}	-0.076	-0.098^{***}	-0.072	-0.166^{***}	-0.045	0.019
	(0.07)	(0.05)	(0.04)	(0.06)	(0.06)	(0.04)	(0.05)
Leverage	0.094	0.038	-0.005	0.015	0.088	-0.110	0.024
	(0.10)	(0.06)	(0.07)	(0.07)	(0.09)	(0.07)	(0.07)
lnms	0.037	-0.002	0.006	0.036^{*}	0.033	-0.004	0.022
	(0.02)	(0.02)	(0.01)	(0.02)	(0.02)	(0.01)	(0.02)
lnbs	-7.921	-3.748	-99.661	3.927	1.726	-6.836	-13.208
	(6.82)	(4.30)	(111.31)	(2.86)	(3.49)	(10.60)	(8.99)
Observations	314	314	314	314	314	279	314

Panel C: Province Level Governance Measure: mile

	(1)	(2)	(3)	(4)	(5)	(6)	(7)
mile	-0.012	-0.002	0.005	-0.024^{***}	-0.017^{*}	0.000	-0.004
	(0.01)	(0.01)	(0.01)	(0.01)	(0.01)	(0.01)	(0.01)
Shrcr2_10	0.001	0.002	0.000	0.001	0.004^{**}	-0.002	0.000
	(0.00)	(0.00)	(0.00)	(0.00)	(0.00)	(0.00)	(0.00)
shrz	-0.000	-0.005^{**}	-0.000	0.000	0.000	-0.000	-0.000
	(0.00)	(0.00)	(0.00)	(0.00)	(0.00)	(0.00)	(0.00)
shrhfd10	0.000	0.000	0.000^{**}	0.000	0.000^{**}	-0.000	0.000
	(0.00)	(0.00)	(0.00)	(0.00)	(0.00)	(0.00)	(0.00)
Board size	0.015	0.015^{*}	0.006	-0.008	-0.003	-0.001	-0.001
	(0.01)	(0.01)	(0.01)	(0.01)	(0.01)	(0.01)	(0.01)
Board_ind	-0.085	-0.525	-0.072	0.487	0.268	0.311	0.718^{*}
	(0.52)	(0.44)	(0.29)	(0.39)	(0.46)	(0.27)	(0.41)
Duality	-0.145^{*}	0.034	0.073^{**}	0.004	-0.142^{**}		0.034
	(0.08)	(0.05)	(0.04)	(0.06)	(0.07)		(0.06)
MTB_t-1	-0.024	-0.024	0.001	-0.028^{*}	0.011	-0.020	-0.067^{**}
	(0.02)	(0.02)	(0.01)	(0.02)	(0.01)	(0.02)	(0.03)

continued

Model	(1)	(2)	(3)	(4)	(5)	(6)	(7)
	dexp	dsh2	drel	dac	dpro5	dpol4	dpol7
ROA_t − 1	−0.129	−0.176	−0.052	−0.479	−0.336	0.206	−0.096
	(0.41)	(0.25)	(0.24)	(0.30)	(0.32)	(0.21)	(0.26)
Firm size	−0.079 ***	−0.054 ***	0.000	−0.031	−0.029	0.020	−0.010
	(0.03)	(0.02)	(0.01)	(0.02)	(0.03)	(0.02)	(0.02)
Firm age	−0.198 ***	−0.077	−0.104 ***	−0.062	−0.175 ***	−0.054	0.010
	(0.08)	(0.05)	(0.04)	(0.06)	(0.07)	(0.04)	(0.06)
Leverage	0.096	0.040	−0.011	0.021	0.090	−0.113	0.034
	(0.10)	(0.06)	(0.07)	(0.07)	(0.09)	(0.08)	(0.07)
lnms	0.039	−0.001	0.003	0.040 **	0.034	−0.005	0.021
	(0.02)	(0.02)	(0.01)	(0.02)	(0.02)	(0.01)	(0.02)
lnbs	−7.682	−3.876	−133.881	4.407	1.126	−11.113	−16.405
	(6.57)	(4.41)	(113.16)	(2.84)	(3.46)	(17.42)	(10.92)
Observations	314	314	314	314	314	279	314

Panel D: Province Level Governance Measure: in_dev

	(1)	(2)	(3)	(4)	(5)	(6)	(7)
in_dev	−0.023 **	−0.020 **	0.014 **	−0.025 ***	−0.006	0.009	0.005
	(0.01)	(0.01)	(0.01)	(0.01)	(0.01)	(0.01)	(0.01)
Shrcr2_10	0.001	0.002	0.000	0.001	0.004 **	−0.001	0.000
	(0.00)	(0.00)	(0.00)	(0.00)	(0.00)	(0.00)	(0.00)
shrz	−0.000	−0.005 **	−0.000	0.000	0.000	0.000	−0.000
	(0.00)	(0.00)	(0.00)	(0.00)	(0.00)	(0.00)	(0.00)
shrhfd10	0.000	0.000	0.000 **	0.000	0.000 *	−0.000	0.000
	(0.00)	(0.00)	(0.00)	(0.00)	(0.00)	(0.00)	(0.00)
Board size	0.014	0.013	0.008	−0.008	−0.002	0.001	−0.000
	(0.01)	(0.01)	(0.01)	(0.01)	(0.01)	(0.01)	(0.01)
Board_ind	−0.059	−0.422	−0.116	0.453	0.218	0.311	0.710 *
	(0.52)	(0.38)	(0.31)	(0.39)	(0.45)	(0.26)	(0.42)
Duality	−0.134	0.053	0.064 *	0.014	−0.152 **		0.031
	(0.08)	(0.05)	(0.04)	(0.07)	(0.07)		(0.06)

continued

Model	(1)	(2)	(3)	(4)	(5)	(6)	(7)
	dexp	*dsh2*	*drel*	*dac*	*dpro5*	*dpol4*	*dpol7*
MTB_t-1	-0.026	-0.031	0.003	-0.031*	0.010	-0.017	-0.064**
	(0.02)	(0.02)	(0.01)	(0.02)	(0.01)	(0.02)	(0.03)
ROA_t-1	-0.107	-0.097	-0.057	-0.479	-0.343	0.208	-0.112
	(0.41)	(0.26)	(0.24)	(0.30)	(0.32)	(0.21)	(0.26)
Firm size	-0.074***	-0.051**	-0.005	-0.027	-0.031	0.016	-0.014
	(0.03)	(0.02)	(0.01)	(0.02)	(0.03)	(0.02)	(0.02)
Firm age	-0.196***	-0.067	-0.106***	-0.070	-0.190***	-0.069*	-0.002
	(0.07)	(0.05)	(0.03)	(0.06)	(0.06)	(0.04)	(0.06)
Leverage	0.096	0.036	-0.011	0.017	0.089	-0.110	0.038
	(0.10)	(0.07)	(0.07)	(0.07)	(0.09)	(0.07)	(0.07)
lnms	0.036	-0.000	0.004	0.033*	0.029	-0.002	0.021
	(0.02)	(0.02)	(0.01)	(0.02)	(0.02)	(0.01)	(0.02)
lnbs	-7.106	-3.008	-149.145	3.996	0.192	-11.575	-18.245
	(6.18)	(3.87)	(113.87)	(2.85)	(3.52)	(22.14)	(11.14)
Observations	314	314	314	314	314	279	314

Panel E: Province Level Governance Measure: *ipr*

ipr	-0.003	0.001	0.002	-0.008**	-0.006*	-0.000	-0.001
	(0.00)	(0.00)	(0.00)	(0.00)	(0.00)	(0.00)	(0.00)
Shrcr2_10	0.001	0.002	0.000	0.001	0.004**	-0.002	0.000
	(0.00)	(0.00)	(0.00)	(0.00)	(0.00)	(0.00)	(0.00)
shrz	-0.000	-0.005**	-0.000	0.000	0.000	-0.000	-0.000
	(0.00)	(0.00)	(0.00)	(0.00)	(0.00)	(0.00)	(0.00)
shrhfd10	0.000	0.000	0.000**	0.000	0.000**	-0.000	0.000
	(0.00)	(0.00)	(0.00)	(0.00)	(0.00)	(0.00)	(0.00)
Board size	0.016	0.015*	0.006	-0.006	-0.002	-0.001	-0.001
	(0.01)	(0.01)	(0.01)	(0.01)	(0.01)	(0.01)	(0.01)
Board_ind	-0.097	-0.557	-0.070	0.482	0.270	0.309	0.720*
	(0.52)	(0.44)	(0.28)	(0.39)	(0.46)	(0.27)	(0.41)

continued

Model	(1)	(2)	(3)	(4)	(5)	(6)	(7)
	dexp	dsh2	drel	dac	dpro5	dpol4	dpol7
Duality	−0.149 *	0.032	0.074 **	0.003	−0.145 **		0.034
	(0.08)	(0.05)	(0.04)	(0.07)	(0.07)		(0.06)
MTB_t − 1	−0.023	−0.023	0.001	−0.026	0.011	−0.021	−0.067 **
	(0.02)	(0.02)	(0.01)	(0.02)	(0.01)	(0.02)	(0.03)
ROA_t − 1	−0.134	−0.195	−0.056	−0.479	−0.334	0.207	−0.095
	(0.41)	(0.25)	(0.24)	(0.29)	(0.32)	(0.20)	(0.26)
Firm size	−0.080 ***	−0.053 ***	0.001	−0.034	−0.031	0.021	−0.011
	(0.03)	(0.02)	(0.01)	(0.02)	(0.03)	(0.02)	(0.02)
Firm age	−0.204 ***	−0.086 *	−0.105 ***	−0.065	−0.175 ***	−0.051	0.010
	(0.08)	(0.05)	(0.04)	(0.06)	(0.07)	(0.04)	(0.06)
Leverage	0.097	0.042	−0.010	0.022	0.090	−0.114	0.035
	(0.10)	(0.06)	(0.07)	(0.07)	(0.09)	(0.08)	(0.07)
lnms	0.038	−0.003	0.003	0.040 **	0.035 *	−0.004	0.021
	(0.02)	(0.02)	(0.01)	(0.02)	(0.02)	(0.01)	(0.02)
lnbs	−8.115	−4.299	−128.997	4.002	1.005	−11.152	−16.560
	(6.87)	(4.76)	(111.86)	(2.91)	(3.46)	(16.86)	(11.14)
Observations	314	314	314	314	314	279	314

Note: This table reports probit estimates [columns (1), (2), (3), (4), (5), (6), and (7)] for examining the types of factors influencing the changes of director characteristics through CV adoption, based on the CV firms that adopted CV in between 2002 and 2005. The reported coefficients are marginal effects estimated with a probit model and computed at the mean of the independent variables. All regressions contain a constant term (not reported). Robust standard errors are in parentheses. *** , ** , and * denote significance at the 1% , 5% , and 10% levels, respectively.

1.7　Discussion

This study carries out two parts of analysis to examine the influence of the CV voting rule. In the first part, we investigate the changes CV has brought to the power structure of the corporate board and the individual characteristics of the board members. We find that the CV – elected boards manifest more balanced representativeness of shareholder interests than non – CV – elected boards. In addition, CV – elected directors have stronger professional background and educational qualifications than the non – CV – elected directors, and CV – elected independent directors are more independent in the sense of having less close relations with corporate executives. For example, the proportion of CV executive directors having executive experience is greater than that of non – CV directors; the proportion of CV executive directors with prior work experience in the same industry is higher than that of non – CV executive directors; and the proportion of CV independent directors having close relations with former colleagues or fellow alumni/alumnae among corporate executives is smaller and thus implies a higher degree of independence compared with non – CV independent directors. These findings indicate that CV adoption produces improvements in the quality of board directors elected.

In the second part of the empirical analysis, we find that CV firms located in provinces and which exhibit relatively weak outer governance environments in terms of the five indices defined previously are likely to elect better directors in terms of director personal characteristics. In general, province – and firm – level governance are substitutes in that CV firms belonging to provinces with weak governance settings exhibit high probability to generate better CV – elected directors in terms of director personal attributes. Moreover, firms with only one person acting as both CEO and chairman form a barrier to the positive changes in firm – level governance. In addition, Firm age is generally negatively related to the changes in director characteristics, and the ratio of the share ownership of the largest shareholders to that of the second one increases the probability that the proportion of directors as representatives of the second shareholders increases after CV adoption by 0. 05. Furthermore, the sum of shareholdings among the second to the tenth shareholders positively affects the increase in the number of professional directors. Firms with bad performance are also strongly motivated to enhance firm – level governance to change existing bad situations.

These findings largely suggest that CV implementation truly improves, to some extent, the balance of representativeness in the board, the professionalism and educational qualifications of directors, and the independence of independent directors.

1. 8   Conclusion

Similar to most emerging markets, corporate China is plagued with the problem of the expropriation of minority shareholders by the controlling shareholders. The Chinese regulatory authority introduced a host of Western governance institutions in the early 2000s to strengthen the protection of minority shareholder interests. One prominent measure is the adoption of the CV rule, which is designed to enable minority shareholders, especially the large minority shareholders or non – controlling substantial shareholders, to elect their representatives into the corporate board to enhance corporate governance.

A salient difficulty in research on corporate governance is "endogeneity" or "self selection" problem. This study attempts to address this issue using the matching methods for constructing a control group and by running DID – style regressions to further reduce econometrical confoundedness. We employ two different matching methods for constructing two samples and increasing the robustness of our main empirical results; the sample from the BL matching is used to yield all of the main conclusions. In Appendix A, we provide the main estimated results using the sample from the CEM process, which are consistent with those from the sample through the BL method.

The most important contribution of this study lies in the use of hand – collected unique data to analyze the differences in the personal characteristics of directors under different voting mechanisms. To the best of our knowledge, this study is the first work to tackle the issue at the individual level of directors. Using a sub – sample in which the top 10 large shareholders were not related, we find that the percentage of CV – elected directors who represented the second largest shareholder was significantly higher than that of non – CV – elected directors, thus showing that CV implementation did work to some extent as the regulators had originally intended. The same result is obtained when we control for other firm characteristics. Second, we find that the percentage of directors with previous experience as CEO or chairman was positively related to CV adoption.

This result also holds after we control for other firm characteristics. Third, the percentage of directors who worked in the same industry was positively associated with CV use, which remains true after controlling for other firm characteristics. Fourth, the educational qualifications of directors increased after the adoption of CV, which still holds after we control for other firm characteristics. Fifth, a smaller proportion of CV – elected directors had previous experience in the central government, the national committee of CPPCC, and the National People's Congress compared with non – CV – elected directors.

Moreover, our regression results indicate that the percentage of independent directors exhibiting close relations with controlling shareholders decreased in the post – CV period. This result is invariant when controlling for other firm characteristics. The aforementioned conclusions are robust in that the regression results from the two samples generated by the BL matching and the CEM matching are consistent.

A growing literature has been endeavoring to establish interactions between firm level and country – level governance in various settings. This line of literature principally attempts to identify this relation with a global view based on data across countries. However, relevant findings from this line of work are inconsistent. We find that firm – level and province – level governance in China are substitutes with a relatively micro view.

Our findings indicate that CV use has engendered several positive changes to the quality of directors and the independence of independent directors. In addition, different province – level governance settings exhibit important effects on the validity of CV adoption. The Chinese experience may have useful implications for other emerging market economies characterized by weak legal institutions and weak investor protection.

Chapter 2　Cumulative Voting, Firm Performance, and Corporate Policies

2.1　Introduction

In Chapter1, we report the results of the investigation on whether CV adoption positively changes the boardroom in terms of the personal characteristics of directors. We find several salient and positive changes in the personal characteristics of directors after CV implementation. We also obtain evidence that shareholder power structure in corporate boards has been changed slightly on a subsample basis after the use of CV. The matter that logically follows from the previous discussion concerns whether the adoption of CV and the changes in the characteristics of board directors have affected firm performance. Another concern is how CV shaped corporate policy changes. These major issues are discussed in this chapter.

Using an unbalanced panel dataset covering 2002 – 2008, we examine the effects of CV on four indicators of firm performance, namely, industry – adjusted Tobin's Q, industry – adjusted market – to – book ratio ($AMTB$), industry – adjusted ROA, and industry – adjusted return on equity (ROE). Using the DID – style regression analysis, no consistently significant evidence could show that the use of CV significantly enhances firm performance. The results from the two samples generated by BL matching and CEM matching are consistent with each other.

We explore how CV shapes corporate policy changes to understand the rationale for CV influence on corporate performance. We focus on whether CV adoption affects the tunneling or propping – up activities from the controlling shareholder, as well as other corporate financial and investment policies. We cannot find strong evidence that the use of CV could effectively curb tunneling activities, thereby suggesting that the improvement in the power structure following CV implementation is still too small to generate fundamental changes in corporate policies and firm performance.

This study contributes to the literature on shareholder voting mechanisms. Previous studies (Bhagat and Brickley, 1984; Harris and Raviv, 1988; Grossman and Hart, 1988; DeAngelo and DeAngelo, 1985; Klapper and Love, 2004; Zingales, 1994, 1995; Bethel and Gillan, 2002; Klapper et al., 2006; Bebchuk et al., 2009; Iliev et al., 2011) have investigated the effects of different shareholder voting mechanisms on corporate governance. Several earlier investigations indicate that CV positively affects corporate valuation, but these studies cannot identify the channels through which CV influences firm performance. Thus, the results might be affected by confounding factors. This research fills the void by introducing the personal characteristics of elected directors under different voting mechanisms into regressions to determine whether CV can enhance firm performance or curb tunneling activities.

This study is related to a large body of literature on law and finance. For instance, La Porta et al. (1998) investigate the legal rules and investor protection measures in 47 countries and reveal that only 27% of their sample countries have laws for CV or proportional representation, with countries of German legal origin having the highest percentage (33%). This study tests the theory developed by La Porta et al. (2002) at the firm – level in one country, which indicates that strong investor protection is associated with high firm value among different countries. ① Klapper and Love (2004) report a wide variation in firm – level governance and point out that the average firm – level governance is lower in countries with weak legal systems than in those with strong legal systems based on data on firm – level corporate governance rankings across 14 emerging markets. Klapper and Love (2004) also provide evidence that provisions in firm – level corporate governance matter more in countries with weak legal environments. In addition, Price et al. (2011) examine the relationship between the efforts of Mexico to improve corporate governance and firm performance and transparency, and demonstrate

---

① In their model, they derive an explicit positive relation between Tobin's Q and investor protection.

that a single reform on corporate governance launched by regulators alone is insufficient to fundamentally change economic behavior. The objective of the current paper is to determine whether firm – level corporate governance provisions, such as CV, matter in China, a country with weak legal environments.

This study also enriches the literature on corporate policies, especially on tunneling and propping – up activities. For instance, Cheung et al. (2006) examine related party transactions between Hong Kong SAR listed companies and their controlling shareholders. They argue that firm announcing related party transactions earn significant negative excess returns, which are significantly lower than those of firms announcing similar arm's length transactions. In addition, Jiang et al. (2010) investigate a particular form of tunneling activities (through intercorporate loans) in China and indicate that the minority shareholder expropriation problem in China is quite severe. The present study attempts to verify whether CV implementation can effectively contain tunneling activities or encourage propping – up activities. We also attempt to examine whether CV adoption exerts substantial effects on other corporate polices, such as executive compensation, firm Leverage, and corporate capital expenditure.

The rest of the chapter proceeds as follows. Section 2.2 discusses the empirical methods adopted in this study. Section 2.3 describes the variables and the data used, and Section 2.4 discusses the influence of CV implementation on firm performance. Section 2.5 shows the investigation of the effects of CV adoption on corporate policy changes, and Section 2.6 discusses the findings. Section 2.7 concludes.

2. 2   Methodology

As in Chapter 1, we initially apply control – group methods, and then conduct DID style analysis to overcome or reduce the "endogeneity" problem to the maximum limit. In other words, our analysis in this chapter is based on BL and CEM matching processes. The details of the matching methods are already discussed in Chapter 1.

We perform DID – style regression analysis to further reduce the "self – selection" bias. Our identification strategy follows the principles of DID in that we primarily compare the changes in the treatment – group firms before and after the CV implementation prior to comparing the changes in the treatment – group firms with those in the control – group firms. The DID – style regressions can remove biases in the comparisons between CV users and non – CV users in the post – CV period that could result from the permanent differences between these two groups. The regressions can also preclude the biases over time in the CV – using firms as a result of the time trends.

Our baseline regression model is as follows:

$$Y_{it} = \alpha_i + \alpha_t + \beta CV_{it} + \delta CV_{it} \times z + \gamma X_{it} + \varepsilon_{it} \qquad (2-1)$$

where i indexes firms and t indexes time; Y_{it} is the outcome variable; CV_{it} is an indicator variable that equals 1 if firm i has used CV in director election by year t, and 0 otherwise; X_{it} is a vector of control variables; α_i and α_t represent firm and year fixed effects respectively; and ε_{it} is the error term. Variable z equals 0 in our basic regressions without incorporating any director attributes, but it equals a dummy variable d when director characteristics are introduced into the analysis. We select the CV firms in which the change in several characteristics of the directors that may be beneficial to firm performance or conducive to curbing tunneling activities, and we define a dummy d for those firms as equal to 1 once the change occurs.

2. 3   Data and Variables

We identify the firms that adopted CV and the directors elected through CV from the information on shareholder meetings in The Disclosure by Listed Companies available from SHSE and SZSE. The firm – level accounting, financial, corporate ownership, and corporate governance data are obtained from CSMAR database.

The basic sample is obtained by combining the BL (CEM) sample in Chapter1 and firm – level accounting and corporate governance data for 2002 – 2008. The sample used from the BL method consists of around 3900 firm – year observations, whereas the sample used from CEM process consists of 5600 firm – year observations. ①

The definitions of the main variables used in the empirical analysis are listed in Table B1 of Appendix B.

In the set of regressions on the relationship between CV and firm value, the control variables include both financial variables and corporate governance variables. As suggested by Doidge et al. (2004), Bebchuk et al. (2011) and Lu and Shi (2012) firm size, firm age, and firm Leverage are closely related to firm value and included as important financial variables. In addition, the nature of ownership variables Sd (dummy of State – holding firms) and Fd (dummy of Foreign – holding firms) also may influence firm value and are thus included as covariates in this set of regressions.

In the process of exploring the influence of CV use on firm tunneling activities, we select two commonly used measures on tunneling based on the previous literature. Similar to Berkman et al. (2011) and Qian and Zhao (2011), we adopt the annual aggregate value of related – party transactions for each firm divided by the year – end total assets (TRPT) of the firm. Base on Cheung et al. (2006, 2009), TRPT in turn can be divided into two components, one of which is potentially beneficial for the listed company if it received cash, loans, or guarantees from the related party (BRPT), and the other is the harmful related – party transactions (HRPT) that equal TRPT subtracted by BRPT. Our second proxy for expropriation by controlling shareholders is the ratio of other receivables over total book assets (OAR). Jiang et al. (2010) find this ratio to be highly related to the extent of the tunneling activities of the controlling shareholders.

We also follow the previous literature on tunneling during the selection of our control variables (Jiang et al. , 2010; Qian and Zhao, 2011). Based on the recent literature on tunneling, we incorporate firm age, firm Leverage, firm size, market to book ratio, the percentage of shares held by controlling shareholders, and ownership structure into our regression equations as control variables. Moreover, we also control CEO/chairman duality, board size, and board independence. We winsorize all of the financial variables at the 1% and 99% levels for each year.

---

① The precise number of firm – year observations depends on the dependent variables and regression models, which are shown in relevant tables later.

2. 4   CV and Firm Performance

In this section, we mainly discuss the effects of CV adoption on firm performance. We consider a sub – sample consisting of all CV firms that adopted CV in 2005 and their controls for preliminary analysis. This sub – sample is used as a benchmark case because the number of CV firms reached its peak (253) in 2005 in our BL sample, accounting for approximately 72% of total CV firms in 2002 – 2005. We examine the effect of CV adoption on firm performance through the following simple pictures based on this sub – sample.

In Figure 2. 1 – 2. 4, no strong evidence shows that the use of CV can effectively enhance firm performance. Considering that a director typically holds office for three years, we principally consider the three years after the adoption year (2005). In the subsequent three years, the differences in firm performance between CV firms and their controls are almost negligible, whereas the differences in firm performance in the years before the adoption year are also insignificant. For example, with regard to industry –

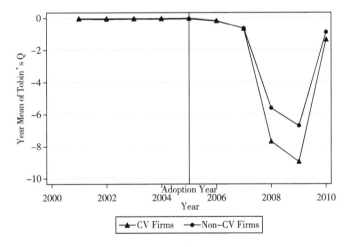

Figure 2. 1   This figure describes the relationship between CV adoption and Tobin's Q (industry – adjusted) after CV adoption.

adjusted ROA, the difference in firm performance both in the years before the adoption year and in the subsequent three years after the adoption year is almost 0. These four figures show that the use of CV does not produce salient influence on firm performance, at least for this sub – sample case.

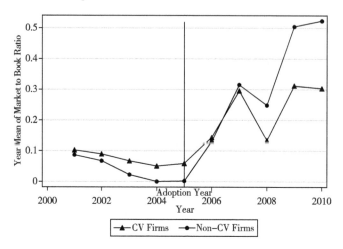

Figure 2. 2   This figure describes the relationship between CV adoption and market to book ratio (industry – adjusted) after CV adoption

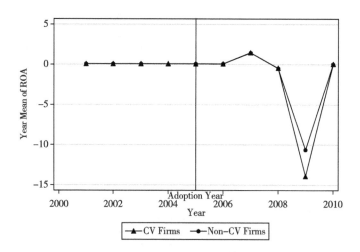

Figure 2. 3   This figure describes the relationship between CV adoption and ROA (industry – adjusted) after CV adoption.

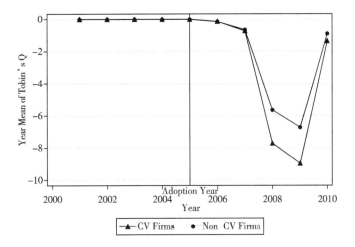

Figure 2. 4   This figure describes the relationship between CV adoption and ROE (industry – adjusted) after CV adoption.

We also conduct DID – style analysis based on this sub – sample. If CV – elected directors play a role in improving firm performance, firms require time to absorb such a role from CV – directors. Thus, we incorporate six dummy variables into our regression analysis. We use variables $d\_1 - d4$ to represent the year before adoption of CV, years $0 - 3$ after CV adoption, and year 4 forward for CV firms; these dummy variables equal 1 for CV firms when relevant time constraints hold (i. e. , $d1 = 1$ if a firm is a CV firm and time variable $year = 2006$; 0 otherwise). Table $2 - 1$ presents this line of analysis using a panel dataset that covers $2002 - 2010$ based on this sub – sample. Columns (1) – (4) show the regression results, where the firm performance indicators include the industry – adjusted Tobin's Q, industry – adjusted market – to – book ratio, industry – adjusted ROA, and industry – adjusted ROE, respectively. Based on the table, no evidence indicates that CV adoption exerts a significant effect on firm performance. This result remains to be true regardless of the firm performance measure used, as shown in the four columns of Table $2 - 1$, and does not depend on the choices of time lags or leads either. Therefore, both the previous visual check and this more precise regressions indicate that the use of CV does not generate considerable effects on firm performance.

Table 2 – 1   CV Adoption and Firm Performance: Sub – Sample Case.

Model	(1)	(2)	(3)	(4)
	Tobin's Q	AMTB	ROA	ROE
Intercept	– 18. 823	11. 483 ***	– 24. 428 *	– 0. 696 **
	(16. 87)	(0. 75)	(13. 47)	(0. 34)
d_1	0. 035	– 0. 001	0. 034	– 0. 035
	(0. 18)	(0. 03)	(0. 20)	(0. 04)
d0	0. 086	– 0. 008	– 0. 011	0. 073
	(0. 25)	(0. 03)	(0. 27)	(0. 05)
d1	0. 156	– 0. 006	0. 043	– 0. 085
	(0. 24)	(0. 05)	(0. 24)	(0. 10)
d2	– 0. 077	– 0. 021	– 0. 025	– 0. 015
	(0. 37)	(0. 10)	(0. 56)	(0. 06)
d3	– 2. 671	– 0. 029	– 0. 250	0. 037
	(3. 10)	(0. 06)	(0. 44)	(0. 06)
d4	– 1. 516	– 0. 135	– 2. 172	0. 005
	(2. 01)	(0. 12)	(2. 90)	(0. 04)
Sd	– 0. 425	– 0. 161 *	0. 437	0. 057
	(1. 76)	(0. 09)	(2. 09)	(0. 05)
Fd	– 20. 203	– 0. 396 **	– 18. 705	0. 122
	(19. 22)	(0. 18)	(18. 45)	(0. 26)
Firm size	0. 841	– 0. 567 ***	1. 263 *	0. 030 *
	(0. 81)	(0. 04)	(0. 66)	(0. 02)
Firm age	– 0. 230	0. 196 **	– 2. 090	– 0. 084 ***
	(1. 55)	(0. 10)	(2. 16)	(0. 03)
Leverage	3. 878 **	0. 657 ***	2. 980 **	0. 057
	(1. 54)	(0. 13)	(1. 42)	(0. 07)
Observations	3773	3773	3741	3796
Adj. R^2	0. 056	0. 195	0. 051	0. 047

Note: This table reports the DID (panel data for 2002 – 2010with fixed effects) regressions [columns (1), (2), (3), and (4)] to test whether the use of CV can enhance firm performance or value, using the sample constructed through the BL method in 2005. All outcome variables in the table are industry – adjusted (by subtracting the industry mean of the original variable, for example, the industry – adjusted Tobin's Q is defined as the common Tobin's Q minus its industry mean for each year). Standard errors (in parentheses) are heteroskedasticity consistent and clustered at the firm level. *** , ** , and * denote significance at the 1% , 5% , and 10% levels, respectively.

To thoroughly examine this issue, we conduct additional complete analyses on all of the CV firms that adopted CV between 2002 and 2005. Table 2 – 2 presents the regression results based on the panel data for 2002 – 2008 generated by the BL process. All of the regressions reported in the table include year and firm fixed effects. We allow for the clustering of the observations at the firm level to account for the presence of serial correlations in the data. Columns (1) – (4) present the regression results, where the firm performance indicators are the industry – adjusted Tobin's Q, AMTB, the industry – adjusted ROA, and the industry – adjusted ROE, respectively. Clearly, none of the regression results produce significant estimates for CV adoption, that is, we do not find statistically significant effects of CV implementation on firm performance. Thus, no consistent evidence shows that the use of CV exerts significant and positive effects on firm performance. This finding is consistent with our preliminary analysis.

Table 2 – 2   CV Adoption and Firm Performance

Model	(1) Tobin's Q	(2) AMTB	(3) ROA	(4) ROE
Intercept	– 12. 326 (13. 40)	5. 843 *** (0. 80)	– 4. 108 (3. 61)	0. 172 (1. 14)
CV_{it}	– 0. 006 (0. 79)	– 0. 013 (0. 03)	0. 016 (0. 12)	0. 010 (0. 03)
Sd	– 0. 629 (1. 15)	– 0. 018 (0. 06)	– 0. 022 (0. 28)	– 0. 033 (0. 07)
Fd	– 18. 281 (17. 60)	– 0. 095 (0. 14)	2. 673 (2. 83)	0. 314 (0. 44)
Firm size	0. 662 (0. 64)	– 0. 295 *** (0. 04)	0. 270 (0. 17)	– 0. 017 (0. 06)
Firm age	– 1. 498 (1. 36)	0. 088 (0. 06)	– 0. 934 *** (0. 24)	– 0. 001 (0. 04)

continued

Model	(1)	(2)	(3)	(4)
	Tobin's Q	*AMTB*	*ROA*	*ROE*
Leverage	1.975 **	0.713 ***	− 0.141	0.117
	(0.86)	(0.08)	(0.23)	(0.08)
Year fixed effects	Yes	Yes	Yes	Yes
Firm fixed effects	Yes	Yes	Yes	Yes
Observations	3946	3946	3890	3960
Adj. R^2	0.054	0.179	0.094	0.046

Note: This table reports the DID (panel data for 2002 – 2008 with fixed effects) regressions [columns (1), (2), (3), and (4)] to test whether the use of CV can enhance firm performance or value, using the sample constructed through the BL method. All outcome variables in the table are industry – adjusted (by subtracting the industry mean of the original variable, for example, the industry – adjusted Tobin's Q is defined as the common Tobin's Q minus its industry mean for each year). Standard errors (in parentheses) are heteroskedasticity consistent and clustered at the firm level. ***, **, and * denote significance at the 1%, 5%, and 10% levels, respectively.

The effects of CV on firm performance may likely to be different between firms with high ownership concentration and those with low ownership concentration. We divide the sample into two parts to determine whether this case applies to firms. One part consists of firms where the percentage of shares held by the controlling largest shareholder is less than 30% (voluntary group), and the other consists of firms where the percentage is equal to or more than 30% (regulatory group). CV is possibly effective in containing the dominant controlling shareholder in the regulatory group and thus exhibits strong influence on firm performance.

For these two groups, we conduct the same regression analysis separately. The results in Tables 2 – 3 and 2 – 4 indicate that the use of CV exerts no statistically significant effects at all on firm performance. For robustness check, we re – run all of the regressions using the sample constructed through the CEM process, which produce qualitatively equivalent results, as shown in Appendix B.

Table 2 – 3   CV Adoption and Firm Performance: Voluntary Group

Model	(1) Tobin's Q	(2) AMTB	(3) ROA	(4) ROE
Intercept	– 10. 710 (23. 60)	5. 728 *** (1. 86)	– 6. 006 (8. 14)	– 1. 741 (1. 21)
CV_{it}	– 0. 617 (1. 37)	0. 084 (0. 09)	0. 148 (0. 34)	0. 112 (0. 09)
Sd	– 0. 614 (0. 73)	– 0. 039 (0. 21)	– 0. 536 (0. 57)	0. 031 (0. 14)
Fd	0. 359 (1. 35)	– 0. 122 (0. 22)	5. 574 (3. 41)	0. 292 (0. 69)
Firm size	0. 583 (1. 12)	– 0. 315 *** (0. 08)	0. 362 (0. 39)	0. 073 (0. 06)
Firm age	– 1. 405 (2. 96)	0. 401 * (0. 23)	– 0. 732 (0. 57)	– 0. 084 (0. 12)
Leverage	2. 264 (1. 55)	0. 706 *** (0. 13)	– 0. 298 (0. 47)	0. 278 ** (0. 14)
Year fixed effects	Yes	Yes	Yes	Yes
Firm fixed effects	Yes	Yes	Yes	Yes
Observations	1084	1084	1082	1093
Adj. R^2	0. 036	0. 265	0. 135	0. 073

Note: This table reports the DID (panel data for 2002 – 2008 with fixed effects) regressions [columns (1), (2), (3), and (4)] to test whether the use of CV can enhance firm performance or value, using the subsample with the percentage of shares held by the largest shareholder less than 30% from the sample constructed through the BL method. All outcome variables in the table are industry – adjusted (by subtracting the industry mean of the original variable, for example, the industry – adjusted Tobin's Q is defined as the common Tobin's Q minus its industry mean for each year). Standard errors (in parentheses) are heteroskedasticity consistent and clustered at the firm level. *** , ** , and * denote significance at the 1% , 5% , and 10% levels, respectively.

Table 2 - 4   CV Adoption and Firm Performance: Regulatory Group

Model	(1)	(2)	(3)	(4)
	Tobin's Q	AMTB	ROA	ROE
Intercept	- 15. 469	5. 266 ***	- 4. 992 *	0. 193
	(17. 84)	(0. 89)	(3. 02)	(1. 07)
CV_{it}	0. 305	- 0. 008	0. 150	- 0. 029
	(1. 03)	(0. 03)	(0. 13)	(0. 04)
Sd	0. 134	- 0. 070	0. 494	0. 080 *
	(1. 55)	(0. 04)	(0. 32)	(0. 04)
Fd	- 0. 745	- 0. 168	0. 227	- 0. 003
	(0. 64)	(0. 15)	(0. 18)	(0. 06)
Firm size	0. 741	- 0. 262 ***	0. 306 **	- 0. 013
	(0. 82)	(0. 04)	(0. 15)	(0. 05)
Firm age	- 0. 420	0. 023	- 0. 842 ***	- 0. 036
	(1. 59)	(0. 06)	(0. 28)	(0. 04)
Leverage	0. 928	0. 664 ***	- 0. 447 *	0. 037
	(1. 17)	(0. 13)	(0. 23)	(0. 09)
Year fixed effects	Yes	Yes	Yes	Yes
Firm fixed effects	Yes	Yes	Yes	Yes
Observations	2862	2862	2808	2867
Adj. R^2	0. 050	0. 116	0. 081	0. 033

Note: This table reports the DID (panel data for 2002 – 2008 with fixed effects) regressions [columns (1), (2), (3), and (4)] to test whether the use of CV can enhance firm performance or value, using the sub – sample with the percentage of shares held by the largest shareholder larger than or equal to 30% from the sample constructed through the BL method. All outcome variables in the table are industry – adjusted (by subtracting the industry mean of the original variable, for example, the industry – adjusted Tobin's Q is defined as the common Tobin's Q minus its industry mean for each year). Standard errors (in parentheses) are heteroskedasticity consistent and clustered at the firm level. *** , ** , and * denote significance at the 1% , 5% , and 10% levels, respectively.

We apply the seven dummy variables defined in Section 1. 6 of Chapter 1, namely, *dexp*, *dsh2*, *drel*, *dpro5*, *dac*, *dpol*1 and *dpol*7 to indicate the changes in the individual attributes of directors and verify whether CV could affect firm performance
through the changes in the characteristics of directors after CV adoption. We include the
interaction terms between the variable CV_{it} and the seven indicators separately into our regressions, as shown in Tables 2 – 5 – 2 – 11, to examine whether CV implementation
affects firm performance through the changes in the attributes of elected directors.
Clearly, almost all of the interaction terms in all of the tables are insignificant, except
for the one in Table 2 – 9. The result in column (3) of Table 2 – 9 demonstrates that
CV adoption may affect firm performance through the decrease in the proportion of independent directors from academe with weak significance. However, this result is not robust in that it ceases to be true when we repeat the exercise based on the CEM sample.
Thus, no evidence shows that CV adoption affects firm performance through the changes
in director attributes. [1]

Table 2 – 5　　**Executive Experience and Firm Performance**

Model	(1)	(2)	(3)	(4)
	Tobin's Q	*AMTB*	*ROA*	*ROE*
Intercept	– 12. 085	5. 861 ***	– 4. 106	0. 173
	(13. 31)	(0. 80)	(3. 61)	(1. 14)
CV_{it}	– 0. 481	– 0. 041	0. 020	0. 007
	(0. 92)	(0. 04)	(0. 14)	(0. 04)
dexp	0. 911	0. 009	– 0. 031	– 0. 001
	(0. 89)	(0. 05)	(0. 18)	(0. 05)
$CV_{it} * dexp$	0. 892	0. 077	0. 006	0. 011
	(1. 64)	(0. 07)	(0. 25)	(0. 07)
Sd	– 0. 629	– 0. 017	– 0. 021	– 0. 033
	(1. 14)	(0. 06)	(0. 28)	(0. 07)

[1]　We also do the similar exercises using continuous variables, instead of dummy variables, and the main results do not
change.

continued

Model	(1) Tobin's Q	(2) AMTB	(3) ROA	(4) ROE
Fd	- 18. 093 (17. 59)	- 0. 087 (0. 14)	2. 669 (2. 83)	0. 315 (0. 44)
Firm size	0. 655 (0. 63)	- 0. 295 *** (0. 04)	0. 270 (0. 17)	- 0. 017 (0. 06)
Firm age	- 1. 548 (1. 36)	0. 086 (0. 06)	- 0. 933 *** (0. 24)	- 0. 001 (0. 04)
Leverage	1. 914 ** (0. 85)	0. 711 *** (0. 08)	0. 140 (0. 23)	0. 117 (0. 08)
Year fixed effects	Yes	Yes	Yes	Yes
Firm fixed effects	Yes	Yes	Yes	Yes
Observations	3946	3946	3890	3960
Adj. R^2	0. 054	0. 180	0. 093	0. 045

Note: This table reports the DID (panel data for 2002 – 2008 with fixed effects) regressions including interaction term $CV_{it} \times dexp$ [columns (1), (2), (3), and (4)] to test whether the use of CV can enhance firm performance or value, using the sample constructed through the BL method, where dummy variable $dexp$ equals 1 from the treatment period if the difference of variable Exe_exp between the treatment period and the pretreatment period is positive, and 0 otherwise. All outcome variables in the table are industry – adjusted (by subtracting the industry mean of the original variable, for example, the industry – adjusted Tobin's Q is defined as the common Tobin's Q minus its industry mean for each year). Standard errors (in parentheses) are heteroskedasticity consistent and clustered at the firm level. *** , ** , and * denote significance at the 1% , 5% , and 10% levels, respectively.

Table 2 – 6   Second Shareholders' Representatives and Firm Performance

Model	(1) Tobin's Q	(2) AMTB	(3) ROA	(4) ROE
Intercept	- 12. 829 (13. 49)	5. 843 *** (0. 80)	- 4. 164 (3. 60)	0. 169 (1. 14)
CV_{it}	- 0. 306 (0. 90)	- 0. 015 (0. 03)	0. 053 (0. 13)	0. 008 (0. 03)

continued

Model	(1) Tobin's Q	(2) AMTB	(3) ROA	(4) ROE
dsh2	1. 439 *** (0. 52)	− 0. 002 (0. 07)	0. 411 (0. 35)	0. 001 (0. 10)
$CV_{it} \times dsh2$	0. 819 (1. 06)	0. 009 (0. 09)	− 0. 491 (0. 41)	0. 012 (0. 11)
Sd	− 0. 634 (1. 14)	− 0. 018 (0. 06)	− 0. 021 (0. 28)	− 0. 033 (0. 07)
Fd	− 18. 294 (17. 60)	0. 095 (0. 14)	2. 648 (2. 84)	0. 314 (0. 44)
Firm size	0. 691 (0. 64)	− 0. 295 *** (0. 04)	0. 272 (0. 17)	− 0. 017 (0. 06)
Firm age	− 1. 537 (1. 37)	0. 088 (0. 06)	− 0. 918 *** (0. 23)	− 0. 001 (0. 04)
Leverage	1. 872 ** (0. 85)	0. 713 *** (0. 08)	− 0. 150 (0. 23)	0. 117 (0. 08)
Year fixed effects	Yes	Yes	Yes	Yes
Firm fixed effects	Yes	Yes	Yes	Yes
Observations	3946	3946	3890	3960
Adj. R^2	0. 054	0. 179	0. 094	0. 045

Note: This table reports the DID (panel data for 2002 – 2008 with fixed effects) regressions including interaction term $CV_{it} \times dsh2$ [columns (1), (2), (3), and (4)] to test whether the use of CV can enhance firm performance or value, using the sample constructed through the BL method, where dummy variable dsh2 equals 1 from the treatment period if the difference of variable Share2 between the treatment period and the pretreatment period is positive, and 0 otherwise. All outcome variables in the table are industry – adjusted (by subtracting the industry mean of the original variable, for example, the industry – adjusted Tobin's Q is defined as the common Tobin's Q minus its industry mean for each year). Standard errors (in parentheses) are heteroskedasticity consistent and clustered at the firm level. *** , ** , and * denote significance at the 1% , 5% , and 10% levels, respectively.

Table 2 – 7 **Director Independence and Firm Performance**

Model	(1)	(2)	(3)	(4)
	Tobin's Q	AMTB	ROA	ROE
Intercept	– 13. 323	5. 809 ***	– 4. 292	0. 186
	(13. 36)	(0. 80)	(3. 61)	(1. 14)
CV_{it}	0. 498	– 0. 014	0. 058	0. 003
	(0. 70)	(0. 03)	(0. 12)	(0. 03)
drel	– 0. 841	– 0. 108	– 0. 371 *	0. 021
	(2. 65)	(0. 08)	(0. 21)	(0. 09)
$CV_{it} \times drel$	– 7. 386	0. 027	– 0. 572	0. 096
	(6. 64)	(0. 10)	(0. 48)	(0. 21)
Sd	– 0. 971	– 0. 022	– 0. 059	– 0. 028
	(1. 02)	(0. 06)	(0. 28)	(0. 07)
Fd	– 17. 737	– 0. 090	2. 736	0. 306
	(17. 77)	(0. 14)	(2. 81)	(0. 44)
Firm size	0. 674	– 0. 294 ***	0. 273	– 0. 017
	(0. 63)	(0. 04)	(0. 17)	(0. 06)
Firm age	– 1. 049	0. 100	– 0. 852 ***	– 0. 008
	(1. 39)	(0. 06)	(0. 24)	(0. 05)
Leverage	2. 113 **	0. 715 ***	– 0. 122	0. 115
	(0. 86)	(0. 08)	(0. 23)	(0. 08)
Year fixed effects	Yes	Yes	Yes	Yes
Firm fixed effects	Yes	Yes	Yes	Yes
Observations	3946	3946	3890	3960
Adj. R^2	0. 057	0. 180	0. 095	0. 046

Note: This table reports the DID (panel data for 2002 – 2008 with fixed effects) regressions including interaction term $CV_{it} \times drel$ [columns (1), (2), (3), and (4)] to test whether the use of CV can enhance firm performance or value, using the sample constructed through the BL method, where dummy variable drel equals 1 from the treatment period if the difference of variable Exe_rel3 between the treatment period and the pretreatment period is positive, and 0 otherwise. All outcome variables in the table are industry – adjusted (by subtracting the industry mean of the original variable, for example, the industry – adjusted Tobin's Q is defined as the common Tobin's Q minus its industry mean for each year). Standard errors (in parentheses) are heteroskedasticity consistent and clustered at the firm level. *** , ** , and * denote significance at the 1% , 5% , and 10% levels, respectively.

Table 2 −8   **Professional Experience and Firm Performance**

Model	(1)	(2)	(3)	(4)
	Tobin's Q	AMTB	ROA	ROE
Intercept	− 11. 898	5. 855 ***	− 4. 104	0. 178
	(13. 44)	(0. 80)	(3. 61)	(1. 15)
CV_{it}	0. 095	− 0. 014	0. 010	0. 015
	(0. 87)	(0. 03)	(0. 13)	(0. 03)
dpro5	− 1. 238	− 0. 072	− 0. 088	0. 018
	(1. 54)	(0. 05)	(0. 22)	(0. 07)
$CV_{it} \times dpro5$	0. 271	0. 046	0. 083	− 0. 031
	(2. 18)	(0. 08)	(0. 29)	(0. 09)
Sd	− 0. 633	− 0. 019	− 0. 023	− 0. 033
	(1. 15)	(0. 06)	(0. 28)	(0. 07)
Fd	− 18. 357	− 0. 097	2. 671	0. 313
	(17. 61)	(0. 14)	(2. 83)	(0. 44)
Firm size	0. 635	− 0. 295 ***	0. 270	− 0. 017
	(0. 64)	(0. 04)	(0. 17)	(0. 06)
Firm age	− 1. 423	0. 092	− 0. 932 ***	− 0. 001
	(1. 36)	(0. 06)	(0. 24)	(0. 04)
Leverage	2. 034 **	0. 716 ***	− 0. 138	0. 116
	(0. 87)	(0. 08)	(0. 23)	(0. 08)
Year fixed effects	Yes	Yes	Yes	Yes
Firm fixed effects	Yes	Yes	Yes	Yes
Observations	3946	3946	3890	3960
Adj. R^2	0. 053	0. 179	0. 094	0. 045

Note: This table reports the DID (panel data for 2002 – 2008 with fixed effects) regressions including interaction term $CV_{it} \times dpro5$ [columns (1), (2), (3), and (4)] to test whether the use of CV can enhance firm performance or value, using the sample constructed through the BL method, where dummy variable dpro5 equals 1 from the treatment period if the difference of variable Pro5 between the treatment period and the pretreatment period is positive, and 1 otherwise. All outcome variables in the table are industry – adjusted (by subtracting the industry mean of the original variable, for example, the industry – adjusted Tobin's Q is defined as the common Tobin's Q minus its industry mean for each year). Standard errors (in parentheses) are heteroskedasticity consistent and clustered at the firm level. *** , ** , and * denote significance at the 1% , 5% , and 10% levels, respectively.

Table 2 – 9 Academic Independent Directors and Firm Performance

Model	(1)	(2)	(3)	(4)
	Tobin's Q	AMTB	ROA	ROE
Intercept	– 11. 630	5. 861 ***	– 3. 931	0. 180
	(13. 68)	(0. 81)	(3. 57)	(1. 14)
CV_{it}	– 0. 260	– 0. 004	– 0. 006	0. 011
	(0. 88)	(0. 03)	(0. 13)	(0. 03)
dac	– 2. 680	– 0. 007	– 0. 538 ***	– 0. 020
	(2. 01)	(0. 08)	(0. 15)	(0. 06)
$CV_{it} \times dac$	2. 882	– 0. 044	0. 426 *	0. 007
	(2. 52)	(0. 09)	(0. 25)	(0. 08)
Sd	– 0. 607	– 0. 017	– 0. 013	– 0. 033
	(1. 14)	(0. 06)	(0. 28)	(0. 07)
Fd	– 18. 272	– 0. 097	2. 670	0. 314
	(17. 60)	(0. 14)	(2. 83)	(0. 44)
Firm size	0. 621	– 0. 295 ***	0. 261	– 0. 018
	(0. 65)	(0. 04)	(0. 17)	(0. 05)
Firm age	– 1. 421	0. 088	– 0. 923 ***	– 0. 000
	(1. 35)	(0. 06)	(0. 24)	(0. 04)
Leverage	2. 162 **	0. 714 ***	– 0. 102	0. 119
	(0. 88)	(0. 08)	(0. 23)	(0. 08)
Year fixed effects	Yes	Yes	Yes	Yes
Firm fixed effects	Yes	Yes	Yes	Yes
Observations	3946	3946	3890	3960
Adj. R^2	0. 054	0. 179	0. 094	0. 045

Note: This table reports the DID (panel data for 2002 – 2008 with fixed effects) regressions including interaction term $CV_{it} \times dac$ [columns (1), (2), (3), and (4)] to test whether the use of CV can enhance firm performance or value, using the sample constructed through the BL method, where dummy variable dac equals 1 from the treatment period if the difference of directors from academic world between the treatment period and the pretreatment period is negative, and 0 otherwise. All outcome variables in the table are industry – adjusted (by subtracting the industry mean of the original variable, for example, the industry – adjusted Tobin's Q is defined as the common Tobin's Q minus its industry mean for each year). Standard errors (in parentheses) are heteroskedasticity consistent and clustered at the firm level. *** , ** , and * denote significance at the 1% , 5% , and 10% levels, respectively.

Table 2 – 10　　Central Government Experience and Firm Performance

Model	(1)	(2)	(3)	(4)
	Tobin's Q	AMTB	ROA	ROE
Intercept	– 12. 257	5. 844 ***	– 4. 133	0. 181
	(13. 40)	(0. 80)	(3. 60)	(1. 14)
CV_{it}	– 0. 137	– 0. 013	0. 029	0. 011
	(0. 82)	(0. 03)	(0. 12)	(0. 03)
dpol1	– 0. 039	0. 020	– 0. 188	0. 154 **
	(1. 53)	(0. 11)	(0. 24)	(0. 08)
$CV_{it} \times dpol1$	2. 140	– 0. 023	– 0. 090	– 0. 103
	(1. 95)	(0. 13)	(0. 28)	(0. 10)
Sd	– 0. 633	– 0. 018	– 0. 022	– 0. 033
	(1. 14)	(0. 06)	(0. 28)	(0. 07)
Fd	– 18. 209	– 0. 095	2. 662	0. 316
	(17. 61)	(0. 14)	(2. 82)	(0. 44)
Firm size	0. 661	– 0. 295 ***	0. 271	– 0. 017
	(0. 64)	(0. 04)	(0. 17)	(0. 06)
Firm age	– 1. 535	0. 088	– 0. 929 ***	– 0. 005
	(1. 37)	(0. 06)	(0. 24)	(0. 04)
Leverage	1. 991 **	0. 713 ***	– 0. 145	0. 119
	(0. 85)	(0. 08)	(0. 23)	(0. 08)
Year fixed effects	Yes	Yes	Yes	Yes
Firm fixed effects	Yes	Yes	Yes	Yes
Observations	3946	3946	3890	3960
Adj. R^2	0. 053	0. 179	0. 094	0. 046

Note: This table reports the DID (panel data for 2002 – 2008 with fixed effects) regressions including interaction term $CV_{it} \times dpol1$ [columns (1), (2), (3), and (4)] to test whether the use of CV can enhance firm performance or value, using the sample constructed through the BL method, where dummy variable dpol1 equals 1 from the treatment period if the difference of variable Pol1 for independent directors between the treatment period and the pretreatment period is positive, and 0 otherwise. All outcome variables in the table are industry – adjusted (by subtracting the industry mean of the original variable, for example, the industry – adjusted Tobin's Q is defined as the common Tobin's Q minus its industry mean for each year). Standard errors (in parentheses) are heteroskedasticity consistent and clustered at the firm level. ***, **, and * denote significance at the 1%, 5%, and 10% levels, respectively.

Table 2 – 11   **Political Connection and Firm Performance**

Model	(1) Tobin's Q	(2) AMTB	(3) ROA	(4) ROE
Intercept	– 12. 195 (13. 41)	5. 855 *** (0. 80)	– 4. 058 (3. 60)	0. 178 (1. 14)
CV_{it}	0. 006 (0. 85)	– 0. 014 (0. 03)	0. 048 (0. 13)	0. 015 (0. 03)
dpol7	– 1. 089 (1. 73)	– 0. 115 * (0. 06)	– 0. 326 ** (0. 14)	– 0. 018 (0. 07)
$CV_{it} \times dpol7$	0. 487 (2. 72)	0. 067 (0. 09)	– 0. 074 (0. 23)	– 0. 027 (0. 11)
Sd	– 0. 635 (1. 15)	– 0. 019 (0. 06)	– 0. 023 (0. 28)	– 0. 034 (0. 07)
Fd	– 18. 328 (17. 61)	– 0. 099 (0. 14)	2. 647 (2. 82)	0. 311 (0. 44)
Firm size	0. 656 (0. 64)	– 0. 295 *** (0. 04)	0. 268 (0. 17)	– 0. 017 (0. 06)
Firm age	– 1. 504 (1. 36)	0. 087 (0. 06)	– 0. 934 *** (0. 24)	– 0. 001 (0. 04)
Leverage	1. 962 ** (0. 86)	0. 712 *** (0. 08)	– 0. 148 (0. 23)	0. 116 (0. 08)
Year fixed effects	Yes	Yes	Yes	Yes
Firm fixed effects	Yes	Yes	Yes	Yes
Observations	3946	3946	3890	3960
Adj. R^2	0. 053	0. 180	0. 094	0. 045

Note: This table reports the DID (panel data for 2002 – 2008 with fixed effects) regressions including interaction term $CV_{it} \times dpol7$ [columns (1), (2), (3), and (4)] to test whether the use of CV can enhance firm performance or value, using the sample constructed through the BL method, where dummy variable dpol7 equals 1 from the treatment period if the difference of variable Pol7 for independent directors between the treatment period and the pretreatment period is positive, and 0 otherwise. All outcome variables in the table are industry – adjusted (by subtracting the industry mean of the original variable, for example, the industry – adjusted Tobin's Q is defined as the common Tobin's Q minus its industry mean for each year). Standard errors (in parentheses) are heteroskedasticity consistent and clustered at the firm level. ***, **, and * denote significance at the 1%, 5%, and 10% levels, respectively.

The results are based on the sample consisting of all of the CV firms that adopted CV between 2002 and 2005, as well as their controls, and their firm performance observations for 2002 – 2008. One issue that may arise from this decision to extend the observation period concerns the previous results remaining true with more observations. To this end, we consider all of the CV firms that adopted CV between 2002 and 2010, and we use the same methods (BL and CEM) to construct control groups as before. Based on this enlarged sample, we conducted similar empirical analysis as in Tables 2 – 2, 2 – 3, and 2 – 4. Tables 2 – 12, 2 – 13, and 2 – 14 deliver the estimate results based upon this extended sample constructed through the BL method. From the three tables, we do not find evidence that CV adoption significantly affects firm performance, which is highly consistent with the previous empirical results from our original sample that covers a relatively short sample period. We also conduct the same exercise using the extended sample constructed through the CEM method, and the preceding conclusion remains true, which again shows the robustness of our empirical inference.

Table 2 – 12   CV Adoption and Firm Performance

Model	(1)	(2)	(3)	(4)
	Tobin's Q	AMTB	ROA	ROE
Intercept	− 3.784	15.292 ***	− 23.282 **	− 0.816 **
	(9.20)	(0.90)	(10.90)	(0.39)
CV_{it}	1.355 **	0.009	0.902	0.007
	(0.69)	(0.04)	(0.81)	(0.02)
Sd	1.350	− 0.042	0.604	− 0.041
	(1.11)	(0.07)	(1.37)	(0.04)
Fd	− 11.104	− 0.004	− 10.694	0.054
	(11.58)	(0.16)	(11.60)	(0.16)
Firm size	0.193	− 0.755 ***	1.177 **	0.034 *
	(0.44)	(0.04)	(0.51)	(0.02)
Firm age	− 1.119	0.263 ***	− 1.489	− 0.056 **
	(0.93)	(0.05)	(1.34)	(0.02)

continued

Model	(1)	(2)	(3)	(4)
	Tobin's Q	AMTB	ROA	ROE
Leverage	1.501 *	0.663 ***	0.930	−0.003
	(0.81)	(0.08)	(0.78)	(0.04)
Year fixed effects	Yes	Yes	Yes	Yes
Firm fixed effects	Yes	Yes	Yes	Yes
Observations	11897	11897	11497	11989
Adj. R^2	0.054	0.255	0.056	0.052

Note: This table reports the DID (panel data for 2002 – 2010 with fixed effects) regressions [columns (1), (2), (3), and (4)] to test whether the use of CV can enhance firm performance or value, using the sample constructed through the BL method. All outcome variables in the table are industry – adjusted (by subtracting the industry mean of the original variable, for example, the industry – adjusted Tobin's Q is defined as the common Tobin's Q minus its industry mean for each year). Standard errors (in parentheses) are heteroskedasticity consistent and clustered at the firm level. *** , ** , and * denote significance at the 1% , 5% , and 10% levels, respectively.

Table 2 – 13   CV Adoption and Firm Performance: Voluntary Group

Model	(1)	(2)	(3)	(4)
	Tobin's Q	AMTB	ROA	ROE
Intercept	−5.101	17.770 ***	−39.889 *	−1.449 **
	(18.83)	(2.20)	(22.95)	(0.62)
CV_{it}	1.689	0.075	0.335	−0.001
	(1.39)	(0.08)	(2.00)	(0.05)
Sd	0.376	0.095	−1.895	−0.027
	(1.78)	(0.11)	(2.13)	(0.07)
Fd	−4.509	0.259	−5.449	0.065
	(7.36)	(0.19)	(8.08)	(0.23)
Firm size	0.155	−0.888 ***	1.933 *	0.055 *
	(0.90)	(0.11)	(1.07)	(0.03)
Firm age	0.307	0.404 ***	−0.836	−0.043
	(1.97)	(0.12)	(3.06)	(0.07)

continued

Model	(1)	(2)	(3)	(4)
	Tobin's Q	*AMTB*	*ROA*	*ROE*
Leverage	0.991	0.475 ***	1.549	0.091
	(1.43)	(0.12)	(1.40)	(0.07)
Year fixed effects	Yes	Yes	Yes	Yes
Firm fixed effects	Yes	Yes	Yes	Yes
Observations	4176	4176	4122	4241
Adj. R^2	0.065	0.344	0.072	0.081

Note: This table reports the DID (panel data for 2002 – 2010 with fixed effects) regressions [columns (1), (2), (3), and (4)] to test whether the use of CV can enhance firm performance or value, using the subsample with the percentage of shares held by the largest shareholder less than 30% from the sample constructed through the BL method. All outcome variables in the table are industry – adjusted (by subtracting the industry mean of the original variable, for example, the industry – adjusted Tobin's Q is defined as the common Tobin's Q minus its industry mean for each year). Standard errors (in parentheses) are heteroskedasticity consistent and clustered at the firm level. *** , ** , and * denote significance at the 1% , 5% , and 10% levels, respectively.

Table 2 – 14   CV Adoption and Firm Performance: Regulatory Group

Model	(1)	(2)	(3)	(4)
	Tobin's Q	*AMTB*	*ROA*	*ROE*
Intercept	– 6.926	11.694 ***	– 21.405	– 0.560
	(11.73)	(1.04)	(14.16)	(0.53)
CV_{it}	1.408 *	0.021	1.292	0.005
	(0.84)	(0.04)	(0.92)	(0.02)
Sd	2.250	– 0.123	2.468	– 0.027
	(1.61)	(0.08)	(2.12)	(0.05)
Fd	– 1.423 *	– 0.379	– 1.295	0.001
	(0.78)	(0.42)	(1.10)	(0.05)
Firm size	0.286	– 0.576 ***	0.996	0.026
	(0.56)	(0.05)	(0.68)	(0.03)
Firm age	– 0.407	0.189 ***	– 0.302	– 0.052 **
	(1.01)	(0.05)	(1.44)	(0.02)

continued

Model	(1)	(2)	(3)	(4)
	Tobin's Q	AMTB	ROA	ROE
Leverage	2. 169 * (1. 12)	0. 614 *** (0. 10)	0. 851 (1. 08)	− 0. 065 (0. 06)
Year fixed effects	Yes	Yes	Yes	Yes
Firm fixed effects	Yes	Yes	Yes	Yes
Observations	7721	7721	7375	7748
Adj. R^2	0. 047	0. 143	0. 045	0. 034

Note: This table reports the DID (panel data for 2002 – 2010 with fixed effects) regressions [columns (1), (2), (3), and (4)] to test whether the use of CV can enhance firm performance or value, using the sub – sample with the percentage of shares held by the largest shareholder larger than or equal to 30% from the sample constructed through the BL method. All outcome variables in the table are industry – adjusted (by subtracting the industry mean of the original variable, for example, the industry – adjusted Tobin's Q is defined as the common Tobin's Q minus its industry mean for each year). Standard errors (in parentheses) are heteroskedasticity consistent and clustered at the firm level. *** , ** , and * denote significance at the 1% , 5% , and 10% levels, respectively.

Clearly, the introduction of the CV rule into director elections does not produce significantly positive effects on firm performance. One plausible explanation for this result is that the positive changes in board structure and board composition may be still too small to produce substantial improvements in corporate monitoring and advising. For instance, Panel A of Table 1 – 4 in Chapter 1 presents the comparison results in the pre – and post – CV periods between the proportion of representatives of the controlling shareholder and that of the second largest shareholder, that of the second to the fifth largest shareholders, and that of the second to the tenth largest shareholders. No significant decline is noted in the dominance of the representativeness of the controlling shareholder in the boardroom after the implementation of CV. Sometimes the representativeness of the controlling shareholder in the boardroom even increases in the post – CV period. Moreover, an increase in the representativeness of the second largest shareholder in the board is observed in a fairly small sub – sample, as shown in Table 1 – 4. Considering that the use of CV does not really undermine the relative control power of the controlling shareholders, we cannot expect CV to produce substantial effects on firm performance. These results and implications are consistent with those of Price et al.

(2011), who find no evidence that firm performance has improved as a result of governance reform regardless of the efforts of regulators to push for the best practice of corporate governance in Mexico; such reforms include the extensive disclosure of different aspects of governance (e. g. , structure of the board, internal control, and executive compensation) similar to that of the Sarbanes Oxley Act in the United States. Price et al. (2011) argue that the broad institutional and legal environment in Mexico remains weak and renders the effects of any legal reform alone limited. In the case of China, the weak institutional and legal setting is similar to that of Mexico. In addition, the financial market of China remains in its infancy stage, and large and inefficient State – owned firms enjoy advantages in many aspects, such as easier access to external finance than efficient private firms. Furthermore, regulators in China play the dual roles of both referees and players in the market, thus resulting in distorted incentives, numerous loopholes, and regulation inefficiency, as Allen et al. (2005) discussed. These detrimental factors in the institutions and financial system substantially weaken the effects of government reform.

2.5   CV and Corporate Policy Changes

2.5.1   CV and Tunneling Activities

An important angle in understanding the influence of CV adoption on firm performance is the examination of whether CV implementation has induced noteworthy changes to corporate policies. One central category of corporate policies is related to the changes in related party transactions and other receivables, which are extensively regarded as strong indicators of tunneling or propping – up activities conducted by block shareholders. We construct four variables in this category, namely, the ratio of the aggregate value of total related – party transactions to the firm's year – end total assets (*TRPT*), the ratio of aggregate value of beneficial related – party transactions to the firm's year – end

total assets ($BRPT$), the ratio of the aggregate value of harmful related – party transactions to the firm's year – end total assets ($HRPT$), and other receivables deflated by
year – end total assets (OAR). $HRPT$ and OAR are typically interpreted as tunneling
activities, whereas $BRPT$ can be treated as propping – up activities.

Table 2 – 15 presents regressions based on the panel data for 2002 – 2008 generated by the BL method. All of the regression models include firm and year fixed effects.
We allow for the clustering of the observations at the firm level to account for the presence of serial correlations in the data. All of the coefficients of the explanatory variable
CV_{it} on tunneling variables in the table are not statistically significant. This result indicates that the use of CV does not play an important role in curbing tunneling. However,
the strong statistical significance of the coefficient of variable CV_{it} in column (2) shows
that CV adoption may encourage prop – up activities in terms of potentially beneficial related party transactions.

Table 2 – 15   Propping and Tunneling Effects

Model	(1)	(2)	(3)	(4)
	$TRPT$	$BRPT$	$HRPT$	OAR
Intercept	3. 759 ***	0. 481 *	3. 119 ***	0. 281
	(1. 08)	(0. 28)	(1. 06)	(0. 21)
CV_{it}	0. 022	0. 022 ***	– 0. 009	0. 007
	(0. 04)	(0. 01)	(0. 04)	(0. 00)
Firm size	– 0. 188 ***	– 0. 024 *	– 0. 152 ***	– 0. 014
	(0. 05)	(0. 01)	(0. 05)	(0. 01)
Leverage	0. 146	0. 036	0. 063	0. 140 ***
	(0. 10)	(0. 03)	(0. 09)	(0. 03)
Firm age	0. 063	0. 020	0. 045	0. 027 ***
	(0. 09)	(0. 01)	(0. 08)	(0. 01)
Duality	– 0. 006	0. 017	0. 012	– 0. 009
	(0. 07)	(0. 01)	(0. 06)	(0. 01)
Board size	0. 001	0. 000	0. 004	– 0. 001
	(0. 01)	(0. 00)	(0. 01)	(0. 00)

continued

Model	(1)	(2)	(3)	(4)
	TRPT	BRPT	HRPT	OAR
Board_ind	0.273	−0.036	0.242	−0.068 **
	(0.33)	(0.06)	(0.32)	(0.03)
MTB	0.053	0.002	0.013	−0.012 *
	(0.06)	(0.01)	(0.05)	(0.01)
Sd	0.074 *	−0.008	0.066	0.002
	(0.04)	(0.01)	(0.04)	(0.01)
Fd	−0.040	0.087	−0.122	0.020
	(0.08)	(0.07)	(0.13)	(0.01)
Shrcr1	0.002	0.001 *	0.000	0.000
	(0.00)	(0.00)	(0.00)	(0.00)
Year fixed effects	Yes	Yes	Yes	Yes
Firm fixed effects	Yes	Yes	Yes	Yes
Observations	3687	3687	3687	3893
Adj. R^2	0.021	0.032	0.015	0.165

Note: This table reports the DID (panel data for 2002 – 2008 with fixed effects) regressions [columns (1), (2), (3), and (4)] to test whether the use of CV can curb tunneling activities or promote propping activities, using the sample constructed through the BL method. Standard errors (in parentheses) are heteroskedasticity consistent and clustered at the firm level. ***, **, and * denote significance at the 1%, 5%, and 10% levels, respectively.

We also re – run this set of regressions in the two sub – samples (voluntary and regulatory groups) partitioned as before. The results in Tables 2 – 16 and 2 – 17 indicate that CV adoption still has no statistically significant influence in most of the regressions. Nonetheless, the coefficients of variable CV_{it} in column (2) of Tables 2 – 16 and 2 – 17 indicate that CV adoption increases the potentially beneficial related party transactions in both the voluntary and regulatory groups. For robustness, we rerun all of the regressions using the sample constructed through the CEM process in Appendix B, which produce qualitatively equivalent results. The result suggests that CV – elected directors in the voluntary group might have helped to the firms in introducing beneficial related party transactions.

Table 2 – 16 **Propping and Tunneling Effects: Voluntary Group**

Model	(1)	(2)	(3)	(4)
	TRPT	BRPT	HRPT	OAR
Intercept	4.776 **	0.107	3.885 *	0.160
	(2.29)	(0.45)	(2.32)	(0.49)
CV_{it}	0.013	0.026 *	-0.013	0.013
	(0.08)	(0.01)	(0.08)	(0.01)
Firm size	-0.283 ***	-0.005	-0.240 ***	-0.010
	(0.08)	(0.02)	(0.08)	(0.02)
Leverage	0.151	0.049	0.106	0.157 **
	(0.13)	(0.03)	(0.13)	(0.06)
Firm age	0.251	0.002	0.242	0.038
	(0.39)	(0.02)	(0.39)	(0.02)
Duality	-0.108	0.018	-0.124 *	-0.022
	(0.07)	(0.02)	(0.07)	(0.02)
Board size	0.029	-0.002	0.032	-0.001
	(0.03)	(0.00)	(0.03)	(0.00)
Board_ind	0.991	-0.040	1.030	-0.095
	(1.01)	(0.07)	(1.01)	(0.07)
MTB	0.051	-0.009	0.065	-0.014 *
	(0.08)	(0.01)	(0.08)	(0.01)
Sd	0.139	0.022	0.118	-0.013
	(0.10)	(0.02)	(0.09)	(0.02)
Fd	-0.124	0.151	-0.245	0.005
	(0.12)	(0.11)	(0.19)	(0.02)
Shrcr1	0.008	0.001	0.006	0.002
	(0.01)	(0.00)	(0.01)	(0.00)
Year fixed effects	Yes	Yes	Yes	Yes
Firm fixed effects	Yes	Yes	Yes	Yes
Observations	956	956	956	1055
Adj. R^2	0.038	0.058	0.027	0.198

Note: This table reports the DID (panel data for 2002 – 2008 with fixed effects) regressions [columns (1), (2), (3), and (4)] to test whether the use of CV can curb tunneling activities or promote propping activities, using the sub – sample with the percentage of shares held by the controlling shareholders less than 30% from the sample constructed through the BL method. Standard errors (in parentheses) are heteroskedasticity consistent and clustered at the firm level. *** , ** , and * denote significance at the 1% , 5% , and 10% levels, respectively.

Table 2 – 17   Propping and Tunneling Effects: Regulatory Group

Model	(1)	(2)	(3)	(4)
	TRPT	BRPT	HRPT	OAR
Intercept	3. 121 ***	0. 654 **	2. 328 **	0. 284
	(1. 13)	(0. 30)	(0. 94)	(0. 18)
CV_{it}	0. 011	0. 018 *	− 0. 019	0. 004
	(0. 05)	(0. 01)	(0. 05)	(0. 01)
Firm size	− 0. 147 ***	− 0. 032 **	− 0. 104 **	− 0. 014
	(0. 05)	(0. 01)	(0. 04)	(0. 01)
Leverage	0. 211	0. 061	0. 042	0. 124 ***
	(0. 16)	(0. 04)	(0. 13)	(0. 03)
Firm age	0. 007	0. 024	− 0. 014	0. 025 ***
	(0. 07)	(0. 02)	(0. 06)	(0. 01)
Duality	0. 085	0. 015	0. 117	− 0. 003
	(0. 11)	(0. 01)	(0. 10)	(0. 01)
Board size	− 0. 012	0. 001	− 0. 008	− 0. 003 **
	(0. 02)	(0. 00)	(0. 02)	(0. 00)
Board_ind	0. 098	− 0. 060	0. 096	− 0. 060 *
	(0. 33)	(0. 07)	(0. 31)	(0. 03)
MTB	0. 056	0. 002	− 0. 018	− 0. 009
	(0. 09)	(0. 01)	(0. 05)	(0. 01)
Sd	0. 044	− 0. 026	0. 054	0. 000
	(0. 05)	(0. 02)	(0. 05)	(0. 01)
Fd	0. 215 ***	− 0. 014	0. 218 **	− 0. 008 **
	(0. 08)	(0. 02)	(0. 10)	(0. 00)
Shrcr1	0. 002	0. 001	0. 001	0. 000
	(0. 00)	(0. 00)	(0. 00)	(0. 00)
Year fixed effects	Yes	Yes	Yes	Yes
Firm fixed effects	Yes	Yes	Yes	Yes
Observations	2731	2731	2731	2838
Adj. R^2	0. 018	0. 027	0. 014	0. 136

Note: This table reports the DID (panel data for 2002 – 2008 with fixed effects) regressions [columns (1), (2), (3), and (4)] to test whether the use of CV can curb tunneling activities, using the sub – sample with the percentage of shares held by the controlling shareholders equal to or more than 30% from the sample constructed through the BL method. Standard errors (in parentheses) are heteroskedasticity consistent and clustered at the firm level. *** , ** , and * denote significance at the 1% , 5% , and 10% levels, respectively.

We also attempt to examine whether CV adoption affects tunneling or proppingup activities through the characteristics of independent directors. We incorporate into regressions the interaction terms between the CV dummy and the dummy variables *dexp*, *dsh2*, *drel*, *dpro5*, *dac*, *dpol1* and *dpol7* as previously mentioned. As shown in Tables 2 – 18 – 2 – 24, the CV – using firms that elected more directors with corporate executive experience actually display an increase in *BRPT*. The CV – using firms that have more independent directors with working experience in the central government exhibit a decrease in both the *TRPT* and *HRPT*. These results suggest that the use of CV may play a role in containing tunneling activities or encouraging propping – up activities through several channels, such as the increase in the number of executive directors with corporate executive experience or the increase in the proportion of independent directors with central government work experience, as we identified.

Table 2 – 18   Executive Experience and Propping and Tunneling Effects

Model	(1)	(2)	(3)	(4)
	TRPT	*BRPT*	*HRPT*	*OAR*
Intercept	3. 785 ***	0. 490 *	3. 123 ***	0. 281
	(1. 07)	(0. 28)	(1. 06)	(0. 21)
CV_{it}	– 0. 005	0. 009	– 0. 013	0. 006
	(0. 05)	(0. 01)	(0. 04)	(0. 00)
dexp	0. 005	– 0. 015	0. 007	– 0. 001
	(0. 05)	(0. 01)	(0. 05)	(0. 01)
$CV_{it} \times dexp$	0. 076	0. 046 **	0. 006	0. 003
	(0. 08)	(0. 02)	(0. 08)	(0. 01)
Firm size	– 0. 189 ***	– 0. 024 *	– 0. 153 ***	– 0. 014
	(0. 05)	(0. 01)	(0. 05)	(0. 01)
Leverage	0. 146	0. 036	0. 063	0. 140 ***
	(0. 10)	(0. 03)	(0. 09)	(0. 03)

continued

Model	(1) TRPT	(2) BRPT	(3) HRPT	(4) OAR
Firm age	0.061 (0.09)	0.019 (0.01)	0.045 (0.08)	0.027 *** (0.01)
Duality	-0.003 (0.07)	0.018 (0.01)	0.013 (0.06)	-0.009 (0.01)
Board size	0.002 (0.01)	0.000 (0.00)	0.004 (0.01)	-0.001 (0.00)
Board_ind	0.270 (0.33)	-0.036 (0.06)	0.241 (0.32)	-0.068 ** (0.03)
MTB	0.052 (0.06)	0.001 (0.01)	0.013 (0.05)	-0.012 * (0.01)
Sd	0.074 * (0.04)	-0.007 (0.01)	0.066 (0.04)	0.002 (0.01)
Fd	-0.033 (0.08)	0.089 (0.07)	-0.120 (0.13)	0.020 (0.01)
Shrcr1	0.002 (0.00)	0.001 * (0.00)	0.000 (0.00)	0.000 (0.00)
Year fixed effects	Yes	Yes	Yes	Yes
Firm fixed effects	Yes	Yes	Yes	Yes
Observations	3687	3687	3687	3893
Adj. R^2	0.021	0.034	0.014	0.164

Note: This table reports the DID (panel data for 2002 – 2008 with fixed effects) regressions with interaction term $CV_{it} \times dexp$ [columns (1), (2), (3), and (4)] to test whether the use of CV can curb tunneling activities or promote propping activities, using the sample constructed through the BL method, where dummy variable *dexp equals* 1 *from the treatment period if the difference of variable Exe_exp* between the treatment period and the pretreatment period is positive, and zero otherwise. Standard errors (in parentheses) are heteroskedasticity consistent and clustered at the firm level. *** , ** , and * denote significance at the 1% , 5% , and 10% levels, respectively.

Table 2 – 19   Second Shareholders' Representatives and

Propping and Tunneling Effects

Model	(1) TRPT	(2) BRPT	(3) HRPT	(4) OAR
Intercept	3. 762 *** (1. 08)	0. 482 * (0. 28)	3. 127 *** (1. 06)	0. 283 (0. 21)
CV_{it}	− 0. 008 (0. 04)	0. 022 ** (0. 01)	− 0. 032 (0. 04)	0. 007 (0. 01)
dsh2	− 0. 079 (0. 06)	− 0. 005 (0. 03)	− 0. 082 (0. 05)	− 0. 006 (0. 01)
$CV_{it} \times dsh2$	0. 226 (0. 14)	0. 000 (0. 03)	0. 185 (0. 13)	0. 001 (0. 01)
Firm size	− 0. 188 *** (0. 05)	− 0. 024 * (0. 01)	− 0. 153 *** (0. 05)	− 0. 014 (0. 01)
Leverage	0. 144 (0. 10)	0. 036 (0. 02)	0. 062 (0. 08)	0. 140 *** (0. 03)
Firm age	0. 059 (0. 09)	0. 020 (0. 01)	0. 042 (0. 08)	0. 027 *** (0. 01)
Duality	− 0. 006 (0. 07)	0. 017 (0. 01)	0. 012 (0. 06)	− 0. 009 (0. 01)
Board size	0. 002 (0. 01)	0. 000 (0. 00)	0. 004 (0. 01)	− 0. 001 (0. 00)
Board_ind	0. 262 (0. 33)	− 0. 034 (0. 06)	0. 237 (0. 32)	− 0. 067 ** (0. 03)
MTB	0. 053 (0. 06)	0. 002 (0. 01)	0. 014 (0. 05)	− 0. 012 * (0. 01)
Sd	0. 074 * (0. 04)	− 0. 008 (0. 01)	0. 066 (0. 04)	0. 002 (0. 01)
Fd	− 0. 030 (0. 09)	0. 088 (0. 07)	− 0. 113 (0. 13)	0. 020 (0. 01)

continued

Model	(1)	(2)	(3)	(4)
	TRPT	*BRPT*	*HRPT*	*OAR*
Shrcr1	0.002	0.001 *	0.000	0.000
	(0.00)	(0.00)	(0.00)	(0.00)
Year fixed effects	Yes	Yes	Yes	Yes
Firm fixed effects	Yes	Yes	Yes	Yes
Observations	3687	3687	3687	3893
Adj. R^2	0.021	0.032	0.015	0.164

Note: This table reports the DID (panel data for 2002 – 2008 with fixed effects) regressions with interaction term $CV_{it} \times dsh2$ [columns (1), (2), (3), and (4)] to test whether the use of CV can curb tunneling activities, using the sample constructed through the BL method, where dummy variable *dsh2* equals 1 from the treatment period if the difference of variable *Share2* between the treatment period and the pretreatment period is positive, and zero otherwise. Standard errors (in parentheses) are heteroskedasticity consistent and clustered at the firm level. ***, **, and * denote significance at the 1%, 5%, and 10% levels, respectively.

Table 2 – 20　Director Independence and Propping and Tunneling Effects

Model	(1)	(2)	(3)	(4)
	TRPT	*BRPT*	*HRPT*	*OAR*
Intercept	3.773 ***	0.484 *	3.130 ***	0.283
	(1.07)	(0.28)	(1.06)	(0.21)
CV_{it}	0.013	0.019 **	-0.018	0.006
	(0.04)	(0.01)	(0.04)	(0.00)
drel	-0.004	-0.004	-0.012	0.004
	(0.06)	(0.02)	(0.06)	(0.01)
$CV_{it} \times drel$	0.122	0.036	0.122	0.015
	(0.24)	(0.03)	(0.23)	(0.03)
Firm size	-0.188 ***	-0.024 *	-0.153 ***	-0.014
	(0.05)	(0.01)	(0.05)	(0.01)
Leverage	0.145	0.036	0.062	0.139 ***
	(0.10)	(0.03)	(0.08)	(0.03)

continued

Model	(1)	(2)	(3)	(4)
	TRPT	BRPT	HRPT	OAR
Firm age	0.057	0.018	0.040	0.026 ***
	(0.09)	(0.01)	(0.09)	(0.01)
Duality	− 0.006	0.017	0.012	− 0.009
	(0.07)	(0.01)	(0.06)	(0.01)
Board size	0.002	0.000	0.004	− 0.001
	(0.01)	(0.00)	(0.01)	(0.00)
Board_ind	0.265	− 0.038	0.234	− 0.070 **
	(0.33)	(0.06)	(0.32)	(0.03)
MTB	0.053	0.002	0.014	− 0.012 *
	(0.06)	(0.01)	(0.05)	(0.01)
Sd	0.078 *	− 0.006	0.071 *	0.003
	(0.04)	(0.01)	(0.04)	(0.01)
Fd	− 0.048	0.085	− 0.129	0.020
	(0.09)	(0.07)	(0.13)	(0.01)
Shrcr1	0.002	0.001 *	0.000	0.000
	(0.00)	(0.00)	(0.00)	(0.00)
Year fixed effects	Yes	Yes	Yes	Yes
Firm fixed effects	Yes	Yes	Yes	Yes
Observations	3687	3687	3687	3893
Adj. R^2	0.021	0.032	0.015	0.165

Note: This table reports the DID (panel data for 2002 – 2008 with fixed effects) regressions with interaction term $CV_{it} \times$ drel [columns (1), (2), (3), and (4)] to test whether the use of CV can curb tunneling activities, using the sample constructed through the BL method, where dummy variable *drel* equals 1 from the treatment period if the difference of variable *Exe_rel3* between the treatment period and the pretreatment period is positive, and zero otherwise. Standard errors (in parentheses) are heteroskedasticity consistent and clustered at the firm level. ***, **, and * denote significance at the 1%, 5%, and 10% levels, respectively.

Table 2 – 21   Professional Experience and Propping

and Tunneling Effects

Model	(1)	(2)	(3)	(4)
	TRPT	BRPT	HRPT	OAR
Intercept	3. 791 ***	0. 474 *	3. 161 ***	0. 283
	(1. 07)	(0. 28)	(1. 05)	(0. 21)
CV_{it}	0. 037	0. 017 **	0. 012	0. 007
	(0. 05)	(0. 01)	(0. 04)	(0. 01)
dpro5	− 0. 029	− 0. 006	− 0. 032	− 0. 009
	(0. 07)	(0. 02)	(0. 06)	(0. 01)
$CV_{it} \times pro5$	− 0. 056	0. 024	− 0. 079	0. 005
	(0. 09)	(0. 03)	(0. 07)	(0. 01)
Firm size	− 0. 190 ***	− 0. 024 *	− 0. 155 ***	− 0. 014
	(0. 05)	(0. 01)	(0. 05)	(0. 01)
Leverage	0. 149	0. 036	0. 066	0. 140 ***
	(0. 10)	(0. 03)	(0. 09)	(0. 03)
Firm age	0. 066	0. 019	0. 049	0. 027 ***
	(0. 09)	(0. 01)	(0. 08)	(0. 01)
Duality	− 0. 007	0. 017	0. 011	− 0. 009
	(0. 07)	(0. 01)	(0. 06)	(0. 01)
Board size	0. 001	0. 000	0. 004	− 0. 001
	(0. 01)	(0. 00)	(0. 01)	(0. 00)
Board_ind	0. 285	− 0. 037	0. 257	− 0. 068 **
	(0. 33)	(0. 06)	(0. 32)	(0. 03)
MTB	0. 052	0. 002	0. 013	− 0. 012 *
	(0. 06)	(0. 01)	(0. 05)	(0. 01)
Sd	0. 075 *	− 0. 008	0. 068 *	0. 002
	(0. 04)	(0. 01)	(0. 04)	(0. 01)
Fd	− 0. 046	0. 089	− 0. 129	0. 019
	(0. 08)	(0. 07)	(0. 13)	(0. 01)

continued

Model	(1)	(2)	(3)	(4)
	TRPT	*BRPT*	*HRPT*	*OAR*
Shrcr1	0.002 (0.00)	0.001* (0.00)	0.000 (0.00)	0.000 (0.00)
Year fixed effects	Yes	Yes	Yes	Yes
Firm fixed effects	Yes	Yes	Yes	Yes
Observations	3687	3687	3687	3893
Adj. R^2	0.021	0.032	0.015	0.165

Note: This table reports the DID (panel data for 2002 – 2008 with fixed effects) regressions with interaction term $CV_{it} \times pro5$ [columns (1), (2), (3), and (4)] to test whether the use of CV can curb tunneling activities, using the sample constructed through the BL method, where dummy variable *dpro5* equals 1 from the treatment period if the difference of variable *Pro5* for independent directors between the treatment period and the pretreatment period is positive, and zero otherwise. Standard errors (in parentheses) are heteroskedasticity consistent and clustered at the firm level. ***, **, and * denote significance at the 1%, 5%, and 10% levels, respectively.

Table 2 – 22   Academic Independent Directors and
Propping and Tunneling Effects

Model	(1)	(2)	(3)	(4)
	TRPT	*BRPT*	*HRPT*	*OAR*
Intercept	3.799*** (1.07)	0.487* (0.28)	3.166*** (1.06)	0.285 (0.21)
CV_{it}	0.036 (0.05)	0.026*** (0.01)	0.006 (0.04)	0.007 (0.01)
dac	−0.044 (0.07)	0.007 (0.03)	−0.059 (0.06)	−0.009 (0.01)
$CV_{it} \times dac$	−0.054 (0.09)	−0.024 (0.03)	−0.051 (0.07)	0.003 (0.01)
Firm size	−0.190*** (0.05)	−0.024* (0.01)	−0.155*** (0.05)	−0.014 (0.01)
Leverage	0.150 (0.10)	0.036 (0.02)	0.067 (0.09)	0.140*** (0.03)

continued

Model	(1)	(2)	(3)	(4)
	TRPT	BRPT	HRPT	OAR
Firm age	0.064	0.020	0.047	0.027 ***
	(0.09)	(0.01)	(0.08)	(0.01)
Duality	−0.005	0.017	0.013	−0.009
	(0.07)	(0.01)	(0.06)	(0.01)
Board size	0.001	0.000	0.004	−0.001
	(0.01)	(0.00)	(0.01)	(0.00)
Board_ind	0.289	−0.032	0.259	−0.067 **
	(0.33)	(0.06)	(0.32)	(0.03)
MTB	0.052	0.001	0.013	−0.012 *
	(0.06)	(0.01)	(0.05)	(0.01)
Sd	0.076 *	−0.007	0.069 *	0.002
	(0.04)	(0.01)	(0.04)	(0.01)
Fd	−0.043	0.087	−0.126	0.019
	(0.08)	(0.07)	(0.13)	(0.01)
Shrcr1	0.002	0.001 *	0.000	0.000
	(0.00)	(0.00)	(0.00)	(0.00)
Year fixed effects	Yes	Yes	Yes	Yes
Firm fixed effects	Yes	Yes	Yes	Yes
Observations	3687	3687	3687	3893
Adj. R^2	0.021	0.032	0.015	0.165

Note: This table reports the DID (panel data for 2002 – 2008 with fixed effects) regressions with interaction term $CV_{it} \times dac$ [columns (1), (2), (3), and (4)] to test whether the use of CV can curb tunneling activities, using the sample constructed through the BL method, where dummy variable dac equals 1 from the treatment period if the difference of variable Academy for independent directors between the treatment period and the pretreatment period is positive, and zero otherwise. Standard errors (in parentheses) are heteroskedasticity consistent and clustered at the firm level. ***, **, and * denote significance at the 1%, 5%, and 10% levels, respectively.

Table 2 – 23 **Central Government Experience and**
Propping and Tunneling Effects

Model	(1)	(2)	(3)	(4)
	TRPT	*BRPT*	*HRPT*	*OAR*
Intercept	3.765 ***	0.482 *	3.122 ***	0.280
	(1.07)	(0.28)	(1.06)	(0.21)
CV_{it}	0.033	0.020 **	−0.000	0.007
	(0.04)	(0.01)	(0.04)	(0.01)
*dpol*1	0.046	0.036 **	−0.001	−0.012
	(0.05)	(0.01)	(0.05)	(0.01)
$CV_{it} \times dpol1$	−0.212 *	0.003	−0.151 *	0.010
	(0.12)	(0.04)	(0.09)	(0.02)
Firm size	−0.188 ***	−0.024 *	−0.153 ***	−0.014
	(0.05)	(0.01)	(0.05)	(0.01)
Leverage	0.145	0.037	0.061	0.139 ***
	(0.10)	(0.03)	(0.09)	(0.03)
Firm age	0.065	0.019	0.047	0.027 ***
	(0.09)	(0.01)	(0.08)	(0.01)
Duality	−0.007	0.018	0.011	−0.009
	(0.07)	(0.01)	(0.06)	(0.01)
Board size	0.002	0.000	0.004	−0.001
	(0.01)	(0.00)	(0.01)	(0.00)
Board_ind	0.258	−0.033	0.229	−0.069 **
	(0.33)	(0.06)	(0.32)	(0.03)
MTB	0.053	0.002	0.013	−0.012 *
	(0.06)	(0.01)	(0.05)	(0.01)
Sd	0.074 *	−0.008	0.067	0.002
	(0.04)	(0.01)	(0.04)	(0.01)
Fd	−0.046	0.089	−0.127	0.019
	(0.08)	(0.07)	(0.13)	(0.01)

continued

Model	(1)	(2)	(3)	(4)
	TRPT	*BRPT*	*HRPT*	*OAR*
*Shrcr*1	0.002	0.001 *	0.000	0.000
	(0.00)	(0.00)	(0.00)	(0.00)
Year fixed effects	Yes	Yes	Yes	Yes
Firm fixed effects	Yes	Yes	Yes	Yes
Observations	3687	3687	3687	3893
Adj. R^2	0.021	0.033	0.015	0.164

Note: This table reports the DID (panel data for 2002 – 2008 with fixed effects) regressions with interaction term $CV_{it} \times dpol1$ [columns (1), (2), (3), and (4)] to test whether the use of CV can curb tunneling activities, using the sample constructed through the BL method, where dummy variable *dpol*1 equals 1 from the treatment period if the difference of variable *Pol*1 for independent directors between the treatment period and the pretreatment period is positive, and zero otherwise. Standard errors (in parentheses) are heteroskedasticity consistent and clustered at the firm level. ***, **, and * denote significance at the 1%, 5%, and 10% levels, respectively.

Table 2 – 24   Political Connection and Propping and Tunneling Effects

Model	(1)	(2)	(3)	(4)
	TRPT	*BRPT*	*HRPT*	*OAR*
Intercept	3.753 ***	0.464 *	3.136 ***	0.278
	(1.08)	(0.28)	(1.06)	(0.21)
CV_{it}	0.021	0.016 *	− 0.003	0.005
	(0.04)	(0.01)	(0.04)	(0.01)
*dpol*7	0.015	0.021	− 0.020	− 0.003
	(0.07)	(0.02)	(0.06)	(0.01)
$CV_{it} \times dpol7$	− 0.001	0.035	− 0.038	0.016
	(0.12)	(0.03)	(0.10)	(0.02)
Firm size	− 0.188 ***	− 0.023 *	− 0.153 ***	− 0.014
	(0.05)	(0.01)	(0.05)	(0.01)
Leverage	0.147	0.037	0.062	0.140 ***
	(0.10)	(0.03)	(0.09)	(0.03)
Firm age	0.063	0.020	0.045	0.027 ***
	(0.09)	(0.01)	(0.08)	(0.01)

continued

Model	(1)	(2)	(3)	(4)
	TRPT	*BRPT*	*HRPT*	*OAR*
Duality	-0.006	0.018	0.011	-0.009
	(0.07)	(0.01)	(0.06)	(0.01)
Board size	0.002	0.000	0.004	-0.001
	(0.01)	(0.00)	(0.01)	(0.00)
Board_ind	0.274	-0.034	0.240	-0.068**
	(0.33)	(0.06)	(0.32)	(0.03)
MTB	0.053	0.002	0.013	-0.012*
	(0.06)	(0.01)	(0.05)	(0.01)
Sd	0.074	-0.007	0.066	0.002
	(0.04)	(0.01)	(0.04)	(0.01)
Fd	-0.039	0.091	-0.125	0.020
	(0.08)	(0.07)	(0.13)	(0.01)
Shrcr1	0.002	0.001*	0.000	0.000
	(0.00)	(0.00)	(0.00)	(0.00)
Year fixed effects	Yes	Yes	Yes	Yes
Firm fixed effects	Yes	Yes	Yes	Yes
Observations	3687	3687	3687	3893
Adj. R^2	0.021	0.034	0.014	0.165

Note: This table reports the DID (panel data for 2002 – 2008 with fixed effects) regressions with interaction term $CV_{it} \times$ dpol7 [columns (1), (2), (3), and (4)] to test whether the use of CV can curb tunneling activities, using the sample constructed through the BL method, where dummy variable *dpol7* equals 1 from the treatment period if the difference of variable *Pol7* for independent directors between the treatment period and the pretreatment period is positive, and zero otherwise. Standard errors (in parentheses) are heteroskedasticity consistent and clustered at the firm level. ***, **, and * denote significance at the 1%, 5%, and 10% levels, respectively.

We also consider all CV firms that adopted CV between 2002 and 2010, and we use the same methods (BL and CEM) for constructing control groups as before. Based on this enlarged sample, we conduct similar empirical analysis as in Tables 2 – 15, 2 – 16, and 2 – 17. Tables 2 – 25, 2 – 26, and 2 – 27 presents the estimate results based on the extended sample constructed through the BL method. From the three tables, we do not find evidence that the CV adoption exerts a significant effect on tunneling or propping up activities, which is mainly consistent with the previous empirical results in Tables 2 – 15, 2 – 16, and 2 – 17. We also perform the same exercise, using the extended sample constructed through the CEM method, and the preceding conclusion still holds.

Table 2 – 25　　　　**Propping and Tunneling Effects**

Model	(1) TRPT	(2) BRPT	(3) HRPT	(4) OAR
Intercept	3. 300 *** (1. 04)	0. 644 *** (0. 17)	2. 207 ** (0. 88)	0. 299 *** (0. 11)
CV_{it}	– 0. 015 (0. 03)	0. 008 (0. 01)	– 0. 023 (0. 03)	0. 003 (0. 00)
Firm size	– 0. 170 *** (0. 06)	– 0. 028 *** (0. 01)	– 0. 119 ** (0. 05)	– 0. 013 *** (0. 01)
Leverage	0. 267 * (0. 14)	– 0. 018 (0. 02)	0. 291 ** (0. 14)	0. 140 *** (0. 01)
Firm age	0. 053 * (0. 03)	0. 015 * (0. 01)	0. 042 * (0. 03)	0. 033 *** (0. 00)
Duality	0. 001 (0. 04)	0. 015 (0. 01)	– 0. 010 (0. 03)	0. 003 (0. 00)
Board size	0. 002 (0. 01)	– 0. 001 (0. 00)	0. 005 (0. 01)	– 0. 001 (0. 00)
Board_ind	– 0. 023 (0. 24)	– 0. 170 *** (0. 05)	0. 169 (0. 21)	– 0. 066 ** (0. 03)
MTB	0. 059 *** (0. 02)	0. 019 *** (0. 01)	0. 010 (0. 01)	– 0. 009 *** (0. 00)
Sd	0. 019 (0. 04)	– 0. 001 (0. 01)	0. 004 (0. 04)	– 0. 003 (0. 00)
Fd	– 0. 150 (0. 14)	0. 003 (0. 04)	– 0. 130 (0. 15)	0. 016 * (0. 01)

continued

Model	(1)	(2)	(3)	(4)
	TRPT	BRPT	HRPT	OAR
Shrcr1	0.004 ***	0.000	0.003 ***	−0.001 ***
	(0.00)	(0.00)	(0.00)	(0.00)
Year fixed effects	Yes	Yes	Yes	Yes
Firm fixed effects	Yes	Yes	Yes	Yes
Observations	11144	11144	11144	11683
Adj. R^2	0.033	0.055	0.022	0.212

Note: This table reports the DID (panel data for 2002 – 2010 with fixed effects) regressions [columns (1), (2), (3), and (4)] to test whether the use of GV can curb tunneling activities or promote propping activities, using the sample constructed through the BL method. Standard errors (in parentheses) are heteroskedasticity consistent and clustered at the firm level. ***, **, and * denote significance at the 1%, 5%, and 10% levels, respectively.

Table 2 – 26   Propping and Tunneling Effects: Voluntary Group

Model	(1)	(2)	(3)	(4)
	TRPT	BRPT	HRPT	OAR
Intercept	4.744 *	1.124 ***	2.596	0.147
	(2.44)	(0.38)	(2.02)	(0.22)
CV_{it}	0.013	0.027	−0.020	0.009
	(0.05)	(0.02)	(0.04)	(0.01)
Firm size	−0.247 *	−0.046 **	−0.152	−0.007
	(0.13)	(0.02)	(0.11)	(0.01)
Leverage	0.377	−0.027	0.461 *	0.151 ***
	(0.25)	(0.03)	(0.25)	(0.02)
Firm age	0.054	0.027	0.013	0.044 ***
	(0.07)	(0.02)	(0.05)	(0.01)
Duality	−0.063	0.018	−0.090 **	0.004
	(0.05)	(0.02)	(0.04)	(0.01)
Board size	0.007	0.000	0.006	−0.002
	(0.01)	(0.00)	(0.01)	(0.00)
Board_ind	−0.037	−0.302 ***	0.521	−0.061
	(0.50)	(0.11)	(0.46)	(0.05)

continued

Model	(1)	(2)	(3)	(4)
	TRPT	BRPT	HRPT	OAR
MTB	0. 091 ***	0. 014	0. 038 **	− 0. 013 ***
	(0. 03)	(0. 01)	(0. 02)	(0. 00)
Sd	0. 075	0. 001	0. 069 **	− 0. 012
	(0. 05)	(0. 02)	(0. 03)	(0. 01)
Fd	− 0. 013	0. 068	− 0. 078	0. 009
	(0. 06)	(0. 06)	(0. 09)	(0. 01)
Shrcr1	0. 003	− 0. 005 **	0. 007 *	− 0. 000
	(0. 00)	(0. 00)	(0. 00)	(0. 00)
Year fixed effects	Yes	Yes	Yes	Yes
Firm fixed effects	Yes	Yes	Yes	Yes
Observations	3761	3761	3761	4055
Adj. R^2	0. 087	0. 076	0. 058	0. 216

Note: This table reports the DID (panel data for 2002 – 2010 with fixed effects) regressions [columns (1), (2), (3), and (4)] to test whether the use of CV can curb tunneling activities, using the subsample with the percentage of shares held by the controlling shareholders less than 30% from the sample constructed through the BL method. Standard errors (in parentheses) are heteroskedasticity consistent and clustered at the firm level. *** , ** , and * denote significance at the 1% , 5% , and 10% levels, respectively.

Table 2 – 27   Propping and Tunneling Effects: Regulatory Group

Model	(1)	(2)	(3)	(4)
	TRPT	BRPT	HRPT	OAR
Intercept	2. 046 ***	0. 375 **	1. 481 ***	0. 258 **
	(0. 58)	(0. 17)	(0. 45)	(0. 10)
CV_{it}	− 0. 001	0. 010	− 0. 015	0. 001
	(0. 04)	(0. 01)	(0. 04)	(0. 00)
Firm size	− 0. 099 ***	− 0. 015 *	− 0. 075 ***	− 0. 012 **
	(0. 03)	(0. 01)	(0. 02)	(0. 00)
Leverage	0. 103	− 0. 023	0. 110 *	0. 113 ***
	(0. 09)	(0. 03)	(0. 06)	(0. 02)

continued

Model	(1) TRPT	(2) BRPT	(3) HRPT	(4) OAR
Firm age	0.056 (0.04)	0.020 ** (0.01)	0.047 (0.03)	0.025 *** (0.00)
Duality	0.031 (0.05)	0.014 (0.01)	0.026 (0.05)	-0.000 (0.01)
Board size	-0.001 (0.01)	-0.002 (0.00)	0.004 (0.01)	-0.002 * (0.00)
Board ind	0.066 (0.27)	-0.141 ** (0.06)	0.159 (0.23)	-0.036 * (0.02)
MTB	0.033 (0.03)	0.023 ** (0.01)	-0.017 (0.01)	-0.002 (0.00)
Sd	-0.053 (0.06)	0.004 (0.01)	-0.079 (0.06)	0.000 (0.00)
Fd	-0.580 (0.45)	-0.152 (0.10)	-0.303 (0.50)	0.020 (0.02)
Shrcr1	0.002 (0.00)	0.000 (0.00)	0.001 (0.00)	-0.000 (0.00)
Year fixed effects	Yes	Yes	Yes	Yes
Firm fixed effects	Yes	Yes	Yes	Yes
Observations	7383	7383	7383	7628
Adj. R^2	0.017	0.040	0.014	0.148

Note: This table reports the DID (panel data for 2002 – 2010 with fixed effects) regressions [columns (1), (2), (3), and (4)] to test whether the use of CV can curb tunneling activities, using the sub – sample with the percentage of shares held by the controlling shareholders equal to or more than 30% from the sample constructed through the BL method. Standard errors (in parentheses) are heteroskedasticity consistent and clustered at the firm level. *** , ** , and * denote significance at the 1% , 5% , and 10% levels, respectively.

In conclusion, CV adoption is ineffective in curbing tunneling activities probably because the incremental improvements in the representation of non – controlling substantial shareholders and the attributes of board members in the CV – using firms could not diminish to a large extent the dominance of the controlling shareholder in the boardroom, change corporate policies, and thus curb the tunneling activities of the controlling largest shareholder. Thus, the regulatory requirement of CV adoption and CV implementation cannot play a salient role in curbing the expropriation of minority shareholders by the controlling largest shareholder in China, where governance institutions are weak as in most emerging markets. Our findings on tunneling activities in the post – CV period are basically consistent with Qian and Zhao (2011), although regression designs and sampling methods differ between theirs and ours.

2. 5. 2 CV and Other Corporate Policies

We also examine a few other corporate policies including executive compensation, financial policy (debt finance), and capital expenditure. [1]We construct the variable of the logarithm of the sum of the compensation of the top three executives plus 1, as an indicator of executive compensation; the variable of the industry – adjusted Leverage ratio of long – term debt to total assets as an indicator of debt finance policy; and the variable of the ratio of industry – adjusted capital expenditure to total assets as a measure of capital expenditure.

As shown in Table 2 – 28, CV implementation does not exhibit significant effects on corporate policies. In unreported results, we do not find significant effects of CV on the corporate policies in either the voluntary or the regulatory group. We also investigate whether CV adoption affects corporate policies through the changes in the attributes of the elected directors. We include into regressions the interaction terms of the CV dummy and the aforementioned dummy variables $dexp$, $dsh2$, $drel$, $dpro5$, dac, $dpol1$ and $dpol7$. Most of the regressions do not generate statistically significant results. columns (2) and (3) of Table 2 – 28 present regressions with significant estimated results. In column (2), the CV – using firms with increased executive director professional experience exhibit a decrease in top executive compensation. In column (3), the CV – using firms with increased professional independent director ratio show a decrease in top executive compensation. Similar to previous empirical analyses, we also

---

① All results on firm leverage and capital expenditure exclude financial firms.

consider the extended sample that includes more observations. Table 2 – 29 reports relevant estimates. Clearly, we do not find any indication that CV adoption exerts an important effect on this line of corporate policies.

Table 2 – 28   **CV and Other Corporate Policies**

Model	(1)	(2)	(3)	(4)	(5)
	Compen	Compen	Compen	ALeverage	Acapex
Intercept	7.551 *** (0.89)	7.621 *** (0.89)	7.604 *** (0.89)	-0.607 (0.47)	-11.121 *** (2.01)
CV_{it}	0.017 (0.06)	-0.053 (0.06)	0.060 (0.06)	0.004 (0.01)	0.019 (0.08)
ROA_t-1	0.029 (0.35)	0.032 (0.35)	0.028 (0.35)		
Firm size	0.253 *** (0.04)	0.250 *** (0.04)	0.250 *** (0.04)	0.026 (0.02)	0.540 *** (0.10)
Leverage	-0.513 *** (0.19)	-0.514 *** (0.19)	-0.516 *** (0.19)		-0.604 ** (0.25)
MTB	0.032 (0.03)	0.029 (0.03)	0.032 (0.03)	0.096 *** (0.02)	0.038 (0.03)
Duality	-0.089 (0.09)	-0.084 (0.09)	-0.089 (0.09)		
Board size	0.017 (0.01)	0.018 (0.01)	0.018 (0.01)		
Board_ind	-0.031 (0.28)	-0.032 (0.28)	-0.028 (0.28)		
Sd	0.094 * (0.05)	0.096 * (0.05)	0.097 ** (0.05)	0.017 (0.02)	
Fd	0.440 (0.30)	0.457 (0.31)	0.432 (0.30)	-0.059 (0.04)	
Shrcr1	-0.008 *** (0.00)	-0.008 *** (0.00)	-0.008 *** (0.00)		
dexp		-0.017 (0.08)			

continued

Model	(1)	(2)	(3)	(4)	(5)
	Compen	Compen	Compen	ALeverage	Acapex
$CV_{it} \times dexp$		0.215 * (0.12)			
dpro5			0.143 (0.11)		
$CV_{it} \times pro5$			-0.288 ** (0.13)		
Profit				-0.001 *** (0.00)	
Cratio				-0.364 *** (0.07)	
Liquidity				-0.012 *** (0.00)	
Cflow					-2.206 *** (0.00)
Year fixed effects	Yes	Yes	Yes	Yes	Yes
Firm fixed effects	Yes	Yes	Yes	Yes	Yes
Observations	3678	3678	3678	3908	3647
Adj. R^2	0.270	0.272	0.271	0.130	1.000

Note: This table reports the DID (panel data for 2002 – 2008 with fixed effects) regressions [columns (1), (2), (3), (4), and (5)] to test whether the use of CV can change corporate policies, using the sample constructed through the BL method. We add the interaction terms $CV_{it} \times dexp$ and $CV_{it} \times pro5$ in models (2) and (3), respectively, to see whether they have effects on executive compensation, where dummy variable dexp equals 1 from the treatment period if the difference of variable *Exe_exp* between the treatment period and the pretreatment period is positive, and zero otherwise; and dummy variable dpro5 equals 1 from the treatment period if the difference of variable *Pro5* for independent directors between the treatment period and the pretreatment period is positive, and zero otherwise. Variable *Compen* is the logarithm of the sum of the compensation of the top three executives plus 1; variable *ALeverage* is industry – adjusted (by subtracting industry mean) *Leverage* that is defined as long term debt divided by total assets; and variable *Acapex* is industry – adjusted (by subtracting industry mean) capital expenditure that equals the ratio of capital expenditure to total assets. $ROA\_t - 1$ is return of asset with order of lag one. *Profit* is operating profit deflated by total assets. *Cratio* is cash divided by total assets. *Liquidity* is the ratio of total current assets divided by total current liabilities. *Cflow* is defined as pre – tax profit plus depreciation divided by total assets. Standard errors (in parentheses) are heteroskedasticity consistent and clustered at the firm level. *** , ** , and * denote significance at the 1% , 5% , and 10% levels, respectively.

Table 2 – 29　　　　**CV and Other Corporate Policies**

Model	(1)	(2)	(3)
	Compen	ALeverage	Acapex
Intercept	7. 602 *** (0. 69)	0. 618 * (0. 33)	– 1153. 455 (1165. 69)
CV_{it}	0. 006 (0. 03)	0. 005 (0. 01)	1. 031 (1. 67)
$ROA\_t - 1$	0. 000 *** (0. 00)		
Firm size	0. 235 *** (0. 03)	– 0. 029 * (0. 02)	54. 725 (55. 49)
Leverage	– 0. 299 *** (0. 08)		– 5. 501 (15. 93)
MTB	0. 030 *** (0. 01)	0. 038 *** (0. 01)	3. 882 (4. 03)
Duality	0. 014 (0. 04)		
Board size	0. 012 (0. 01)		
Board_ind	– 0. 069 (0. 23)		
Sd	0. 080 ** (0. 03)	0. 006 (0. 01)	
Fd	0. 288 * (0. 17)	– 0. 027 (0. 03)	
Shrcr1	– 0. 001 (0. 00)		
Profit		– 0. 000 *** (0. 00)	
Cratio		– 0. 296 *** (0. 05)	

continued

Model	(1)	(2)	(3)
	Compen	*ALeverage*	*Acapex*
Liquidity		-0.020*** (0.01)	
Cflow			-2.107*** (0.02)
Year fixed effects	Yes	Yes	Yes
Firm fixed effects	Yes	Yes	Yes
Observations	10569	11761	10777
Adj. R^2	0.321	0.120	0.946

Note: This table reports the DID (panel data for 2002 – 2010 with fixed effects) regressions [columns (1), (2), and (3)] to test whether the use of CV can change corporate policies, using the sample constructed through the BL method. Variable *Compen* is the logarithm of the sum of the compensation of the top three executives plus 1; variable *Aleverage* is industry – adjusted (by subtracting industry mean) *Leverage* that is defined as long term debt divided by total assets; and variable *Acapex* is industry – adjusted (by subtracting industry mean) capital expenditure that equals the ratio of capital expenditure to total assets. *ROA_t* – 1 is return of asset with order of lag one. *Profit* is operating profit deflated by total assets. *Cratio* is cash divided by total assets. *Liquidity* is the ratio of total current assets divided by total current liabilities. *Cflow* is defined as pre – tax profit plus depreciation divided by total assets. Standard errors (in parentheses) are heteroskedasticity consistent and clustered at the firm level. ***, **, and * denote significance at the 1%, 5%, and 10% levels, respectively.

2.6   Discussion

This chapter presents the two parts of analysis to examine the influence of CV implementation. In the first part, we investigate whether CV use has a substantial effect on firm valuation. We find that CV adoption does not exert consistently significant and positive effects on firm performance on average. When we link the improvement in director characteristics after the CV adoption with firm performance, we still cannot find positive results. Thus, CV implementation does not produce significant and positive effects on firm performance through board restructuring.

In the second part of the empirical analysis, we explore the effects of CV adoption on tunneling activities and other corporate policies. We do not find any evidence to show that the use of CV can curb the tunneling activities of the controlling largest shareholders. However, we find that CV implementation did encourage firm proppingup activities in that potentially beneficial related party transactions increased after CV adoption.

These findings indicate that the incremental improvements found in Chapter1 have not substantially improved the representativeness of large minority shareholders in the board. For example, although the proportion of the representatives from the second largest shareholders in the board has increased in a small sub – sample, the relative control power of the controlling largest shareholder does not exhibit salient changes. Similarly, the improvements in the professionalism and independence of directors are not sufficiently high to generate positive changes in corporate governance, corporate policy making, and firm performance.

2. 7　Conclusion

As with most emerging markets, corporates of China is plagued with the problem of the expropriation of minority shareholders by the controlling shareholders. To strengthen the protection of minority shareholder interests, the Chinese regulatory authority introduced a host of Western governance institutions in the early 2000s. One prominent measure is the adoption of the CV rule, which is designed to enable minority shareholders, especially the large minority shareholders or non – controlling substantial shareholders, to elect their representatives into the corporate board and enhance corporate governance.

A salient difficulty in corporate governance research is "endogeneity" or "self selection" problem. This study attempts to address this issue using the matching method for constructing a control group and the DID – style regressions to further reduce econometrical confoundedness. To increase the robustness of our main empirical results, we use two different matching methods for constructing two samples, of which the sample from the BL matching is used to yield all of the major conclusions. In AppendixB, we provide the main estimated results using the sample from the CEM process, which are consistent with those from the sample through the BL method.

The growing literature has been attempting to establish a causal relationship between firm value and corporate governance in a wide variety of settings. This line of literature mainly endeavors to identify this relationship with a global view, based on data across countries. A general conclusion is that firm value is positively related to the improvement of minority shareholder rights. This study investigates this issue with a micro view, which entails using firm – level data in one country environment to identify such a relationship. This study does not find evidence that CV use as a firm – level governance mechanism improves corporate valuation and firm performance. Controlling shareholder tunneling behaviors in various contexts have also been reported extensively in the literature. This study explores this issue to determine whether CV adoption can curb the tunneling activities of controlling shareholders. We find no evidence to justify that the use of CV alone in a weak governance environment such as China can reduce the expropriation of minority shareholders by controlling shareholders.

Our findings indicate that the incremental improvements are insufficient to curb tunneling activities and generate substantial positive effects on firm performance. The Chinese experience may have some useful implications for other emerging market economies characterized by weak legal institutions and weak investor protection.

Chapter 3   Do Investors from Different Institutional Backgrounds Exhibit Different Concerns towards Corporate Governance?

—Evidence from Cross – listed Companies in China

3. 1   Introduction

Corporate governance has become an essential tool for improving firm performance and developing financial markets in both developed countries, such as the United States, and developing countries, such as China. Good corporate governance practices maintain the integrity of business transactions and in so doing strengthen the rule of law and democratic governance. As a powerful antidote to corruption, corporate governance clarifies private rights and public interests and prevents the abuses of both. Recently, the quality of corporate governance has captured the attention of various parties from the academic, business, and political spheres. Since the 1997 Asian financial crisis, investors have increasingly paid more attention to corporate governance. Better corporate frameworks may benefit firms through greater access to financing, lower cost of capital, better performance, and more favorable treatment of all stakeholders. For example, La Porta et al. (1997) find that countries with poor investor protections, measured by both the character of legal rules and the quality of law enforcement, have smaller and narrower capital markets. Several researchers have investigated whether good corporate governance increases corporate valuation. For instance, La Porta et al. (2002) argue that a higher valuation of firms, as measured by Tobin's Q, is evident in countries with better protection of minority shareholders and in firms with higher cash – flow ownership by the controlling shareholder, based on a sample consisting of 27 wealthy economies. Additionally, Bai et al. (2004) find strong evidence that better corporate governance is associated with higher Tobin's Q, on the basis of data from the financial market of China.

In general, there are two common approaches, in both advanced markets and emerging markets, for protecting their benefits when investors recognize that they are facing possible expropriation from insiders or controlling shareholders. One approach is "voting with hand", that is, investors use their voting rights to affect firm decisions. The other approach is "voting with feet", which denotes that investors opt to avoid firms that are characterized by weak governance. The implementation premise of "voting with hand" is complete, effective and strong institutional environment, whereas the implementation of "voting with feet" depends on investors' close attention to and positive feedback on the quality of corporate governance. Therefore, the institutional and legal environments, as well as investors' concerns on corporate governance, may endogenously influence the quality of corporate governance. In advanced markets equipped with complete legal systems and sophisticated investors, minority shareholders can protect their benefits through both mechanisms. In the United States, for example, the market has a strict system of disclosure of information and a complete class action shareholder lawsuit system. Minority shareholders can capture firm operating situations through disclosed information as required by relevant laws. Moreover, investors in the United States typically pay more attention to the quality of corporate governance and are, at the same time, strongly conscious of the need to safeguard their legal rights. Under such conditions, stocks with different structures of voting rights (including Class A and Class B shares[1]) coexisting in the United States market is not a surprise. Similarly, investors from Hong Kong SAR root in a relatively complete, effective, and strong institutional and legal environment compared with infant financial markets, such as the stock market of mainland China. Hence the question on whether differences exist

---

[1]   A classification of common stock that may be accompanied by more or fewer voting rights than Class A shares. Although Class A shares are often thought to carry more voting rights than Class B shares, this is not always the case. Companies will often try to disguise the disadvantages associated with owning shares with fewer voting rights by naming those shares "Class A," and those with more voting rights "Class B. " See http: //www. investopedia. com/terms/c/classbshares. asp.

in terms of concern about the quality of corporate governance arises, which may be reflected in corporate valuation. One important point is whether A – share and H – share investors differ in the sense that they pay different levels of attention to the quality of corporate governance, which is the key issue that this work attempts to address.

The literature has explored the effects of corporate governance on capital market development, firm performance, and corporate valuation. To our best knowledge, very few researchers have investigated whether investor differences, in terms of institutional and legal environments, induce diverse attitudes toward the quality of corporate governance. In the literature on cross – border portfolio investment flows, Kim et al. (2011) examines whether the difference, characterized by varying degrees of control ownership disparity, in the home countries of investors affects their portfolio choice in an emerging market. Data from Korea demonstrate that investors from low – disparity countries disfavor high – disparity stocks, but investors from high – disparity countries are indifferent. The researchers conclude that the nature of corporate governance in the home countries of international investors affects their portfolio choice abroad. The present research is related to the work of Kim et al. (2011) in terms of consideration for investor heterogeneity in the context of corporate governance in their home countries, although the topics explored in the two studies are quite different. The question the current study attempts to address is whether the nature of corporate governance in the home countries of investors affects their concern for the quality of corporate governance, which may, in turn, be reflected in firm valuation. This topic is an important but unsolved question, and no literature has discussed it thus far.

Theoretically, no clear framework can predict whether investors from countries with strong governance environments pay more attention to the quality of corporate governance than those from countries with weak governance settings. Empirically, we cannot find any attempt to probe this problem or evidence to show clear conclusions. This study attempts to examine whether different concerns exist on the quality of corporate governance between two types of investors from strikingly different institutional and legal environments owing to differences in governance environments. If such type of differences does exist, then we intend to further investigate whether or not investors from strong governance background are more concerned about the quality of corporate governance. Therefore, we do not develop any clear hypotheses on this question ex ante, but explore it instead as an open issue.

We analyze the question based on public companies cross – listed in the stock markets of both Hong Kong SAR and mainland China. Essentially, such companies are firms of China. Based on A + H share framework that is a unique feature of the Chinese stock market, endogeneity, which is a common problem in corporate governance research, is subtly avoided, where A + H shares refer to a firm listed in the stock markets of both mainland China and Hong Kong SAR. First, we set the Tobin's Q for A – and H – shares for each company in the sample spanning from 2002 to 2013. Second, we let the Tobin's Q of A – and H – shares be the dependent variables, and the related corporate governance variables and control variables as independent variables. We subsequently run separate regressions using these two groups of variables to verify whether significant differences exist between these two estimates. We also use the log – ratio of market capitalization to total assets as an equity valuation measure, followingBai et al. (2014) for examining the existence of such differences. In addition, we use the ratio of the Tobin's Q of H – share to that of A – share as a dependent variable to run similar regressions. However, we do not find strong evidence to show a significant difference in the concern for the quality of corporate governance between these two types of investors.

This study contributes to the literature on corporate governance and corporate valuation. Numerous studies (e. g. La Porta et al. , 2002; Bai et al. , 2004; Black et al. , 2006; Brown and Caylor, 2006; Chhaochharia and Grinstein, 2007; Lu and Shi, 2012) have investigated the effects of corporate governance mechanisms on corporate valuation. Most of the studies suggest that strong corporate governance increases corporate valuation. None of them, however, explores whether differences exist in the effects of corporate governance on firm valuation resulting from different types of investors from different countries with pronounced disparities in legal and governance settings. To our knowledge, this study is the first work to attempt checking if such differences exist. Using data from Korea, Kim et al. (2011) demonstrate that investors from different countries, whose home markets manifest different degrees of strength, hold various investment portfolios in terms of different degrees of firm – level governance.

However, Kim et al. (2011) do not investigate the effects of such differences on corporate valuations, which is the crucial issue that the current study attempts to explore.

This paper is also related to the growing body of literature on cross – listed companies. Increasing evidence shows that institutional and legal environments play an important role in corporate valuation and access to finance (e. g. La Porta et al. , 1997, 1998, 2000). On the basis of this evidence, dual – listing in countries with strong institutional and legal settings has been suggested as a means for firms from countries with weak governance environment of surmounting these effects. This idea is called bonding hypothesis. Numerous studies (e. g. Coffee Jr, 1998, 2002; Burns et al. , 2007; Charitou et al. , 2007; Lel and Miller, 2008) have focused on this hypothesis to thoroughly explore the relationship between corporate governance and cross – listing. For example, Charitou et al. (2007) find that cross – listing elevates firm – level governance in terms of board and audit committee independence, based on data from Canadian firms. By contrast, the current study attempts to investigate the relationship between dual – listing and corporate governance focusing on the difference in investor concern for the quality of corporate governance arising from their different home markets and different degrees of legal institutional frameworks.

The rest of the study proceeds as follows. Section 3. 2 discusses the institutional environment and conceptual framework. Section 3. 3 describes the data and sample used in the study and illustrates econometric models applied in the next section. Section 3. 4 presents the main findings on the effects of corporate governance on firm valuation from different from the viewpoint of H – shares and A – shares. Section 3. 5 concludes.

3. 2　Institutional Background

The China stock market started in the early 1990s. At present, three types of shares are issued by Chinese firms, namely, A – , B – , and H – shares. Both A – and B – shares are listed and traded in SHSE and SZSE. Traded in the domestic market, A – shares are restricted to domestic investors. Being foreign – invested shares,

B – shares are subscribed and traded in foreign currencies and, until February 2001, were only available to foreign investors. Chinese companies are also allowed to issue shares overseas to access external finance. Most Chinese offshore stocks are traded on the Stock Exchange of Hong Kong Limited (SEHK), that is, H – shares, except on a few on other foreign markets, such as the New York, London, and Singapore Stock Exchanges. Both B – and H – shares are foreign shares, but one important difference between them is that B – shares are listed and traded on the domestic market, whereas H – shares are not. For this line of basic background information, see alsoWang and Jiang (2004).

China, similar to many emerging markets, has weak legal institutions and an incomplete and infant financial market infrastructure. Thus, investor attention to corporate governance is potentially important for developing and completing capital markets. Owing to strict capital control, A – share market and H – share market are segmented almost completely, whereas A and H cross – listed shares can be simultaneously traded in both markets by two groups of investors. A – and H – shares of cross – listed companies provide the same voting and cash flow rights. The three stock exchanges involved in listing these dual – listed shares require firms to disclose identical information to investors, regardless of local or foreign investors. This study maximizes these unique control features of legal institutional settings, information disclosure systems, and accounting standards to explore whether differences exist between these two types of investors in their concern for and sensitivity to corporate governance.

The legal institutional environments of H – and A – shares are strikingly different. The SEHK is well established, more internationalized, more open, and more rigorous in listing systems, accounting standards, and disclosure of information compared with the SHSE and SZSE. For example, as Wang and Jiang (2004) mentioned, the SEHK has set additional listing rules for companies that operate and have headquarters in mainland China. Owing to lacking ownership restrictions and capital control, H – shares have attracted more institutional and foreign investors. By contrast, the history of A – shares is relatively short, and the China Chinese has imposed various restrictions on ownership for domestic investors. In addition, the legal system, information disclosure rules, and listing requirements are not well established. The Chinese government has likewise imposed rigorous capital control on the market. In sum, the governance environment in terms of institutions and legal systems at the general level is weaker than that of Hong Kong SAR. Thus, differences in attitude toward the quality of corporate governance at the firm – level may exist between the two classes of investors, which may, in turn, result in different firm valuations.

3.3   Data and Methodology

3.3.1   Data

We construct our sample of A – and H – share financial data from Wind database, which is a dominant financial data supplier in China. Wind database supplies detailed financial information on H and A cross – listed firms. Our corporate governance data are obtained from the CSMAR database. Following convention in corporate governance research, we exclude all firms belonging to the financial industry. Our basic sample consists of all non – financial, dual – listed firms in the SEHK and SHSE (or SZSE) in the period 2002 – 2013, which forms an unbalanced panel dataset on the year basis. Our basic sample consists of 540 firm – year observations. Additionally, we also construct a balanced panel dataset that comprises 26 firms starting from 2002 and ending in 2013, which is composed of 312 firm – year observations in total.

3.3.2   Variables

Following convention (e. g. Bai et al. , 2004), Tobin's Q is selected as a measure of corporate valuation. Allowing for existing substantial non – tradable shares in Chinese public firms, similar to Zhang (2008), we define Tobin's Q for H shares as $htq = [$ (the circulation market value of H – shares + total liabilities)/(book value of equity $\times$ the proportion of the floating H – shares over total shares + total liabilities) $]$.

In a similar manner, we define Tobin's Q for A – shares as atq = [(the circulation market value of A – shares + total liabilities)/(book value of equity × the proportion of the floating A – shares over total shares + total liabilities)] . Market value is the number of tradable shares multiplied by the closed price per share at the end of each year. Alternatively, following Bai et al. (2014), we also consider the log – ratio of market capitalization to total assets as our second equity valuation measure for robustness. As pointed out by Bai et al. (2014), taking logs can alleviate skewness and is usually better – behaved. Furthermore, as shown in their model, the log – ratio of market capitalization to total assets can well measure equity price informativeness. For the sake of consistency, we translate all variables denominated by HKD into those by RMB using the central bank rate, where exchange rate data are derived from Wind database. We also use the ratio (tqr) of htq to atq as explained variable to further explore whether the relative valuation of firms between the two types of investors differs.

The main corporate governance variables in the study include the percentage of ownership of the largest shareholders $sh1$, board independence b_ind measured by the number of independent directors over the number of all directors in a board, CEOchairman *Duality dual*, and the natural logarithm of the sum of squares of the percentage points of shares held by the second to the tenth largest shareholders ($cstr2\_10$). Variable $sh1$ measures both the largest shareholder interest in a company and also the largest shareholder power in the board. As discussed in Bai et al. (2004), the relationship between firm valuation and $sh1$ may not be linear; thus we add the square of $sh1$ ($sh1\_sq$) to the set of regressors. Variable *dual* equals 1 if the CEO and board chairman in a firm are the same person, and 0 otherwise, which is also a commonly used governance variable in the previous literature. Variable $cstr2\_10$ measures the market for corporate control by the concentration of shares in the hands of the second to the tenth largest shareholders. As argued in Bai et al. (2004), this variable should have a positive effect on corporate valuation. We also incorporate *TRPT* and *HRPT*[1] into regression models as measures for tunneling activities.

---

[1]   Following Cheung et al. (2006, 2009), harmful related party transactions is calculated as the difference between total related party transactions and potentially beneficial related party transactions, where a related party transaction is potentially beneficial for a firm if it received cash, loans or guarantees from the related party.

Finally, we include capital – to – sales ratio (cs), operating profit – to – sales ratio (os), Firm size (measured by the natural logarithm of total sales plus 1), Firm age (defined as current year minus firm established year), and firm Leverage (measured by total liabilities over total assets) as control variables, which are quite standard controls in corporate governance study. The variable definitions are summarized in Table 3 – 1.

Table 3 – 1　　　　　　　　　**Variables and Definitions**

Variable	Definition
htq	Tobin's Q in H share market: (the circulation market value of H shares + total liabilities)/(book value of equity * the proportion of the floating H shares over total shares + total liabilities)
atq	Tobin's Q in A share market: (the circulation market value of A shares + total liabilities)/(book value of equity * the proportion of the floating A shares over total shares + total liabilities)
tqr	htq/atq
sh1	The Stake of the largest shareholder (%)
sh1_sq	The Square of sh1
dual	An indicator equals 1 if the CEO and the board chairman in a firm is the same person, and 0 otherwise
b_ind	Board independence: the number of independent directors divided by the total number of directors in a board
cstr2_10	The natural logarithm of the sum of squares of the percentage points of shareholding by the second to the tenth largest shareholders
TRPT	Total related party transactions deflated by total assets
HRPT	Potentially harmful related party transactions deflated by total assets
cs	Capital to sales ratio
os	Operating profit/total sales
fsize	Firm size: log (sales + 1)
age	Firm age: current year – firm established year
lev	Firm leverage: total liabilities/total assets

Note: This table briefly defines the main variables used in the empirical analysis.

3. 3. 3 Descriptive Statistics

Table 3 − 2 reports the basic descriptive statistics of explained variables and main explanatory variables. Based on the table, the mean (median) of the firm valuation of H − shares is less than that of A − shares for all years, which implies that the mean (median) of variable *tqr* is less than 1 for all years, as shown in column (5). The table also describes the distribution of dual − listed firms over the years, which assumes an evident increasing trend from 26 firms in 2002 to 68 firms in 2013, excluding all financial companies for all years. One possible interpretation for the difference in corporate valuation between the two markets for the same firm is that H − share market is well established and features rich and diversified investment channels, whereas A − share market is not well established and is characterized by poor and limited investment channels that may boost the valuation of firms. The mean (median) of *sh*1 is larger than 45% for all years, which indicates that corporate ownership concentration is prevalent in the dual − listed companies, which should be a primary concern for corporate governance for investors. We winsorize all of the financial variables at the 1% and 99% levels for each year.

Table 3 − 2   **Descriptive Statistics**

Year	Stats	*htq*	*atq*	*tqr*	*sh*1	*dual*	*b_ind*	*cstr2_*10
2002	mean	0. 917	1. 243	0. 756	0. 482	0. 115	0. 298	− 2. 593
	median	0. 915	1. 143	0. 760	0. 497	0. 000	0. 317	− 2. 438
	sd	0. 087	0. 230	0. 131	0. 116	0. 326	0. 084	0. 689
	N	26	26	26	26	26	26	26
2003	mean	1. 153	1. 257	0. 925	0. 475	0. 071	0. 333	− 2. 534
	median	1. 075	1. 193	0. 914	0. 492	0. 000	0. 333	− 2. 431
	sd	0. 249	0. 201	0. 170	0. 116	0. 262	0. 069	0. 635
	N	28	28	28	28	28	28	28

continued

Year	Stats	*htq*	*atq*	*tqr*	*sh1*	*dual*	*b_ind*	*cstr2_10*
2004	mean	1. 100	1. 156	0. 948	0. 478	0. 069	0. 350	− 2. 567
	median	1. 053	1. 136	0. 934	0. 489	0. 000	0. 364	− 2. 427
	sd	0. 270	0. 134	0. 162	0. 113	0. 258	0. 049	0. 675
	N	29	29	29	29	29	29	29
2005	mean	1. 045	1. 091	0. 960	0. 472	0. 067	0. 365	− 2. 565
	median	1. 008	1. 067	0. 966	0. 482	0. 000	0. 360	− 2. 421
	sd	0. 164	0. 106	0. 127	0. 119	0. 254	0. 048	0. 683
	N	30	30	30	30	30	30	30
2006	mean	1. 181	1. 202	0. 986	0. 455	0. 059	0. 370	− 2. 641
	median	1. 140	1. 153	1. 009	0. 464	0. 000	0. 364	− 2. 504
	sd	0. 273	0. 195	0. 166	0. 120	0. 239	0. 054	0. 688
	N	34	34	34	34	34	34	34
2007	mean	1. 415	1. 757	0. 833	0. 469	0. 140	0. 370	− 2. 767
	median	1. 268	1. 704	0. 819	0. 478	0. 000	0. 364	− 2. 568
	sd	0. 459	0. 578	0. 215	0. 142	0. 351	0. 060	0. 730
	N	43	43	43	43	43	43	43
2008	mean	1. 015	1. 138	0. 900	0. 463	0. 102	0. 388	− 2. 779
	median	1. 007	1. 075	0. 919	0. 482	0. 000	0. 364	− 2. 581
	sd	0. 201	0. 202	0. 137	0. 142	0. 306	0. 077	0. 688
	N	49	49	49	49	49	49	49
2009	mean	1. 195	1. 537	0. 824	0. 457	0. 098	0. 389	− 2. 809
	median	1. 105	1. 341	0. 849	0. 472	0. 000	0. 364	− 2. 592
	sd	0. 355	0. 583	0. 209	0. 140	0. 300	0. 083	0. 718
	N	51	51	51	51	51	51	51
2010	mean	1. 178	1. 555	0. 819	0. 442	0. 109	0. 384	− 2. 784
	median	1. 100	1. 335	0. 843	0. 452	0. 000	0. 357	− 2. 753
	sd	0. 267	0. 641	0. 206	0. 145	0. 315	0. 078	0. 645
	N	55	55	55	55	55	55	55

continued

Year	Stats	htq	atq	tqr	sh1	dual	b_ind	cstr2_10
2011	mean	1.020	1.260	0.856	0.438	0.119	0.386	−2.755
	median	0.982	1.124	0.905	0.431	0.000	0.364	−2.613
	sd	0.179	0.469	0.165	0.143	0.326	0.072	0.621
	N	59	59	59	59	59	59	59
2012	mean	1.052	1.237	0.892	0.441	0.132	0.385	−2.800
	median	1.003	1.087	0.923	0.436	0.000	0.364	−2.624
	sd	0.185	0.441	0.154	0.141	0.341	0.073	0.725
	N	68	68	68	68	68	68	68
2013	mean	1.059	1.243	0.911	0.440	0.118	0.395	−2.806
	median	0.988	1.050	0.975	0.427	0.000	0.364	−2.683
	sd	0.228	0.545	0.178	0.142	0.325	0.083	0.669
	N	68	68	68	68	68	68	68
Pooling	mean	1.110	1.320	0.880	0.455	0.106	0.375	−2.731
	median	1.030	1.157	0.907	0.464	0.000	0.364	−2.578
	sd	0.282	0.481	0.181	0.135	0.308	0.075	0.681
	N	540	540	540	540	540	540	540

Note: This table presents basic summary statistics for dependent variables and main explanatory variables.

3.3.4   Methodology

This study adopts the static panel data model as its econometric approach. We apply both the fixed – effects and random – effects models to our data. The fixed – effects model can alleviate, but does not necessarily eliminate, the endogeneity problem. Several corporate governance variables are time invariant so that their effects on firm valuation cannot be identified in a fixed – effects model. By contrast, the random – effects model can identify the influence of these time – constant variables, as explained inBai et al. (2004).

3.4   Empirical Analysis

We empirically investigate whether the attitude toward the quality of corporate governance from H – share investors is different from that of A – share investors in terms of the sensitivity of corporate valuation to a set of governance variables. We primarily use three different measures of market valuation, namely, *htq*, *atq*, and *tqr*, as explained variables. The explanatory variables and control variables consist of those listed in Table 3 – 1. China started non – tradable shares reform in 2005, which is expected to exert salient effects on corporate governance. We take a sub – sample comprising all of the observations in 2002 – 2004 to insulate such effect. We estimate both fixed – effects and random – effects models using the first three – year unbalanced panel data, as shown in Table 3 – 3.

Table 3 – 3   Corporate Governance and Market Valuation from

Different Types of Investors: Sub – Sample Case

(Unbalanced Panel)

	(1)	(2)	(3)	(4)	(5)	(6)
	htq (*fe*)	*atq* (*fe*)	*htq* (*re*)	*atq* (*re*)	*tqr* (*fe*)	*tqr* (*re*)
*sh*1	− 3.6723 *	1.6289	1.5292	− 0.3739	− 3.6987 ***	1.4437
	(2.076)	(1.266)	(1.129)	(1.117)	(1.223)	(0.924)
*sh*1_*sq*	1.7329	− 1.2195	− 2.0716	0.1869	1.9802 *	− 1.7405 *
	(1.703)	(1.003)	(1.296)	(1.223)	(0.987)	(1.030)
b_ind	0.7678	0.3974	0.6474	0.0433	0.2949	0.4426 **
	(0.668)	(0.372)	(0.427)	(0.229)	(0.291)	(0.203)
*cstr*2_10	0.4924 **	0.1708 *	0.1224 *	− 0.0337	0.3348 **	0.0997 **
	(0.224)	(0.097)	(0.065)	(0.044)	(0.159)	(0.049)
cs	− 0.0046	0.0451	− 0.0455	− 0.0335 *	− 0.0168	− 0.0087
	(0.046)	(0.058)	(0.028)	(0.019)	(0.030)	(0.018)
os	0.5140	0.4850	0.8951 **	0.3781 **	0.0654	0.4362 *
	(0.605)	(0.316)	(0.423)	(0.164)	(0.276)	(0.260)

continued

	(1)	(2)	(3)	(4)	(5)	(6)
	htq (fe)	atq (fe)	htq (re)	atq (re)	tqr (fe)	tqr (re)
fsize	0. 1813 *	0. 2398 **	0. 0540 **	-0. 0740 ***	0. 0328	0. 0913 ***
	(0. 102)	(0. 107)	(0. 025)	(0. 018)	(0. 081)	(0. 019)
age	0. 0145	-0. 1107 ***	0. 0234 *	-0. 0190 *	0. 0722 ***	0. 0302 ***
	(0. 023)	(0. 032)	(0. 013)	(0. 011)	(0. 022)	(0. 009)
lev	-0. 4939	-1. 4963 ***	-0. 0625	-0. 4770 ***	0. 4236	0. 2682
	(0. 331)	(0. 328)	(0. 248)	(0. 156)	(0. 269)	(0. 178)
dual			-0. 0402	0. 0105		-0. 0442
			(0. 076)	(0. 044)		(0. 064)
Intercept	-0. 5748	-2. 8212	-0. 4482	3. 3111 ***	1. 4182	-1. 7277 ***
	(2. 222)	(2. 359)	(0. 489)	(0. 586)	(1. 791)	(0. 427)
N	83	83	83	83	83	83
r2_w	0. 408	0. 538	0. 360	0. 357	0. 588	0. 505
r2_b	0. 064	0. 005	0. 337	0. 561	0. 073	0. 438
r2_o	0. 098	0. 000	0. 346	0. 466	0. 005	0. 452

Note: This table reports regression results from both the fixed effects and the random effects models, based on a sub – sample consisting of all observations in the period 2002 – 2004. "fe" and "re" in parentheses denote the fixed effect and the random effect models, respectively. $r2\_w$, $r2\_b$, and $r2\_o$ represent within, between, and overall R – squared, respectively. Standard errors (in parentheses) are heteroskedasticity consistent and clustered at the firm level. *** , ** , and * denote significance at the 1% , 5% , and 10% levels, respectively.

In light of the fixed – effects model, the significantly negative coefficient of $sh1$ at the 10% level in column 1 of Table 3 – 3 indicates that H – share investors regard the concentration of ownership of the largest shareholders as a detrimental factor to firm valuation. Intuitively, concentrated equity ownership endows the largest shareholders with substantial discretionary power to use the firm resources for personal gain at the expense of other shareholders, which prompts sophisticated investors to disgust firms with high concentration of ownership of the largest share reflected in market valuation. By contrast, the result in row 1 column (2) indicates that the investors from A – shares do not care about the concentration of ownership of the largest shareholders when they value firms, and the sign of the coefficient is even positive. The corresponding result in column (5) further substantiates this finding, which demonstrates the negative effects of the concentration of ownership of the largest shareholders on the relative valuation of firms being statistically significant at least at the 1% level. column 5 also shows U – shaped relationship between relative firm value and ownership concentration among firms. A simple but intuitive interpretation is that free – rider problem is serious when the ownership concentration measured by $sh1$ is low; an increase in $sh1$ may eliminate or alleviate free – rider problem, which increases firm value. When ownership concentration is increased further, the constraint tunneling activities of the largest shareholder is relaxed, which in turn decreases firm value. If ownership concentration is increased even further,[1] then the net gains from tunneling for the largest shareholder eventually must be negative after some cutoff value of $sh1$, which will decrease tunneling activities and thus improve firm value. Furthermore, ownership concentration is high in China; therefore, a U – shaped curve occurs. Considering this set of regressions with fixed – effects model and based on this subsample, the investors of H – shares are more sensitive to the negative effects of corporate ownership concentration on corporate valuation than the investors of A – shares. The coefficient of $cstr2\_10$ in column (1) is positive and significant at the 5% level, whereas the corresponding coefficient in column (2) is also positive but at a lower significance level of 10%. This result suggests that H – share investors pay more attention to the efficiency of the market for corporate control than A – share investors. The positive effects on firm valuation can be illustrated by several reasons. First, block shareholders other than the largest one form obstacles to expropriation activities from the largest shareholder because they have sufficient stake in the firm so that they have sufficient incentive to monitor and curb the largest shareholder. Second, the power from block shareholders can enhance the efficiency of the market for corporate control because these block shareholders can initiate or assist a fight for corporate control when the current management underperforms. Moreover, these block shareholders have motivations to directly monitor the management. Put differently, $cstr2\_10$ measures the balance of power between the largest shareholder and other share-

---

[1] For instance, consider an extreme case in which $sh1 = 100\%$. The largest shareholder has no incentives to conduct tunneling activities that are detrimental to firm value at all in this case. In our sample, the mean (median) of $sh1$ is higher than 45% for all years.

holders, or the constraint on the largest shareholder power. As discussed in Bai et al. (2004), the concentration of shareholdings in the hands of these block shareholders should have a positive effect on corporate valuation. More importantly, the results in columns (1) and (2) also suggest that H – share investors are more concerned than A – share investors in terms of the effect of $cstr1\_10$ on valuation of firms, which is also strengthened by the result in column (5), where the positive and significant coefficient of $cstr2\_10$ indicates an important effect on the relative valuation of firms. Additionally, the estimates from the random effects model shown in columns (3), (4), and (6) are relatively weak, compared with the aforementioned results. Overall, however, the estimates are consistent.

We use both the fixed effects and the random effects models to conduct similar exercises, based on the full sample with all observations in the period 2002 – 2013. We present the estimates with no year fixed effects and with year fixed effects in Tables 3 – 4 and 3 – 5, respectively. From these two tables, we determine that all of the significant results discussed above disappear. One possible reason for this outcome is the non – persistent concern for corporate governance from H – share market. Another explanation may be that the non – tradable shares reform[①] starting from 2005, which have affected Chinese corporate governance to a large degree. The coefficient of $dual$ in column (1) in both tables is positive and significant at 1%, which shows that, at least to some extent, H – share investors feel that a firm whose CEO and board chairman are the same person performs better. This result is not consistent with Bai et al. (2004), who provide evidence that this variable has a significant and negative effect on the valuation of firms. Should the CEO also be the chairman? This problem remains unsolved. CEO Duality exists when the CEO is simultaneously the board chairman. Views differ on whether Duality or independence is conducive to firm valuation. Ruigrok et al. (2006) strongly advocate the joint Duality structure in which the CEO and board chairman are the same person. They point out that, "such clear cut leadership removes any ambiguity of accountability and responsibility for firm processes and outcomes. The advantages of clear leadership might be the most valuable in situations where a company has

---

① To examine the effects of this reform on corporate governance and firm valuation, we will conduct detailed analysis later.

to overcome a crisis, as this situation requires fast decisions and clear strategic orientation" (p. 1208). However, this opinion remains controversial in both academic and business worlds. By contrast, Kang and Zardkoohi (2005) emphasize that whether CEO Duality can enhance or lower firm performance rests on its fit with the internal and external conditions of the firm. Elsayed (2007) reveals that the effect of CEO Duality on firm performance varies with industry context. In sum, the significantly positive result on this variable is not strange, which is consistent with both agency theory and stewardship theory, as illustrated by Elsayed (2007). In this series of estimates, we do not find consistent and significant results as previously mentioned in the sub – sample case.

Table 3 – 4   Corporate Governance and Market Valuation

from Different Types of Investors: Full Sample Case

(Unbalanced Panel) without Year Fixed Effects

	(1)	(2)	(3)	(4)	(5)	(6)
	htq (fe)	atq (fe)	htq (re)	atq (re)	tqr (fe)	tqr (re)
sh1	– 1. 4905	– 1. 7072	– 0. 2945	– 0. 9739	0. 1850	0. 3005
	(2. 370)	(3. 275)	(0. 768)	(1. 449)	(0. 988)	(0. 567)
sh1_sq	1. 2975	0. 9785	0. 1733	0. 6965	0. 1635	– 0. 1621
	(2. 223)	(3. 212)	(0. 731)	(1. 536)	(1. 035)	(0. 586)
dual	0. 1305 ***	0. 2712 *	0. 0533	0. 1174	0. 0074	0. 0059
	(0. 043)	(0. 156)	(0. 041)	(0. 113)	(0. 054)	(0. 040)
b_ind	0. 4459	0. 4801	0. 3499 *	0. 8814 **	0. 1978	0. 0059
	(0. 335)	(0. 407)	(0. 179)	(0. 420)	(0. 176)	(0. 150)
cstr2_10	– 0. 0352	– 0. 1226	0. 0065	– 0. 0510	0. 0113	0. 0159
	(0. 044)	(0. 093)	(0. 031)	(0. 051)	(0. 024)	(0. 022)
cs	– 0. 0437 **	– 0. 0575	– 0. 0445 ***	– 0. 0626 ***	– 0. 0096	0. 0018
	(0. 021)	(0. 044)	(0. 012)	(0. 019)	(0. 009)	(0. 006)
os	0. 7659 ***	0. 7784 ***	0. 7544 ***	0. 4338 *	0. 0775	0. 2017 **
	(0. 159)	(0. 265)	(0. 138)	(0. 225)	(0. 099)	(0. 080)
fsize	– 0. 0738 **	– 0. 2445 *	– 0. 0052	– 0. 0867 **	0. 0136	0. 0294 ***
	(0. 031)	(0. 135)	(0. 014)	(0. 042)	(0. 030)	(0. 010)

continued

	(1) htq (fe)	(2) atq (fe)	(3) htq (re)	(4) atq (re)	(5) tqr (fe)	(6) tqr (re)
age	0.0094 (0.007)	0.0514 ** (0.024)	0.0002 (0.004)	0.0169 * (0.009)	-0.0080 (0.006)	-0.0059 ** (0.003)
lev	-0.1087 (0.182)	-0.5035 * (0.265)	-0.0527 (0.123)	-0.3777 * (0.208)	0.2170 * (0.111)	0.1876 ** (0.081)
Intercept	2.9139 *** (0.994)	6.7691 ** (3.036)	1.2463 *** (0.318)	3.2440 *** (0.964)	0.3884 (0.687)	0.0754 (0.273)
Year FE	No	No	No	No	No	No
N	540	540	540	540	540	540
r2_w	0.152	0.167	0.128	0.128	0.060	0.036
r2_b	0.019	0.245	0.205	0.303	0.246	0.428
r2_o	0.040	0.147	0.158	0.200	0.133	0.254

Note: This table reports regression results from both the fixed effects and the random effects models with no year fixed effects, based on the full sample consisting of all observations in the period 2002 – 2013. "fe" and "re" in parentheses denote the fixed effect and the random effect models, respectively. $r2\_w$, $r2\_b$, and $r2\_o$ represent within, between, and overall R – squared, respectively. Standard errors (in parentheses) are heteroskedasticity consistent and clustered at the firm level. ***, **, and * denote significance at the 1%, 5%, and 10% levels, respectively.

Table 3 – 5   Corporate Governance and Market Valuation

from Different Types of Investors: Full Sample Case

(Unbalanced Panel) with Year Fixed Effects

	(1) htq (fe)	(2) atq (fe)	(3) htq (re)	(4) atq (re)	(5) tqr (fe)	(6) tqr (re)
sh1	-0.5349 (1.880)	0.1933 (2.390)	-0.1480 (0.752)	-0.4620 (1.277)	-0.2038 (0.885)	0.2097 (0.536)
sh1_sq	0.4403 (1.770)	-0.5247 (2.411)	0.0568 (0.708)	0.3416 (1.404)	0.4047 (0.972)	-0.1243 (0.577)
dual	0.0855 *** (0.030)	0.1757 (0.131)	0.0497 (0.034)	0.1009 (0.101)	0.0300 (0.047)	0.0217 (0.037)
b_ind	-0.1270 (0.363)	0.0853 (0.490)	0.0650 (0.222)	0.4545 (0.408)	0.0041 (0.179)	-0.0348 (0.150)

continued

	(1)	(2)	(3)	(4)	(5)	(6)
	htq (fe)	atq (fe)	htq (re)	atq (re)	tqr (fe)	tqr (re)
cstr2_10	− 0. 0409	− 0. 1207	− 0. 0044	− 0. 0654	0. 0039	0. 0112
	(0. 034)	(0. 081)	(0. 028)	(0. 051)	(0. 021)	(0. 019)
cs	− 0. 0364 **	− 0. 0429	− 0. 0359 ***	− 0. 0534 **	− 0. 0125	0. 0001
	(0. 018)	(0. 040)	(0. 011)	(0. 024)	(0. 009)	(0. 006)
os	0. 5275 ***	0. 3293	0. 5384 ***	0. 1508	0. 1387	0. 2245 ***
	(0. 133)	(0. 235)	(0. 117)	(0. 207)	(0. 091)	(0. 075)
fsize	− 0. 0993 ***	− 0. 2832 **	− 0. 0161	− 0. 1345 **	0. 0162	0. 0394 ***
	(0. 026)	(0. 132)	(0. 017)	(0. 064)	(0. 031)	(0. 013)
age	0. 0320 ***	0. 0542 **	− 0. 0027	0. 0005	0. 0070	− 0. 0024
	(0. 008)	(0. 023)	(0. 005)	(0. 007)	(0. 007)	(0. 003)
lev	− 0. 2003	− 0. 7256 ***	− 0. 1362	− 0. 5531 ***	0. 2744 ***	0. 2315 ***
	(0. 166)	(0. 204)	(0. 126)	(0. 190)	(0. 096)	(0. 071)
Intercept	3. 1448 ***	7. 2960 **	1. 3795 ***	4. 3511 ***	0. 2713	− 0. 2591
	(0. 842)	(2. 882)	(0. 381)	(1. 436)	(0. 683)	(0. 313)
Year FE	Yes	Yes	Yes	Yes	Yes	Yes
N	540	540	540	540	540	540
r2_w	0. 408	0. 431	0. 386	0. 401	0. 311	0. 298
r2_b	0. 001	0. 249	0. 150	0. 332	0. 131	0. 480
r2_o	0. 048	0. 224	0. 272	0. 373	0. 198	0. 399

Note: This table reports regression results from both the fixed effects and the random effects models with year fixed effects, based on the full sample consisting of all observations in the period 2002 – 2013. "fe" and "re" in parentheses denote the fixed effect and the random effect models, respectively. $r2\_w$, $r2\_b$, and $r2\_o$ represent within, between, and overall R – squared, respectively. Standard errors (in parentheses) are heteroskedasticity consistent and clustered at the firm level. *** , ** , and * denote significance at the 1% , 5% , and 10% levels, respectively.

The extant literature (e. g. Cheung et al. , 2006) shows that related party transactions as a type of tunneling activities often from the controlling shareholders, inflict harm on minority shareholder interests, hence the need to figure out whether differences exist in the effects of tunneling activities on corporate valuation between the two types of investors. To this end, we also incorporate common measures on related party transactions into our regression equations to run similar regressions as before. Following Berkman et al. (2011), we adopt the TRPT as a measure on tunneling. We likewise incorporate HRPT as an additional measure of tunneling activities from the controlling shareholders, according to Cheung et al. (2006, 2009). We provide relevant results on this aspect of corporate governance in Tables 3 − 6 and 3 − 7. From Table 3 − 6, no significant result is evident on the effects of TRPT on firm valuation, although all of the regressions yield the expected sign on the TRPT coefficient. By contrast, the results in columns (1), (2), (3), and (4) of Table 3 − 7 are all significant at least at the 5% level. Moreover, in light of the estimates from the fixed effects models, as shown in columns (1) and (2), the significance level (1%) in column (1) is considerably higher than that of in column (2) (5%), which may suggest that H − share investors pay more attention to the effects of harmful related transactions on firm valuation than A − share investors.

Table 3 − 6   The Effects of Tunneling Activities on Market Valuation

from Different Types of Investors: Full Sample Case

(Unbalanced Panel)

	(1)	(2)	(3)	(4)	(5)	(6)
	htq (fe)	atq (fe)	htq (re)	atq (re)	tqr (fe)	tqr (re)
$sh1$	− 0.5655	0.9137	− 0.1672	− 0.4095	− 0.5367	0.1063
	(1.972)	(2.476)	(0.779)	(1.240)	(0.905)	(0.547)
$sh1\_sq$	0.4514	− 1.5319	0.0446	0.1326	0.7941	0.0052
	(1.910)	(2.537)	(0.743)	(1.304)	(1.010)	(0.584)
$dual$	0.0820 **	0.0712	0.0363	0.0086	0.0514	0.0339
	(0.034)	(0.119)	(0.033)	(0.080)	(0.049)	(0.038)
b_ind	− 0.1350	0.2643	0.0591	0.4990	− 0.0407	− 0.0523
	(0.383)	(0.456)	(0.230)	(0.417)	'(0.180)	(0.150)
$cstr2\_10$	− 0.0312	− 0.0963	0.0044	− 0.0351	0.0086	0.0133
	(0.036)	(0.067)	(0.028)	(0.040)	(0.020)	(0.019)
$TRPT$	− 0.0015	− 0.0025	− 0.0019	− 0.0027	0.0001	− 0.0002
	(0.001)	(0.003)	(0.002)	(0.003)	(0.001)	(0.001)
cs	− 0.0348 *	− 0.0316	− 0.0347 ***	− 0.0490 ***	− 0.0131	0.0000
	(0.018)	(0.032)	(0.011)	(0.019)	(0.009)	(0.006)

continued

	(1)	(2)	(3)	(4)	(5)	(6)
	htq (fe)	atq (fe)	htq (re)	atq (re)	tqr (fe)	tqr (re)
os	0.5381 ***	0.3573	0.5516 ***	0.2111	0.1251	0.2152 ***
	(0.130)	(0.233)	(0.116)	(0.183)	(0.097)	(0.077)
fsize	-0.0835 ***	-0.1765 **	-0.0066	-0.0883 ***	0.0084	0.0357 ***
	(0.029)	(0.080)	(0.016)	(0.033)	(0.030)	(0.012)
age	0.0298 ***	0.0340 **	-0.0020	0.0034	0.0090	-0.0026
	(0.009)	(0.015)	(0.005)	(0.006)	(0.006)	(0.003)
lev	-0.2000	-0.7035 ***	-0.1309	-0.5372 ***	0.2709 ***	0.2363 ***
	(0.169)	(0.231)	(0.124)	(0.198)	(0.097)	(0.071)
Intercept	2.8413 ***	4.9042 ***	1.1976 ***	3.4024 ***	0.5282	-0.1512
	(0.893)	(1.689)	(0.350)	(0.789)	(0.637)	(0.274)
Year FE	Yes	Yes	Yes	Yes	Yes	Yes
N	527	527	527	527	527	527
r2_w	0.405	0.428	0.388	0.409	0.313	0.297
r2_b	0.002	0.257	0.189	0.372	0.041	0.452
r2_o	0.058	0.240	0.286	0.383	0.129	0.367

Note: This table reports regression results of the effects of total related party transactions on corporate valuation from both the fixed effects and the random effects models with year fixed effects, based on the full sample consisting of all observations in the period 2002 – 2013. "fe" and "re" in parentheses denote the fixed effect and the random effect models, respectively. $r2\_w$, $r2\_b$, and $r2\_o$ represent within, between, and overall R – squared, respectively. Standard errors (in parentheses) are heteroskedasticity consistent and clustered at the firm level. *** , ** , and * denote significance at the 1% , 5% , and 10% levels, respectively.

Table 3 – 7   The Effects of Harmful Related Party Transactions
on Market Valuation from Different Types of
Investors: Full Sample Case (Unbalanced Panel)

	(1)	(2)	(3)	(4)	(5)	(6)
	htq (fe)	atq (fe)	htq (re)	atq (re)	tqr (fe)	tqr (re)
sh1	-0.5690	0.9073	-0.1671	-0.4075	-0.5362	0.1060
	(1.971)	(2.473)	(0.778)	(1.240)	(0.905)	(0.547)
sh1_sq	0.4541	-1.5270	0.0438	0.1289	0.7938	0.0057
	(1.908)	(2.535)	(0.742)	(1.305)	(1.010)	(0.584)

continued

	(1)	(2)	(3)	(4)	(5)	(6)
	htq (*fe*)	*atq* (*fe*)	*htq* (*re*)	*atq* (*re*)	*tqr* (*fe*)	*tqr* (*re*)
dual	0. 0819 **	0. 0711	0. 0361	0. 0084	0. 0515	0. 0340
	(0. 034)	(0. 119)	(0. 033)	(0. 080)	(0. 049)	(0. 038)
b_ind	− 0. 1350	0. 2643	0. 0589	0. 4980	− 0. 0407	− 0. 0522
	(0. 383)	(0. 456)	(0. 230)	(0. 417)	(0. 180)	(0. 150)
cstr2_10	− 0. 0309	− 0. 0959	0. 0046	− 0. 0348	0. 0086	0. 0133
	(0. 036)	(0. 067)	(0. 028)	(0. 040)	(0. 020)	(0. 019)
HRPT	− 0. 0023 ***	− 0. 0041 **	− 0. 0028 **	− 0. 0045 **	0. 0002	0. 0000
	(0. 001)	(0. 002)	(0. 001)	(0. 002)	(0. 001)	(0. 001)
cs	− 0. 0348 *	− 0. 0316	− 0. 0346 ***	− 0. 0490 ***	− 0. 0131	0. 0000
	(0. 018)	(0. 032)	(0. 011)	(0. 019)	(0. 009)	(0. 006)
os	0. 5378 ***	0. 3567	0. 5513 ***	0. 2103	0. 1251	0. 2152 ***
	(0. 130)	(0. 233)	(0. 116)	(0. 183)	(0. 097)	(0. 077)
fsize	− 0. 0835 ***	− 0. 1765 **	− 0. 0065	− 0. 0882 ***	0. 0084	0. 0357 ***
	(0. 029)	(0. 080)	(0. 016)	(0. 033)	(0. 030)	(0. 012)
age	0. 0298 ***	0. 0339 **	− 0. 0020	0. 0034	0. 0090	− 0. 0026
	(0. 009)	(0. 015)	(0. 005)	(0. 006)	(0. 006)	(0. 003)
lev	− 0. 2000	− 0. 7034 ***	− 0. 1310	− 0. 5376 ***	0. 2709 ***	0. 2363 ***
	(0. 169)	(0. 231)	(0. 124)	(0. 198)	(0. 097)	(0. 071)
Intercept	2. 8425 ***	4. 9067 ***	1. 1963 ***	3. 4006 ***	0. 5278	− 0. 1509
	(0. 893)	(1. 690)	(0. 350)	(0. 789)	(0. 637)	(0. 275)
Year FE	Yes	Yes	Yes	Yes	Yes	Yes
N	527	527	527	527	527	527
r2_w	0. 405	0. 428	0. 388	0. 409	0. 313	0. 297
r2_b	0. 002	0. 258	0. 190	0. 372	0. 041	0. 452
r2_o	0. 058	0. 240	0. 286	0. 383	0. 129	0. 367

Note: This table reports regression results of the effects of harmful related party transactions on corporate valuation from both the fixed effects and the random effects models with year fixed effects, based on the full sample consisting of all observations in the period 2002 – 2013. "fe" and "re" in parentheses denote the fixed effect and the random effect models, respectively. *r2_w*, *r2_b*, and *r2_o* represent within, between, and overall R – squared, respectively. Standard errors (in parentheses) are heteroskedasticity consistent and clustered at the firm level. ***, **, and * denote significance at the 1%, 5%, and 10% levels, respectively.

Finally, we find evidence in the previous discussions that H – share investors pay more attention to corporate governance, as seen in a sub – sample that includes all of the observations in the period 2002 – 2004, whereas all of the significant results no longer continually hold when we run the same regressions based on the full sample spanning from 2002 to 2013; thus, we wonder whether the non – tradable shares reform that started from 2005 improves the entire governance level in Chinese firms so that the attitudes of investors change. Given that the reform started in 2005, we define a dummy variable d_06 that is equal to 1 from year 2006, and 0 otherwise. We incorporate this dummy variable into our regression models and conduct random effects analysis. Allowing for possible contagion from other confounding events or factors, we respectively partition different sample periods for separate regressions. In Table 3 – 8, we report our regression results based on sample periods 2002 – 2007 [columns (1), (4), and (7)], 2002 – 2009 [columns (2), (5), and (8)], and 2002 – 2013 [columns (3), (6), and (9)]. columns (2) – (6) show that the non – tradable shares reform has a significantly positive effect on corporate valuation at least at the 1%, which implies that investors strongly regard the reform as an effective measure for enhancing corporate governance and improving firm performance whether they are from H – or A – shares. All of the estimates from different sample periods are highly consistent, as shown in the table. We also use other sample periods and obtain similar results. In the last three columns, we determine that the coefficients of dummy variable d_06 are all negative and significant, which may indicate that A – share investors care more about the reform. In sum, the evidence in Table 3 – 8 shows that the non – tradable shares reform is good news at least from the viewpoint of market reactions in terms of the valuation of firms from different types of investors.

For robustness check, we consider a balanced panel dataset for 2002 – 2013 with 26 firms for each year, as discussed in Section 3. 3. 1. We use this dataset to run a series of regressions as above. We relegate all of the estimate results based on this balanced panel dataset to Appendix C. The estimates based on this sample are highly consistent with those we have reported thus far. In other words, the main results remain to be true. We also conduct similar empirical exercises on the basis of our alternative equity valuation measure, which is also placed in Appendix C. The main empirical findings

Table 3 – 8　　The Effects of Non – tradable Shares Reform on Market Valuation from Different Types of Investors (Unbalanced Panel)

	(1) htq	(2) htq	(3) htq	(4) atq	(5) atq	(6) atq	(7) tqr	(8) tqr	(9) tqr
sh1	-0.7614 (1.714)	-0.8720 (1.161)	-0.2057 (0.742)	-1.2761 (1.456)	-1.6227 (1.552)	-0.6998 (1.276)	0.1423 (0.746)	0.1062 (0.641)	0.2573 (0.536)
sh1_sq	0.5048 (1.542)	0.6667 (1.019)	0.1719 (0.701)	0.6712 (1.427)	1.1713 (1.441)	0.5891 (1.380)	0.0018 (0.749)	-0.0152 (0.624)	-0.1535 (0.556)
dual	0.1316 (0.109)	0.0555 (0.075)	0.0510 (0.038)	0.2798 (0.235)	0.1503 (0.158)	0.1136 (0.105)	-0.0780* (0.045)	-0.0368 (0.048)	0.0090 (0.039)
b_ind	0.1259 (0.413)	0.1087 (0.289)	0.0802 (0.195)	0.0138 (0.397)	0.0183 (0.255)	0.2804 (0.398)	0.1954 (0.186)	0.2357 (0.156)	0.1295 (0.160)
cstr2_10	0.0790 (0.056)	0.0371 (0.046)	0.0005 (0.031)	-0.0470 (0.047)	-0.0308 (0.042)	-0.0632 (0.050)	0.0594* (0.031)	0.0378 (0.026)	0.0172 (0.021)
d_06	0.1652*** (0.038)	0.1583*** (0.038)	0.1901*** (0.035)	0.3638*** (0.062)	0.3277*** (0.060)	0.3995*** (0.075)	-0.0725*** (0.022)	-0.0795*** (0.019)	-0.0822*** (0.019)
cs	-0.0081 (0.010)	-0.0379*** (0.010)	-0.0476*** (0.012)	-0.0400*** (0.012)	-0.0482*** (0.013)	-0.0704*** (0.022)	0.0027 (0.009)	-0.0018 (0.005)	0.0032 (0.006)
os	0.6785*** (0.227)	0.7540*** (0.141)	0.7432*** (0.130)	0.4401 (0.281)	0.3716** (0.172)	0.4378** (0.207)	0.3087*** (0.132)	0.3238*** (0.087)	0.2028** (0.079)

continued

	(1)	(2)	(3)	(4)	(5)	(6)	(7)	(8)	(9)
	htq	htq	htq	atq	atq	atq	tqr	tqr	tqr
fsize	0.0856***	0.0101	-0.0306**	-0.0504**	-0.0770**	-0.1376**	0.0657***	0.0474***	0.0397***
	(0.023)	(0.018)	(0.014)	(0.025)	(0.033)	(0.049)	(0.014)	(0.012)	(0.011)
age	0.0073	-0.0040	-0.0105***	-0.0130	-0.0028	-0.0042	0.0106*	0.0013	-0.0013
	(0.010)	(0.006)	(0.004)	(0.010)	(0.005)	(0.007)	(0.006)	(0.003)	(0.003)
lev	-0.0984	-0.0668	-0.0770	-0.3781***	-0.4029***	-0.4214**	0.1705*	0.2076***	0.1966**
	(0.158)	(0.147)	(0.118)	(0.136)	(0.134)	(0.190)	(0.096)	(0.066)	(0.078)
Intercept	-0.5416	1.1893***	1.8769***	2.9602***	3.5820***	4.4893***	-0.7725***	-0.3385	-0.1859
(0.410)	(0.620)	(0.410)	(0.374)	(0.736)	(0.857)	(1.114)	(0.294)	(0.268)	(0.279)
N	190	290	540	190	290	540	190	290	540
r2_w	0.376	0.150	0.209	0.249	0.177	0.213	0.111	0.072	0.059
r2_b	0.304	0.377	0.117	0.423	0.392	0.314	0.484	0.512	0.473
r2_o	0.317	0.238	0.155	0.323	0.257	0.256	0.339	0.307	0.293

Note: This table reports the regression results of the effects of non-tradable shares reform on corporate valuation with the random effects model. The estimates in columns (1), (4) and (7) come from a sub-sample with observations in the period 2002-2007; the results in columns (2), (5), and (8) are based on a subsample with observations in the period 2002-2009; and the estimates in columns (3), (6), and (9) are from the full sample with all observations in the period 2002-2013. $r2\_w$, $r2\_b$, and $r2\_o$ represent within, between, and overall $R-$squared, respectively. Standard errors (in parentheses) are heteroskedasticity consistent and clustered at the firm level. ***, **, and * denote significance at the 1%, 5%, and 10% levels, respectively.

from this line of analysis are consistent with our previous discussion. For example, as shown in Table C7, the coefficients of *cstr2_10* in columns (1) and (3) are both significant at least at the 1% level, whereas those in columns (2) and (4) are both insignificant, thereby showing evidence similar to what we find in Table 3 – 3 that H – share investors pay more attention to the efficiency of the market for corporate control compared with A – share investors.

3. 5   Conclusion

In this study, we analyze the question on whether H – share investors and A – share investors hold different beliefs on the quality of corporate governance based on the public companies of China cross – listed both in Hong Kong SAR and mainland China stock markets. Essentially, such companies are firms of China. Based on A + H share framework, which is the unique feature of the China stock market, "endogeneity" problem is avoided subtly, where A + H shares refer to firms listed both in the stock markets of mainland China and Hong Kong SAR. We set the Tobin's Q of A – and H – shares for each company in the sample spanning 2002 to 2013. We let the Tobin's Q of A – and H – shares be the dependent variables, and the related corporate governance variables and the control variables as independent variables. We subsequently run separate regressions using these two groups of variables to verify whether significant differences exist between these two estimates. We also use the ratio of the Tobin's Q of H – share to that of A – share as a dependent variable in running similar regressions. In the sub – sample with observations from 2002 – 2004, we find that H – share investors care more about the concentration of ownership of the largest shareholders than A – share investors do. Moreover, we find that the concentration of ownership in the hands of the second to the tenth shareholders exhibits a more important influence on the corporate valuation of H – share market than A – share market.

The evidence from the sub – sample seems to demonstrate that when valuing firms, H – share investors pay more attention to the quality of corporate governance compared with A – share investors. However, this evidence disappears after conducting a full sample analysis, that is, our findings from the sub – sample do not hold at all. We do not find strong evidence to show that a significant difference exists in the concern for the quality of corporate governance between these two types of investors. We also incorporate related party transaction variables into our empirical framework to determine whether H – share investors dislike tunneling activities from the controlling shareholders more compared with A – share investors; we find only weak evidence that H – share investors disgust harmful related party transactions more than A – share investors in terms of different statistical significance levels.

We also consider that the non – tradable shares reform launched in 2005 may play an important role in the entire level of corporate governance in China. We introduce a dummy variable to represent possible effects from the reform into our empirical design under the framework of random effects. In this series of empirical analyses, we find that the reform exerts important effects on market valuation based on different sample periods, which shows the robustness of our regressions. However, we do not find that H – share investors care more about the effects of this policy on corporate valuation compared with A – share investors.

Alternatively, for robustness, we also conduct similar analyses based on a new equity valuation measure, that is, the log – ratio of market capitalization to total assets. As shown in Tables C7 – C18 of Appendix C, the empirical results based on the subsample indicate that compared with A – share investors, H – share investors care more about the quality of corporate governance when they value firms. For instance, Table C7 indicates that H – share investors pay more attention to the efficiency of the market for corporate control than A – share investors. This conclusion, however, does not hold any longer when we prolong the sample period to include additional time periods. Moreover, the results on the effects of the non – tradable shares reform on corporate governance and firm valuation suggest that the reform is good news for both H – and A – share investors. For example, Table C12 shows that the reform has significantly positive effects on corporate valuation at least at the 1% level, which implies that investors strongly regard the reform as an effective measure for enhancing corporate governance and improving firm performance whether they are from H – or A – shares. In sum, the conclusions from this line of alternative analysis are highly consistent with our explanation in the text.

To sum up, in this study, we find weak evidence that H – share investors care more than A – share investors about governance variables, based on a sub – sample. However, this effect is not persistent. We do not find strong evidence to support the existence of a significant difference between H – and A – share investors in their concern for the quality of corporate governance.

Appendix A Additional Tables and Results from CEM Sample

A. 1 Variable Definitions, Summary Statistics, and Further Results from BL Sample

Table A1   Brief Definitions and Sources of Main Variables

Variable Name	Definition	Source
	Panel A: Main Outcome Variables on Director Characteristics	
Share1	Percentage of executive directors as representatives of the controlling shareholders.	ASINA
Share2	Percentage of executive directors as representatives of the second shareholders.	ASINA
Share2_5	Percentage of executive directors as representatives of the second to the fifth shareholders.	ASINA
CEO_exp	Percentage of executive directors with CEO work experience.	ASINA
Chair_exp	Percentage of executive directors with board chairman work experience.	ASINA
Exe_exp	Percentage of executive directors with CEO or chairman work experience.	ASINA
Ind_exp	Percentage of directors with work experience in the same industry.	ASINA
Pro_exp	Percentage of directors with advanced professional experience (Accountant, lawyer, engineer, economist, etc.).	ASINA
Edu1	Percentage of directors whose educational qualifications are technical secondary school, or lower.	ASINA
Edu2	Percentage of directors with a junior college diploma.	ASINA
Edu3	Percentage of directors whose educational qualifications are junior college, or below.	ASINA

continued

Variable Name	Definition	Source
Edu4	Percentage of directors with a bachelor degree.	ASINA
Edu5	Percentage of directors with a master's degree.	ASINA
Edu6	Percentage of directors with a doctorate degree.	ASINA
Edu7	Percentage of directors whose educational qualifications are master, or higher.	ASINA
Pol1	Percentage of directors with central government work experience.	ASINA
pol2	Percentage of directors with local government work experience.	ASINA
pol3	Percentage of directors who are members of the national committee of CPPCC.	ASINA
pol4	Percentage of directors who are members of the local committee of CP-PCC.	ASINA
pol5	Percentage of directors who are members of deputy to the National People's Congress.	ASINA
Pol6	Percentage of directors who are members of deputy to the local People's Congress.	ASINA
Pol7	Percentage of directors who have at least one of Pol1 −6 experience.	ASINA
Academe	Proportion of independent directors from academic institutions.	ASINA
Match	Percentage of independent directors whose research fields match the business of the firms served when they come from academic institutions.	ASINA
Dir_age	Average age of directors.	ASINA
Exe_rel1	Percentage of independent directors who former colleagues of the current firm's CEO or chairman.	ASINA
Exe_rel2	Percentage of independent directors who are college alumni or alumnae of the current firm's CEO or chairman.	ASINA
Exe_rel	Percentage of independent directors who are either former colleagues or college alumni/alumnae of the current firm's CEO or chairman.	ASINA
CV	A dummy variable takes the value of 1 if a firm is a CV user, and 0 otherwise.	ASINA
t	A time dummy takes the value of 1 for the years when CV users adopt CV, and 0 otherwise.	

continued

Variable Name	Definition	Source
	Panel B: Main Control Variables	
Firm size	Log (book value of total assets).	CSMAR
Leverage	Long term debt divided by total assets.	CSMAR
Firm age	Log (the number of listing years + 1)	CSMAR
MTB	Market – to – book ratio, calculated as the market value of equity plus book value of debt divided by total assets.	CSMAR
Duality	A binary variable equals 1 if the CEO of a company is also the chairman of the board of the directors, and 0 otherwise.	CSMAR
Board size	The number of directors in the board of directors in a firm.	CSMAR
Board_ind	Board independence, defined as the number of independent directors over Board size for each company.	CSMAR
Related	A categorical variable indicating whether related parties among the top ten shareholders exist, which equals 1 if there is no relation among the top ten shareholders, equals 2 if such relation exist, and equals 3 if it is uncertainty (no public information available on this).	CSMAR
Shrcr1	The controlling shareholders' ownership (percentage) at the year – end.	CSMAR
Shrcr2_10	Percentage of shares held by the second to the tenth shareholders.	CSMAR
sd	An indicator variable, the nature of the controlling shareholder, equals 1 if the firma's controlling shareholder is government – related, and 0 otherwise.	CSMAR
Fd	A dummy variable, the nature of the controlling shareholder, equals 1 if a firm is controlled by Foreigners, and 0 otherwise.	CSMAR
Regulatory	A binary variable indicating the concentration of the controlling shareholder equals 1 if the percentage of shares held by the controlling shareholder is equal or more than 30% , and 0 otherwise.	CSMAR

Note: This table briefly defines the main variables used in the empirical analysis. The data sources are as follows: (i) ASINA: Extraction from director resumes obtained from firm annual reports disclosed by SHSE, SZSE and SINA FINANCE, (ii) CSMAR: the China Stock Market & Accounting Research database.

Table A2   Summary Statistics

Variable	Mean	Median	Standard Deviation	Minimum	Maximum	Number of Observations
Panel A: Summary Statistics on Director Characteristics						
Pretreatment Period: Control Group						
*Share*1	55. 393	50. 000	25. 404	0. 000	100. 000	294
*Share*2	6. 849	0. 000	11. 410	0. 000	66. 667	294
*Share*2_5	13. 934	11. 111	17. 104	0. 000	83. 333	294
CEO_exp	34. 135	33. 333	19. 663	0. 000	100. 000	294
Chair_exp	24. 889	22. 222	17. 839	0. 000	77. 778	294
Exe_exp	43. 249	40. 000	20. 910	0. 000	100. 000	294
Ind_exp	94. 572	100. 000	10. 913	30. 000	100. 000	294
Ind_exp'	6. 533	0. 000	10. 044	0. 000	50. 000	294
Pro_exp	69. 227	76. 389	27. 661	0. 000	100. 000	294
Pro_exp'	50. 746	50. 000	30. 063	0. 000	100. 000	274
*Pol*1	1. 892	0. 000	6. 349	0. 000	66. 667	294
*pol*2	14. 743	10. 000	18. 843	0. 000	85. 714	294
*pol*3	0. 426	0. 000	2. 989	0. 000	33. 333	294
*pol*4	1. 244	0. 000	4. 722	0. 000	33. 333	294
*pol*5	2. 000	0. 000	5. 662	0. 000	40. 000	294
*Pol*6	1. 978	0. 000	5. 483	0. 000	28. 571	294
*Pol*7	21. 439	16. 667	20. 390	0. 000	85. 714	294
*Pol*1'	11. 336	0. 000	21. 199	0. 000	100. 000	274
*Pol*2'	19. 280	0. 000	25. 452	0. 000	100. 000	274
*Pol*3'	1. 502	0. 000	7. 778	0. 000	66. 667	274
*Pol*4'	2. 792	0. 000	9. 829	0. 000	50. 000	274
*Pol*5'	0. 967	0. 000	5. 900	0. 000	50. 000	274
*Pol*6'	1. 502	0. 000	6. 573	0. 000	33. 333	274
*Pol*7'	32. 501	33. 333	30. 958	0. 000	100. 000	274
Academe	45. 196	45. 000	35. 731	0. 000	200. 000	274
Match	7. 373	0. 000	15. 977	0. 000	100. 000	274
*Edu*1	4. 637	0. 000	9. 437	0. 000	50. 000	294

continued

Variable	Mean	Median	Standard Deviation	Minimum	Maximum	Number of Observations
Edu2	18.924	16.667	19.590	0.000	83.333	294
Edu3	23.561	16.667	22.341	0.000	88.889	294
Edu4	40.925	40.000	22.348	0.000	100.000	294
Edu5	30.283	28.571	21.795	0.000	87.500	294
Edu6	5.231	0.000	9.653	0.000	50.000	294
Edu7	35.514	33.333	23.766	0.000	100.000	294
Edu1'	1.588	0.000	7.908	0.000	66.667	274
Edu2'	6.776	0.000	17.348	0.000	100.000	274
Edu3'	8.364	0.000	19.183	0.000	100.000	274
Edu4'	32.457	33.333	29.358	0.000	100.000	274
Edu5'	27.879	33.333	27.225	0.000	100.000	274
Edu6'	31.300	33.333	29.942	0.000	100.000	274
Edu7'	59.179	66.667	32.985	0.000	100.000	274
Dir_age	46.394	46.155	4.221	33.833	61.333	294
Exe_rel1	5.827	0.000	14.500	0.000	66.667	274
Exe_rel2	11.169	0.000	21.343	0.000	100.000	274
Exe_rel3	16.753	0.000	23.671	0.000	100.000	274
Treatment Period: Control group						
Share1	55.300	50.000	25.570	0.000	100.000	296
Share2	7.331	0.000	12.047	0.000	71.429	296
Share2_5	14.281	10.000	17.629	0.000	71.429	296
CEO_exp	34.479	33.333	20.177	0.000	100.000	296
Chair_exp	26.090	20.000	18.621	0.000	85.714	296
Exe_exp	44.153	42.857	21.591	0.000	100.000	296
Ind_exp	95.255	100.000	10.282	30.000	100.000	296
Ind_exp'	6.813	0.000	10.161	0.000	50.000	296
Pro_exp	68.365	74.167	28.678	0.000	100.000	296
Pro_exp'	51.162	50.000	29.058	0.000	100.000	295
Pol1	1.988	0.000	7.243	0.000	80.000	296

continued

Variable	Mean	Median	Standard Deviation	Minimum	Maximum	Number of Observations
pol2	14. 319	10. 000	18. 610	0. 000	87. 500	296
pol3	0. 547	0. 000	3. 831	0. 000	50. 000	296
pol4	1. 388	0. 000	5. 455	0. 000	50. 000	296
pol5	2. 228	0. 000	6. 127	0. 000	40. 000	296
Pol6	1. 903	0. 000	5. 322	0. 000	28. 571	296
Pol7	21. 520	16. 667	21. 223	0. 000	100. 000	296
Pol1'	10. 128	0. 000	19. 265	0. 000	100. 000	295
Pol2'	18. 811	0. 000	24. 929	0. 000	100. 000	295
Pol3'	1. 209	0. 000	6. 580	0. 000	66. 667	295
Pol4'	3. 124	0. 000	10. 565	0. 000	50. 000	295
Pol5'	0. 910	0. 000	5. 385	0. 000	50. 000	295
Pol6'	1. 136	0. 000	5. 643	0. 000	33. 333	295
Pol7'	30. 571	33. 333	29. 529	0. 000	100. 000	295
Academe	45. 080	40. 000	33. 745	0. 000	100. 000	295
Match	6. 831	0. 000	15. 069	0. 000	100. 000	295
Edu1	4. 901	0. 000	9. 901	0. 000	50. 000	296
Edu2	17. 298	16. 667	18. 674	0. 000	87. 500	296
Edu3	22. 199	16. 667	21. 414	0. 000	87. 500	296
Edu4	40. 241	40. 000	22. 726	0. 000	100. 000	296
Edu5	32. 147	33. 333	21. 903	0. 000	87. 500	296
Edu6	5. 413	0. 000	10. 606	0. 000	66. 667	296
Edu7	37. 560	33. 333	24. 230	0. 000	100. 000	296
Edu1'	1. 898	0. 000	8. 495	0. 000	66. 667	295
Edu2'	5. 746	0. 000	15. 854	0. 000	100. 000	295
Edu3'	7. 644	0. 000	18. 120	0. 000	100. 000	295
Edu4'	32. 249	33. 333	28. 989	0. 000	100. 000	295
Edu5'	28. 408	33. 333	25. 678	0. 000	100. 000	295
Edu6'	31. 699	33. 333	29. 423	0. 000	100. 000	295
Edu7'	60. 107	66. 667	32. 065	0. 000	100. 000	295

continued

Variable	Mean	Median	Standard Deviation	Minimum	Maximum	Number of Observations
Dir_age	46.723	46.600	4.321	34.333	62.333	296
Exe_rel1	6.045	0.000	14.654	0.000	75.000	295
Exe_rel2	10.970	0.000	21.012	0.000	100.000	295
Exe_rel3	16.902	0.000	23.857	0.000	100.000	295
Pretreatment Period: Treated Group						
Share1	55.726	60.000	28.973	0.000	100.000	348
Share2	7.688	0.000	12.741	0.000	83.333	348
Share2_5	13.952	0.000	19.152	0.000	88.889	348
CEO_exp	35.288	33.333	21.101	0.000	100.000	348
Chair_exp	24.057	20.000	17.696	0.000	83.333	348
Exe_exp	43.881	41.429	21.969	0.000	100.000	348
Ind_exp	94.888	100.000	13.257	0.000	100.000	348
Ind_exp'	7.242	0.000	11.319	0.000	50.000	348
Pro_exp	71.211	78.889	27.290	0.000	100.000	348
Pro_exp'	56.202	60.000	28.999	0.000	100.000	323
Pol1	2.922	0.000	8.405	0.000	66.667	348
pol2	12.495	0.000	17.269	0.000	83.333	348
pol3	0.469	0.000	2.648	0.000	25.000	348
pol4	1.479	0.000	5.380	0.000	50.000	348
pol5	1.741	0.000	5.258	0.000	33.333	348
Pol6	2.021	0.000	6.263	0.000	40.000	348
Pol7	20.877	16.667	20.484	0.000	100.000	348
Pol1'	7.678	0.000	17.108	0.000	100.000	323
Pol2'	17.709	0.000	23.119	0.000	100.000	323
Pol3'	0.903	0.000	5.479	0.000	50.000	323
Pol4'	2.384	0.000	8.705	0.000	50.000	323
Pol5'	1.146	0.000	6.976	0.000	66.667	323
Pol6'	1.641	0.000	7.255	0.000	50.000	323
Pol7'	28.013	33.333	28.469	0.000	100.000	323

continued

Variable	Mean	Median	Standard Deviation	Minimum	Maximum	Number of Observations
Academe	50. 650	50. 000	33. 140	0. 000	150. 000	323
Match	8. 184	0. 000	17. 389	0. 000	100. 000	323
*Edu*1	5. 469	0. 000	12. 090	0. 000	100. 000	348
*Edu*2	22. 477	16. 667	21. 852	0. 000	100. 000	348
*Edu*3	27. 946	23. 611	24. 446	0. 000	100. 000	348
*Edu*4	37. 124	33. 333	22. 362	0. 000	92. 308	348
*Edu*5	30. 520	28. 571	22. 598	0. 000	100. 000	348
*Edu*6	4. 411	0. 000	9. 521	0. 000	66. 667	348
*Edu*7	34. 930	33. 333	24. 844	0. 000	100. 000	348
*Edu*1	2. 688	0. 000	10. 303	0. 000	66. 667	323
*Edu*2′	7. 337	0. 000	15. 923	0. 000	100. 000	323
*Edu*3′	10. 026	0. 000	18. 403	0. 000	100. 000	323
*Edu*4′	33. 359	33. 333	28. 113	0. 000	100. 000	323
*Edu*5′	26. 362	25. 000	26. 389	0. 000	100. 000	323
*Edu*6′	30. 253	33. 333	28. 255	0. 000	100. 000	323
*Edu*7′	56. 615	60. 000	30. 908	0. 000	100. 000	323
Dir_age	46. 634	46. 919	4. 580	33. 000	58. 667	348
*Exe_rel*1	4. 267	0. 000	14. 370	0. 000	100. 000	323
*Exe_rel*2	9. 009	0. 000	19. 138	0. 000	100. 000	323
*Exe_rel*3	13. 277	0. 000	22. 723	0. 000	100. 000	323
Treatment Period: Treated group						
*Share*1	57. 084	57. 143	31. 776	0. 000	100. 000	353
*Share*2	9. 380	0. 000	16. 754	0. 000	100. 000	353
*Share*2_5	15. 009	0. 000	21. 915	0. 000	100. 000	353
CEO_exp	38. 856	37. 500	21. 743	0. 000	100. 000	350
Chair_exp	27. 405	25. 000	20. 650	0. 000	100. 000	350
Exe_exp	48. 762	50. 000	22. 571	0. 000	100. 000	350
Ind_exp	98. 804	100. 000	5. 283	50. 000	100. 000	350
Ind_exp′	7. 736	0. 000	12. 380	0. 000	100. 000	350

continued

Variable	Mean	Median	Standard Deviation	Minimum	Maximum	Number of Observations
Pro_exp	70.117	76.389	28.796	0.000	100.000	350
Pro_exp'	62.265	66.667	28.306	0.000	100.000	326
Pol1	2.202	0.000	6.759	0.000	37.500	350
pol2	13.176	0.000	18.315	0.000	100.000	350
pol3	0.519	0.000	3.313	0.000	33.333	350
pol4	1.624	0.000	5.550	0.000	33.333	350
pol5	1.481	0.000	4.984	0.000	25.000	350
Pol6	2.201	0.000	6.309	0.000	40.000	350
Pol7	20.978	16.667	22.141	0.000	100.000	350
Pol1'	8.574	0.000	18.614	0.000	100.000	326
Pol2'	17.296	0.000	23.464	0.000	100.000	326
Pol3'	0.869	0.000	5.198	0.000	33.333	326
Pol4'	2.950	0.000	10.560	0.000	100.000	326
Pol5'	1.033	0.000	6.180	0.000	66.667	326
Pol6'	1.299	0.000	6.432	0.000	50.000	326
Pol7'	28.916	33.333	28.554	0.000	100.000	326
Academe	45.552	36.667	36.555	0.000	200.000	326
Match	7.428	0.000	15.459	0.000	80.000	326
Edu1	4.266	0.000	11.652	0.000	100.000	350
Edu2	16.766	14.286	19.398	0.000	83.333	350
Edu3	21.032	16.667	21.846	0.000	100.000	350
Edu4	37.010	33.333	25.025	0.000	100.000	350
Edu5	36.559	33.333	26.065	0.000	100.000	350
Edu6	5.399	0.000	11.672	0.000	100.000	350
Edu7	41.958	40.000	27.157	0.000	100.000	350
Edu1'	3.487	0.000	12.288	0.000	100.000	326
Edu2'	7.106	0.000	16.688	0.000	100.000	326
Edu3'	10.593	0.000	20.219	0.000	100.000	326
Edu4'	33.558	33.333	28.803	0.000	100.000	326

continued

Variable	Mean	Median	Standard Deviation	Minimum	Maximum	Number of Observations
Edu5′	26. 074	25. 000	26. 625	0. 000	100. 000	326
Edu6′	29. 775	33. 333	27. 295	0. 000	100. 000	326
Edu7′	55. 849	66. 667	30. 501	0. 000	100. 000	326
Dir_age	46. 129	46. 429	4. 093	34. 333	57. 000	350
Exe_rel1	2. 797	0. 000	12. 230	0. 000	100. 000	326
Exe_rel2	7. 362	0. 000	17. 363	0. 000	100. 000	326
Exe_rel3	10. 056	0. 000	20. 472	0. 000	100. 000	326

Panel B: Control Variable Summary Statistics

Pretreatment Period: Control Group

Firm size	21. 247	21. 115	0. 940	19. 130	26. 441	294
Leverage	0. 467	0. 461	0. 199	0. 073	1. 518	294
ROA	0. 017	0. 023	0. 023	− 0. 163	0. 056	294
Firm age	1. 737	1. 946	0. 642	0. 000	2. 708	289
MTB	0. 928	0. 773	0. 812	− 1. 175	9. 902	291
Duality	0. 119	0. 000	0. 324	0. 000	1. 000	294
Board size	9. 846	9. 000	2. 264	3. 000	17. 000	293
Board_ind	0. 293	0. 333	0. 104	0. 000	0. 500	293
Related	2. 247	2. 000	0. 773	1. 000	3. 000	288
Shrcr1	44. 547	42. 810	15. 642	10. 050	81. 820	294
Shrcr2_10	17. 217	13. 920	13. 173	0. 320	55. 790	293
sd	0. 126	0. 000	0. 332	0. 000	1. 000	294
Fd	0. 003	0. 000	0. 058	0. 000	1. 000	294
Regulatory	0. 759	1. 000	0. 429	0. 000	1. 000	294

Treatment Period: Control group

Firm size	21. 327	21. 164	0. 975	19. 089	26. 599	296
Leverage	0. 504	0. 494	0. 265	0. 078	2. 685	296
ROA	0. 013	0. 019	0. 025	− 0. 092	0. 054	296
Firm age	1. 910	2. 079	0. 541	0. 000	2. 773	293
MTB	0. 759	0. 621	0. 606	− 0. 531	5. 199	295

continued

Variable	Mean	Median	Standard Deviation	Minimum	Maximum	Number of Observations
Duality	0. 115	0. 000	0. 319	0. 000	1. 000	296
Board size	9. 837	9. 000	2. 223	5. 000	17. 000	294
Board_ind	0. 332	0. 333	0. 061	0. 000	0. 600	294
Related	2. 414	3. 000	0. 687	1. 000	3. 000	290
*Shrcr*1	43. 599	42. 460	15. 408	10. 050	81. 820	295
Shrcr2_10	17. 699	14. 480	13. 243	0. 800	57. 200	295
sd	0. 125	0. 000	0. 331	0. 000	1. 000	296
Fd	0. 003	0. 000	0. 058	0. 000	1. 000	296
Regulatory	0. 764	1. 000	0. 426	0. 000	1. 000	296
Pretreatment Period: Treated Group						
Firm size	21. 252	21. 142	0. 924	19. 130	26. 043	348
Leverage	0. 484	0. 488	0. 234	0. 073	2. 342	348
ROA	0. 018	0. 023	0. 020	− 0. 163	0. 056	348
Firm age	1. 753	1. 792	0. 602	0. 000	2. 708	348
MTB	0. 933	0. 704	1. 044	− 1. 862	11. 842	348
Duality	0. 115	0. 000	0. 319	0. 000	1. 000	348
Board size	9. 718	9. 000	2. 261	5. 000	18. 000	348
Board_ind	0. 301	0. 333	0. 107	0. 000	0. 600	348
Related	2. 360	2. 000	0. 701	1. 000	3. 000	339
*Shrcr*1	48. 104	48. 985	16. 098	11. 030	84. 690	348
Shrcr2_10	15. 944	10. 750	13. 412	0. 390	66. 030	347
sd	0. 178	0. 000	0. 383	0. 000	1. 000	348
Fd	0. 003	0. 000	0. 054	0. 000	1. 000	348
Regulatory	0. 839	1. 000	0. 368	0. 000	1. 000	348
Treatment Period: Treated Group						
Firm size	21. 377	21. 306	1. 026	18. 878	26. 588	353
Leverage	0. 519	0. 502	0. 296	0. 070	2. 685	353
ROA	0. 011	0. 019	0. 047	− 0. 500	0. 105	353
Firm age	2. 014	2. 079	0. 477	0. 693	2. 890	353

continued

Variable	Mean	Median	Standard Deviation	Minimum	Maximum	Number of Observations
MTB	0. 937	0. 615	1. 810	− 13. 802	19. 774	353
Duality	0. 108	0. 000	0. 310	0. 000	1. 000	353
Board size	9. 480	9. 000	1. 994	4. 000	15. 000	352
Board_ind	0. 339	0. 333	0. 054	0. 182	0. 750	352
Related	2. 446	3. 000	0. 634	1. 000	3. 000	350
*Shrcr*1	45. 375	44. 490	15. 916	8. 700	76. 470	353
*Shrcr*2_10	15. 961	11. 235	13. 279	0. 520	59. 590	352
sd	0. 187	0. 000	0. 390	0. 000	1. 000	353
Fd	0. 006	0. 000	0. 075	0. 000	1. 000	353
Regulatory	0. 796	1. 000	0. 404	0. 000	1. 000	353

Note: This table reports the summary statistics for the variables included in tableA1, using the sample constructed by the BL method. The variables with prime ' ″ correspond to independent directors, while corresponding variables but without prime correspond to executive directors. The units used for variables are percentage except for the variable *Dir_age*. We winsorize all of the financial variables at the 1% and 99% levels for each year.

Table A3   The Power Distribution in the Board: Binary Case

Model	(1)	(2)	(3)	(4)	(5)	(6)
	*Share*1*d*	*Share*2*d*	*Share*2_5*d*	*Share*1*d*	*Share*2*d*	*Share*2_5*d*
Intercept	− 2. 399 ***	0. 149	0. 888	− 2. 368 *	0. 482	1. 399
	(0. 59)	(0. 66)	(0. 63)	(1. 40)	(1. 32)	(1. 28)
CV	− 0. 073	0. 091	0. 054	− 0. 027	− 0. 132	0. 182
	(0. 06)	(0. 08)	(0. 07)	(0. 16)	(0. 19)	(0. 15)
t	0. 024	0. 019	0. 003	− 0. 165	− 0. 073	0. 078
	(0. 02)	(0. 04)	(0. 03)	(0. 14)	(0. 11)	(0. 11)
CV × *t*	0. 002	0. 067	0. 060	0. 071	0. 499 **	0. 075
	(0. 04)	(0. 06)	(0. 05)	(0. 22)	(0. 20)	(0. 18)
Regulatory	0. 017	0. 147	0. 072	0. 001	0. 178	0. 094
	(0. 08)	(0. 11)	(0. 09)	(0. 20)	(0. 22)	(0. 20)

continued

Model	(1)	(2)	(3)	(4)	(5)	(6)
	Share1d	Share2d	Share2_5d	Share1d	Share2d	Share2_5d
Board size	-0.024*	0.020	0.042***	-0.014	0.078***	0.062**
	(0.01)	(0.01)	(0.01)	(0.03)	(0.03)	(0.03)
Board_ind	0.088	0.393	0.441	0.354	0.421	0.669
	(0.29)	(0.36)	(0.30)	(0.52)	(0.58)	(0.52)
Duality	-0.077	0.063	0.035	0.083	-0.104	0.020
	(0.08)	(0.08)	(0.09)	(0.23)	(0.21)	(0.24)
Related	-0.042	-0.048	-0.082**			
	(0.03)	(0.04)	(0.03)			
Shrcr1	0.018***	-0.012***	-0.012***	0.021***	-0.014*	-0.019**
	(0.00)	(0.00)	(0.00)	(0.01)	(0.01)	(0.01)
Shrcr2_10	-0.005	0.019***	0.024***	-0.006	0.019***	0.028***
	(0.00)	(0.00)	(0.00)	(0.01)	(0.01)	(0.01)
Sd	-0.022	-0.029	-0.008	0.086	0.218	-0.064
	(0.07)	(0.08)	(0.07)	(0.24)	(0.18)	(0.17)
Fd	-0.150	0.453*	0.496**	-0.365	-0.172	-0.018
	(0.15)	(0.26)	(0.24)	(0.34)	(0.28)	(0.28)
Firm size	0.096***	-0.082**	-0.105***	0.086	-0.116**	-0.151***
	(0.03)	(0.03)	(0.03)	(0.06)	(0.06)	(0.05)
Leverage	-0.194	0.147	0.128	-0.472	-0.433*	0.009
	(0.12)	(0.15)	(0.13)	(0.32)	(0.26)	(0.23)
Firm age	0.101*	-0.083	-0.125**	0.097	-0.021	0.010
	(0.05)	(0.06)	(0.06)	(0.16)	(0.13)	(0.14)
ROA	-0.011	-0.418	0.045	1.034	1.192	3.192***
	(0.28)	(0.30)	(0.26)	(1.12)	(1.28)	(1.05)
Observations	8077	8077	8077	1040	1040	1040

Note: This table reports the nonlinear (probit) DID regression estimates [columns (1), (2) (3), (4) and (5)] to test whether minority shareholders can elect their representatives into the board of directors with binary outcome variables at individual director level, using the sample constructed via BL method. columns (1), (2), and (3) use all the sample, while columns (4), (5), and (6) exclude the observations in which the top ten shareholders are related. All outcome variables in the table are binary. Standard errors (in parentheses) are heteroskedasticity consistent and clustered at the firm level. ***, **, and * denote significance at the 1%, 5%, and 10% levels, respectively.

Table A4   Professional Experience of Executive Directors: Binary Case

Model	(1)	(2)	(3)	(4)
	CEO_exp_d	Chair_exp_d	Ind_exp_d	Edu
Intercept	− 1. 168 ***	− 0. 217	− 0. 416	
	(0. 41)	(0. 53)	(1. 16)	
CV	0. 042	− 0. 021	0. 068	− 0. 085 *
	(0. 04)	(0. 05)	(0. 10)	(0. 05)
t	− 0. 020	0. 009	0. 051	0. 010
	(0. 02)	(0. 02)	(0. 05)	(0. 02)
$CV \times t$	0. 093 ***	0. 081 **	0. 592 ***	0. 112 ***
	(0. 03)	(0. 04)	(0. 10)	(0. 03)
Regulatory	− 0. 055	0. 056	0. 069	0. 065
	(0. 06)	(0. 08)	(0. 16)	(0. 08)
Board size	− 0. 034 ***	− 0. 040 ***	− 0. 035	− 0. 002
	(0. 01)	(0. 01)	(0. 02)	(0. 01)
Board ind	0. 474 **	0. 857 ***	0. 446	0. 859 ***
	(0. 20)	(0. 22)	(0. 44)	(0. 24)
Duality	− 0. 096	0. 051	0. 082	− 0. 120 *
	(0. 07)	(0. 07)	(0. 12)	(0. 07)
Related	− 0. 023	0. 004	0. 112 **	− 0. 077 ***
	(0. 02)	(0. 02)	(0. 05)	(0. 03)
Shrcr1	− 0. 006 ***	− 0. 005 **	0. 002	0. 003
	(0. 00)	(0. 00)	(0. 01)	(0. 00)
Shrcr2_10	0. 001	0. 001	− 0. 006	0. 003
	(0. 00)	(0. 00)	(0. 00)	(0. 00)
Sd	0. 046	0. 033	− 0. 336 ***	0. 090 *
	(0. 05)	(0. 06)	(0. 11)	(0. 05)
Fd	− 0. 796 **	− 0. 139	0. 246	0. 616 ***
	(0. 31)	(0. 18)	(0. 59)	(0. 15)

continued

Model	(1)	(2)	(3)	(4)
	CEO_exp_d	Chair_exp_d	Ind_exp_d	Edu
Firm size	0.061 ***	−0.002	0.117 **	0.079 ***
	(0.02)	(0.03)	(0.06)	(0.02)
Leverage	0.012	0.066	−0.167	−0.145
	(0.08)	(0.09)	(0.18)	(0.09)
Firm age	−0.021	−0.093 **	−0.222 **	0.067
	(0.04)	(0.05)	(0.11)	(0.04)
ROA	0.301 *	0.573 **	−0.093	0.058
	(0.21)	(0.25)	(0.43)	(0.20)
cut1 Intercept1				0.345 (0.51)
cut2 Intercept2				1.305 ** (0.51)
cut3 Intercept3				2.349 *** (0.51)
cut4 Intercept4				3.694 *** (0.51)
Observations	8077	8077	8077	8077
Pseudo R^2	0.013	0.012	0.068	0.010

Note: This table reports the nonlinear DID regression estimates [columns (1), (2) (3), and (4)] to test whether executive directors elected via CV have more likelihood to have richer professional experience and better educational background, using the sample constructed via BL method. We obtain estimates in columns (1), (2), and (3), using probit DID model, while we obtain estimates in column (4) via ordered probit DID model, because Edu is an ordered categorical variable. CEO_exp_d denotes whether a director has CEO experiences; Chair_exp_d denotes whether a director has chairman experiences; and Ind_exp_d represents whether a director has work experience in the same industry. Edu is a categorical variable, which takes 1 if a director is a graduate from technical secondary school, or lower, takes 2 if a director holds a junior college diploma, takes 3 if a director holds a bachelor degree; takes 4 if a director holds a master degree; and takes 5 if a director holds a doctor degree. All outcome variables in the table are binary except variable Edu. Standard errors (in parentheses) are heteroskedasticity consistent and clustered at the firm level. ***, **, and * denote significance at the 1%, 5%, and 10% levels, respectively.

Table A5   Political Connections of Executive Directors: Binary Case

Model	(1) Pol1	(2) pol2	(3) pol3	(4) pol4	(5) pol5	(6) Pol6	(7) pol7
Intercept	−4.195 *** (1.04)	−1.855 ** (0.77)	−6.754 *** (1.39)	−1.859 (1.26)	−5.026 *** (1.05)	−0.514 (1.01)	−1.669 ** (0.67)
CV	0.195 * (0.11)	−0.080 (0.08)	0.226 (0.17)	0.083 (0.13)	−0.050 (0.10)	0.081 (0.11)	0.022 (0.06)
t	−0.034 (0.04)	−0.016 (0.03)	0.045 (0.07)	−0.017 (0.04)	0.036 (0.04)	0.003 (0.04)	−0.008 (0.03)
CV × t	−0.137 ** (0.07)	0.019 (0.05)	−0.215 ** (0.10)	0.056 (0.07)	−0.118 * (0.06)	0.016 (0.06)	−0.027 (0.04)
Regulatory	0.198 (0.15)	−0.015 (0.11)	0.026 (0.22)	0.277 (0.18)	0.066 (0.16)	0.048 (0.15)	0.060 (0.10)
Board size	−0.027 (0.02)	−0.036 ** (0.01)	−0.073 ** (0.04)	0.021 (0.03)	−0.025 (0.02)	0.006 (0.02)	−0.034 *** (0.01)
Board_ind	0.794 (0.56)	−0.562 (0.36)	0.630 (0.68)	1.482 ** (0.62)	0.844 (0.53)	0.554 (0.46)	−0.041 (0.33)
Duality	−0.291 * (0.16)	0.121 (0.09)	0.203 (0.20)	0.000 (0.20)	0.258 * (0.14)	0.387 *** (0.14)	0.204 ** (0.09)
Related	−0.041 (0.06)	−0.003 (0.04)	−0.168 * (0.09)	0.039 (0.06)	0.033 (0.06)	0.043 (0.06)	0.007 (0.03)
Shrcr1	0.002 (0.00)	−0.003 (0.00)	−0.013 * (0.01)	−0.012 (0.01)	−0.006 (0.00)	−0.010 * (0.01)	−0.005 * (0.00)
Shrcr2_10	0.015 *** (0.00)	0.001 (0.00)	−0.005 (0.01)	−0.004 (0.01)	−0.009 * (0.01)	−0.008 (0.01)	0.001 (0.00)
Sd	0.056 (0.12)	−0.119 (0.08)	−0.436 ** (0.21)	−0.034 (0.14)	−0.110 (0.14)	−0.184 (0.18)	−0.109 (0.08)
Fd	0.314 (0.28)	−0.112 (0.29)		0.170 (0.46)			−0.218 (0.25)
Firm size	0.088 * (0.05)	0.060 (0.04)	0.275 *** (0.08)	−0.026 (0.06)	0.181 *** (0.05)	−0.055 (0.05)	0.064 ** (0.03)
Leverage	−0.367 (0.25)	0.023 (0.14)	−0.184 (0.36)	0.034 (0.18)	−0.611 ** (0.25)	0.059 (0.16)	−0.028 (0.13)
Firm age	0.006 (0.09)	0.102 (0.08)	−0.137 (0.11)	−0.150 (0.10)	−0.195 ** (0.09)	−0.148 (0.10)	0.017 (0.06)

continued

Model	(1)	(2)	(3)	(4)	(5)	(6)	(7)
	*Pol*1	*pol*2	*pol*3	*pol*4	*pol*5	*Pol*6	*pol*7
ROA	0.692	0.169	0.369	−0.287	−0.252	−0.116	0.043
	(0.51)	(0.24)	(0.35)	(0.36)	(0.51)	(0.38)	(0.23)
Observations	8077	8077	8037	8077	8037	8037	8077
Pseudo R^2	0.041	0.010	0.079	0.021	0.032	0.027	0.009

Note: This table reports the nonlinear (probit) DID regression estimates [columns (1), (2), (3), (4), (5), (6), and (7)] to test whether the political connections of directors elected via CV are different from those elected via straight voting, using the sample constructed via BL method. Variable *pol*1 is a dummy variable to indicate whether an executive director has central government work experience; *pol*2 is a dummy variable to indicate whether an executive director has local government work experience; *pol*3 is a dummy variable to indicate whether an executive director is a member of the national committee of CPPCC; *pol*4 is a dummy variable to indicate whether an executive director is a member of the local committee of CPPCC; *pol*5 is a dummy variable to indicate whether an executive director is a member of deputy to the National People's Congress; *pol*6 is a dummy variable to indicate whether an executive director is a member of deputy to the local People's Congress; and *pol*7 is a dummy variable to indicate whether an executive director has at least one of the above experience. Standard errors (in parentheses) are heteroskedasticity consistent and clustered at the firm level. ***, **, and * denote significance at the 1%, 5%, and 10% levels, respectively.

Table A6   Relationship between Independent Directors and Executives: Binary Case

Model	(1)	(2)	(3)
	*Exe_rel*1_*d*	*Exe_rel*2_*d*	*Exe_rel*3_*d*
Intercept	−2.521 **	−2.260 **	−2.148 **
	(1.27)	(1.10)	(0.93)
CV	−0.109	−0.128	−0.139
	(0.12)	(0.10)	(0.09)
t	0.009	0.018	0.021
	(0.05)	(0.04)	(0.03)
$CV \times t$	−0.202 *	−0.079	−0.144 **
	(0.11)	(0.07)	(0.07)
Regulatory	−0.018	−0.020	−0.010
	(0.19)	(0.16)	(0.14)
Board size	−0.006	−0.005	−0.003
	(0.03)	(0.02)	(0.02)

continued

Model	(1) Exe_rel1_d	(2) Exe_rel2_d	(3) Exe_rel3_d
Board_ind	- 0. 775 (0. 91)	1. 083 (0. 69)	0. 474 (0. 62)
Duality	- 0. 141 (0. 18)	- 0. 050 (0. 12)	- 0. 096 (0. 11)
Related	- 0. 115* (0. 06)	0. 041 (0. 05)	- 0. 026 (0. 05)
Shrcr1	0. 010* (0. 01)	0. 007 (0. 00)	0. 009** (0. 00)
Shrcr2_10	0. 007 (0. 01)	- 0. 001 (0. 00)	0. 003 (0. 00)
Sd	- 0. 447*** (0. 15)	0. 139 (0. 11)	- 0. 029 (0. 10)
Fd	1. 055 (0. 67)		0. 452 (0. 59)
Firm size	0. 041 (0. 06)	0. 020 (0. 06)	0. 031 (0. 05)
Leverage	- 0. 431 (0. 27)	0. 383** (0. 17)	0. 144 (0. 17)
Firm age	0. 177 (0. 12)	- 0. 162* (0. 09)	- 0. 053 (0. 08)
ROA	- 0. 087 (0. 43)	0. 080 (0. 38)	- 0. 051 (0. 35)
Observations	3688	3669	3688
Pseudo R^2	0. 041	0. 020	0. 016

Note: This table reports the DID regression estimates [columns (1), (2) and (3)] to examine whether the independent directors elected under the CV rule with close relation with firm's CEO or chairman have less likelihood than those elected under straight voting, using the sample constructed via BL method. We measure the relation by three different dummy variables—Exe_rel1_d, Exe_rel2_d, and Exe_rel_d, respectively. Here Exe_rel1_d takes 1 if a independent director worked in the same institution or firm with the current firm's CEO or chairman, and zero otherwise; Exe_re2_d takes 1 if a independent director and the current firm's CEO or chairman are in the same old boy network, and zero otherwise; and Exe_rel_d takes 1 if one of the above relations exists, and zero otherwise. Standard errors (in parentheses) are heteroskedasticity consistent and clustered at the firm level. ***, **, and * denote significance at the 1%, 5%, and 10% levels, respectively.

Table A7   Political Connections of Independent Directors: Binary Case

Model	(1)	(2)	(3)	(4)	(5)	(6)	(7)
	Pol1	pol2	pol3	pol4	pol5	Pol6	Pol7
Intercept	-3.527*** (0.94)	-1.576* (0.81)	-5.871** (2.45)	-3.981*** (1.28)	-0.556 (2.07)	-2.386 (1.56)	-1.805** (0.71)
CV	-0.195* (0.10)	-0.063 (0.09)	-0.200 (0.20)	-0.101 (0.15)	0.089 (0.19)	-0.002 (0.16)	-0.127 (0.08)
t	-0.020 (0.04)	-0.028 (0.03)	-0.106 (0.08)	0.067 (0.05)	0.012 (0.05)	-0.136** (0.07)	-0.042 (0.03)
CV×t	0.078 (0.06)	-0.024 (0.05)	0.083 (0.12)	0.062 (0.09)	-0.066 (0.10)	0.090 (0.09)	0.055 (0.05)
Regulatory	0.117 (0.16)	-0.039 (0.13)	-0.303 (0.24)	-0.131 (0.23)	-0.353 (0.25)	-0.138 (0.22)	-0.026 (0.12)
Board size	0.012 (0.02)	0.009 (0.02)	-0.041 (0.03)	-0.024 (0.03)	0.026 (0.04)	0.037 (0.03)	0.009 (0.02)
Board_ind	-1.118* (0.65)	-0.091 (0.56)	-1.375 (1.19)	-0.784 (1.19)	0.594 (1.21)	1.997* (1.10)	-0.490 (0.47)
Duality	-0.129 (0.17)	-0.007 (0.11)	-0.173 (0.26)	0.062 (0.17)	0.164 (0.22)	-0.045 (0.23)	0.010 (0.10)
Related	-0.012 (0.05)	0.029 (0.05)	-0.104 (0.08)	-0.106* (0.06)	0.081 (0.11)	0.074 (0.08)	0.013 (0.04)
Shrcr1	0.006 (0.00)	0.002 (0.00)	0.021*** (0.01)	0.014*** (0.01)	0.004 (0.01)	-0.001 (0.01)	0.005 (0.00)
Shrcr2_10	0.007 (0.00)	-0.002 (0.00)	0.019* (0.01)	0.009 (0.01)	-0.008 (0.01)	-0.003 (0.01)	0.002 (0.00)
Sd	-0.083 (0.11)	0.059 (0.09)	0.033 (0.26)	-0.031 (0.17)	0.160 (0.20)	-0.178 (0.20)	0.034 (0.09)
Fd	0.155 (0.47)	-0.195 (0.51)					-0.144 (0.20)
Firm size	0.108** (0.05)	0.021 (0.04)	0.167 (0.12)	0.099 (0.06)	-0.098 (0.10)	-0.033 (0.08)	0.055 (0.03)
Leverage	-0.260 (0.24)	-0.101 (0.15)	-0.870* (0.52)	0.102 (0.30)	-0.119 (0.30)	0.234 (0.19)	-0.129 (0.14)
Firm age	-0.060 (0.09)	0.072 (0.08)	0.295 (0.19)	-0.044 (0.12)	-0.066 (0.17)	-0.104 (0.13)	0.009 (0.07)

continued

Model	(1)	(2)	(3)	(4)	(5)	(6)	(7)
	*Pol*1	*pol*2	*pol*3	*pol*4	*pol*5	*Pol*6	*Pol*7
ROA	0.559 *	− 0.074	− 0.219	0.984 *	0.284	0.540 *	0.316
	(0.33)	(0.31)	(0.47)	(0.58)	(0.51)	(0.30)	(0.31)
Observations	3688	3688	3669	3669	3669	3669	3688
Pseudo R^2	0.030	0.003	0.085	0.035	0.023	0.020	0.008

Note: This table reports the nonlinear (probit) DID regressions [columns (1), (2), (3), (4), (5), (6), and (7)] to test whether the political connections of independent directors elected via CV are different from those elected via straight voting, using the sample constructed via BL method. Variable *pol*1 is a dummy variable to indicate whether an independent director has central government work experience; *pol*2 is a dummy variable to indicate whether an independent director has local government work experience; *pol*3 is a dummy variable to indicate whether an independent director is a member of the national committee of CPPCC; *pol*4 is a dummy variable to indicate whether an independent director is a member of the local committee of CPPCC; *pol*5 is a dummy variable to indicate whether an independent director is a member of deputy to the National People's Congress; *pol*6 is a dummy variable to indicate whether an independent director is a member of deputy to the local People's Congress; and *pol*7 is a dummy variable to indicate whether an independent director has at least one of the above experience. Standard errors (in parentheses) are heteroskedasticity consistent and clustered at the firm level. *** , ** , and * denote significance at the 1% , 5% , and 10% levels, respectively.

Table A8   Professional Experience of Independent Directors : Binary Case

Model	(1)	(2)	(3)	(4)	(5)	(6)
	*pro*1	*pro*2	*pro*3	*pro*4	*pro*5	*ind_exp*
Intercept	0.047	− 2.593 ***	− 2.591 ***	− 1.826 *	− 0.350	− 2.523 ***
	(0.46)	(0.75)	(0.85)	(1.01)	(0.61)	(0.96)
CV	0.160 ***	0.119	− 0.027	− 0.187 *	0.145 **	0.092
	(0.05)	(0.09)	(0.09)	(0.10)	(0.07)	(0.09)
t	0.045 *	0.016	0.023	− 0.072 **	0.018	− 0.046
	(0.02)	(0.04)	(0.04)	(0.03)	(0.03)	(0.04)
CV × t	0.050	0.035	0.060	0.061	0.117 ***	0.059
	(0.04)	(0.05)	(0.06)	(0.07)	(0.04)	(0.06)
Regulatory	0.075	− 0.057	0.001	0.432 ***	0.125	0.069
	(0.07)	(0.12)	(0.13)	(0.15)	(0.10)	(0.13)
Board size	− 0.051 ***	0.017	0.034 *	0.014	− 0.015	0.017
	(0.01)	(0.02)	(0.02)	(0.02)	(0.01)	(0.02)

continued

Model	(1)	(2)	(3)	(4)	(5)	(6)
	pro1	pro2	pro3	pro4	pro5	ind_exp
Board_ind	−1.116***	0.968*	−0.339	−0.064	−0.504	0.629
	(0.34)	(0.59)	(0.64)	(0.76)	(0.46)	(0.58)
Duality	−0.088	−0.045	0.084	−0.005	−0.019	−0.002
	(0.06)	(0.13)	(0.12)	(0.13)	(0.10)	(0.10)
Related	0.020	−0.030	0.016	−0.059	0.001	−0.015
	(0.02)	(0.04)	(0.05)	(0.05)	(0.03)	(0.05)
Shrcr1	−0.000	0.001	0.002	−0.002	0.000	0.002
	(0.00)	(0.00)	(0.00)	(0.00)	(0.00)	(0.00)
Shrcr2_10	0.002	0.000	−0.004	0.003	0.001	0.001
	(0.00)	(0.00)	(0.00)	(0.00)	(0.00)	(0.00)
Sd	−0.082	0.133	−0.080	−0.196	−0.080	−0.039
	(0.05)	(0.10)	(0.12)	(0.13)	(0.07)	(0.10)
Fd	0.000	−0.156		−0.240	−0.465*	0.374
	(0.12)	(0.35)		(0.62)	(0.28)	(0.61)
Firm size	−0.004	0.034	0.065	0.003	0.022	0.054
	(0.02)	(0.03)	(0.04)	(0.05)	(0.03)	(0.05)
Leverage	0.113	0.169	−0.056	−0.324*	0.104	−0.422**
	(0.09)	(0.15)	(0.18)	(0.20)	(0.13)	(0.19)
Firm age	0.033	−0.018	−0.165**	0.173*	0.032	0.004
	(0.04)	(0.07)	(0.08)	(0.09)	(0.06)	(0.08)
ROA	0.050	−0.271	−0.057	0.197	0.056	−0.004
	(0.14)	(0.28)	(0.41)	(0.37)	(0.25)	(0.34)
Observations	3688	3688	3669	3688	3688	3688
Pseudo R^2	0.013	0.010	0.015	0.023	0.011	0.01

Note: This table reports the DID regressions [columns (1), (2), (3), (4), (5), and (6)] to test whether the professional experience of independent directors elected via CV is different from those elected via straight voting, using the sample constructed via BL method. Dummy variable pro1 denotes whether an independent director is an accountant; dummy variable pro2 denotes whether an independent director is a lawyer; dummy variable pro3 denotes whether an independent director is an engineer; dummy variable pro4 denotes whether an independent director is an economist; dummy variable pro5 denotes whether an independent director has at least one of titles listed above; and dummy variable ind_exp denotes whether an independent director has the same industry work experience as the firms in which they work as independent directors. Standard errors (in parentheses) are heteroskedasticity consistent and clustered at the firm level. ***, **, and * denote significance at the 1%, 5%, and 10% levels, respectively.

Table A9　Academic Independent Directors: Binary Case

Model	(1)	(2)	(3)	(4)	(5)
	Academe	*Econ*	*Acco*	*Law*	*Match*
Intercept	1.254 * (0.67)	-0.002 (0.72)	-0.722 (0.73)	-0.669 (1.12)	-1.556 * (0.90)
CV	0.109 (0.08)	0.060 (0.07)	0.062 (0.08)	0.057 (0.12)	0.059 (0.10)
t	0.032 (0.03)	-0.007 (0.03)	0.007 (0.03)	0.103 * (0.06)	0.016 (0.04)
CV × t	-0.098 ** (0.05)	-0.052 (0.05)	-0.031 (0.05)	-0.174 * (0.09)	0.083 (0.06)
Regulatory	0.083 (0.11)	-0.040 (0.11)	0.275 ** (0.12)	0.355 ** (0.17)	-0.218 (0.15)
Board size	0.010 (0.01)	0.004 (0.01)	-0.043 *** (0.02)	0.043 ** (0.02)	0.049 ** (0.02)
Board_ind	-0.573 (0.50)	-0.139 (0.47)	-1.250 ** (0.49)	0.247 (0.82)	0.296 (0.72)
Duality	-0.074 (0.10)	-0.078 (0.11)	-0.218 ** (0.11)	0.067 (0.14)	0.223 (0.15)
Related	-0.023 (0.04)	-0.046 (0.04)	0.010 (0.04)	-0.070 (0.06)	0.005 (0.05)
Shrcr1	-0.008 ** (0.00)	-0.001 (0.00)	-0.006 ** (0.00)	-0.007 (0.01)	-0.004 (0.01)
Shrcr2_10	-0.007 ** (0.00)	-0.002 (0.00)	-0.004 (0.00)	0.002 (0.01)	-0.009 * (0.00)
Sd	-0.004 (0.09)	0.013 (0.09)	0.077 (0.09)	0.230 * (0.14)	-0.217 * (0.11)
Fd	-0.910 *** (0.17)	-0.348 (0.39)	-0.368 (0.33)		-0.443 (0.36)
Firm size	-0.037 (0.03)	-0.036 (0.04)	0.022 (0.03)	-0.090 (0.05)	0.025 (0.04)
Leverage	-0.022 (0.15)	0.037 (0.14)	-0.080 (0.16)	-0.038 (0.24)	0.184 (0.19)

continued

Model	(1)	(2)	(3)	(4)	(5)
	Academe	*Econ*	*Acco*	*Law*	*Match*
Firm age	-0.041	0.040	0.048	0.180*	-0.382***
	(0.06)	(0.07)	(0.08)	(0.10)	(0.08)
ROA	0.042	-0.152	0.179	0.426	0.175
	(0.30)	(0.26)	(0.30)	(0.32)	(0.38)
Observations	3688	3688	3688	3669	3688
Pseudo R^2	0.007	0.003	0.014	0.027	0.035

Note: This table reports the probit DID regression estimates [columns (1), (2), (3), (4), and (5)] on academic backgrounds of independent directors, using the sample constructed via BL method. Dummy variable *Academe* represents whether an independent director comes from academic world; dummy variable *Econ* denotes whether an independent director specializes in economics, finance or management when coming from academic world; dummy variables *Acco* and *Law* denote in respective whether an independent director specializes in accounting and law when coming from academic world; and dummy variable *Match* stands for whether an independent director's research field matches to the business of the firm he or she works for. Standard errors (in parentheses) are heteroskedasticity consistent and clustered at the firm level. ***, **, and * denote significance at the 1%, 5%, and 10% levels, respectively.

A.2   CEM Method

A.2.1   CEM Matching Process

We also employ a novel matching approach called "coarsened exact matching" (CEM) for robustness. Generating a comparable control group is a quite difficult but very important task for non – experimental data. Fortunately, there are several matching methods developed to construct control group for non – experimental data. CEM is a relatively novel matching method with lots of good statistical properties, developed by Iacus et al. (2012). The reason that we apply this method is just because of its various advantages. As Iacus et al. (2012) noted, CEM is part of general class methods termed "monotonic imbalance bounding" (MIB) (Iacus et al., 2011), which has advantageous statistical properties as compared to widely used current matching methods, such as propensity score and Mahalanobis matching, which belong to the class of matching methods known as "equal percent bias reducing" (EPBR) models (Rubin, 1976). MIB eliminates many of assumptions required for unbiased estimates of treatment effects and dominates commonly used existing (EPBR and other) matching methods in its ability to reduce imbalance, model dependence, estimation error, bias, variance, mean square error, and other criteria, as Iacus et al. (2012) mentioned. A crucial difference in practice rests with the order of data pre – possessing: EPBR models such as propensity score matching require determining ex ante the matched sample size, and then producing some level of reduction in imbalance between the treated and control groups ex post, whereas CEM determines the imbalance between the matched treated and control groups ex ante. Moreover, CEM works in sample and requires no assumptions on the data generating process.

The basic idea of CEM is to "coarsen" each variable of a set of observable covariates by recoding so that substantively indistinguishable values are grouped and assigned the same numerical value, then to apply the "exact matching" algorithm to the coarsened data to determine the matches and to "prune" unmatched observations, and run estimations using the original but pruned uncoarsened data. The main goal of any matching process is to guarantee that the treated and control groups are constructed as balanced as possible in the sense that the empirical joint distributions of their covariates are as similar as possible.

In our environment, ownership concentration is an essential variable to impact CV adoption as aforementioned. So we first divided our raw data into two groups— voluntary and regulatory groups as before. As suggested by Doidge et al. (2004), Bebchuk et al. (2011) and Lu and Shi (2012) *Firmsize*, *Firmage*, and *Leverage* are closely related to both firm value and different corporate governance variables. Then we focus on the three key pre – treatment covariates, Firm size, firm leverage, and Firm age, coarsening them year by year to generate treated and control group samples. Following Iacus et al. (2011), we use the L_1 distance to measure the multivariate differences between the empirical distributions of treated and control groups both before and after the CEM process. The multivariate imbalance measure L_1 is defined as

$$L_1(f,g) = \frac{1}{2} \sum_{l_1,\cdots,l_k \in H(X)} |f_{l_1\cdots l_k} - g_{l_1\cdots l_k}| \qquad (\text{A}-1)$$

where f and g are the relative empirical frequency distributions for the treated and control groups. In equation (A. 1), $H(X)$ is the Cartesian product $H(X_1) \times \cdots \times H(X_k)$, while $H(X_i)$ be the set of distinct values generated by binning on the covariate X_i, that is, the set of intervals into which the support of variable X_i has been cut. Denote by f^m and g^m the empirical distributions for the matched treated and control groups after the CEM process corresponding to the unmatched f and g distributions before the CEM process. Then a desirable matching method should have $L_1(f^m, g^m) \leqslant L_1(f, g)$. A nice interpretation is as follows. If the two distributions of data are completely different, then $L_1 = 1$; if the two distributions are exactly the same, then $L_1 = 0$. In all other cases, $L_1 \in (0, 1)$. The values of L_1 provides relative information on our matching results. If, for example, $L_1 = 0.4$, then 60% of the density of the two distributions overlap. We show the outcome of our application of the CEM process in table A10 as follows.

Table A10   Comparison of the Imbalance before and after the CEM Process

Year	Voluntary Group		Regulatory Group	
	Before L_1	After L_1	Before L_1	After L_1
2002	0. 951	0. 000	0. 908	0. 185
2003	0. 907	0. 333	0. 790	0. 321
2004	0. 978	0. 000	0. 860	0. 217
2005	0. 707	0. 386	0. 653	0. 551

Note: This table reports the comparison of data imbalance in terms of the three key variables, *Firm size*, *Leverage*, and *Firm age* before and after the CEM process. We divide our raw data into two subsamples according to the magnitude of the proportion of shares held by the largest shareholders for each firm. The partition rule is that if the largest shareholder holds shares less than 30% of firm total shares, then the firm belongs to the "Voluntary Group" in the table, and it falls in the "Regulatory Group" otherwise.

After the CEM process, the imbalance between treated and control firms is improved strikingly for the two sub – samples and for all years, and the least improvement exceeds 10%, while the most improvement reaches 98%, measured by L_1 metric, as shown in table A10. Therefore, our application of the CEM method seems to be successful.

To further show that the CEM process does generate desirable results in terms of the balance between the treated and control groups in our sample generated by the CEM method, we also execute the nearest neighbor propensity score matching (PSM), using the same covariates. The comparison between PSM and CEM methods via L_1 distance is given in table A11. Clearly the performance of the CEM method is better than that of the PSM method for all years and for both sub – samples. In conclusion, the matching results strongly support our application of the CEM method.

Table A11   Comparison of the Imbalance between

PSM and CEM Methods

Year	Voluntary Group		Regulatory Group	
	PSM L_1	CEM L_1	PSM L_1	CEM L_1
2002	0. 000	0. 000	0. 621	0. 185
2003	0. 333	0. 333	0. 515	0. 321
2004	0. 333	0. 000	0. 400	0. 217
2005	0. 521	0. 386	0. 637	0. 551

Note: This table reports the comparison of data imbalance in terms of the three key variables, *Firm size*, *Leverage*, and *Firm age* between the nearest neighbor PSM matching and the CEM process. We divide our raw data into two sub – samples according to the magnitude of the proportion of shares held by the largest shareholders for each firm. The partition rule is that if the largest shareholder holds shares less than 30% of firm total shares, then the firm belongs to the "Voluntary Group" in the table, and it falls in the "Regulatory Group" otherwise.

Under the CEM matching process, both CV users and non – CV users have been pruned to balance the three key pretreatment covariates. After this process, 278 CV firms constitute the treated group at period $t = 1$. A total of 278 matches belong to the control group at this period, but no relevant information on directors is available for three of the 278 matches at the treatment period; thus, we eventually obtain 275 matches left in the treatment period. The number and composition of the treated and control groups at period $t = 0$ are 273 and 278, respectively. Data on five of the 278 CV firms in the pretreatment period are unavailable; thus, the CEM matching process builds a sample with 1, 106 firm – year observations in total.

A. 2. 2   Empirical Results Based on the CEM Sample

In this section, we presents main results from the sample derived from the CEM process, which correspond to the results we have discussed in the text from the sample constructed by the BL method.

CV and Personal Characteristics of Directors

Table A12　　Representatives from Minority Shareholders

Model	(1)	(2)	(3)	(4)	(5)	(6)
	Share1	Share2	Share2_5	Share1	Share2	Share2_5
Intercept	-38.540*	28.492***	49.335***	27.710	0.297	31.960
	(22.30)	(10.39)	(13.59)	(72.49)	(38.86)	(38.70)
CV	-1.400	1.183	0.880	7.385	-4.202	-2.740
	(2.32)	(0.98)	(1.37)	(7.28)	(2.69)	(3.73)
t	0.676	-0.017	0.154	-5.850	-2.418	-2.286
	(1.03)	(0.47)	(0.62)	(5.10)	(2.67)	(3.11)
CV * t	1.641	2.133**	1.874	-0.529	11.046**	8.715*
	(1.78)	(0.97)	(1.18)	(9.06)	(4.25)	(4.81)
Regulatory	0.934	-0.349	-1.728	1.740	-1.558	-4.228
	(3.47)	(2.02)	(2.52)	(9.68)	(5.02)	(6.27)
Board size	-0.858*	0.220	0.818***	0.389	0.832	1.310**
	(0.49)	(0.20)	(0.28)	(1.26)	(0.53)	(0.62)
Board_ind	2.972	-2.073	2.680	24.891	0.465	8.131
	(11.72)	(4.44)	(6.51)	(25.23)	(8.81)	(13.14)
Duality	-4.543	1.606	-0.353	-9.253	1.260	-0.272
	(3.29)	(1.65)	(2.18)	(7.90)	(3.03)	(4.95)
Related	-1.217	0.195	-0.627			
	(1.30)	(0.61)	(0.75)			
Shrcr1	0.587***	-0.064	-0.166***	0.969***	-0.056	-0.060
	(0.11)	(0.04)	(0.06)	(0.28)	(0.10)	(0.16)
Shrcr2_10	-0.206*	0.337***	0.640***	0.054	0.375***	0.799***
	(0.12)	(0.06)	(0.08)	(0.32)	(0.12)	(0.19)
Sd	-2.191	1.579	2.589	0.230	10.061**	6.696
	(2.91)	(1.53)	(1.89)	(7.60)	(4.70)	(4.71)
Fd	-16.047**	23.983*	18.307	-7.006	49.365***	36.111***
	(7.63)	(12.52)	(11.16)	(13.82)	(6.16)	(7.23)

continued

Model	(1)	(2)	(3)	(4)	(5)	(6)
	Share1	Share2	Share2_5	Share1	Share2	Share2_5
Firm size	3. 426 ***	− 1. 288 **	− 1. 891 ***	− 1. 941	0. 467	− 1. 084
	(1. 14)	(0. 52)	(0. 65)	(3. 48)	(1. 57)	(1. 57)
Leverage	− 7. 390	1. 805	2. 667	− 10. 197	− 2. 206	− 3. 280
	(4. 52)	(1. 65)	(2. 68)	(10. 50)	(3. 34)	(3. 65)
Firm age	5. 845 **	− 0. 135	− 3. 105 *	8. 244	− 6. 013	− 6. 939
	(2. 28)	(1. 08)	(1. 61)	(7. 33)	(4. 04)	(4. 50)
ROA	13. 851 *	− 1. 435	1. 532	38. 257	4. 126	16. 806 *
	(7. 78)	(3. 50)	(5. 03)	(29. 57)	(6. 84)	(9. 50)
Observations	1051	1051	1051	140	140	140
adj. R^2	0. 216	0. 202	0. 355	0. 184	0. 304	0. 425

Note: This table reports the DID regression estimates [columns (1), (2), (3), (4), (5), and (6)] to test whether minority shareholders can elect their representatives into the board of directors, using the sample constructed via CEM method. columns (1), (2) and (3) use all the sample, while columns (4), (5), and (6) exclude the observations in which the top ten shareholders are related. Standard errors (in parentheses) are heteroskedasticity consistent and clustered at the firm level. ***, **, and * denote significance at the 1%, 5%, and 10% levels, respectively.

Table A13   Educational Background of Directors

Model	(1)	(2)	(3)	(4)	(5)	(6)	(7)
	Edu1	Edu2	Edu3	Edu4	Edu5	Edu6	Edu7
Intercept	16. 466 **	93. 960 ***	110. 426 ***	67. 666 ***	− 61. 095 **	− 16. 997 *	− 78. 092 ***
	(7. 35)	(20. 64)	(22. 07)	(22. 09)	(25. 70)	(9. 38)	(26. 05)
CV	1. 690 *	− 1. 524	0. 166	0. 292	− 0. 542	0. 084	− 0. 458
	(1. 02)	(2. 08)	(2. 29)	(2. 06)	(2. 06)	(0. 92)	(2. 21)
t	− 0. 466	− 2. 091 ***	− 2. 556 ***	0. 729	1. 669 *	0. 158	1. 827 *
	(0. 36)	(0. 80)	(0. 90)	(0. 89)	(0. 91)	(0. 46)	(0. 95)
CV × t	− 0. 557	− 2. 329 *	− 2. 886 *	0. 126	2. 682 *	0. 078	2. 760 *
	(0. 78)	(1. 31)	(1. 49)	(1. 54)	(1. 56)	(0. 66)	(1. 58)
Regulatory	− 1. 176	− 0. 339	− 1. 515	1. 838	− 1. 197	0. 874	− 0. 323
	(1. 63)	(3. 13)	(3. 35)	(3. 33)	(3. 18)	(1. 44)	(3. 35)
Board size	− 0. 024	− 0. 271	− 0. 295	0. 767 *	− 0. 388	− 0. 083	− 0. 472
	(0. 16)	(0. 39)	(0. 42)	(0. 44)	(0. 37)	(0. 21)	(0. 42)

continued

Model	(1)	(2)	(3)	(4)	(5)	(6)	(7)
	Edu1	Edu2	Edu3	Edu4	Edu5	Edu6	Edu7
Board_ind	-4.260 (3.80)	-29.670*** (9.60)	-33.930*** (10.62)	3.708 (9.56)	14.012* (8.40)	16.210*** (5.69)	30.222*** (8.78)
Duality	2.279 (1.85)	-2.467 (2.55)	-0.188 (3.02)	-1.592 (3.10)	3.447 (3.58)	-1.666 (1.08)	1.780 (3.74)
Related	0.361 (0.46)	0.991 (1.09)	1.351 (1.18)	-0.320 (1.12)	-0.068 (1.08)	-0.964* (0.49)	-1.031 (1.15)
Shrcr1	-0.062 (0.06)	-0.053 (0.10)	-0.115 (0.11)	0.035 (0.11)	0.110 (0.09)	-0.030 (0.04)	0.080 (0.10)
Shrcr2_10	-0.037 (0.05)	-0.006 (0.10)	-0.043 (0.10)	-0.063 (0.10)	0.100 (0.11)	0.006 (0.05)	0.105 (0.11)
Sd	0.193 (1.15)	-1.993 (2.54)	-1.800 (2.74)	-2.170 (2.55)	3.683 (2.78)	0.287 (1.10)	3.970 (2.86)
Fd	-5.475*** (1.67)	1.084 (7.14)	-4.392 (7.20)	-16.397*** (6.27)	-0.120 (8.17)	20.909*** (7.64)	20.789*** (5.77)
Firm size	-0.276 (0.35)	-2.631** (1.02)	-2.908*** (1.08)	-1.533 (1.10)	3.389*** (1.29)	1.051** (0.46)	4.440*** (1.31)
Leverage	3.914* (2.22)	1.984 (3.69)	5.898 (4.25)	2.964 (4.88)	-6.198 (4.07)	-2.664* (1.42)	-8.862** (4.25)
Firm age	-1.983* (1.10)	-1.283 (1.99)	-3.266 (2.14)	-4.763** (2.12)	8.265*** (2.15)	-0.236 (1.10)	8.029*** (2.23)
ROA	1.296 (3.49)	0.382 (6.69)	1.679 (7.49)	0.971 (14.91)	-0.973 (11.47)	-1.676 (2.45)	-2.650 (11.97)
Observations	1051	1051	1051	1051	1051	1051	1051
Adj. R^2	0.019	0.046	0.057	0.014	0.069	0.050	0.097

Note: This table reports the DID regression estimates [columns (1), (2), (3), (4), (5), (6), and (7)] to test whether the educational background of executive directors elected via CV is different from those elected via straight voting, using the sample constructed via CEM method. Standard errors (in parentheses) are heteroskedasticity consistent and clustered at the firm level. ***, **, and * denote significance at the 1%, 5%, and 10% levels, respectively.

Table A14   Professional Experience of Directors

Model	(1) CEO_exp	(2) Chair_exp	(3) Exe_exp	(4) Ind_exp	(5) Pro_exp	(6) Dir_age
Intercept	− 0. 183 (15. 00)	− 16. 439 (18. 82)	− 6. 276 (17. 97)	49. 685 *** (10. 90)	− 1. 200 (6. 80)	22. 343 *** (2. 99)
CV	4. 641 ** (1. 85)	0. 394 (1. 57)	4. 621 ** (1. 87)	3. 332 *** (1. 10)	0. 454 (0. 70)	− 0. 190 (0. 36)
t	0. 497 (0. 85)	0. 038 (0. 65)	1. 386 * (0. 84)	0. 662 (0. 64)	− 0. 164 (0. 65)	0. 029 (0. 16)
CV × t	1. 825 (1. 56)	2. 729 ** (1. 26)	2. 685 * (1. 63)	2. 864 *** (1. 02)	1. 220 (1. 10)	− 0. 879 *** (0. 28)
Regulatory	− 3. 610 (2. 58)	− 1. 840 (2. 62)	− 3. 506 (2. 74)	3. 410 * (1. 86)	1. 316 (1. 09)	0. 554 (0. 53)
Board size	− 0. 805 ** (0. 33)	− 0. 625 * (0. 33)	− 0. 784 ** (0. 35)	− 0. 413 * (0. 22)	− 0. 478 ** (0. 18)	0. 095 (0. 07)
Board_ind	14. 826 * (8. 20)	25. 797 *** (6. 25)	24. 817 *** (8. 58)	10. 416 * (5. 85)	16. 179 *** (4. 36)	− 0. 410 (1. 61)
Duality	− 1. 646 (2. 42)	− 1. 415 (2. 38)	− 3. 064 (2. 65)	− 0. 065 (1. 62)	0. 631 (1. 06)	− 0. 728 (0. 51)
Related	0. 916 (0. 98)	0. 150 (0. 81)	1. 155 (0. 97)	0. 723 (0. 67)	− 0. 706 (0. 45)	0. 021 (0. 19)
Shrcr1	− 0. 217 *** (0. 08)	− 0. 135 * (0. 07)	− 0. 308 *** (0. 08)	0. 063 (0. 05)	− 0. 011 (0. 03)	− 0. 020 (0. 02)
Shrcr2_10	− 0. 061 (0. 08)	0. 080 (0. 08)	− 0. 030 (0. 09)	− 0. 042 (0. 05)	− 0. 088 *** (0. 03)	− 0. 049 *** (0. 02)
Sd	3. 226 (2. 20)	0. 093 (1. 88)	3. 936 * (2. 24)	− 0. 901 (1. 30)	− 0. 588 (0. 91)	− 0. 428 (0. 45)
Fd	− 5. 650 (10. 25)	− 16. 264 * (9. 59)	− 9. 364 (9. 11)	3. 533 (3. 31)	1. 004 (7. 93)	− 1. 747 (1. 19)
Firm size	2. 407 *** (0. 76)	2. 329 ** (0. 94)	3. 404 *** (0. 91)	1. 972 *** (0. 55)	0. 766 ** (0. 35)	1. 161 *** (0. 15)
Leverage	− 0. 011 (3. 33)	1. 437 (3. 00)	− 0. 094 (3. 20)	− 1. 642 (2. 58)	− 3. 260 ** (1. 40)	− 0. 925 (0. 62)

continued

Model	(1)	(2)	(3)	(4)	(5)	(6)
	CEO_exp	Chair_exp	Exe_exp	Ind_exp	Pro_exp	Dir_age
Firm age	-2.716	-3.415 **	-6.420 ***	-2.765 ***	-0.751	0.503
	(1.66)	(1.57)	(1.74)	(0.83)	(0.72)	(0.33)
ROA	11.037	17.301 *	8.516	6.025	-7.721 ***	4.080 ***
	(9.77)	(9.36)	(9.52)	(5.02)	(2.67)	(1.05)
Observations	1051	1051	1051	1051	1051	1051
Adj. R^2	0.072	0.077	0.119	0.155	0.054	0.146

Note: This table reports the DID regression estimates [columns (1), (2), (3), (4), (5), and (6)] to test whether the professional experience of executive directors elected via CV is different from those elected via straight voting, and whether there are differences in director average age under the two different voting rules, using the sample constructed via CEM method. Standard errors (in parentheses) are heteroskedasticity consistent and clustered at the firm level. ***, **, and * denote significance at the 1%, 5%, and 10% levels, respectively.

Table A15　　　　**Political Connections of Executive Directors**

Model	(1)	(2)	(3)	(4)	(5)	(6)	(7)
	Pol1	pol2	pol3	pol4	pol5	Pol6	Pol7
Intercept	-14.666	1.514	-8.907	2.206	-7.618	8.956 **	-5.040
	(9.63)	(17.71)	(6.16)	(3.53)	(4.73)	(4.38)	(20.06)
CV	1.282 *	-1.281	0.150	-0.028	-0.223	0.246	0.611
	(0.76)	(1.76)	(0.28)	(0.39)	(0.54)	(0.55)	(1.94)
t	0.389	-0.694	0.042	-0.108	0.042	-0.199	-0.407
	(0.30)	(0.83)	(0.15)	(0.22)	(0.15)	(0.16)	(0.87)
CV × t	-1.355 ***	0.468	-0.103	0.326	-0.531 *	0.328	-0.639
	(0.51)	(1.20)	(0.20)	(0.32)	(0.28)	(0.35)	(1.38)
Regulatory	0.272	-1.118	0.053	0.452	0.504	1.378	1.325
	(1.07)	(2.69)	(0.46)	(0.74)	(0.76)	(0.94)	(3.03)
Board size	0.051	-0.855 **	-0.072	0.054	-0.078	0.041	-0.982 **
	(0.14)	(0.36)	(0.07)	(0.10)	(0.12)	(0.12)	(0.41)
Board_ind	3.435	-12.024	1.035	5.093 **	3.713 **	4.085 **	-1.611
	(2.88)	(8.00)	(0.95)	(2.07)	(1.86)	(2.08)	(8.86)

continued

Model	(1) Pol1	(2) pol2	(3) pol3	(4) pol4	(5) pol5	(6) Pol6	(7) Pol7
Duality	− 1.014 (0.72)	1.461 (2.57)	0.822 (0.62)	1.169 (0.85)	− 0.139 (0.67)	2.047 * (1.14)	2.898 (2.88)
Related	0.136 (0.34)	0.118 (0.97)	− 0.201 (0.16)	− 0.297 (0.24)	0.087 (0.25)	0.145 (0.26)	0.049 (1.04)
Shrcr1	− 0.014 (0.03)	− 0.113 (0.08)	− 0.040 * (0.02)	− 0.069 *** (0.02)	− 0.019 (0.03)	− 0.070 ** (0.03)	− 0.286 *** (0.09)
Shrcr2_10	0.064 ** (0.03)	− 0.003 (0.09)	− 0.018 (0.01)	− 0.053 ** (0.02)	− 0.020 (0.03)	− 0.027 (0.03)	− 0.026 (0.11)
Sd	− 0.195 (0.81)	− 0.781 (2.04)	− 0.259 (0.33)	− 0.474 (0.43)	− 0.650 (0.63)	− 0.555 (0.67)	− 1.637 (2.43)
Fd	5.550 (3.71)	− 2.554 (16.63)	− 2.535 * (1.34)	− 0.377 (1.33)	− 2.815 *** (0.83)	− 2.017 ** (0.91)	− 2.805 (15.12)
Firm size	0.884 * (0.51)	1.323 (0.99)	0.607 * (0.35)	0.086 (0.19)	0.596 ** (0.23)	− 0.223 (0.22)	2.530 ** (1.06)
Leverage	− 2.336 ** (1.14)	2.864 (3.34)	− 0.131 (0.42)	0.141 (0.56)	− 2.231 *** (0.83)	− 0.563 (0.85)	1.271 (4.00)
Firm age	− 1.727 ** (0.87)	0.828 (1.60)	− 0.324 (0.30)	− 0.432 (0.43)	− 0.791 (0.49)	− 0.850 (0.57)	− 2.621 (1.86)
ROA	− 0.306 (2.57)	0.527 (6.70)	− 0.374 (0.53)	− 0.567 (0.86)	− 0.266 (1.10)	− 0.038 (1.61)	− 0.965 (6.58)
Observations	1051	1051	1051	1051	1051	1051	1051
Adj. R^2	0.038	0.012	0.038	0.032	0.024	0.017	0.031

Note: This table reports the DID regression estimates [columns (1), (2), (3), (4), (5), (6), and (7)] to test whether the political connections of executive directors elected via CV are different from those elected via straight voting, using the sample constructed via CEM method. Standard errors (in parentheses) are heteroskedasticity consistent and clustered at the firm level. *** , ** , and * denote significance at the 1% , 5% , and 10% levels, respectively.

Table A16 **Relationships between Independent Directors and Executives**

Model	(1)	(2)	(3)
	*Exe_rel*1	*Exe_rel*2	*Exe_rel*3
Intercept	9.627 (16.40)	-16.245 (18.49)	-3.264 (22.56)
CV	-3.072* (1.60)	-1.560 (2.03)	-3.986* (2.38)
t	-0.372 (0.53)	0.971 (1.02)	0.693 (1.08)
CV × t	-1.007 (1.03)	-3.574** (1.46)	-4.716*** (1.72)
Regulatory	-0.098 (2.14)	-2.573 (2.99)	-2.604 (3.48)
Board size	0.215 (0.32)	-0.015 (0.45)	0.301 (0.54)
Board_ind	-8.441 (11.61)	15.226 (14.27)	8.220 (17.33)
Duality	-1.866 (1.60)	0.226 (2.48)	-1.433 (2.76)
Related	-1.715** (0.73)	0.451 (1.05)	-0.947 (1.20)
Shrcr1	0.068 (0.07)	0.086 (0.09)	0.135 (0.10)
Shrcr2_10	0.001 (0.07)	-0.009 (0.08)	-0.021 (0.10)
Sd	-2.921** (1.26)	-0.316 (2.32)	-2.996 (2.41)
Fd	13.061 (14.95)	-13.634*** (3.68)	0.113 (14.36)
Firm size	-0.090 (0.84)	0.841 (1.04)	0.506 (1.22)

continued

Model	(1) Exe_rel1	(2) Exe_rel2	(3) Exe_rel3
Leverage	− 1. 629 (2. 53)	3. 794 (3. 52)	2. 944 (4. 34)
Firm age	1. 507 (1. 33)	0. 195 (2. 02)	1. 507 (2. 20)
ROA	− 4. 061 (5. 31)	0. 417 (5. 26)	− 3. 334 (6. 65)
Observations	991	991	991
Adj. R^2	0. 025	0. 004	0. 017

Note: This table reports the DID regression estimates [columns (1), (2) and (3)] to examine whether the independent directors elected under the CV rule with close relation with firm's CEO or chairman have less likelihood than those elected under straight voting, using the sample constructed via CEM method. We measure the relation by three different variables—Exe_rel1, Exe_rel2, and Exe_rel3, respectively. Standard errors (in parentheses) are heteroskedasticity consistent and clustered at the firm level. ***, **, and * denote significance at the 1%, 5%, and 10% levels, respectively.

Table A17   Educational Background of Independent Directors

Model	(1) Edu1	(2) Edu2	(3) Edu3	(4) Edu4	(5) Edu5	(6) Edu6	(7) Edu7
Intercept	10. 997 * (6. 59)	21. 647 (14. 96)	32. 644 * (17. 06)	− 16. 218 (25. 89)	53. 744 ** (20. 79)	29. 831 (26. 67)	83. 575 *** (28. 94)
CV	0. 998 (1. 00)	0. 119 (1. 58)	1. 117 (1. 83)	− 1. 695 (2. 93)	0. 787 (2. 67)	− 0. 209 (3. 09)	0. 579 (3. 12)
t	0. 038 (0. 37)	0. 468 (0. 86)	0. 506 (0. 91)	− 1. 414 (1. 25)	0. 192 (1. 02)	0. 717 (1. 14)	0. 908 (1. 27)
CV × t	0. 337 (0. 77)	− 0. 584 (1. 38)	− 0. 247 (1. 55)	0. 312 (2. 09)	− 0. 218 (1. 92)	0. 154 (2. 17)	− 0. 065 (2. 27)
Regulatory	− 0. 481 (1. 65)	0. 141 (2. 50)	− 0. 340 (2. 93)	− 8. 029 * (4. 40)	9. 005 ** (3. 79)	− 0. 636 (4. 14)	8. 369 * (4. 69)
Board size	− 0. 061 (0. 21)	− 0. 112 (0. 38)	− 0. 173 (0. 42)	− 0. 637 (0. 64)	0. 372 (0. 56)	0. 437 (0. 66)	0. 810 (0. 68)

continued

Model	(1)	(2)	(3)	(4)	(5)	(6)	(7)
	Edu1	Edu2	Edu3	Edu4	Edu5	Edu6	Edu7
Board_ind	-9.616	-4.738	-14.354	-7.826	1.987	20.193	22.180
	(10.15)	(10.50)	(13.76)	(24.24)	(18.20)	(19.45)	(23.19)
Duality	1.919	4.186 *	6.105 **	1.684	-2.177	-5.612 *	-7.789 *
	(1.69)	(2.33)	(2.84)	(4.00)	(3.52)	(3.38)	(4.16)
Related	-1.208 *	0.016	-1.192	2.542	-0.753	-0.597	-1.350
	(0.69)	(0.91)	(1.10)	(1.59)	(1.41)	(1.56)	(1.71)
Shrcr1	-0.014	-0.015	-0.030	0.053	-0.172	0.149	-0.024
	(0.05)	(0.07)	(0.09)	(0.13)	(0.12)	(0.13)	(0.14)
Shrcr2_10	-0.015	-0.041	-0.057	0.008	0.071	-0.023	0.048
	(0.04)	(0.07)	(0.09)	(0.13)	(0.12)	(0.12)	(0.14)
Sd	-0.033	-6.443 ***	-6.476 ***	-3.920	-2.059	12.455 ***	10.395 ***
	(1.33)	(1.25)	(1.81)	(3.49)	(3.24)	(4.43)	(3.84)
Fd	-3.448 **	-8.284 ***	-11.732 ***	-21.723	23.378 *	10.077 *	33.455 ***
	(1.58)	(2.91)	(3.32)	(13.54)	(14.12)	(5.80)	(12.75)
Firm size	-0.069	-0.326	-0.395	2.339 *	-1.533	-0.412	-1.945
	(0.36)	(0.73)	(0.86)	(1.34)	(1.02)	(1.34)	(1.49)
Leverage	0.831	6.547 *	7.379 *	-0.423	-5.163	-1.793	-6.956
	(1.73)	(3.58)	(4.34)	(5.34)	(4.57)	(6.29)	(6.21)
Firm age	-0.060	-2.875 *	-2.935	3.946	2.578	-3.589	-1.011
	(0.84)	(1.62)	(1.82)	(2.80)	(2.49)	(2.90)	(2.98)
ROA	8.915	6.597	15.513	-10.113	-9.215	3.816	-5.399
	(6.59)	(8.12)	(13.71)	(8.33)	(8.30)	(10.87)	(13.04)
Observations	991	991	991	991	991	991	991
Adj. R^2	0.008	0.021	0.024	0.010	0.007	0.021	0.022

Note: This table reports the DID regression estimates [columns (1), (2), (3), (4), (5), (6), and (7)] to test whether the educational background of independent directors elected via CV is different from those elected via straight voting, using the sample constructed via CEM method. Standard errors (in parentheses) are heteroskedasticity consistent and clustered at the firm level. ***, **, and * denote significance at the 1%, 5%, and 10% levels, respectively.

Table A18   Professional Experience of Independent Directors

Model	(1)	(2)	(3)	(4)	(5)	(6)
	Pro1	Pro2	Pro3	Pro4	Pro5	Ind_exp
Intercept	49. 466 ***	12. 911	− 30. 850 *	9. 969	48. 186	− 14. 213
	(16. 48)	(15. 54)	(15. 76)	(16. 54)	(30. 22)	(29. 43)
CV	4. 369 **	0. 214	− 2. 036	0. 391	4. 178	3. 074
	(1. 77)	(1. 76)	(1. 75)	(1. 44)	(2. 91)	(2. 25)
t	− 0. 682	− 0. 939	− 0. 631	0. 067	− 2. 036	0. 671
	(0. 95)	(0. 73)	(0. 85)	(0. 63)	(1. 33)	(0. 85)
CV × t	3. 840 **	2. 040	2. 421 *	0. 570	8. 351 ***	0. 360
	(1. 67)	(1. 33)	(1. 33)	(1. 20)	(2. 09)	(1. 67)
Regulatory	4. 297	0. 667	− 1. 647	4. 454 **	7. 508 *	2. 393
	(2. 70)	(2. 37)	(2. 36)	(2. 19)	(4. 41)	(3. 22)
Board size	− 1. 368 ***	0. 144	0. 646	− 0. 303	− 0. 941	0. 323
	(0. 39)	(0. 34)	(0. 42)	(0. 34)	(0. 63)	(0. 45)
Board_ind	− 30. 815 **	− 0. 747	− 11. 111	− 15. 143	− 48. 850 **	− 17. 555
	(15. 19)	(14. 23)	(15. 03)	(12. 99)	(20. 49)	(21. 21)
Duality	− 0. 830	− 4. 484 **	− 1. 394	0. 964	− 4. 162	1. 307
	(2. 24)	(2. 02)	(2. 22)	(2. 17)	(3. 80)	(2. 59)
Related	1. 063	− 1. 121	0. 184	− 1. 714 *	− 0. 461	0. 082
	(1. 01)	(0. 97)	(0. 88)	(0. 88)	(1. 49)	(1. 26)
Shrcr1	− 0. 102	− 0. 045	0. 025	− 0. 060	− 0. 194	0. 108
	(0. 08)	(0. 08)	(0. 08)	(0. 06)	(0. 13)	(0. 09)
Shrcr2_10	0. 008	0. 031	− 0. 144 *	0. 032	− 0. 102	0. 026
	(0. 08)	(0. 08)	(0. 08)	(0. 07)	(0. 13)	(0. 10)
Sd	− 3. 622	1. 400	− 3. 292 *	− 3. 144 *	− 7. 338 **	− 6. 235 ***
	(2. 26)	(2. 19)	(1. 87)	(1. 61)	(3. 58)	(2. 19)
Fd	4. 694	8. 851	− 16. 225 ***	− 2. 822	− 2. 047	8. 480
	(6. 15)	(6. 71)	(5. 07)	(5. 39)	(8. 96)	(15. 45)
Firm size	− 0. 258	− 0. 202	2. 086 ***	0. 096	0. 994	0. 696
	(0. 83)	(0. 73)	(0. 79)	(0. 86)	(1. 51)	(1. 52)

continued

Model	(1) Pro1	(2) Pro2	(3) Pro3	(4) Pro4	(5) Pro5	(6) Ind_exp
Leverage	0.497 (4.02)	-1.075 (3.78)	2.124 (3.21)	-0.534 (2.36)	3.689 (5.60)	-3.135 (4.41)
Firm age	2.231 (1.70)	3.035* (1.55)	-2.138 (1.58)	2.916** (1.37)	6.617** (2.82)	4.866** (2.05)
ROA	3.444 (5.17)	-6.775 (4.50)	-2.667 (5.25)	10.560* (5.93)	5.932 (9.08)	3.243 (10.36)
Observations	991	991	991	991	991	991
Adj. R^2	0.052	0.008	0.033	0.018	0.047	0.021

Note: This table reports the DID regression estimates [columns (1), (2), (3), (4), (5), and (6)] to test whether the professional experience of directors elected via CV is different from those elected via straight voting, using the sample constructed via CEM method. Standard errors (in parentheses) are heteroskedasticity consistent and clustered at the firm level. ***, **, and * denote significance at the 1%, 5%, and 10% levels, respectively.

Table A19   Political Connections of Independent Directors

Model	(1) Pol1	(2) pol2	(3) pol3	(4) pol4	(5) pol5	(6) Pol6	(7) Pol7
Intercept	-46.026*** (15.93)	-21.674 (19.64)	-7.209 (7.26)	7.508 (9.35)	3.461 (4.24)	-0.849 (6.52)	-29.362 (25.65)
CV	-2.293 (1.68)	-0.484 (2.29)	0.437 (0.60)	-0.441 (0.97)	0.492 (0.51)	0.900 (0.65)	-1.760 (2.79)
t	0.040 (0.72)	-0.110 (0.86)	-0.015 (0.23)	0.380 (0.42)	0.078 (0.24)	-0.099 (0.16)	0.366 (1.07)
CV×t	0.605 (1.17)	-0.469 (1.63)	-0.277 (0.33)	0.457 (0.75)	-0.134 (0.36)	-0.188 (0.40)	0.443 (1.95)
Regulatory	1.547 (2.40)	-3.059 (3.48)	0.461 (0.58)	-0.684 (1.30)	-0.412 (0.55)	-0.969 (0.79)	-0.131 (4.20)
Board size	0.331 (0.36)	-0.366 (0.47)	0.064 (0.10)	-0.018 (0.23)	0.092 (0.08)	0.059 (0.14)	-0.120 (0.57)

continued

Model	(1)	(2)	(3)	(4)	(5)	(6)	(7)
	Pol1	pol2	pol3	pol4	pol5	Pol6	Pol7
Board_ind	3.997	-7.274	-2.843	-19.001	4.500	6.145	-11.422
	(13.41)	(16.11)	(2.75)	(11.94)	(3.66)	(4.50)	(20.65)
Duality	-1.235	-1.488	-0.536	0.384	-0.438	-0.351	-2.462
	(2.59)	(3.82)	(0.37)	(1.51)	(0.46)	(0.82)	(4.33)
Related	0.419	0.579	-0.365	0.301	0.211	0.088	0.620
	(0.86)	(1.28)	(0.28)	(0.67)	(0.22)	(0.22)	(1.53)
Shrcr1	0.074	0.038	0.032	0.017	0.014	0.003	0.070
	(0.08)	(0.10)	(0.02)	(0.03)	(0.02)	(0.02)	(0.12)
Shrcr2_10	0.117	-0.020	0.047	-0.012	-0.019	-0.015	0.091
	(0.08)	(0.10)	(0.03)	(0.04)	(0.02)	(0.02)	(0.12)
Sd	-3.123*	4.252	-1.002**	-0.118	0.544	-0.793	0.410
	(1.60)	(3.34)	(0.43)	(1.07)	(0.71)	(0.56)	(3.94)
Fd	-14.011***	-13.452*	12.129	-2.841	0.399	-2.156	-12.434
	(3.26)	(7.86)	(9.99)	(1.81)	(0.72)	(1.33)	(8.30)
Firm size	2.261***	2.029*	0.267	0.045	-0.258	0.030	2.782**
	(0.83)	(1.04)	(0.34)	(0.49)	(0.21)	(0.29)	(1.34)
Leverage	-3.280	5.146	-1.856*	1.837	-0.640	2.041*	2.486
	(2.76)	(4.05)	(1.01)	(1.75)	(0.76)	(1.16)	(4.82)
Firm age	-1.233	-0.177	1.038*	-0.635	-0.014	-0.844	-1.154
	(1.65)	(1.98)	(0.55)	(0.97)	(0.47)	(0.55)	(2.63)
ROA	12.057**	-0.437	-0.218	4.219	-0.040	2.474	15.797
	(5.82)	(9.01)	(1.22)	(3.42)	(1.36)	(1.98)	(11.00)
Observations	991	991	991	991	991	991	991
Adj. R^2	0.044	0.009	0.042	0.002	0.002	0.003	0.003

Note: This table reports the DID regression estimates [columns (1), (2), (3), (4), (5), (6), and (7)] to test whether the political connections of independent directors elected via CV are different from those elected via straight voting, using the sample constructed via CEM method. Standard errors (in parentheses) are heteroskedasticity consistent and clustered at the firm level. ***, **, and * denote significance at the 1%, 5%, and 10% levels, respectively.

Table A20   **Academic Independent Directors**

Model	(1)	(2)	(3)	(4)	(5)
	Academe	*Econ*	*Acco*	*Law*	*Match*
Intercept	102.274 ***	39.360 **	25.196 *	− 1.027	25.134 *
	(30.47)	(19.66)	(15.26)	(10.28)	(13.16)
CV	5.170	1.661	3.011 *	− 0.356	1.684
	(3.42)	(2.28)	(1.66)	(1.14)	(1.65)
t	1.424	− 0.173	0.966	0.310	0.441
	(1.16)	(0.89)	(0.71)	(0.41)	(0.84)
CV × t	− 6.491 ***	− 1.851	− 2.373 *	− 0.953	− 0.631
	(2.32)	(1.61)	(1.34)	(0.82)	(1.18)
Regulatory	2.864	− 0.837	2.591	1.760	− 2.774
	(5.14)	(3.42)	(2.45)	(1.64)	(2.35)
Board size	0.446	− 0.086	− 0.540	0.305	0.522
	(0.74)	(0.49)	(0.38)	(0.24)	(0.40)
Board_ind	15.914	13.514	− 8.994	1.769	5.662
	(22.14)	(14.90)	(12.43)	(9.91)	(12.18)
Duality	− 0.245	− 2.615	− 3.102	0.050	3.698
	(4.25)	(2.79)	(2.26)	(1.45)	(2.39)
Related	− 1.374	0.133	0.120	− 0.926	− 0.089
	(1.74)	(1.15)	(0.92)	(0.63)	(0.79)
Shrcr1	− 0.113	0.048	− 0.061	− 0.047	0.027
	(0.16)	(0.10)	(0.08)	(0.05)	(0.07)
Shrcr2_10	− 0.232	0.016	− 0.139 **	− 0.013	− 0.014
	(0.15)	(0.10)	(0.07)	(0.05)	(0.06)
Sd	5.301	2.030	3.890 *	3.366 *	− 1.681
	(4.58)	(2.61)	(2.28)	(1.80)	(1.86)
Fd	6.757	− 0.775	7.659	5.589	0.550
	(15.15)	(9.83)	(8.11)	(10.14)	(4.50)
Firm size	− 2.273	− 0.953	− 0.313	0.176	− 0.872
	(1.63)	(1.00)	(0.77)	(0.50)	(0.65)
Leverage	− 6.802	− 3.115	− 1.997	− 0.350	0.273
	(6.35)	(3.76)	(4.85)	(2.09)	(2.61)
Firm age	− 3.754	− 2.070	2.313	0.311	− 3.227 **
	(3.32)	(2.42)	(1.61)	(0.87)	(1.48)

continued

Model	(1) Academe	(2) Econ	(3) Acco	(4) Law	(5) Match
ROA	-2.885 (11.48)	-7.056 (6.03)	2.050 (6.70)	-0.028 (2.48)	3.679 (4.44)
Observations	991	991	991	991	991
Adj. R^2	0.007	0.005	0.025	0.011	0.012

Note: This table reports the DID regression estimates [columns (1), (2), (3), (4), and (5)] to test whether personal characteristics of independent directors from academic institutions elected via CV is different from those elected via straight voting, using the sample constructed via CEM method. Variable *Academe* represents the proportion of independent directors from academic institutions; variable *Econ* denotes the percentage of independent directors specializing in economics, finance or management when they come from academic institutions; variable *Acco* denotes the percentage of independent directors specializing in accounting when they come from academic institutions; variable *Law* denotes the percentage of independent directors specializing in law when they come from academic institutions; and variable *Match* stands for the percentage of independent directors whose specializations match to the business of firms when they come from academic institutions. Standard errors (in parentheses) are heteroskedasticity consistent and clustered at the firm level. ***, **, and * denote significance at the 1%, 5%, and 10% levels, respectively.

Individual Director Level Analysis

Table A21   Representatives from Minority Shareholders: Binary Case

Model	(1) Share1d	(2) Share2d	(3) Share2_5d	(4) Share1d	(5) Share2d	(6) Share2_5d
Intercept	-2.622 *** (0.62)	0.298 (0.72)	0.762 (0.63)	-1.048 (1.83)	-2.088 (1.98)	0.714 (1.59)
CV	-0.027 (0.06)	0.078 (0.08)	0.028 (0.07)	0.145 (0.18)	-0.297 (0.21)	-0.110 (0.18)
t	0.027 (0.03)	-0.011 (0.04)	-0.000 (0.03)	-0.155 (0.13)	-0.237 (0.19)	-0.204 (0.14)
CV × t	-0.002 (0.05)	0.116 ** (0.06)	0.091 * (0.05)	-0.053 (0.22)	0.701 *** (0.24)	0.421 ** (0.19)
Regulatory	-0.026 (0.09)	0.138 (0.11)	0.110 (0.09)	-0.005 (0.23)	0.092 (0.25)	0.054 (0.23)

continued

Model	(1) Share1d	(2) Share2d	(3) Share2_5d	(4) Share1d	(5) Share2d	(6) Share2_5d
Board size	-0.030** (0.01)	0.010 (0.01)	0.043*** (0.01)	0.007 (0.03)	0.047 (0.03)	0.059** (0.03)
Board_ind	0.083 (0.31)	-0.048 (0.32)	0.200 (0.30)	0.681 (0.61)	0.094 (0.50)	0.381 (0.53)
Duality	-0.119 (0.09)	0.062 (0.10)	-0.041 (0.10)	-0.226 (0.22)	-0.032 (0.19)	-0.145 (0.23)
Related	-0.030 (0.03)	0.004 (0.04)	-0.056 (0.03)			
Shrcr1	0.017*** (0.00)	-0.011*** (0.00)	-0.014*** (0.00)	0.026*** (0.01)	-0.009 (0.01)	-0.012 (0.01)
Shrcr2_10	-0.005* (0.00)	0.021*** (0.00)	0.025*** (0.00)	0.003 (0.01)	0.021*** (0.01)	0.028*** (0.01)
Sd	-0.054 (0.08)	0.095 (0.10)	0.143* (0.08)	0.036 (0.18)	0.494*** (0.16)	0.334** (0.16)
Fd	-0.305** (0.15)	0.652** (0.29)	0.356 (0.26)	-0.325 (0.35)	1.581*** (0.33)	1.177*** (0.28)
Firm size	0.106*** (0.03)	-0.098*** (0.04)	-0.098*** (0.03)	-0.025 (0.09)	0.024 (0.08)	-0.092 (0.07)
Leverage	-0.245* (0.13)	0.168 (0.11)	0.217* (0.13)	-0.391 (0.28)	0.098 (0.25)	0.045 (0.23)
Firmage	0.151** (0.06)	0.015 (0.07)	-0.130* (0.07)	0.207 (0.17)	-0.240 (0.15)	-0.286* (0.16)
ROA	0.161 (0.26)	0.026 (0.29)	0.336 (0.26)	0.716 (0.75)	0.778 (0.65)	1.623*** (0.62)
Observations	6903	6903	6903	946	946	946
Pseudo R^2	0.062	0.087	0.127	0.074	0.112	0.145

Note: This table reports the nonlinear (probit) DID regression estimates [columns (1), (2) (3), (4) and (5)] to test whether minority shareholders can elect their representatives into the board of directors with binary outcome variables at individual director level, using the sample constructed via CEM method. columns (1), (2), and (3) use all the sample, while columns (4), (5), and (6) exclude the observations in which the top ten shareholders are related. All outcome variables in the table are binary. Standard errors (in parentheses) are heteroskedasticity consistent and clustered at the firm level. ***, **, and * denote significance at the 1%, 5%, and 10% levels, respectively.

Table A22   Professional Experience of Executive

Directors: Binary Case

Model	(1)	(2)	(3)	(4)
	CEO_exp_d	Chair_exp_d	Ind_exp_d	Edu
Intercept	− 1. 346 ***	− 2. 405 ***	− 1. 933 *	
	(0. 39)	(0. 59)	(0. 99)	
CV	0. 120 **	0. 019	0. 308 ***	− 0. 018
	(0. 05)	(0. 05)	(0. 09)	(0. 05)
t	0. 019	0. 009	0. 038	0. 048 **
	(0. 02)	(0. 02)	(0. 05)	(0. 02)
CV × t	0. 069 *	0. 084 **	0. 420 ***	0. 059
	(0. 04)	(0. 04)	(0. 13)	(0. 04)
Regulatory	− 0. 079	− 0. 122	0. 158	0. 055
	(0. 07)	(0. 08)	(0. 14)	(0. 08)
Board size	− 0. 025 ***	− 0. 024 **	− 0. 036 *	− 0. 003
	(0. 01)	(0. 01)	(0. 02)	(0. 01)
Board_ind	0. 514 **	1. 023 ***	0. 986 **	0. 993 ***
	(0. 24)	(0. 23)	(0. 44)	(0. 22)
Duality	− 0. 047	− 0. 053	− 0. 022	− 0. 022
	(0. 07)	(0. 08)	(0. 13)	(0. 08)
Related	0. 030	0. 006	0. 060	− 0. 039
	(0. 03)	(0. 03)	(0. 05)	(0. 03)
Shrcr1	− 0. 006 ***	− 0. 004	0. 010 **	0. 002
	(0. 00)	(0. 00)	(0. 00)	(0. 00)
Shrcr2_10	− 0. 001	0. 003	− 0. 003	0. 003
	(0. 00)	(0. 00)	(0. 00)	(0. 00)
Sd	0. 098 *	− 0. 005	− 0. 119	0. 033
	(0. 06)	(0. 06)	(0. 11)	(0. 06)
Fd	− 0. 177	− 0. 683 ***	0. 413	0. 695 ***
	(0. 23)	(0. 24)	(0. 50)	(0. 17)

continued

Model	(1) CEO_exp_d	(2) Chair_exp_d	(3) Ind_exp_d	(4) Edu
Firm size	0. 064 *** (0. 02)	0. 093 *** (0. 03)	0. 154 *** (0. 05)	0. 104 *** (0. 02)
Leverage	0. 011 (0. 09)	− 0. 005 (0. 10)	− 0. 123 (0. 18)	− 0. 216 ** (0. 10)
Firm age	− 0. 075 * (0. 04)	− 0. 109 ** (0. 05)	− 0. 229 *** (0. 09)	0. 148 *** (0. 05)
ROA	0. 211 (0. 22)	0. 323 (0. 28)	0. 679 (0. 47)	− 0. 019 (0. 20)
cut1 Intercept1				1. 050 ** (0. 51)
cut2 Intercept2				2. 127 *** (0. 51)
cut3 Intercept3				3. 128 *** (0. 51)
cut4 Intercept4				4. 473 *** (0. 51)
Observations	6903	6903	6903	6903
Pseudo R^2	0. 014	0. 020	0. 114	0. 015

Note: This table reports the nonlinear DID regression estimates [columns (1), (2) (3), and (4)] to test whether executive directors elected via CV have more likelihood to have richer professional experience and better educational background, using the sample constructed via CEM method. We obtain estimates in columns (1), (2), and (3), using probit DID model, while we obtain estimates in column (4) via ordered probit DID model, because Edu is an ordered categorical variable. CEO_exp_d denotes whether a director has CEO experiences; Chair_exp_d denotes whether a director has chairman experiences; and Ind_exp_d represents whether a director has work experience in the same industry. Edu is a categorical variable, which takes 1 if a director is a graduate from technical secondary school, or lower, takes 2 if a director holds a junior college diploma, takes 3 if a director holds a bachelor degree; takes 4 if a director holds a master degree; and takes 5 if a director holds a doctor degree. All outcome variables in the table are binary except variable Edu. Standard errors (in parentheses) are heteroskedasticity consistent and clustered at the firm level. *** , ** , and * denote significance at the 1% , 5% , and 10% levels, respectively.

Table A23   Political Connections of Executive Directors: Binary Case

Model	(1)	(2)	(3)	(4)	(5)	(6)	(7)
	Pol1	pol2	pol3	pol4	pol5	Pol6	pol7
Intercept	-4. 570 ***	-1. 927 ***	-6. 696 ***	-1. 563	-4. 267 ***	0. 197	-1. 771 ***
	(1. 01)	(0. 74)	(1. 01)	(1. 20)	(0. 93)	(1. 07)	(0. 62)
CV	0. 173	-0. 046	0. 276	0. 046	-0. 080	0. 070	0. 034
	(0. 13)	(0. 08)	(0. 18)	(0. 14)	(0. 11)	(0. 12)	(0. 06)
t	0. 035	-0. 015	0. 066	0. 016	0. 005	-0. 050	-0. 002
	(0. 05)	(0. 04)	(0. 10)	(0. 07)	(0. 03)	(0. 04)	(0. 03)
CV × t	-0. 193 **	0. 027	0. 251 *	0. 088	-0. 125 *	0. 038	-0. 026
	(0. 08)	(0. 05)	(0. 14)	(0. 11)	(0. 06)	(0. 07)	(0. 05)
Regulatory	-0. 025	-0. 063	0. 035	0. 206	0. 141	0. 384 **	0. 028
	(0. 17)	(0. 12)	(0. 22)	(0. 21)	(0. 19)	(0. 18)	(0. 10)
Board size	0. 001	-0. 043 ***	-0. 030	0. 029	-0. 019	0. 001	-0. 039 ***
	(0. 02)	(0. 02)	(0. 04)	(0. 03)	(0. 02)	(0. 02)	(0. 01)
Board_ind	0. 871 *	-0. 505	1. 318 *	1. 386 *	1. 136 **	0. 932 **	-0. 013
	(0. 51)	(0. 35)	(0. 71)	(0. 72)	(0. 49)	(0. 45)	(0. 30)
Duality	-0. 221	0. 013	0. 335	0. 369 **	0. 074	0. 398 ***	0. 087
	(0. 17)	(0. 10)	(0. 21)	(0. 18)	(0. 17)	(0. 15)	(0. 09)
Related	0. 014	-0. 006	-0. 095	-0. 080	0. 022	0. 037	-0. 000
	(0. 07)	(0. 04)	(0. 09)	(0. 07)	(0. 06)	(0. 06)	(0. 03)
Shrcr1	-0. 004	-0. 005	-0. 022 ***	-0. 021 ***	-0. 005	-0. 017 ***	-0. 010 ***
	(0. 00)	(0. 00)	(0. 01)	(0. 01)	(0. 01)	(0. 01)	(0. 00)
Shrcr2_10	0. 008 *	0. 000	-0. 007	-0. 012 **	-0. 006	-0. 005	-0. 000
	(0. 00)	(0. 00)	(0. 00)	(0. 01)	(0. 01)	(0. 01)	(0. 00)
Sd	-0. 022	-0. 063	-0. 311	-0. 206	-0. 212	-0. 099	-0. 072
	(0. 15)	(0. 09)	(0. 24)	(0. 16)	(0. 19)	(0. 17)	(0. 08)
Fd	0. 397 **	-0. 601		0. 054			-0. 439 **
	(0. 18)	(0. 41)		(0. 30)			(0. 22)

continued

Model	(1)	(2)	(3)	(4)	(5)	(6)	(7)
	Pol1	pol2	pol3	pol4	pol5	Pol6	pol7
Firm size	0. 150 ***	0. 076 *	0. 261 ***	− 0. 016	0. 136 ***	− 0. 088 *	0. 093 ***
	(0. 05)	(0. 04)	(0. 06)	(0. 05)	(0. 05)	(0. 05)	(0. 03)
Leverage	− 0. 824 ***	0. 073	− 0. 434	0. 049	− 0. 887 ***	− 0. 025	0. 017
	(0. 30)	(0. 14)	(0. 33)	(0. 19)	(0. 26)	(0. 19)	(0. 14)
Firm age	− 0. 267 **	0. 038	− 0. 157	− 0. 072	− 0. 131	− 0. 167	− 0. 095
	(0. 11)	(0. 07)	(0. 13)	(0. 13)	(0. 10)	(0. 11)	(0. 06)
ROA	0. 361	− 0. 127	− 0. 140	− 0. 342	0. 215	0. 151	− 0. 115
	(0. 64)	(0. 31)	(0. 61)	(0. 48)	(0. 35)	(0. 40)	(0. 26)
Observations	6903	6903	6855	6903	6855	6855	6903
Pseudo R^2	0. 061	0. 012	0. 136	0. 062	0. 040	0. 038	0. 015

Note: This table reports the nonlinear (probit) DID regression estimates [columns (1), (2), (3), (4), (5), (6), and (7)] to test whether the political connections of executive directors elected via CV are different from those elected via straight voting, using the sample constructed via CEM method. Variable pol1 is a dummy variable to indicate whether an executive director has central government work experience; pol2 is a dummy variable to indicate whether an executive director has local government work experience; pol3 is a dummy variable to indicate whether an executive director is a member of the national committee of CPPCC; pol4 is a dummy variable to indicate whether an executive director is a member of the local committee of CPPCC; pol5 is a dummy variable to indicate whether an executive director is a member of deputy to the National People's Congress; pol6 is a dummy variable to indicate whether an executive director is a member of deputy to the local People's Congress; and pol7 is a dummy variable to indicate whether an executive director has at least one of the above experience. Standard errors (in parentheses) are heteroskedasticity consistent and clustered at the firm level. *** , ** , and * denote significance at the 1% , 5% , and 10% levels, respectively.

Table A24   Relationship between Independent Directors and Executives: Binary Case

Model	(1)	(2)	(3)
	Exe_rel1_d	Exe_rel2_d	Exe_rel3_d
Intercept	− 1. 424	− 2. 176 **	− 1. 487 *
	(1. 23)	(0. 97)	(0. 85)
CV	− 0. 161	− 0. 069	− 0. 106
	(0. 13)	(0. 10)	(0. 09)

continued

Model	(1) *Exe_rel1_d*	(2) *Exe_rel2_d*	(3) *Exe_rel3_d*
t	0. 013 (0. 04)	0. 034 (0. 05)	0. 030 (0. 04)
CV × t	− 0. 245 ** (0. 10)	− 0. 159 ** (0. 08)	− 0. 211 *** (0. 07)
Regulatory	− 0. 089 (0. 20)	− 0. 138 (0. 17)	− 0. 144 (0. 15)
Board size	0. 011 (0. 03)	− 0. 003 (0. 03)	0. 007 (0. 02)
Board_ind	− 1. 067 (0. 91)	0. 763 (0. 81)	0. 192 (0. 73)
Duality	− 0. 241 (0. 20)	0. 009 (0. 14)	− 0. 080 (0. 13)
Related	− 0. 138 ** (0. 06)	0. 023 (0. 06)	− 0. 031 (0. 05)
Shrcr1	0. 010 * (0. 01)	0. 006 (0. 00)	0. 008 * (0. 00)
Shrcr2_10	0. 003 (0. 01)	− 0. 001 (0. 00)	0. 000 (0. 00)
Sd	− 0. 342 ** (0. 17)	− 0. 007 (0. 13)	− 0. 122 (0. 11)
Fd	1. 087 * (0. 62)		0. 310 (0. 51)
Firm size	− 0. 007 (0. 07)	0. 021 (0. 05)	0. 003 (0. 05)
Leverage	− 0. 197 (0. 27)	0. 258 (0. 20)	0. 143 (0. 19)
Firm age	0. 175 (0. 12)	− 0. 004 (0. 11)	0. 064 (0. 09)

continued

Model	(1)	(2)	(3)
	Exe_rel1_d	Exe_rel2_d	Exe_rel3_d
ROA	-0.341	0.171	-0.006
	(0.57)	(0.36)	(0.35)
Observations	3090	3073	3090
Pseudo R^2	0.042	0.010	0.014

Note: This table reports the DID regression estimates [columns (1), (2) and (3)] to examine whether the independent directors elected under the CV rule with close relation with firm's CEO or chairman have less likelihood than those elected under straight voting, using the sample constructed via CEM method. We measure the relation by three different dummy variables—Exe_rel1_d, Exe_rel2_d, and Exe_rel3_d, respectively. Here Exe_rel1_d takes 1 if a independent director worked in the same institution or firm with the current firm's CEO or chairman, and zero otherwise; Exe_re2_d takes 1 if a independent director and the current firm's CEO or chairman are in the same old boy network, and zero otherwise; and Exe_rel3_d takes 1 if one of the above relations exists, and zero otherwise. Standard errors (in parentheses) are heteroskedasticity consistent and clustered at the firm level. ***, **, and * denote significance at the 1%, 5%, and 10% levels, respectively.

Table A25　Political Connections of Independent Directors: Binary Case

Model	(1)	(2)	(3)	(4)	(5)	(6)	(7)
	Pol1	pol2	pol3	pol4	pol5	Pol6	pol7
Intercept	-4.291 ***	-1.976 ***	-5.589 ***	-0.403	-0.901	-3.244 **	-1.702 **
	(0.83)	(0.66)	(1.92)	(1.53)	(2.10)	(1.63)	(0.67)
CV	-0.165	0.008	0.196	-0.031	0.163	0.262	-0.037
	(0.11)	(0.08)	(0.21)	(0.15)	(0.26)	(0.18)	(0.08)
t	0.007	-0.001	-0.069	0.031	0.010	-0.070	0.011
	(0.04)	(0.03)	(0.13)	(0.06)	(0.09)	(0.06)	(0.03)
CV×t	-0.015	-0.054	-0.059	0.078	-0.022	-0.002	-0.021
	(0.07)	(0.06)	(0.18)	(0.11)	(0.15)	(0.10)	(0.05)
Regulatory	0.053	-0.143	0.239	-0.104	-0.232	-0.327	-0.048
	(0.16)	(0.13)	(0.30)	(0.21)	(0.30)	(0.22)	(0.12)
Board size	0.016	-0.029 *	-0.001	-0.020	0.028	0.021	-0.017
	(0.02)	(0.02)	(0.04)	(0.03)	(0.04)	(0.04)	(0.02)
Board_ind	-0.264	-0.572	-2.392 **	-2.697 *	2.083	2.167 *	-0.646
	(0.83)	(0.55)	(1.20)	(1.39)	(1.65)	(1.20)	(0.54)

continued

Model	(1)	(2)	(3)	(4)	(5)	(6)	(7)
	*Pol*1	*pol*2	*pol*3	*pol*4	*pol*5	*Pol*6	*pol*7
Duality	−0.054	−0.081	−0.455	0.001	−0.304	−0.146	−0.060
	(0.20)	(0.14)	(0.36)	(0.20)	(0.33)	(0.27)	(0.13)
Related	0.014	0.038	−0.149	0.016	0.079	0.042	0.016
	(0.06)	(0.05)	(0.09)	(0.09)	(0.12)	(0.08)	(0.04)
Shrcr1	0.004	0.001	0.010	0.001	0.008	0.003	0.003
	(0.00)	(0.00)	(0.01)	(0.01)	(0.01)	(0.01)	(0.00)
Shrcr2_10	0.005	−0.001	0.013	−0.003	−0.011	−0.002	0.002
	(0.00)	(0.00)	(0.01)	(0.01)	(0.01)	(0.01)	(0.00)
Sd	−0.215*	0.157	−0.637*	−0.070	0.209	−0.214	0.024
	(0.13)	(0.12)	(0.35)	(0.18)	(0.26)	(0.25)	(0.11)
Fd		−0.308	1.238**				−0.180
		(0.39)	(0.58)				(0.20)
Firm size	0.138***	0.067*	0.146	−0.022	−0.126	0.008	0.067*
	(0.04)	(0.03)	(0.11)	(0.07)	(0.10)	(0.07)	(0.03)
Leverage	−0.579**	0.153	−1.318**	0.254	−0.229	0.582**	0.002
	(0.28)	(0.15)	(0.55)	(0.26)	(0.37)	(0.23)	(0.15)
Firm age	−0.058	0.000	0.457*	−0.056	−0.006	−0.223	−0.014
	(0.10)	(0.07)	(0.25)	(0.14)	(0.19)	(0.15)	(0.07)
ROA	0.745***	−0.123	0.184	0.571	0.207	0.685*	0.344
	(0.28)	(0.32)	(0.42)	(0.40)	(0.51)	(0.37)	(0.30)
Observations	3073	3090	3090	3073	3073	3073	3090
Pseudo R^2	0.043	0.007	0.137	0.021	0.052	0.045	0.005

Note: This table reports the nonlinear (probit) DID regression estimates [columns (1), (2), (3), (4), (5), (6), and (7)] to test whether the political connections of independent directors elected via CV are different from those elected via straight voting, using the sample constructed via CEM method. Variable *pol*1 is a dummy variable to indicate whether an independent director has central government work experience; *pol*2 is a dummy variable to indicate whether an independent director has local government work experience; *pol*3 is a dummy variable to indicate whether an independent director is a member of the national committee of CPPCC; *pol*4 is a dummy variable to indicate whether an independent director is a member of the local committee of CPPCC; *pol*5 is a dummy variable to indicate whether an independent director is a member of deputy to the National People's Congress; *pol*6 is a dummy variable to indicate whether an independent director is a member of deputy to the local People's Congress; and *pol*7 is a dummy variable to indicate whether an independent director has at least one of the above experience. Standard errors (in parentheses) are heteroskedasticity consistent and clustered at the firm level. ***, **, and * denote significance at the 1%, 5%, and 10% levels, respectively.

Table A26 Professional Experience of Independent Directors: Binary Case

Model	(1)	(2)	(3)	(4)	(5)	(6)
	pro1	pro2	pro3	pro4	pro5	ind_exp
Intercept	0. 100	- 1. 442 *	- 3. 317 ***	- 1. 400	- 0. 168	- 2. 413 **
	(0. 45)	(0. 77)	(0. 89)	(1. 08)	(0. 77)	(0. 99)
CV	0. 108 **	0. 012	- 0. 064	0. 088	0. 122 *	0. 167 *
	(0. 05)	(0. 09)	(0. 10)	(0. 11)	(0. 07)	(0. 10)
t	- 0. 028	- 0. 054	- 0. 010	- 0. 004	- 0. 044	0. 013
	(0. 02)	(0. 03)	(0. 04)	(0. 05)	(0. 03)	(0. 04)
CV × t	0. 116 ***	0. 096	0. 139 **	- 0. 016	0. 193 ***	0. 015
	(0. 04)	(0. 06)	(0. 07)	(0. 08)	(0. 05)	(0. 07)
Regulatory	0. 117	0. 010	- 0. 078	0. 293 *	0. 153	0. 088
	(0. 07)	(0. 12)	(0. 15)	(0. 16)	(0. 11)	(0. 14)
Board size	- 0. 047 ***	0. 006	0. 039 *	- 0. 020	- 0. 028 *	0. 017
	(0. 01)	(0. 02)	(0. 02)	(0. 02)	(0. 02)	(0. 02)
Board_ind	- 1. 168 ***	0. 346	- 0. 432	- 1. 731 **	- 1. 308 ***	- 0. 868
	(0. 39)	(0. 68)	(0. 78)	(0. 86)	(0. 49)	(0. 82)
Duality	- 0. 056	- 0. 299 **	- 0. 062	0. 068	- 0. 129	0. 071
	(0. 06)	(0. 13)	(0. 15)	(0. 15)	(0. 09)	(0. 11)
Related	0. 021	- 0. 053	0. 001	- 0. 093	- 0. 014	- 0. 023
	(0. 03)	(0. 05)	(0. 05)	(0. 06)	(0. 04)	(0. 05)
Shrcr1	- 0. 003	- 0. 000	0. 001	- 0. 003	- 0. 003	0. 003
	(0. 00)	(0. 00)	(0. 00)	(0. 00)	(0. 00)	(0. 00)
Shrcr2_10	0. 001	0. 004	- 0. 008 *	0. 003	- 0. 001	- 0. 001
	(0. 00)	(0. 00)	(0. 00)	(0. 00)	(0. 00)	(0. 00)
Sd	- 0. 106 *	0. 079	- 0. 265 *	- 0. 241 *	- 0. 184 **	- 0. 307 ***
	(0. 06)	(0. 10)	(0. 14)	(0. 14)	(0. 09)	(0. 11)
Fd	0. 060	0. 425 **		- 0. 049	- 0. 053	0. 393
	(0. 15)	(0. 21)		(0. 41)	(0. 22)	(0. 46)
Firm size	0. 001	- 0. 007	0. 100 **	0. 015	0. 033	0. 047
	(0. 02)	(0. 04)	(0. 05)	(0. 06)	(0. 04)	(0. 05)
Leverage	- 0. 072	- 0. 063	0. 142	- 0. 239	- 0. 007	- 0. 219
	(0. 10)	(0. 19)	(0. 21)	(0. 20)	(0. 15)	(0. 21)

continued

Model	(1)	(2)	(3)	(4)	(5)	(6)
	pro1	pro2	pro3	pro4	pro5	ind_exp
Firm age	0.066	0.165**	-0.138	0.252**	0.159**	0.187**
	(0.05)	(0.08)	(0.09)	(0.11)	(0.07)	(0.09)
ROA	-0.004	-0.359	-0.084	0.371	0.046	0.188
	(0.15)	(0.32)	(0.45)	(0.30)	(0.28)	(0.38)
Observations	3090	3090	3073	3090	3090	3090
Pseudo R^2	0.011	0.011	0.027	0.027	0.015	0.021

Note: This table reports the DID regression estimates [columns (1), (2), (3), (4), (5), and (6)] to test whether the professional experience of independent directors elected via CV is different from those elected via straight voting, using the sample constructed via CEM method. Dummy variable pro1 denotes whether an independent director is an accountant; dummy variable pro2 denotes whether an independent director is a lawyer; dummy variable pro3 denotes whether an independent director is an engineer; dummy variable pro4 denotes whether an independent director is an economist; dummy variable pro5 denotes whether an independent director has at least one of titles listed above; and dummy variable ind_exp denotes whether an independent director has the same industry work experience as the firms in which they work as independent directors. Standard errors (in parentheses) are heteroskedasticity consistent and clustered at the firm level. ***, **, and * denote significance at the 1%, 5%, and 10% levels, respectively.

Table A27   Academic Independent Directors: Binary Case

Model	(1)	(2)	(3)	(4)	(5)
	Academe	Econ	Acco	Law	Match
Intercept	1.174*	0.067	-0.635	-2.925***	-0.281
	(0.71)	(0.68)	(0.71)	(1.09)	(0.95)
CV	0.075	0.029	0.105	-0.058	0.075
	(0.08)	(0.08)	(0.08)	(0.12)	(0.11)
t	0.027	-0.027	0.039	0.032	0.055
	(0.03)	(0.03)	(0.03)	(0.05)	(0.05)
CV × t	-0.096*	-0.020	-0.080	-0.109	0.046
	(0.05)	(0.05)	(0.05)	(0.10)	(0.08)
Regulatory	0.151	0.006	0.182	0.144	-0.145
	(0.13)	(0.12)	(0.12)	(0.18)	(0.17)
Board size	0.022	0.006	-0.036**	0.026	0.062**
	(0.02)	(0.02)	(0.02)	(0.03)	(0.03)

continued

Model	(1)	(2)	(3)	(4)	(5)
	Academe	*Econ*	*Acco*	*Law*	*Match*
Board_ind	0.622	0.508	-0.554	0.747	0.677
	(0.53)	(0.51)	(0.55)	(0.94)	(0.81)
Duality	-0.005	-0.090	-0.190	-0.008	0.333**
	(0.10)	(0.11)	(0.12)	(0.16)	(0.15)
Related	-0.021	0.009	0.002	-0.102	0.031
	(0.04)	(0.04)	(0.04)	(0.07)	(0.06)
Shrcr1	-0.004	0.001	-0.003	-0.003	0.003
	(0.00)	(0.00)	(0.00)	(0.01)	(0.01)
Shrcr2_10	0.006	0.000	-0.006*	0.001	-0.000
	(0.00)	(0.00)	(0.00)	(0.01)	(0.01)
Sd	0.124	0.068	0.159*	0.365***	-0.200
	(0.11)	(0.09)	(0.09)	(0.14)	(0.16)
Fd	0.045	-0.090	0.351	0.152	0.220
	(0.46)	(0.49)	(0.29)	(0.59)	(0.36)
Firm size	-0.061	-0.050	-0.003	0.033	-0.083*
	(0.04)	(0.03)	(0.03)	(0.06)	(0.05)
Leverage	-0.106	-0.060	-0.174	0.026	0.166
	(0.15)	(0.15)	(0.17)	(0.25)	(0.19)
Firm age	-0.108	-0.059	0.089	0.052	-0.281***
	(0.08)	(0.08)	(0.08)	(0.12)	(0.09)
ROA	-0.028	-0.214	0.076	-0.033	0.338
	(0.30)	(0.29)	(0.28)	(0.45)	(0.34)
Observations	3090	3090	3090	3090	3090
Pseudo R^2	0.007	0.003	0.016	0.022	0.032

Note: This table reports the probit DID regression estimates [columns (1), (2), (3), (4), and (5)] to test whether personal characteristics of independent directors from academic institutions elected via CV is different from those elected via straight voting, using the sample constructed via CEM method. Dummy variable *Academe* represents whether an independent director comes from an academic institution; dummy variable Econ denotes whether an independent director specializes in economics, finance or management when coming from an academic institution; dummy variable *Acco* denotes whether an independent director specializes in accounting when coming from an academic institution; dummy variable *Law* denotes whether an independent director specializes in law when coming from an academic institution; and dummy variable *Match* stands for whether an independent director's research field matches to the business of the firm he or she serves for when coming from an academic institution. Standard errors (in parentheses) are heteroskedasticity consistent and clustered at the firm level. ***, **, and * denote significance at the 1%, 5%, and 10% levels, respectively.

Appendix B Additional Tables on Firm Performance and Corporate Policies

B. 1 Variable Definitions

Table B1 Brief Definitions and Sources of Main Variables

Variable Name	Definition	Source
	Panel A: Main Variables on Firm Performance and Corporate Policies	
Tobin's Q	Industry – adjusted Tobin's Q. Original Tobin's Q is a ratio. The numerator is the book value of total assets plus the market value of equity, and then minus the book value of equity. The denominator is the book value of total assets. Then subtract industry median from it to get Industry – adjusted Tobin's Q.	CSMAR
AMTB	Industry – adjusted Market – to – book ratio. The original MTB calculated as the market value of equity plus book value of debt divided by total assets. Then subtract industry median from it to get Industry – adjusted MTB.	CSMAR
ROA	Industry – adjusted ROA, obtained from ROA subtracting industry mean of ROA.	CSMAR
ROE	Industry – adjusted Return on equity.	CSMAR
TRPT	Aggregate value of total related – party transactions divided by the firm's year – end total assets.	CSMAR
BRPT	Aggregate value of potential beneficial related – party transactions divided by the firm's year – end total assets.	CSMAR
HRPT	Aggregate value of harmful related – party transactions divided by the firm's year – end total assets.	CSMAR

continued

Variable Name	Definition	Source
OAR	Other receivable deflated by year – end total assets.	CSMAR
CV_it	A indicator variable that equals 1 if a firm has used CV in director election by year t, and 0 otherwise.	ASINA

Panel B: Main Control Variables

Variable Name	Definition	Source
Firm size	log (book value of total assets).	CSMAR
Leverage	Long term debt divided by total assets.	CSMAR
Firm age	log (the number of listing years + 1)	CSMAR
MTB	Market to book ratio, calculated as the market value of equity plus book value of debt divided by total assets.	CSMAR
Duality	A binary variable equals 1 if the CEO of a company is also the chairman of the board of the directors, and 0 otherwise.	CSMAR
Board size	The number of directors in the board of directors in a firm.	CSMAR
Board_ind	Board independence, defined as the number of independent directors over Board size for each company.	CSMAR
Shrcr1	The controlling shareholder's ownership (percentage) at the year – end.	CSMAR
sd	An indicator variable, the nature of the controlling shareholder, equals 1 if the firm's controlling shareholder is government – related, and 0 otherwise.	CSMAR
Fd	A dummy variable, the nature of the controlling shareholder, equals 1 if a firm is controlled by Foreigners, and 0 otherwise.	CSMAR

Note: This table briefly defines the main variables used in the empirical analysis. The data sources are as follows: (i) ASINA: Extraction from director resumes obtained from firm annual reports disclosed by SHSE, SZSE and SINA FINANCE, (ii) CSMAR: the China Stock Market & Accounting Research database.

B. 2   Main Results from CEM Sample

Table B2   **Firm Performance**

Model	(1)	(2)	(3)	(4)
	Tobin's Q	AMTB	ROA	ROE
Intercept	− 14. 295	7. 528 ***	2. 905	1. 810 **
	(11. 43)	(0. 75)	(2. 66)	(0. 89)
CV_it	0. 247	− 0. 044	0. 092	0. 012
	(0. 69)	(0. 03)	(0. 12)	(0. 03)
Sd	1. 244	0. 017	− 0. 075	− 0. 176 **
	(1. 36)	(0. 06)	(0. 20)	(0. 08)
Fd	− 13. 899	− 0. 023	− 1. 240	− 0. 064
	(14. 44)	(0. 11)	(0. 90)	(0. 31)
Firm size	0. 779	− 0. 379 ***	− 0. 054	− 0. 092 **
	(0. 56)	(0. 04)	(0. 13)	(0. 04)
Firm age	− 1. 942	0. 132 **	− 1. 033 ***	− 0. 001
	(1. 23)	(0. 06)	(0. 23)	(0. 04)
Leverage	1. 510 **	0. 763 ***	− 0. 049	0. 011
	(0. 61)	(0. 07)	(0. 21)	(0. 07)
Year fixed effects	Yes	Yes	Yes	Yes
Firm fixed effects	Yes	Yes	Yes	Yes
Observations	5601	5601	5505	5622
Adj. R^2	0. 044	0. 210	0. 093	0. 058

Note: This table reports the DID (panel data for 2002 – 2008 with fixed effects) regressions [columns (1), (2), (3), and (4)] to test whether the use of CV can enhance firm performance or value, using the sample constructed through the CEM method. All outcome variables in the table are industry – adjusted (by subtracting the industry mean of the original variable, for example, the industry – adjusted Tobin's Q is defined as the common Tobin's Q minus its industry mean for each year). Standard errors (in parentheses) are heteroskedasticity consistent and clustered at the firm level. *** , ** , and * denote significance at the 1% , 5% , and 10% levels, respectively.

Table B3   Firm Performance: Voluntary Group

Model	(1)	(2)	(3)	(4)
	Tobin's Q	AMTB	ROA	ROE
Intercept	− 21. 812 (32. 16)	10. 447 *** (1. 84)	4. 907 (6. 73)	1. 139 (1. 32)
CV_it	− 0. 826 (1. 53)	− 0. 036 (0. 08)	0. 025 (0. 31)	0. 035 (0. 07)
Sd	1. 036 (1. 23)	0. 136 (0. 18)	0. 014 (0. 46)	− 0. 113 (0. 10)
Fd	1. 968 (1. 72)	0. 156 (0. 22)	− 0. 491 (0. 37)	− 0. 369 (0. 35)
Firm size	0. 952 (1. 64)	− 0. 543 *** (0. 09)	− 0. 155 (0. 34)	− 0. 070 (0. 06)
Firm age	0. 949 (2. 20)	0. 424 ** (0. 19)	− 0. 919 (0. 62)	− 0. 014 (0. 07)
Leverage	0. 784 (0. 86)	0. 709 *** (0. 10)	0. 004 (0. 39)	0. 117 (0. 13)
Year fixed effects	Yes	Yes	Yes	Yes
Firm fixed effects	Yes	Yes	Yes	Yes
Observations	1588	1588	1575	1602
Adj. R^2	0. 033	0. 322	0. 119	0. 095

Note: This table reports the DID (panel data for 2002 – 2008 with fixed effects) regressions [columns (1), (2), (3), and (4)] to test whether the use of CV can enhance firm performance or value, using the sample constructed by the CEM method. All outcome variables in the table are industry – adjusted (by subtracting the industry mean of the original variable, for example, the industry – adjusted Tobin's Q is defined as the common Tobin's Q minus its industry mean for each year). Standard errors (in parentheses) are heteroskedasticity consistent and clustered at the firm level. *** , ** , and * denote significance at the 1% , 5% , and 10% levels, respectively.

Table B4　　　　　**Firm Performance: Regulatory Group**

Model	(1)	(2)	(3)	(4)
	Tobin's Q	AMTB	ROA	ROE
Intercept	-17.078	5.785 ***	-0.416	0.983
	(12.02)	(0.72)	(3.15)	(1.23)
CV_it	0.647	-0.023	0.231 *	0.005
	(0.86)	(0.03)	(0.14)	(0.04)
Sd	2.638	-0.053	0.142	-0.202 **
	(1.98)	(0.04)	(0.21)	(0.10)
Fd	-0.594	-0.081	0.039	-0.066
	(0.77)	(0.12)	(0.13)	(0.08)
Firm size	0.846	-0.292 ***	0.094	-0.046
	(0.58)	(0.03)	(0.15)	(0.06)
Firm age	-1.479	0.060	-0.892 ***	-0.027
	(1.38)	(0.04)	(0.25)	(0.05)
Leverage	1.772 **	0.768 ***	-0.347	-0.098
	(0.88)	(0.11)	(0.25)	(0.10)
Year fixed effects	Yes	Yes	Yes	Yes
Firm fixed effects	Yes	Yes	Yes	Yes
Observations	4013	4013	3930	4020
Adj. R^2	0.043	0.150	0.078	0.040

Note: This table reports the DID (panel data for 2002 – 2008 with fixed effects) regressions [columns (1), (2), (3), and (4)] for testing whether the use of CV can enhance firm performance or value, using the sample constructed through the CEM method. All outcome variables in the table are industry – adjusted (by subtracting the industry mean of the original variable, for example, the industry – adjusted Tobin's Q is defined as the common Tobin's Q minus its industry mean for each year). Standard errors (in parentheses) are heteroskedasticity consistent and clustered at the firm level. *** , ** , and * denote significance at the 1% , 5% , and 10% levels, respectively.

211

Table B5 **Executive Experience and Firm Performance**

Model	(1)	(2)	(3)	(4)
	Tobin's Q	AMTB	ROA	ROE
Intercept	− 14. 162 (11. 44)	7. 550*** (0. 75)	2. 882 (2. 68)	1. 816** (0. 90)
CV_it	0. 159 (0. 75)	− 0. 076** (0. 03)	0. 123 (0. 14)	0. 009 (0. 03)
dexp	0. 346 (1. 26)	− 0. 010 (0. 06)	− 0. 111 (0. 21)	0. 033 (0. 06)
CV_it × dexp	0. 170 (2. 00)	0. 161** (0. 08)	− 0. 078 (0. 29)	− 0. 008 (0. 08)
Sd	1. 251 (1. 36)		− 0. 077 (0. 20)	− 0. 176** (0. 08)
Fd	− 13. 860 (14. 44)	− 0. 015 (0. 11)	− 1. 254 (0. 90)	− 0. 061 (0. 31)
Firm size	0. 772 (0. 56)	− 0. 380*** (0. 04)	− 0. 053 (0. 13)	− 0. 093** (0. 04)
Firm age	− 1. 937 (1. 23)	0. 133** (0. 06)	− 1. 036*** (0. 23)	− 0. 001 (0. 04)
Leverage	1. 510** (0. 61)	0. 764*** (0. 07)	− 0. 050 (0. 21)	0. 011 (0. 07)
Year fixed effects	Yes	Yes	Yes	Yes
Firm fixed effects	Yes	Yes	Yes	Yes
Observations	5601	5601	5505	5622
Adj. R^2	0. 044	0. 211	0. 093	0. 058

Note: This table reports the DID (panel data for 2002 − 2008 with fixed effects) regressions including interaction term $CV\_it \times dexp$ [columns (1), (2), (3), and (4)] to test whether the use of CV can enhance firm performance or value, using the sample constructed by the CEM method, where dummy variable dexp equals one from the treatment period if the difference of variable Exe_exp between the treatment period and pretreatment period is positive, and 1 otherwise. All outcome variables in the table are industry − adjusted (by subtracting the industry mean of the original variable, for example, the industry − adjusted Tobin's Q is defined as the common Tobin's Q minus its industry mean for each year). Standard errors (in parentheses) are heteroskedasticity consistent and clustered at the firm level. ***, **, and * denote significance at the 1%, 5%, and 10% levels, respectively.

Table B6   Second Shareholders' Representatives and

Firm Performance

Model	(1) Tobin's Q	(2) AMTB	(3) ROA	(4) ROE
Intercept	- 14. 461 (11. 43)	7. 522 *** (0. 75)	2. 902 (2. 67)	1. 806 ** (0. 90)
CV_it	0. 092 (0. 75)	- 0. 052 * (0. 03)	0. 123 (0. 13)	0. 009 (0. 03)
dsh2	1. 112 * (0. 62)	- 0. 000 (0. 09)	0. 648 (0. 53)	- 0. 013 (0. 16)
CV_it × dsh2	0. 625 (0. 92)	0. 080 (0. 11)	- 0. 842 (0. 58)	0. 044 (0. 17)
Sd	1. 237 (1. 36)	0. 017 (0. 06)	- 0. 077 (0. 20)	- 0. 176 ** (0. 08)
Fd	- 13. 925 (14. 45)	- 0. 021 (0. 11)	- 1. 277 (0. 90)	- 0. 062 (0. 31)
Firm size	0. 788 (0. 56)	- 0. 379 *** (0. 04)	- 0. 054 (0. 13)	- 0. 092 ** (0. 04)
Firm age	- 1. 942 (1. 23)	0. 132 ** (0. 06)	- 1. 032 *** (0. 23)	- 0. 001 (0. 04)
Leverage	1. 468 ** (0. 61)	0. 762 *** (0. 07)	- 0. 060 (0. 22)	0. 011 (0. 07)
Year fixed effects	Yes	Yes	Yes	Yes
Firm fixed effects	Yes	Yes	Yes	Yes
Observations	5601	5601	5505	5622
Adj. R^2	0. 044	0. 209	0. 093	0. 058

Note: This table reports the DID (panel data for 2002 – 2008 with fixed effects) regressions including interaction term $CV\_it \times dsh2$ [columns (1), (2), (3), and (4)] to test whether the use of CV can enhance firm performance or value, using the sample constructed by the CEM method, where dummy variable $dsh2$ equals one from the treatment period if the difference of variable $Share2$ between the treatment period and pretreatment period is positive, and 1 otherwise. All outcome variables in the table are industry – adjusted (by subtracting the industry mean of the original variable, for example, the industry – adjusted Tobin's Q is defined as the common Tobin's Q minus its industry mean for each year). Standard errors (in parentheses) are heteroskedasticity consistent and clustered at the firm level. *** , ** , and * denote significance at the 1% , 5% , and 10% levels, respectively.

Table B7   **Director Independence and Firm Performance**

Model	(1)	(2)	(3)	(4)
	Tobin's Q	AMTB	ROA	ROE
Intercept	-15.061	7.509 ***	2.816	1.830 **
	(11.53)	(0.75)	(2.66)	(0.89)
CV_it	0.594	-0.045	0.122	0.008
	(0.66)	(0.03)	(0.12)	(0.03)
drel	0.238	-0.128	-0.219	0.087
	(3.49)	(0.10)	(0.25)	(0.11)
CV_it × drel	-10.808	0.085	-0.893	0.085
	(9.80)	(0.11)	(0.67)	(0.30)
Sd	1.073	0.016	-0.085	-0.174 **
	(1.29)	(0.06)	(0.20)	(0.08)
Fd	-13.279	-0.021	-1.170	-0.074
	(14.58)	(0.11)	(0.91)	(0.31)
Firm size	0.806	-0.378 ***	-0.052	-0.093 **
	(0.57)	(0.04)	(0.13)	(0.04)
Firm age	-1.837	0.134 **	-1.010 ***	-0.004
	(1.24)	(0.06)	(0.23)	(0.04)
Leverage	1.593 ***	0.764 ***	-0.039	0.010
	(0.62)	(0.07)	(0.21)	(0.07)
Year fixed effects	Yes	Yes	Yes	Yes
Firm fixed effects	Yes	Yes	Yes	Yes
Observations	5601	5601	5505	5622
Adj. R^2	0.047	0.210	0.094	0.058

Note: This table reports the DID (panel data for 2002 – 2008 with fixed effects) regressions including interaction term $CV\_it \times drel$ [columns (1), (2), (3), and (4)] to test whether the use of CV can enhance firm performance or value, using the sample constructed by the CEM method, where dummy variable drel equals one from the treatment period if the difference of variable Exe_rel3 between the treatment period and pretreatment period is positive, and 1 otherwise. All outcome variables in the table are industry – adjusted (by subtracting the industry mean of the original variable, for example, the industry – adjusted Tobin's Q is defined as the common Tobin's Q minus its industry mean for each year). Standard errors (in parentheses) are heteroskedasticity consistent and clustered at the firm level. ***, **, and * denote significance at the 1%, 5%, and 10% levels, respectively.

Table B8   Professional Experience and Firm Performance

Model	(1) Tobin's Q	(2) AMTB	(3) ROA	(4) ROE
Intercept	−14.052 (11.55)	7.537 *** (0.76)	2.925 (2.67)	1.831 ** (0.89)
CV_it	0.279 (0.77)	−0.044 (0.03)	0.094 (0.13)	0.021 (0.03)
dpro5	−1.292 (1.84)	−0.082 (0.07)	−0.115 (0.26)	0.061 (0.10)
CV_it × dpro5	0.775 (2.31)	0.065 (0.09)	0.074 (0.33)	−0.111 (0.12)
Sd	1.246 (1.36)	0.017 (0.06)	−0.075 (0.20)	−0.175 ** (0.08)
Fd	−13.916 (14.44)	−0.024 (0.11)	−1.241 (0.90)	−0.064 (0.31)
Firm size	0.767 (0.57)	−0.379 *** (0.04)	−0.055 (0.13)	−0.093 ** (0.04)
Firm age	−1.933 (1.23)	0.132 ** (0.06)	−1.031 *** (0.23)	−0.001 (0.04)
Leverage	1.531 ** (0.61)	0.765 *** (0.07)	−0.048 (0.21)	0.010 (0.07)
Year fixed effects	Yes	Yes	Yes	Yes
Firm fixed effects	Yes	Yes	Yes	Yes
Observations	5601	5601	5505	5622
Adj. R^2	0.044	0.209	0.093	0.058

Note: This table reports the DID (panel data for 2002 – 2008 with fixed effects) regressions including interaction term $CV\_it \times dpro5$ [columns (1), (2), (3), and (4)] to test whether the use of CV can enhance firm performance or value, using the sample constructed by the CEM method, where dummy variable dpro5 equals one from the treatment period if the difference of variable Pro5 between the treatment period and pretreatment period is positive, and 1 otherwise. All outcome variables in the table are industry – adjusted (by subtracting the industry mean of the original variable, for example, the industry – adjusted Tobin's Q is defined as the common Tobin's Q minus its industry mean for each year). Standard errors (in parentheses) are heteroskedasticity consistent and clustered at the firm level. *** , ** , and * denote significance at the 1% , 5% , and 10% levels, respectively.

Table B9   **Academic Independent Directors and Firm Performance**

Model	(1)	(2)	(3)	(4)
	Tobin's Q	AMTB	ROA	ROE
Intercept	− 14. 044 (11. 49)	7. 535 *** (0. 75)	2. 957 (2. 66)	1. 810 ** (0. 89)
CV_it	0. 338 (0. 76)	− 0. 037 (0. 03)	0. 114 (0. 13)	0. 012 (0. 03)
dac	− 1. 488 (2. 13)	0. 119 (0. 13)	− 0. 393 ** (0. 16)	0. 010 (0. 08)
CV_it × dac	0. 401 (2. 69)	− 0. 151 (0. 13)	0. 119 (0. 20)	− 0. 007 (0. 10)
Sd	1. 258 (1. 36)	0. 017 (0. 06)	− 0. 071 (0. 20)	− 0. 176 ** (0. 08)
Fd	− 13. 925 (14. 44)	− 0. 023 (0. 11)	− 1. 246 (0. 90)	− 0. 064 (0. 31)
Firm size	0. 767 (0. 56)	− 0. 379 *** (0. 04)	− 0. 057 (0. 13)	− 0. 092 ** (0. 04)
Firm age	− 1. 946 (1. 23)	0. 131 ** (0. 06)	− 1. 034 *** (0. 23)	− 0. 001 (0. 04)
Leverage	1. 545 ** (0. 62)	0. 760 *** (0. 07)	− 0. 040 (0. 21)	0. 011 (0. 07)
Year fixed effects	Yes	Yes	Yes	Yes
Firm fixed effects	Yes	Yes	Yes	Yes
Observations	5601	5601	5505	5622
Adj. R^2	0. 044	0. 210	0. 093	0. 058

Note: This table reports the DID (panel data for 2002 – 2008 with fixed effects) regressions including interaction term $CV\_it \times dac$ [columns (1), (2), (3), and (4)] to test whether the use of CV can enhance firm performance or value, using the sample constructed by the CEM method, where dummy variable dac equals one from the treatment period if the difference of directors from academic world between the treatment period and pretreatment period is negative, and 1 otherwise. All outcome variables in the table are industry – adjusted (by subtracting the industry mean of the original variable, for example, the industry – adjusted Tobin's Q is defined as the common Tobin's Q minus its industry mean for each year). Standard errors (in parentheses) are heteroskedasticity consistent and clustered at the firm level. *** , ** , and * denote significance at the 1% , 5% , and 10% levels, respectively.

Table B10   Central Government Experience and Firm Performance

Model	(1)	(2)	(3)	(4)
	Tobin's Q	AMTB	ROA	ROE
Intercept	– 14. 364	7. 528 ***	2. 902	1. 815 **
	(11. 43)	(0. 75)	(2. 66)	(0. 89)
CV_it	0. 196	– 0. 042	0. 100	0. 012
	(0. 71)	(0. 03)	(0. 12)	(0. 03)
dpol1	– 1. 591	– 0. 059	– 0. 166	0. 207 *
	(2. 17)	(0. 07)	(0. 31)	(0. 11)
CV_it × dpol1	2. 629	0. 008	– 0. 117	– 0. 162
	(2. 49)	(0. 10)	(0. 36)	(0. 13)
Sd	1. 236	0. 016	– 0. 075	– 0. 175 **
	(1. 36)	(0. 06)	(0. 20)	(0. 08)
Fd	– 13. 901	– 0. 023	– 1. 242	– 0. 063
	(14. 44)	(0. 11)	(0. 90)	(0. 31)
Firm size	0. 783	– 0. 379 ***	– 0. 054	– 0. 093 **
	(0. 56)	(0. 04)	(0. 13)	(0. 04)
Firm age	– 1. 957	0. 132 **	– 1. 031 ***	– 0. 001
	(1. 24)	(0. 06)	(0. 23)	(0. 04)
Leverage	1. 517 **	0. 763 ***	– 0. 053	0. 013
	(0. 61)	(0. 07)	(0. 21)	(0. 07)
Year fixed effects	Yes	Yes	Yes	Yes
Firm fixed effects	Yes	Yes	Yes	Yes
Observations	5601	5601	5505	5622
Adj. R^2	0. 044	0. 209	0. 093	0. 058

Note: This table reports the DID (panel data for 2002 – 2008 with fixed effects) regressions including interaction term $CV\_it \times dpol1$ [columns (1), (2), (3), and (4)] to test whether the use of CV can enhance firm performance or value, using the sample constructed by the CEM method, where dummy variable $dpol1$ equals one from the treatment period if the difference of variable $Pol1$ for independent directors between the treatment period and pretreatment period is positive, and 1 otherwise. All outcome variables in the table are industry – adjusted (by subtracting the industry mean of the original variable, for example, the industry – adjusted Tobin's Q is defined as the common Tobin's Q minus its industry mean for each year). Standard errors (in parentheses) are heteroskedasticity consistent and clustered at the firm level. *** , ** , and * denote significance at the 1% , 5% , and 10% levels, respectively.

Table B11   **Political Connection and Firm Performance**

Model	(1)	(2)	(3)	(4)
	Tobin's Q	AMTB	ROA	ROE
Intercept	-14.099	7.532 ***	2.956	1.821 **
	(11.48)	(0.75)	(2.66)	(0.89)
CV_it	0.346	-0.042	0.124	0.018
	(0.73)	(0.03)	(0.13)	(0.03)
dpol7	-2.363	-0.074	-0.362 **	0.033
	(2.22)	(0.08)	(0.18)	(0.08)
CV_it × dpol7	0.388	0.028	-0.162	-0.096
	(3.23)	(0.10)	(0.27)	(0.13)
Sd	1.226	0.016	-0.078	-0.176 **
	(1.36)	(0.06)	(0.20)	(0.08)
Fd	-13.959	-0.025	-1.253	-0.065
	(14.44)	(0.11)	(0.90)	(0.31)
Firm size	0.772	-0.379 ***	-0.056	-0.093 **
	(0.56)	(0.04)	(0.13)	(0.04)
Firm age	-1.960	0.131 **	-1.038 ***	-0.001
	(1.23)	(0.06)	(0.23)	(0.04)
Leverage	1.474 **	0.763 ***	-0.058	0.010
	(0.62)	(0.07)	(0.21)	(0.07)
Year fixed effects	Yes	Yes	Yes	Yes
Firm fixed effects	Yes	Yes	Yes	Yes
Observations	5601	5601	5505	5622
Adj. R^2	0.044	0.209	0.094	0.058

Note: This table reports the DID (panel data for 2002 – 2008 with fixed effects) regressions including interaction term $CV\_it \times dpol7$ [columns (1), (2), (3), and (4)] to test whether the use of CV can enhance firm performance or value, using the sample constructed by the CEM method, where dummy variable $dpol7$ equals one from the treatment period if the difference of variable $Pol7$ for independent directors between the treatment period and pretreatment period is positive, and 1 otherwise. All outcome variables in the table are industry – adjusted (by subtracting the industry mean of the original variable, for example, the industry – adjusted Tobin's Q is defined as the common Tobin's Q minus its industry mean for each year). Standard errors (in parentheses) are heteroskedasticity consistent and clustered at the firm level. *** , ** , and * denote significance at the 1%, 5%, and 10% levels, respectively.

Table B12   **Firm Performance**

Model	(1)	(2)	(3)	(4)
	Tobin's Q	*AMTB*	*ROA*	*ROE*
Intercept	− 15. 786	5. 630	− 25. 218	0. 376
	(15. 74)	(11. 36)	(18. 84)	(0. 69)
CV_it	0. 339	− 0. 664 **	0. 309	0. 021
	(0. 80)	(0. 28)	(0. 99)	(0. 03)
Sd	2. 813	0. 718	1. 588	− 0. 051
	(1. 84)	(0. 59)	(2. 34)	(0. 06)
Fd	1. 773	3. 698	0. 744	− 0. 322
	(1. 76)	(3. 87)	(2. 16)	(0. 22)
Firm size	0. 737	− 0. 203	1. 287	− 0. 011
	(0. 73)	(0. 52)	(0. 85)	(0. 03)
Firm age	− 0. 694	0. 491	− 1. 269	− 0. 040
	(1. 37)	(0. 54)	(1. 93)	(0. 04)
Leverage	0. 865	− 0. 556	0. 819	− 0. 119 *
	(1. 10)	(0. 66)	(0. 93)	(0. 07)
Year fixed effect	Yes	Yes	Yes	Yes
Firm fixed effect	Yes	Yes	Yes	Yes
Observations	7342	7341	7210	7391
Adj. R^2	0. 047	0. 080	0. 050	0. 045

Note: This table reports the DID (panel data for 2002 – 2010 with fixed effects) regressions [columns (1), (2), (3), and (4)] to test whether the use of CV can enhance firm performance or value, using the (extended) sample constructed by the CEM method. All outcome variables in the table are industryadjusted (by subtracting the industry mean of the original variable, for example, the industryadjusted Tobin's Q is defined as the common Tobin's Q minus its industry mean for each year). Standard errors (in parentheses) are heteroskedasticity consistent and clustered at the firm level. ***, **, and * denote significance at the 1% , 5% , and 10% levels, respectively.

Table B13   **Firm Performance: Voluntary Group**

Model	(1)	(2)	(3)	(4)
	Tobin's Q	AMTB	ROA	ROE
Intercept	− 26. 576	34. 855 **	− 52. 776	0. 637
	(38. 47)	(16. 00)	(44. 24)	(1. 17)
CV_it	− 0. 197	− 0. 603	− 2. 068	0. 012
	(1. 87)	(0. 71)	(2. 39)	(0. 06)
Sd	− 1. 113	− 0. 588	− 2. 843	− 0. 036
	(2. 15)	(0. 77)	(3. 76)	(0. 08)
Fd	2. 235	5. 560	0. 494	− 0. 477
	(1. 80)	(5. 62)	(3. 49)	(0. 33)
Firm size	1. 296	− 1. 350 **	2. 635	− 0. 033
	(1. 90)	(0. 68)	(2. 07)	(0. 05)
Firm age	− 0. 211	− 0. 690	− 0. 710	0. 000
	(3. 43)	(2. 07)	(4. 91)	(0. 12)
Leverage	− 0. 477	− 2. 737 ***	1. 587	− 0. 008
	(1. 73)	(0. 65)	(1. 36)	(0. 11)
Year fixed effect	Yes	Yes	Yes	Yes
Firm fixed effect	Yes	Yes	Yes	Yes
Observations	2051	2051	2051	2088
Adj. R^2	0. 055	0. 074	0. 062	0. 067

Note: This table reports the DID (panel data for 2002 – 2010 with fixed effects) regressions [columns (1), (2), (3), and (4)] to test whether the use of CV can enhance firm performance or value, using the sub – sample with the percentage of shares held by the largest shareholder less than 30% from the (extended) sample constructed by the CEM method. All outcome variables in the table are industryadjusted (by subtracting the industry mean of the original variable, for example, the industryadjusted Tobin's Q is defined as the common Tobin's Q minus its industry mean for each year). Standard errors (in parentheses) are heteroskedasticity consistent and clustered at the firm level. ***, **, and * denote significance at the 1%, 5%, and 10% levels, respectively.

Table B14   Firm Performance: Regulatory Group

Model	(1)	(2)	(3)	(4)
	Tobin's Q	AMTB	ROA	ROE
Intercept	− 13. 595	− 4. 699	− 15. 453	0. 187
	(16. 72)	(14. 48)	(19. 71)	(0. 90)
CV_it	0. 637	− 0. 714 **	1. 348	0. 019
	(0. 84)	(0. 30)	(1. 01)	(0. 03)
Sd	4. 608 *	1. 116	4. 037	− 0. 067
	(2. 44)	(0. 77)	(2. 96)	(0. 08)
Fd	− 1. 217	− 1. 118	− 0. 837	− 0. 035
	(1. 35)	(1. 61)	(1. 84)	(0. 08)
Firm size	0. 593	0. 183	0. 839	0. 002
	(0. 76)	(0. 66)	(0. 88)	(0. 04)
Firm age	− 0. 876	0. 846 ***	− 1. 668	− 0. 044
	(1. 43)	(0. 29)	(1. 98)	(0. 03)
Leverage	1. 900	0. 802	0. 064	− 0. 217 **
	(1. 25)	(1. 03)	(1. 29)	(0. 10)
Year fixed effect	Yes	Yes	Yes	Yes
Firm fixed effect	Yes	Yes	Yes	Yes
Observations	5291	5290	5159	5303
Adj. R^2	0. 044	0. 094	0. 044	0. 037

Note: This table reports the DID (panel data for 2002 – 2010 with fixed effects) regressions [columns (1), (2), (3), and (4)] to test whether the use of CV can enhance firm performance or value, using the sub – sample with the percentage of shares held by the largest shareholder larger than or equal to 30% from the sample constructed by the CEM method. All outcome variables in the table are industry – adjusted (by subtracting the industry mean of the original variable, for example, the industry – adjusted Tobin's Q is defined as the common Tobin's Q minus its industry mean for each year). Standard errors (in parentheses) are heteroskedasticity consistent and clustered at the firm level. ***, **, and * denote significance at the 1%, 5%, and 10% levels, respectively.

Table B15 Propping – up and Tunneling Effects

Model	(1)	(2)	(3)	(4)
	TRPT	BRPT	HRPT	OAR
Intercept	3. 309 ***	0. 506 ***	2. 757 ***	0. 493 ***
	(0. 73)	(0. 18)	(0. 66)	(0. 14)
CV_it	0. 002	0. 010	− 0. 009	0. 003
	(0. 06)	(0. 01)	(0. 06)	(0. 00)
Firm size	− 0. 159 ***	− 0. 024 ***	− 0. 131 ***	− 0. 024 ***
	(0. 03)	(0. 01)	(0. 03)	(0. 01)
Leverage	0. 148 *	0. 011	0. 097	0. 133 ***
	(0. 08)	(0. 03)	(0. 08)	(0. 02)
Firm age	0. 031	0. 023 **	0. 018	0. 027 ***
	(0. 05)	(0. 01)	(0. 05)	(0. 01)
Duality	− 0. 058	0. 027 **	− 0. 069	− 0. 007
	(0. 07)	(0. 01)	(0. 07)	(0. 01)
Board size	0. 006	0. 001	0. 007	− 0. 001
	(0. 01)	(0. 00)	(0. 01)	(0. 00)
Board_ind	0. 150	− 0. 022	0. 145	− 0. 053 *
	(0. 22)	(0. 05)	(0. 20)	(0. 03)
MTB	− 0. 013	− 0. 003	− 0. 036	− 0. 009 **
	(0. 04)	(0. 00)	(0. 03)	(0. 00)
Sd	− 0. 038	− 0. 004	− 0. 051	0. 003
	(0. 08)	(0. 01)	(0. 08)	(0. 01)
Fd	− 0. 358	− 0. 002	− 0. 363	0. 027 **
	(0. 32)	(0. 01)	(0. 32)	(0. 01)
Shrcr1	0. 001	0. 000	0. 001	− 0. 000
	(0. 00)	(0. 00)	(0. 00)	(0. 00)
Year fixed effects	Yes	Yes	Yes	Yes
Firm fixed effects	Yes	Yes	Yes	Yes
Observations	5225	5225	5225	5514
Adj. R^2	0. 021	0. 031	0. 017	0. 149

Note: This table reports the DID (panel data for 2002 – 2008 with fixed effects) regressions [columns (1), (2), (3), and (4)] to test whether the use of CV can curb tunneling activities or promote propping – up activities, using the sample constructed by the CEM method. Standard errors (in parentheses) are heteroskedasticity consistent and clustered at the firm level. *** , ** , and * denote significance at the 1% , 5% , and 10% levels, respectively.

Table B16   Propping – up and Tunneling Effects: Voluntary Group

Model	(1)	(2)	(3)	(4)
	TRPT	BRPT	HRPT	OAR
Intercept	2. 185 *	0. 102	1. 841	0. 727 **
	(1. 32)	(0. 35)	(1. 19)	(0. 33)
CV_it	– 0. 005	0. 032 **	– 0. 029	0. 002
	(0. 08)	(0. 01)	(0. 08)	(0. 01)
Firm size	– 0. 118 *	0. 001	– 0. 106 *	– 0. 034 **
	(0. 06)	(0. 02)	(0. 06)	(0. 02)
Leverage	0. 264 *	0. 005	0. 233	0. 148 ***
	(0. 14)	(0. 05)	(0. 15)	(0. 04)
Firm age	– 0. 002	– 0. 009	0. 001	0. 031 **
	(0. 09)	(0. 02)	(0. 09)	(0. 01)
Duality	– 0. 097 *	0. 017	– 0. 119 **	– 0. 007
	(0. 06)	(0. 02)	(0. 06)	(0. 01)
Board size	0. 005	0. 004	0. 000	– 0. 000
	(0. 02)	(0. 00)	(0. 02)	(0. 00)
Board_ind	0. 325	– 0. 146 *	0. 473	– 0. 121
	(0. 32)	(0. 08)	(0. 30)	(0. 08)
MTB	0. 001	– 0. 010	0. 010	– 0. 010 *
	(0. 04)	(0. 01)	(0. 04)	(0. 01)
Sd	0. 079	0. 027	0. 030	– 0. 008
	(0. 07)	(0. 03)	(0. 06)	(0. 02)
Fd	– 0. 075	0. 006	– 0. 103	0. 021
	(0. 10)	(0. 02)	(0. 10)	(0. 02)
Shrcr1	0. 007	– 0. 002	0. 010 *	– 0. 001
	(0. 01)	(0. 00)	(0. 01)	(0. 00)
Year fixed effects	Yes	Yes	Yes	Yes
Firm fixed effects	Yes	Yes	Yes	Yes
Observations	1411	1411	1411	1543
Adj. R^2	0. 032	0. 034	0. 026	0. 182

Note: This table reports the DID (panel data for 2002 – 2008 with fixed effects) regressions [columns (1), (2), (3), and (4)] to test whether the use of CV can curb tunneling activities or promote propping – up activities, using the sub – sample with the percentage of shares held by the controlling shareholders less than 30% from the sample constructed by the CEM method. Standard errors (in parentheses) are heteroskedasticity consistent and clustered at the firm level. *** , ** , and * denote significance at the 1% , 5% , and 10% levels, respectively.

Table B17　　Propping – up and Tunneling Effects: Regulatory Group

Model	(1)	(2)	(3)	(4)
	TRPT	BRPT	HRPT	OAR
Intercept	3. 410 ***	0. 479 **	2. 966 ***	0. 445 **
	(1. 05)	(0. 22)	(0. 96)	(0. 17)
CV_it	− 0. 009	0. 001	− 0. 016	0. 003
	(0. 08)	(0. 01)	(0. 08)	(0. 00)
Firm size	− 0. 161 ***	− 0. 025 **	− 0. 135 ***	− 0. 021 **
	(0. 05)	(0. 01)	(0. 05)	(0. 01)
Leverage	0. 107	0. 029	0. 016	0. 125 ***
	(0. 11)	(0. 04)	(0. 10)	(0. 03)
Firm age	0. 018	0. 034 ***	0. 000	0. 029 ***
	(0. 07)	(0. 01)	(0. 06)	(0. 01)
Duality	− 0. 030	0. 027 *	− 0. 026	− 0. 004
	(0. 12)	(0. 01)	(0. 11)	(0. 01)
Board size	0. 006	0. 002	0. 006	− 0. 003 **
	(0. 02)	(0. 00)	(0. 02)	(0. 00)
Board_ind	0. 204	0. 021	0. 140	− 0. 023
	(0. 29)	(0. 05)	(0. 27)	(0. 03)
MTB	− 0. 009	0. 005	− 0. 067	− 0. 005
	(0. 08)	(0. 01)	(0. 05)	(0. 01)
Sd	− 0. 090	− 0. 016	− 0. 102	0. 003
	(0. 12)	(0. 02)	(0. 12)	(0. 01)
Fd	− 0. 896	− 0. 009	− 0. 894	0. 026
	(0. 85)	(0. 01)	(0. 84)	(0. 03)
Shrcr1	0. 002	0. 000	0. 001	− 0. 000
	(0. 00)	(0. 00)	(0. 00)	(0. 00)
Year fixed effects	Yes	Yes	Yes	Yes
Firm fixed effects	Yes	Yes	Yes	Yes
Observations	3814	3814	3814	3971
Adj. R^2	0. 020	0. 029	0. 018	0. 134

Note: This table reports the DID (panel data for 2002 – 2008 with fixed effects) regressions [columns (1), (2), (3), and (4)] to test whether the use of CV can curb tunneling activities, using the sub – sample with the percentage of shares held by the controlling shareholders equal to or more than 30% from the sample constructed by the CEM method. Standard errors (in parentheses) are heteroskedasticity consistent and clustered at the firm level. *** , ** , and * denote significance at the 1% , 5% , and 10% levels, respectively.

Table B18   Executive Experience and Propping – up and Tunneling Effects

Model	(1)	(2)	(3)	(4)
	TRPT	*BRPT*	*HRPT*	*OAR*
Intercept	3. 299 ***	0. 511 ***	2. 729 ***	0. 495 ***
	(0. 73)	(0. 18)	(0. 65)	(0. 14)
CV_it	0. 004	0. 002	0. 008	0. 002
	(0. 07)	(0. 01)	(0. 07)	(0. 00)
dexp	− 0. 036	− 0. 030 *	− 0. 013	− 0. 002
	(0. 05)	(0. 02)	(0. 05)	(0. 01)
CV_it × dexp	0. 017	0. 057 ***	− 0. 070	0. 008
	(0. 09)	(0. 02)	(0. 08)	(0. 01)
Firm size	− 0. 158 ***	− 0. 024 ***	− 0. 129 ***	− 0. 024 ***
	(0. 03)	(0. 01)	(0. 03)	(0. 01)
Leverage	0. 148 *	0. 011	0. 096	0. 133 ***
	(0. 08)	(0. 03)	(0. 08)	(0. 02)
Firm age	0. 031	0. 025 **	0. 017	0. 027 ***
	(0. 05)	(0. 01)	(0. 05)	(0. 01)
Duality	− 0. 058	0. 028 **	− 0. 070	− 0. 007
	(0. 07)	(0. 01)	(0. 07)	(0. 01)
Board size	0. 006	0. 001	0. 007	− 0. 001
	(0. 01)	(0. 00)	(0. 01)	(0. 00)
Board_ind	0. 150	− 0. 024	0. 149	− 0. 053 *
	(0. 22)	(0. 05)	(0. 20)	(0. 03)
MTB	− 0. 013	− 0. 003	− 0. 034	− 0. 009 **
	(0. 04)	(0. 00)	(0. 03)	(0. 00)
Sd	− 0. 039	− 0. 003	− 0. 052	0. 003
	(0. 08)	(0. 01)	(0. 08)	(0. 01)
Fd	− 0. 360	− 0. 002	− 0. 368	0. 027 **
	(0. 32)	(0. 01)	(0. 32)	(0. 01)
Shrcr1	0. 001	0. 000	0. 001	− 0. 000
	(0. 00)	(0. 00)	(0. 00)	(0. 00)
Year fixed effects	Yes	Yes	Yes	Yes
Firm fixed effects	Yes	Yes	Yes	Yes
Observations	5225	5225	5225	5514
Adj. R^2	0. 021	0. 032	0. 017	0. 149

Note: This table reports the DID (panel data for 2002 – 2008 with fixed effects) regressions with interaction term CV_it × dexp [columns (1), (2), (3), and (4)] to test whether the use of CV can curb tunneling activities or promote propping – up activities, using the sample constructed by the CEM method, where dummy variable *dexp* equals 1 from the treatment period if the difference of variable *Exe_exp* between the treatment period and pretreatment period is positive, and 1 otherwise. Standard errors (in parentheses) are heteroskedasticity consistent and clustered at the firm level. *** , ** , and * denote significance at the 1% , 5% , and 10% levels, respectively.

Table B19   **Second Shareholders' Representatives and**

Propping – up and Tunneling Effects

Model	(1)	(2)	(3)	(4)
	TRPT	BRPT	HRPT	OAR
Intercept	3. 311 ***	0. 505 ***	2. 759 ***	0. 493 ***
	(0. 73)	(0. 18)	(0. 66)	(0. 14)
CV_it	− 0. 003	0. 010	− 0. 009	0. 003
	(0. 06)	(0. 01)	(0. 06)	(0. 00)
dsh2	− 0. 063	0. 004	− 0. 080	− 0. 002
	(0. 08)	(0. 05)	(0. 06)	(0. 02)
CV_it × dsh2	0. 102	− 0. 011	0. 065	0. 004
	(0. 13)	(0. 06)	(0. 11)	(0. 02)
Firm size	− 0. 159 ***	− 0. 024 ***	− 0. 131 ***	− 0. 024 ***
	(0. 03)	(0. 01)	(0. 03)	(0. 01)
Leverage	0. 149 *	0. 011	0. 099	0. 133 ***
	(0. 08)	(0. 03)	(0. 08)	(0. 02)
Firm age	0. 032	0. 025 **	0. 018	0. 027 ***
	(0. 05)	(0. 01)	(0. 05)	(0. 01)
Duality	− 0. 058	0. 027 **	− 0. 069	− 0. 007
	(0. 07)	(0. 01)	(0. 07)	(0. 01)
Board size	0. 006	0. 001	0. 007	− 0. 001
	(0. 01)	(0. 00)	(0. 01)	(0. 00)
Board_ind	0. 152	− 0. 022	0. 150	− 0. 053
	(0. 22)	(0. 05)	(0. 20)	(0. 03)
MTB	− 0. 013	− 0. 003	− 0. 036	− 0. 009 **
	(0. 04)	(0. 00)	(0. 03)	(0. 00)
Sd	− 0. 038	− 0. 004	− 0. 051	0. 003
	(0. 08)	(0. 01)	(0. 08)	(0. 01)
Fd	− 0. 353	− 0. 003	− 0. 358	0. 027 **
	(0. 32)	(0. 01)	(0. 32)	(0. 01)
Shrcr1	0. 001	0. 000	0. 001	− 0. 000
	(0. 00)	(0. 00)	(0. 00)	(0. 00)
Year fixed effects	Yes	Yes	Yes	Yes
Firm fixed effects	Yes	Yes	Yes	Yes
Observations	5225	5225	5225	5514
Adj. R^2	0. 021	0. 030	0. 017	0. 149

Note: This table reports the DID (panel data for 2002 – 2008 with fixed effects) regressions with interaction term $CV\_it \times dsh2$ [columns (1), (2), (3), and (4)] to test whether the use of CV can curb tunneling activities, using the sample constructed by the CEM method, where dummy variable $dsh2$ equals 1 from the treatment period if the difference of variable $Share2$ between the treatment period and pre-treatment period is positive, and 1 otherwise. Standard errors (in parentheses) are heteroskedasticity consistent and clustered at the firm level. ***, **, and * denote significance at the 1%, 5%, and 10% levels, respectively.

Table B20   Director Independence and Propping – up and Tunneling Effects

Model	(1) TRPT	(2) BRPT	(3) HRPT	(4) OAR
Intercept	3.282*** (0.73)	0.510*** (0.18)	2.732*** (0.66)	0.497*** (0.14)
CV_it	0.008 (0.06)	0.008 (0.01)	−0.003 (0.06)	0.002 (0.00)
drel	−0.055 (0.06)	−0.013 (0.03)	−0.043 (0.05)	0.009 (0.01)
CV_it × drel	−0.160 (0.14)	0.070 (0.05)	−0.166* (0.10)	0.031 (0.05)
Firm size	−0.158*** (0.03)	−0.024*** (0.01)	−0.130*** (0.03)	−0.024*** (0.01)
Leverage	0.150* (0.08)	0.011 (0.03)	0.098 (0.08)	0.132*** (0.02)
Firm age	0.035 (0.05)	0.024** (0.01)	0.021 (0.05)	0.026*** (0.01)
Duality	−0.059 (0.07)	0.028** (0.01)	−0.070 (0.07)	−0.007 (0.01)
Board size	0.006 (0.01)	0.001 (0.00)	0.006 (0.01)	−0.001 (0.00)
Board_ind	0.155 (0.22)	−0.023 (0.05)	0.150 (0.20)	−0.054* (0.03)
MTB	−0.013 (0.04)	−0.003 (0.00)	−0.036 (0.03)	−0.008** (0.00)
Sd	−0.042 (0.08)	−0.003 (0.01)	−0.054 (0.08)	0.004 (0.01)
Fd	−0.344 (0.33)	−0.006 (0.01)	−0.350 (0.32)	0.027** (0.01)
Shrcr1	0.001 (0.00)	0.000 (0.00)	0.001 (0.00)	−0.000 (0.00)
Year fixed effects	Yes	Yes	Yes	Yes
Firm fixed effects	Yes	Yes	Yes	Yes
Observations	5225	5225	5225	5514
Adj. R^2	0.021	0.031	0.017	0.150

Note: This table reports the DID (panel data for 2002 – 2008 with fixed effects) regressions with interaction term $CV\_it \times drel$ [columns (1), (2), (3), and (4)] to test whether the use of CV can curb tunneling activities, using the sample constructed by the CEM method, where dummy variable *drel* equals 1 from the treatment period if the difference of variable *Exe_rel*3 between the treatment period and pretreatment period is positive, and 1 otherwise. Standard errors (in parentheses) are heteroskedasticity consistent and clustered at the firm level. ***, **, and * denote significance at the 1%, 5%, and 10% levels, respectively.

Table B21 Professional Experience and Propping – up and Tunneling Effects

Model	(1) TRPT	(2) BRPT	(3) HRPT	(4) OAR
Intercept	3.339 *** (0.74)	0.497 *** (0.18)	2.800 *** (0.67)	0.499 *** (0.14)
CV_it	0.012 (0.06)	0.005 (0.01)	0.007 (0.06)	0.005 (0.00)
dpro5	−0.071 (0.09)	−0.027 (0.03)	−0.040 (0.06)	−0.013 (0.01)
CV_it × dpro5	−0.017 (0.12)	0.058 (0.04)	−0.090 (0.10)	0.001 (0.02)
Firm size	−0.160 *** (0.04)	−0.024 *** (0.01)	−0.133 *** (0.03)	−0.024 *** (0.01)
Leverage	0.150 * (0.08)	0.011 (0.03)	0.098 (0.08)	0.133 *** (0.02)
Firm age	0.032 (0.06)	0.025 ** (0.01)	0.019 (0.05)	0.027 *** (0.01)
Duality	−0.059 (0.07)	0.027 ** (0.01)	−0.070 (0.07)	−0.007 (0.01)
Board size	0.006 (0.01)	0.001 (0.00)	0.007 (0.01)	−0.001 (0.00)
Board_ind	0.162 (0.22)	−0.024 (0.05)	0.160 (0.20)	−0.052 (0.03)
MTB	−0.013 (0.04)	−0.003 (0.00)	−0.036 (0.03)	−0.009 ** (0.00)
Sd	−0.037 (0.08)	−0.004 (0.01)	−0.050 (0.08)	0.003 (0.01)
Fd	−0.359 (0.32)	−0.002 (0.01)	−0.366 (0.32)	0.027 ** (0.01)
Shrcr1	0.001 (0.00)	0.000 (0.00)	0.001 (0.00)	−0.000 (0.00)
Year fixed effects	Yes	Yes	Yes	Yes
Firm fixed effects	Yes	Yes	Yes	Yes
Observations	5225	5225	5225	5514
Adj. R^2	0.021	0.031	0.017	0.149

Note: This table reports the DID (panel data for 2002 – 2008 with fixed effects) regressions with interaction term CV_it × dpro5 [columns (1), (2), (3), and (4)] to test whether the use of CV can curb tunneling activities, using the sample constructed by the CEM method, where dummy variable dpro5 equals 1 from the treatment period if the difference of variable Pro5 for independent directors between the treatment period and pretreatment period is positive, and 1 otherwise. Standard errors (in parentheses) are heteroskedasticity consistent and clustered at the firm level. *** , ** , and * denote significance at the 1% , 5% , and 10% levels, respectively.

Table B22   Academic Independent Directors and

Propping – up and Tunneling Effects

Model	(1)	(2)	(3)	(4)
	TRPT	BRPT	HRPT	OAR
Intercept	3. 334 ***	0. 509 ***	2. 789 ***	0. 496 ***
	(0. 74)	(0. 19)	(0. 67)	(0. 14)
CV_it	0. 012	0. 011	0. 003	0. 005
	(0. 06)	(0. 01)	(0. 06)	(0. 00)
dac	− 0. 079	− 0. 003	− 0. 081	− 0. 008
	(0. 11)	(0. 05)	(0. 08)	(0. 02)
CV_it × dac	− 0. 018	− 0. 009	− 0. 040	− 0. 005
	(0. 13)	(0. 05)	(0. 10)	(0. 02)
Firm size	− 0. 160 ***	− 0. 024 ***	− 0. 132 ***	0. 024 ***
	(0. 04)	(0. 01)	(0. 03)	(0. 01)
Leverage	0. 150 *	0. 011	0. 099	0. 133 ***
	(0. 08)	(0. 03)	(0. 08)	(0. 02)
Firm age	0. 031	0. 025 **	0. 017	0. 027 ***
	(0. 05)	(0. 01)	(0. 05)	(0. 01)
Duality	− 0. 059	0. 027 **	− 0. 070	− 0. 007
	(0. 07)	(0. 01)	(0. 07)	(0. 01)
Board size	0. 006	0. 001	0. 007	− 0. 001
	(0. 01)	(0. 00)	(0. 01)	(0. 00)
Board_ind	0. 161	− 0. 021	0. 159	− 0. 052
	(0. 22)	(0. 05)	(0. 20)	(0. 03)
MTB	− 0. 013	− 0. 003	− 0. 036	− 0. 009 **
	(0. 04)	(0. 00)	(0. 03)	(0. 00)
Sd	− 0. 037	− 0. 003	− 0. 049	0. 003
	(0. 08)	(0. 01)	(0. 08)	(0. 01)
Fd	− 0. 359	− 0. 002	− 0. 365	0. 027 **
	(0. 32)	(0. 01)	(0. 32)	(0. 01)
Shrcr1	0. 001	0. 000	0. 001	− 0. 000
	(0. 00)	(0. 00)	(0. 00)	(0. 00)
Year fixed effects	Yes	Yes	Yes	Yes
Firm fixed effects	Yes	Yes	Yes	Yes
Observations	5225	5225	5225	5514
Adj. R^2	0. 021	0. 030	0. 017	0. 149

Note: This table reports the DID (panel data for 2002 – 2008 with fixed effects) regressions with interaction term $CV\_it \times dac$ [columns (1), (2), (3), and (4)] to test whether the use of CV can curb tunneling activities, using the sample constructed by the CEM method, where dummy variable dac equals 1 from the treatment period if the difference of variable *Academy* for independent directors between the treatment period and pretreatment period is positive, and 1 otherwise. Standard errors (in parentheses) are heteroskedasticity consistent and clustered at the firm level. ***, **, and * denote significance at the 1%, 5%, and 10% levels, respectively.

Table B23 **Central Government Experience and Propping – up and Tunneling Effects**

Model	(1) TRPT	(2) BRPT	(3) HRPT	(4) OAR
Intercept	3. 320 *** (0.73)	0. 503 *** (0.18)	2. 766 *** (0.66)	0. 494 *** (0.14)
CV_it	0. 008 (0.06)	0. 009 (0.01)	− 0. 004 (0.06)	0. 004 (0.00)
dpol1	− 0. 028 (0.05)	0. 017 (0.02)	− 0. 048 (0.05)	− 0. 008 (0.02)
CV_it × dpol1	− 0. 146 (0.14)	0. 021 (0.05)	− 0. 102 (0.10)	− 0. 000 (0.02)
Firm size	− 0. 159 *** (0.04)	− 0. 024 *** (0.01)	− 0. 131 *** (0.03)	− 0. 024 *** (0.01)
Leverage	0. 146 * (0.08)	0. 011 (0.03)	0. 095 (0.08)	0. 133 *** (0.02)
Firm age	0. 033 (0.05)	0. 025 ** (0.01)	0. 019 (0.05)	0. 027 *** (0.01)
Duality	− 0. 059 (0.07)	0. 028 ** (0.01)	− 0. 070 (0.07)	− 0. 007 (0.01)
Board size	0. 006 (0.01)	0. 001 (0.00)	0. 007 (0.01)	− 0. 001 (0.00)
Board_ind	0. 142 (0.22)	− 0. 020 (0.05)	0. 138 (0.20)	− 0. 054 * (0.03)
MTB	− 0. 013 (0.04)	− 0. 003 (0.00)	− 0. 036 (0.03)	− 0. 009 ** (0.00)
Sd	− 0. 038 (0.08)	− 0. 004 (0.01)	− 0. 051 (0.08)	0. 003 (0.01)
Fd	− 0. 359 (0.32)	− 0. 002 (0.01)	− 0. 364 (0.32)	0. 027 ** (0.01)
Shrcr1	0. 001 (0.00)	0. 000 (0.00)	0. 001 (0.00)	− 0. 000 (0.00)
Year fixed effects	Yes	Yes	Yes	Yes
Firm fixed effects	Yes	Yes	Yes	Yes
Observations	5225	5225	5225	5514
Adj. R^2	0. 021	0. 031	0. 017	0. 149

Note: This table reports the DID (panel data for 2002 – 2008 with fixed effects) regressions with interaction term $CV\_it \times dpol1$ [columns (1), (2), (3), and (4)] to test whether the use of CV can curb tunneling activities, using the sample constructed by the CEM method, where dummy variable *dpol*1 equals 1 from the treatment period if the difference of variable *Pol*1 for independent directors between the treatment period and pretreatment period is positive, and 1 otherwise. Standard errors (in parentheses) are heteroskedasticity consistent and clustered at the firm level. ***, **, and * denote significance at the 1%, 5%, and 10% levels, respectively.

Table B24　　**Political Connection and Propping – up**

and Tunneling Effects

Model	(1)	(2)	(3)	(4)
	TRPT	*BRPT*	*HRPT*	*OAR*
Intercept	3. 304 ***	0. 491 ***	2. 772 ***	0. 491 ***
	(0. 74)	(0. 18)	(0. 66)	(0. 14)
CV_it	0. 000	0. 005	− 0. 004	0. 002
	(0. 06)	(0. 01)	(0. 06)	(0. 00)
dpol7	− 0. 011	0. 007	− 0. 024	− 0. 002
	(0. 09)	(0. 03)	(0. 07)	(0. 01)
CV_it × dpol7	0. 030	0. 055	− 0. 042	0. 015
	(0. 14)	(0. 04)	(0. 12)	(0. 02)
Firm size	− 0. 158 ***	− 0. 024 ***	− 0. 132 ***	− 0. 023 ***
	(0. 04)	(0. 01)	(0. 03)	(0. 01)
Leverage	0. 149 *	0. 012	0. 095	0. 133 ***
	(0. 08)	(0. 03)	(0. 08)	(0. 02)
Firm age	0. 031	0. 025 **	0. 017	0. 027 ***
	(0. 05)	(0. 01)	(0. 05)	(0. 01)
Duality	− 0. 058	0. 028 **	− 0. 069	− 0. 007
	(0. 07)	(0. 01)	(0. 07)	(0. 01)
Board size	0. 006	0. 001	0. 007	− 0. 001
	(0. 01)	(0. 00)	(0. 01)	(0. 00)
Board_ind	0. 150	− 0. 022	0. 145	− 0. 053 *
	(0. 22)	(0. 05)	(0. 20)	(0. 03)
MTB	− 0. 013	− 0. 003	− 0. 036	− 0. 009 **
	(0. 04)	(0. 00)	(0. 03)	(0. 00)
Sd	− 0. 038	− 0. 003	− 0. 052	0. 003
	(0. 08)	(0. 01)	(0. 08)	(0. 01)
Fd	− 0. 357	− 0. 001	− 0. 364	0. 027 **
	(0. 32)	(0. 01)	(0. 32)	(0. 01)
Shrcr1	0. 001	0. 000	0. 001	− 0. 000
	(0. 00)	(0. 00)	(0. 00)	(0. 00)
Year fixed effects	Yes	Yes	Yes	Yes
Firm fixed effects	Yes	Yes	Yes	Yes
Observations	5225	5225	5225	5514
Adj. R^2	0. 021	0. 032	0. 017	0. 149

Note: This table reports the DID (panel data for 2002 – 2008 with fixed effects) regressions with interaction term $CV\_it \times dpol7$ [columns (1), (2), (3), and (4)] to test whether the use of CV can curb tunneling activities, using the sample constructed by the CEM method, where dummy variable *dpol7* equals 1 from the treatment period if the difference of variable *Pol7* for independent directors between the treatment period and pretreatment period is positive, and 1 otherwise. Standard errors (in parentheses) are heteroskedasticity consistent and clustered at the firm level. ***, **, and * denote significance at the 1%, 5%, and 10% levels, respectively.

Table B25   **Tunneling Effect**

Model	(1)	(2)	(3)	(4)
	TRPT	BRPT	HRPT	OAR
Intercept	3.054 ***	-488.929	1.609 ***	-0.052
	(0.68)	(487.99)	(0.49)	(0.13)
CV_it	-0.017	26.076	-0.019	-0.001
	(0.04)	(25.98)	(0.04)	(0.00)
Firm size	-0.161 ***	15.513	-0.090 ***	0.003
	(0.03)	(15.34)	(0.02)	(0.01)
Leverage	0.144 *	35.635	0.121 *	0.107 ***
	(0.08)	(35.61)	(0.07)	(0.02)
Firm age	0.120 ***	-16.545	0.093 **	0.034 ***
	(0.04)	(16.48)	(0.04)	(0.00)
Duality	-0.033	0.472	-0.050	-0.007
	(0.04)	(1.68)	(0.04)	(0.01)
Board size	0.010	7.459	0.013	-0.002
	(0.01)	(7.47)	(0.01)	(0.00)
Board_ind	0.107	141.157	0.132	-0.079 **
	(0.38)	(141.95)	(0.33)	(0.03)
MTB	0.007	0.855	0.002	0.000
	(0.01)	(0.86)	(0.00)	(0.00)
Sd	-0.053	1.526	-0.058	-0.000
	(0.06)	(2.14)	(0.05)	(0.01)
Fd	-0.064	-19.152	0.095	0.001
	(0.11)	(22.70)	(0.12)	(0.02)
Shrcr1	0.294	102.874	0.151	-0.039
	(0.20)	(102.57)	(0.16)	(0.04)
Year fixed effect	Yes	Yes	Yes	Yes
Firm fixed effect	Yes	Yes	Yes	Yes
Observations	6453	6414	6453	6701
Adj. R^2	0.018	0.001	0.012	0.139

Note: This table reports the DID (panel data for 2002 – 2010 with fixed effects) regressions [columns (1), (2), (3), and (4)] for testing whether the use of CV can curb tunneling activities, using the (extended) sample constructed by the CEM method. Standard errors (in parentheses) are heteroskedasticity consistent and clustered at the firm level. ***, **, and * denote significance at the 1%, 5%, and 10% levels, respectively.

Table B26   **Tunneling Effect: Voluntary Group**

Model	(1)	(2)	(3)	(4)
	TRPT	BRPT	HRPT	OAR
Intercept	2.845 **	-0.169	1.177	-0.218
	(1.30)	(0.62)	(1.05)	(0.23)
CV_it	0.034	0.003	0.007	-0.005
	(0.06)	(0.03)	(0.05)	(0.01)
Firm size	-0.156 **	0.040	-0.082	0.012
	(0.07)	(0.03)	(0.05)	(0.01)
Leverage	0.173	-0.016	0.183	0.104 ***
	(0.14)	(0.04)	(0.13)	(0.03)
Firm age	0.113	0.043	0.087	0.040 ***
	(0.09)	(0.07)	(0.07)	(0.01)
Duality	-0.026	-0.030	-0.057	-0.014
	(0.08)	(0.04)	(0.06)	(0.01)
Board size	0.018	-0.006	0.012	0.001
	(0.02)	(0.01)	(0.01)	(0.00)
Board_ind	-0.058	-0.319	0.145	-0.156 **
	(0.56)	(0.28)	(0.52)	(0.07)
MTB	0.011	-0.003	0.004	-0.000
	(0.01)	(0.00)	(0.01)	(0.00)
Sd	0.066	0.015	0.027	-0.009
	(0.04)	(0.07)	(0.04)	(0.01)
Fd	0.041	-0.044	0.027	-0.011
	(0.08)	(0.14)	(0.06)	(0.02)
Shrcr1	0.094	-0.394	0.760 **	-0.169 **
	(0.50)	(0.37)	(0.38)	(0.08)
Year fixed effect	Yes	Yes	Yes	Yes
Firm fixed effect	Yes	Yes	Yes	Yes
Observations	1775	1766	1775	1888
Adj. R^2	0.036	0.028	0.017	0.146

Note: This table reports the DID (panel data for 2002 – 2010 with fixed effects) regressions [columns (1), (2), (3), and (4)] for exploring whether the use of CV can curb tunneling activities, using the sub – sample with the percentage of shares held by the controlling shareholders less than 30% from the (extended) sample constructed by the CEM method. Standard errors (in parentheses) are heteroskedasticity consistent and clustered at the firm level. ***, **, and * denote significance at the 1%, 5%, and 10% levels, respectively.

Table B27 **Tunneling Effect: Regulatory Group**

Model	(1)	(2)	(3)	(4)
	TRPT	BRPT	HRPT	OAR
Intercept	2.731 ***	−585.678	1.445 **	0.051
	(0.80)	(584.47)	(0.58)	(0.17)
CV_it	−0.034	35.563	−0.028	0.001
	(0.05)	(35.42)	(0.05)	(0.00)
Firm size	−0.146 ***	17.441	−0.080 ***	−0.002
	(0.04)	(17.27)	(0.03)	(0.01)
Leverage	0.115	55.841	0.050	0.119 ***
	(0.11)	(56.30)	(0.07)	(0.03)
Firm age	0.131 **	22.475	0.103 **	0.030 ***
	(0.05)	(22.36)	(0.04)	(0.00)
Duality	−0.028	2.211	−0.041	−0.004
	(0.05)	(3.47)	(0.05)	(0.01)
Board size	0.011	9.443	0.016	−0.003 **
	(0.02)	(9.47)	(0.02)	(0.00)
Board_ind	0.279	188.969	0.186	−0.050
	(0.47)	(190.36)	(0.42)	(0.04)
MTB	0.007	1.211	0.001	0.000
	(0.01)	(1.22)	(0.01)	(0.00)
Sd	−0.098	0.910	−0.097	0.004
	(0.08)	(2.49)	(0.08)	(0.01)
Fd	−0.336	−70.831	0.381	−0.000
	(0.27)	(74.97)	(0.26)	(0.02)
Shrcr1	0.238	120.488	0.062	−0.027
	(0.22)	(120.11)	(0.18)	(0.05)
Year fixed effect	Yes	Yes	Yes	Yes
Firm fixed effect	Yes	Yes	Yes	Yes
Observations	4678	4648	4678	4813
Adj. R^2	0.014	0.001	0.010	0.155

Note: This table reports the DID (panel data from 2002 to 2010 with fixed effects) regressions [columns (1), (2), (3), and (4)] for examining whether the use of CV can curb tunneling activities, using the sub-sample with the percentage of shares held by the controlling shareholders equal to or more than 30% from the (extended) sample constructed by the CEM method. Standard errors (in parentheses) are heteroskedasticity consistent and clustered at the firm level. ***, **, and * denote significance at the 1%, 5%, and 10% levels, respectively.

234

Table B28   **CV and Other Corporate Policies**

Model	(1)	(2)	(3)
	Compen	*ALeverage*	*Acapex*
Intercept	6. 384 ***	− 0. 439	− 14. 806 ***
	(0. 81)	(0. 39)	(3. 03)
CV_it	− 0. 009	0. 010	0. 021
	(0. 05)	(0. 01)	(0. 05)
ROA_t − 1	0. 051		
	(0. 11)		
Firm size	0. 295 ***	0. 019	0. 699 ***
	(0. 04)	(0. 02)	(0. 15)
Leverage	− 0. 334 ***		− 0. 152
	(0. 09)		(0. 31)
MTB	0. 025	0. 088 ***	− 0. 009
	(0. 02)	(0. 02)	(0. 10)
Duality	0. 007		
	(0. 06)		
Board size	0. 009		
	(0. 01)		
Board_ind	0. 058		
	(0. 22)		
Sd	0. 076 *	0. 007	
	(0. 05)	(0. 02)	
Fd	0. 389	0. 003	
	(0. 28)	(0. 02)	
*Shrcr*1	− 0. 003		
	(0. 00)		
Profit		− 0. 102 ***	
		(0. 04)	
Cratio		− 0. 310 ***	
		(0. 07)	
Liquidity		− 0. 019 ***	
		(0. 01)	
Cflow			− 0. 239
			(0. 20)
Year fixed effect	Yes	Yes	Yes

continued

Model	(1)	(2)	(3)
	Compen	ALeverage	Acapex
Firm fixed effect	Yes	Yes	Yes
Observations	5186	5541	5112
Adj. R^2	0. 288	0. 171	0. 055

Note: This table reports the DID (panel data for 2002 – 2008 with fixed effects) regressions [columns (1), (2), and (3)] to test whether the use of CV can change corporate policy, using the sample constructed by the CEM method. Variable *Compen* is logarithm of the sum of the compensation of the top three executives; variable *Aleverage* is industry – adjusted (by subtracting industry mean) Leverage that is defined as long term debt divided by total assets; and variable *Acapex* is industry – adjusted (by subtracting industry mean) capital expenditure that equals the ratio of capital expenditure to total assets. *ROA_t – 1* is return of asset with order of lag one. *Profit* is operating profit deflated by total assets. *Cratio* is cash divided by total assets. *Liquidity* is the ratio of total current assets divided by total current liabilities. *Cflow* is defined as pre – tax profit plus depreciation divided by total assets. All results on firm *Leverage*, cash holdings, and capital expenditure exclude finance industry. Standard errors (in parentheses) are heteroskedasticity consistent and clustered at the firm level. ***, **, and * denote significance at the 1%, 5%, and 10% levels, respectively.

Table B29   CV and Other Corporate Policies

Model	(1)	(2)	(3)
	Compen	ALeverage	Acapex
Intercept	9. 420 ***	0. 555	– 12. 305 ***
	(1. 09)	(0. 42)	(2. 19)
CV_it	– 0. 0412	0. 002	0. 001
	(0. 03)	(0. 01)	(0. 03)
ROA_t – 1	0. 219 *		
	(0. 12)		
Firm size	0. 199 ***	– 0. 019	0. 548 ***
	(0. 05)	(0. 02)	(0. 10)
Leverage	– 0. 265 ***		– 0. 039
	(0. 09)		(0. 40)
MTB	– 0. 001	– 0. 009 ***	0. 005
	(0. 00)	(0. 00)	(0. 03)
Duality	0. 050		
	(0. 05)		

continued

Model	(1)	(2)	(3)
	Compen	*ALeverage*	*Acapex*
Board size	0. 022 *		
	(0. 01)		
Board_ind	− 0. 271		
	(0. 41)		
Sd	0. 003	0. 005	
	(0. 04)	(0. 02)	
Fd	0. 397	− 0. 070	
	(0. 30)	(0. 07)	
Shrcr1	0. 307		
	(0. 36)		
Profit		− 0. 122 ***	
		(0. 03)	
Cratio		− 0. 237 ***	
		(0. 07)	
Liquidity		− 0. 018 ***	
		(0. 01)	
Cflow			− 0. 023
			(0. 12)
Year fixed effect	Yes	Yes	Yes
Firm fixed effect	Yes	Yes	Yes
Observations	5770	7253	6804
Adj. R^2	0. 05	0. 12	0. 02

Note: This table reports the DID (panel data from 2002 to 2010 with fixed effects) regressions [columns (1), (2), and (3)] to test whether the use of CV can change corporate policy, using the (extended) sample constructed by the CEM method. Variable *Compen* is logarithm of the sum of the compensation of the top three executives; variable *Aleverage* is industry – adjusted (by subtracting industry mean) Leverage that is defined as long term debt divided by total assets; and variable *Acapex* is industry – adjusted (by subtracting industry mean) capital expenditure that equals the ratio of capital expenditure to total assets. $ROA\_t - 1$ is return of asset with order of lag one. *Profit* is operating profit deflated by total assets. *Cratio* is cash divided by total assets. *Liquidity* is the ratio of total current assets divided by total current liabilities. *Cflow* is defined as pre – tax profit plus depreciation divided by total assets. All results on firm *Leverage*, cash holdings, and capital expenditure exclude finance industry. Standard errors (in parentheses) are heteroskedasticity consistent and clustered at the firm level. ***, **, and * denote significance at the 1%, 5%, and 10% levels, respectively.

Appendix C   Additional Tables and Results
Based on the Alternative
Equity Valuation Measure

C. 1   Results from Balanced Panel data
Based on Equity Valuation Measure
used in the Body Text

This section reports all relevant estimate results based on the balanced panel data-set consisting of 312 firm – year observations, based on the equity measure discussed in details in the body text.

Table C1   Corporate Governance and Market Valuation from
Different Types of Investors: Sub – Sample Case (Balanced Panel)

	(1)	(2)	(3)	(4)	(5)	(6)
	htq (fe)	atq (fe)	htq (re)	atq (re)	tqr (fe)	tqr (re)
sh1	– 3. 6293*	1. 7663	1. 1023	– 1. 2666	– 3. 7407***	1. 7379
	(2. 072)	(1. 258)	(1. 238)	(1. 077)	(1. 226)	(1. 061)
sh1_sq	1. 6826	– 1. 3509	– 1. 5889	1. 1227	2. 0132*	– 2. 0319*
	(1. 709)	(1. 010)	(1. 359)	(1. 157)	(0. 984)	(1. 159)
b_ind	0. 8172	0. 4943	0. 6391	0. 0079	0. 2803	0. 4605**
	(0. 700)	(0. 420)	(0. 447)	(0. 232)	(0. 308)	(0. 213)
cstr2_10	0. 4828**	0. 1877*	0. 1412*	– 0. 0078	0. 3179*	0. 0959*
	(0. 223)	(0. 097)	(0. 073)	(0. 044)	(0. 157)	(0. 056)
cs	0. 0073	0. 0543	– 0. 0433	– 0. 0353*	– 0. 0126	– 0. 0049
	(0. 049)	(0. 065)	(0. 031)	(0. 020)	(0. 034)	(0. 018)
os	0. 5222	0. 4384	0. 8909*	0. 4288**	0. 0976	0. 3983
	(0. 610)	(0. 289)	(0. 460)	(0. 181)	(0. 294)	(0. 266)

continued

	(1)	(2)	(3)	(4)	(5)	(6)
	htq (fe)	atq (fe)	htq (re)	atq (re)	tqr (fe)	tqr (re)
fsize	0.2020 *	0.2608 **	0.0569 **	− 0.0777 ***	0.0376	0.0967 ***
	(0.110)	(0.115)	(0.026)	(0.020)	(0.089)	(0.019)
age	0.0104	− 0.1187 ***	0.0264 **	− 0.0186 *	0.0734 ***	0.0330 ***
	(0.025)	(0.035)	(0.013)	(0.011)	(0.024)	(0.010)
lev	− 0.4883	− 1.5578 ***	− 0.0779	− 0.5199 ***	0.4620	0.2971
	(0.339)	(0.327)	(0.251)	(0.173)	(0.273)	(0.186)
dual			− 0.0384	0.0188		− 0.0459
			(0.079)	(0.050)		(0.070)
Intercept	− 1.0766	− 3.2202	− 0.4031	3.6792 ***	1.2446	− 1.9748 ***
	(2.404)	(2.565)	(0.546)	(0.590)	(1.924)	(0.458)
N	78	78	78	78	78	78
r2_w	0.409	0.556	0.364	0.366	0.595	0.520
r2_b	0.080	0.013	0.339	0.613	0.082	0.433
r2_o	0.105	0.001	0.343	0.485	0.005	0.453

Note: This table reports the regression results from both the fixed effects and the random effects models, based on a sub – sample consisting of all observations in the period 2002 – 2004 from the balanced sample. "fe" and "re" in parentheses denote the fixed effect and the random effect models, respectively. $r2\_w$, $r2\_b$, and $r2\_o$ represent within, between, and overall R – squared, respectively. Standard errors (in parentheses) are heteroskedasticity consistent and clustered at the firm level. ***, **, and * denote significance at the 1%, 5%, and 10% levels, respectively.

Table C2 Corporate Governance and Market Valuation from Different Types of Investors: Full Sample Case (Balanced Panel) without Year Fixed Effects

	(1)	(2)	(3)	(4)	(5)	(6)
	htq (fe)	atq (fe)	htq (re)	atq (re)	tqr (fe)	tqr (re)
sh1	− 1.7223	− 1.1879	− 1.7108	− 3.5100	0.0209	0.5107
	(2.291)	(2.332)	(2.149)	(2.610)	(0.983)	(1.032)
sh1_sq	1.5294	0.7067	1.4606	3.0684	0.2373	− 0.3732
	(2.153)	(2.389)	(2.017)	(2.742)	(1.022)	(1.054)

continued

	(1)	(2)	(3)	(4)	(5)	(6)
	htq (fe)	atq (fe)	htq (re)	atq (re)	tqr (fe)	tqr (re)
dual	0. 1403 ***	0. 4951 ***	0. 1246 ***	0. 4542 ***	− 0. 0719	− 0. 0782 *
	(0. 046)	(0. 163)	(0. 044)	(0. 168)	(0. 046)	(0. 043)
b_ind	0. 4627	0. 4225	0. 5593	1. 1292 *	0. 2824	0. 1465
	(0. 471)	(0. 546)	(0. 399)	(0. 643)	(0. 216)	(0. 253)
cstr2_10	0. 0018	− 0. 1106	0. 0212	− 0. 0433	0. 0206	0. 0163
	(0. 043)	(0. 105)	(0. 041)	(0. 061)	(0. 031)	(0. 028)
cs	− 0. 0450 *	0. 0497	0. 0134 ***	0. 0566 **	− 0. 0137	− 0. 0026
	(0. 024)	(0. 046)	(0. 016)	(0. 024)	(0. 009)	(0. 006)
os	0. 8576 ***	0. 8020 **	0. 8354 ***	0. 4487 *	0. 1336	0. 2609 **
	(0. 206)	(0. 354)	(0. 188)	(0. 272)	(0. 123)	(0. 109)
fsize	− 0. 0588 *	− 0. 2734 **	− 0. 0123	− 0. 1270 **	0. 0322	0. 0425 ***
	(0. 029)	(0. 126)	(0. 020)	(0. 063)	(0. 027)	(0. 014)
age	0. 0143 *	0. 0727 ***	0. 0071	0. 0425 ***	− 0. 0147 **	− 0. 0135 ***
	(0. 008)	(0. 024)	(0. 006)	(0. 016)	(0. 005)	(0. 004)
lev	0. 0865	− 0. 3960	0. 0864	− 0. 4043 *	0. 2820 **	0. 2750 ***
	(0. 163)	(0. 267)	(0. 152)	(0. 239)	(0. 125)	(0. 103)
Intercept	2. 5196 **	6. 7971 **	1. 5801 **	4. 3661 ***	0. 0884	− 0. 2451
	(0. 920)	(2. 709)	(0. 660)	(1. 514)	(0. 624)	(0. 360)
Year FE	No	No	No	No	No	No
N	312	312	312	312	312	312
r2_w	0. 169	0. 269	0. 161	0. 236	0. 140	0. 124
r2_b	0. 009	0. 288	0. 162	0. 431	0. 302	0. 517
r2_o	0. 055	0. 209	0. 160	0. 299	0. 231	0. 352

Note: This table reports the regression results from both the fixed effects and the random effects models with no year fixed effects, based on the full balanced sample consisting of all observations in the period 2002 – 2013. "fe" and "re" in parentheses denote the fixed effect and the random effect models, respectively. $r2\_w$, $r2\_b$, and $r2\_o$ represent within, between, and overall R – squared, respectively. Standard errors (in parentheses) are heteroskedasticity consistent and clustered at the firm level. ***, **, and * denote significance at the 1%, 5%, and 10% levels, respectively.

Table C3   Corporate Governance and Market Valuation from Different Types of Investors: Full Sample Case (Balanced Panel) with Year Fixed Effects

	(1)	(2)	(3)	(4)	(5)	(6)
	htq (fe)	atq (fe)	htq (re)	atq (re)	tqr (fe)	tqr (re)
sh1	-0.7029	0.0242	-0.6789	-1.4982	0.0137	0.4284
	(1.962)	(2.232)	(1.987)	(2.134)	(0.901)	(0.975)
sh1_sq	0.5746	-0.3190	0.4765	1.1008	0.1848	-0.3048
	(1.852)	(2.301)	(1.861)	(2.260)	(0.992)	(1.034)
dual	0.0839 **	0.3704 **	0.0767 *	0.3716 **	-0.0413	-0.0503
	(0.038)	(0.148)	(0.041)	(0.148)	(0.039)	(0.036)
b_ind	-0.1411	0.3377	-0.0272	0.7207	-0.1053	-0.1298
	(0.500)	(0.633)	(0.421)	(0.561)	(0.213)	(0.214)
cstr2_10	-0.0185	-0.1159	-0.0055	-0.0944	0.0055	0.0083
	(0.036)	(0.096)	(0.041)	(0.077)	(0.026)	(0.026)
cs	-0.0427 *	-0.0457	-0.0425 ***	-0.0615 *	-0.0138	-0.0036
	(0.022)	(0.046)	(0.016)	(0.032)	(0.010)	(0.008)
os	0.6471 ***	0.4146	0.6437 ***	0.2245	0.1652	0.2517 **
	(0.167)	(0.333)	(0.155)	(0.281)	(0.114)	(0.099)
fsize	-0.0883 ***	-0.3000 **	-0.0481 *	-0.2126 **	0.0254	0.0444 **
	(0.026)	(0.133)	(0.025)	(0.090)	(0.030)	(0.020)
age	0.0327 ***	0.0623 **	-0.0310	-0.0729	0.0048	-0.0026
	(0.009)	(0.026)	(0.024)	(0.044)	(0.007)	(0.015)
lev	-0.0528	-0.6534 ***	-0.0262	-0.5403 ***	0.3252 ***	0.3042 ***
	(0.161)	(0.200)	(0.155)	(0.193)	(0.108)	(0.091)
Intercept	2.8438 ***	7.3476 **	2.4498 ***	6.8085 ***	0.0254	-0.4284
	(0.872)	(2.831)	(0.717)	(2.356)	(0.658)	(0.520)
Year FE	Yes	Yes	Yes	Yes	Yes	Yes
N	312	312	312	312	312	312

continued

	(1)	(2)	(3)	(4)	(5)	(6)
	htq (fe)	atq (fe)	htq (re)	atq (re)	tqr (fe)	tqr (re)
r2_w	0.400	0.478	0.394	0.464	0.400	0.390
r2_b	0.002	0.307	0.050	0.506	0.297	0.545
r2_o	0.067	0.298	0.226	0.469	0.340	0.478

Note: This table reports the regression results from both the fixed effects and the random effects models with year fixed effects, based on the full balanced sample consisting of all observations in the period 2002 – 2013. "fe" and "re" in parentheses denote the fixed effect and the random effect models, respectively. $r2\_w$, $r2\_b$, and $r2\_o$ represent within, between, and overall R – squared, respectively. Standard errors (in parentheses) are heteroskedasticity consistent and clustered at the firm level. *** , ** , and * denote significance at the 1%, 5%, and 10% levels, respectively.

Table C4   The Effects of Tunneling Activities on Market

Valuation from Different Types of Investors:

Full Sample Case (Balanced Panel)

	(1)	(2)	(3)	(4)	(5)	(6)
	htq (fe)	atq (fe)	htq (re)	atq (re)	tqr (fe)	tqr (re)
sh1	– 0.7672	0.7038	– 0.7374	– 1.2646	– 0.3367	0.2044
	(2.123)	(2.388)	(2.128)	(2.177)	(0.904)	(1.008)
sh1_sq	0.6217	– 1.2359	0.5048	0.7283	0.5461	– 0.0643
	(2.056)	(2.487)	(2.034)	(2.266)	(1.008)	(1.069)
dual	0.0779*	0.2677*	0.0591	0.2357**	– 0.0373	– 0.0462
	(0.043)	(0.141)	(0.042)	(0.116)	(0.042)	(0.039)
b_ind	– 0.1207	0.6654	– 0.0044	0.9912*	– 0.1717	– 0.1778
	(0.535)	(0.558)	(0.448)	(0.546)	(0.206)	(0.203)
cstr2_10	– 0.0075	– 0.0957	0.0069	– 0.0600	0.0177	0.0183
	(0.039)	(0.079)	(0.044)	(0.063)	(0.025)	(0.026)
TRPT	0.0182	0.0809*	0.0137	0.0624	– 0.0311*	– 0.0305*
	(0.025)	(0.041)	(0.026)	(0.043)	(0.016)	(0.016)
cs	– 0.0390*	– 0.0304	– 0.0389**	– 0.0496**	– 0.0160	– 0.0060
	(0.021)	(0.038)	(0.015)	(0.023)	(0.009)	(0.007)
os	0.6394***	0.3595	0.6454***	0.2271	0.1789	0.2558**
	(0.170)	(0.319)	(0.158)	(0.250)	(0.119)	(0.100)

continued

	(1)	(2)	(3)	(4)	(5)	(6)
	htq (fe)	atq (fe)	htq (re)	atq (re)	tqr (fe)	tqr (re)
fsize	− 0. 0645 **	− 0. 1773 **	− 0. 0292	− 0. 1341 ***	0. 0183	0. 0410 **
	(0. 026)	(0. 081)	(0. 023)	(0. 045)	(0. 030)	(0. 020)
age	0. 0287 ***	0. 0355 **	− 0. 0220	− 0. 0429	0. 0074	− 0. 0016
	(0. 010)	(0. 017)	(0. 024)	(0. 030)	(0. 007)	(0. 015)
lev	− 0. 0598	− 0. 7079 ***	− 0. 0237	− 0. 5122 ***	0. 3570 ***	0. 3279 ***
	(0. 160)	(0. 227)	(0. 149)	(0. 192)	(0. 107)	(0. 089)
Intercept	2. 3855 **	4. 6893 **	2. 0011 ***	4. 7981 ***	0. 2921	− 0. 2705
	(0. 922)	(1. 696)	(0. 696)	(1. 167)	(0. 645)	(0. 513)
Year FE	Yes	Yes	Yes	Yes	Yes	Yes
N	301	301	301	301	301	301
r2_w	0. 397	0. 462	0. 392	0. 451	0. 404	0. 394
r2_b	0. 000	0. 285	0. 092	0. 495	0. 194	0. 492
r2_o	0. 099	0. 311	0. 252	0. 451	0. 283	0. 442

Note: This table reports the regression results of the effects of total related party transactions on corporate valuation from both the fixed effects and the random effects models with year fixed effects, based on the full balanced sample consisting of all observations in the period 2002 – 2013. "fe" and "re" in parentheses denote the fixed effect and the random effect models, respectively. $r2\_w$, $r2\_b$, and $r2\_o$ represent within, between, and overall R – squared, respectively. Standard errors (in parentheses) are heteroskedasticity consistent and clustered at the firm level. *** , ** , and * denote significance at the 1% , 5% , and 10% levels, respectively.

Table C5   The Effects of Harmful Related Party Transactions on

Market Valuation from Different Types of Investors:

Full Sample Case (Balanced Panel)

	(1)	(2)	(3)	(4)	(5)	(6)
	htq (fe)	atq (fe)	htq (re)	atq (re)	tqr (fe)	tqr (re)
sh1	− 0. 7613	0. 7417	− 0. 7031	− 1. 2093	− 0. 3540	0. 2045
	(2. 121)	(2. 409)	(2. 121)	(2. 171)	(0. 895)	(1. 005)
sh1_sq	0. 5889	− 1. 2894	0. 4543	0. 6855	0. 5462	− 0. 0803
	(2. 050)	(2. 517)	(2. 024)	(2. 275)	(0. 998)	(1. 064)

continued

	(1)	(2)	(3)	(4)	(5)	(6)
	htq (fe)	atq (fe)	htq (re)	atq (re)	tqr (fe)	tqr (re)
dual	0.0717	0.2549 *	0.0552	0.2356 **	− 0.0356	− 0.0461
	(0.044)	(0.142)	(0.042)	(0.116)	(0.042)	(0.039)
b_ind	− 0.1314	0.6562	− 0.0138	0.9732 *	− 0.1768	− 0.1812
	(0.533)	(0.557)	(0.445)	(0.544)	(0.207)	(0.203)
cstr2_10	− 0.0044	− 0.0913	0.0095	− 0.0565	0.0181	0.0182
	(0.039)	(0.078)	(0.044)	(0.062)	(0.025)	(0.026)
HRPT	− 0.0049	0.0684	− 0.0066	0.0550	− 0.0465 **	− 0.0450 **
	(0.037)	(0.054)	(0.039)	(0.059)	(0.022)	(0.023)
cs	− 0.0403 *	− 0.0328	− 0.0400 ***	− 0.0513 **	− 0.0157	− 0.0058
	(0.021)	(0.039)	(0.015)	(0.023)	(0.009)	(0.007)
os	0.6539 ***	0.3864	0.6526 ***	0.2321	0.1769	0.2541 **
	(0.167)	(0.321)	(0.155)	(0.251)	(0.120)	(0.102)
fsize	− 0.0674 **	− 0.1822 **	− 0.0295	− 0.1338 ***	0.0184	0.0413 **
	(0.026)	(0.082)	(0.024)	(0.046)	(0.030)	(0.020)
age	0.0295 ***	0.0369 **	− 0.0222	− 0.0418	0.0073	− 0.0021
	(0.010)	(0.017)	(0.023)	(0.030)	(0.007)	(0.015)
lev	− 0.0444	− 0.6767 ***	− 0.0146	− 0.5018 ***	0.3533 ***	0.3242 ***
	(0.158)	(0.222)	(0.150)	(0.195)	(0.107)	(0.089)
Intercept	2.4578 **	4.7928 ***	2.0160 ***	4.7849 ***	0.3008	− 0.2680
	(0.920)	(1.715)	(0.700)	(1.178)	(0.637)	(0.512)
Year FE	Yes	Yes	Yes	Yes	Yes	Yes
N	301	301	301	301	301	301
r2_w	0.396	0.459	0.391	0.448	0.405	0.395
r2_b	0.000	0.288	0.103	0.499	0.186	0.489
r2_o	0.097	0.307	0.256	0.451	0.279	0.441

Note: This table reports the regression results of the effects of harmful related party transactions on corporate valuation from both the fixed effects and the random effects models with year fixed effects, based on the full balanced sample consisting of all observations in the period 2002 – 2013. "fe" and "re" in parentheses denote the fixed effect and the random effect models, respectively. $r2\_w$, $r2\_b$, and $r2\_o$ represent within, between, and overall R – squared, respectively. Standard errors (in parentheses) are heteroskedasticity consistent and clustered at the firm level. ***, **, and * denote significance at the 1%, 5%, and 10% levels, respectively.

Table C6   **The Effects of Non-tradable Shares Reform on Market Valuation from Different Types of Investors (Balanced Panel)**

	(1) htq	(2) htq	(3) htq	(4) atq	(5) atq	(6) atq	(7) tqr	(8) tqr	(9) tqr
sh1	-1.4520 (1.831)	-2.0728 (2.014)	-1.1048 (1.975)	-4.1787** (1.834)	-5.1913*** (1.840)	-2.4453 (2.303)	1.3520* (0.750)	1.1828 (1.063)	0.3613 (1.007)
sh1_sq	1.0272 (1.689)	1.7321 (1.846)	0.9073 (1.847)	3.7931** (1.717)	4.9042*** (1.695)	2.0478 (2.433)	-1.4245** (0.698)	-1.2391 (1.003)	-0.2320 (1.029)
dual	0.1035 (0.118)	0.0617 (0.094)	0.0984** (0.042)	0.2561 (0.228)	0.2891 (0.177)	0.4157*** (0.160)	-0.1361** (0.057)	-0.1252*** (0.046)	-0.0719* (0.043)
b_ind	-0.1002 (0.434)	0.2942 (0.492)	0.3092 (0.396)	-0.0443 (0.369)	0.2718 (0.349)	0.7019 (0.637)	0.1494 (0.207)	0.3219 (0.253)	0.2085 (0.266)
cstr2_10	0.1210** (0.052)	0.0760* (0.043)	0.0139 (0.038)	0.0107 (0.044)	-0.0097 (0.037)	-0.0591 (0.062)	0.0681** (0.032)	0.0542* (0.031)	0.0183 (0.028)
d_06	0.1252*** (0.035)	0.1313*** (0.036)	0.2083*** (0.043)	0.3239*** (0.069)	0.2945*** (0.065)	0.3346*** (0.062)	-0.0851*** (0.018)	-0.0631*** (0.021)	-0.0511** (0.026)
cs	-0.0150 (0.013)	-0.0329*** (0.010)	-0.0436*** (0.014)	-0.0480*** (0.015)	-0.0451*** (0.012)	-0.0594** (0.024)	0.0075 (0.008)	-0.0014 (0.006)	-0.0023 (0.007)
os	0.7422*** (0.268)	0.7925*** (0.174)	0.8249*** (0.165)	0.5642* (0.288)	0.3991** (0.181)	0.4375* (0.243)	0.2533* (0.137)	0.3280*** (0.102)	0.2631** (0.109)

continued

	(1)	(2)	(3)	(4)	(5)	(6)	(7)	(8)	(9)
	htq	htq	htq	atq	atq	atq	tqr	tqr	tqr
fsize	0.0846***	0.0302	-0.0307	-0.0592***	-0.0795***	-0.1563	0.0806***	0.0590***	0.0467***
	(0.023)	(0.019)	(0.019)	(0.022)	(0.030)	(0.066)	(0.013)	(0.014)	(0.014)
Age	0.0240**	-0.0011	-0.0115*	-0.0031	0.0027	0.0128	0.0179**	-0.0033	-0.0089*
	(0.011)	(0.013)	(0.006)	(0.012)	(0.010)	(0.015)	(0.008)	(0.007)	(0.005)
lev	0.0630	0.1715	0.0337	-0.2816**	-0.3131***	-0.4672	0.2201*	0.3032***	0.2856***
	(0.155)	(0.136)	(0.141)	(0.137)	(0.117)	(0.212)	(0.113)	(0.088)	(0.102)
Intercept	-0.3625	0.9504*	2.0560***	3.8050***	4.2869***	5.1012***	-1.3805***	-0.7888***	-0.3547
	(0.636)	(0.529)	(0.705)	(0.804)	(0.908)	(1.600)	(0.307)	(0.344)	(0.383)
N	156	208	312	156	208	312	156	208	312
r2_w	0.405	0.197	0.220	0.269	0.236	0.277	0.192	0.160	0.132
r2_b	0.304	0.378	0.118	0.492	0.539	0.451	0.542	0.534	0.527
r2_o	0.352	0.267	0.173	0.327	0.323	0.334	0.394	0.363	0.362

Note: This table reports the regression results of the effects of non-tradable shares reform on corporate valuation with a random effects model, based on the balanced panel data set. The estimates in columns (1), (4) and (7) come from a sub-sample with observations in the period 2002–2007; the results in columns (2), (5), and (8) are based on a sub-sample with observations in the period 2002–2009; and the estimates in columns (3), (6), and (9) are from the full balanced sample with all observations in the period 2002–2013. $r2\_w$, $r2\_b$, and $r2\_o$ represent within, between, and overall R-squared, respectively. Standard errors (in parentheses) are heteroskedasticity consistent and clustered at the firm level. ***, **, and * denote significance at the 1%, 5%, and 10% levels, respectively.

C. 2   Empirical Results Based on the Log – Ratio of Market Capitalization to Total Assets

This section presents all relevant empirical results based on the alternative equity measure — logratio of market capitalization to total assets for both balanced and unbalanced panel data sets.

Table C7   Corporate Governance and Market Valuation from

Different Types of Investors: Sub – Sample Case

(Unbalanced Panel)

	(1)	(2)	(3)	(4)
	hma (fe)	ama (fe)	hma (re)	ama (re)
sh1	− 20. 8920 ***	− 11. 5987 ***	1. 8969	− 1. 9147
	(3. 225)	(3. 073)	(3. 662)	(2. 291)
sh1_sq	15. 9262 ***	9. 9057 ***	− 3. 5225	1. 0712
	(2. 754)	(2. 457)	(4. 102)	(2. 386)
b_ind	1. 8105	1. 2357 *	1. 5275 **	0. 1665
	(1. 228)	(0. 709)	(0. 665)	(0. 539)
cstr2_10	2. 0193 ***	0. 4440	0. 4602 ***	0. 0779
	(0. 425)	(0. 343)	(0. 129)	(0. 072)
csw	− 0. 0286	0. 0137	− 0. 0895	− 0. 1306 ***
	(0. 113)	(0. 072)	(0. 060)	(0. 041)
osw	0. 6847	0. 9316	2. 1756 **	1. 1332 **
	(1. 218)	(0. 691)	(0. 985)	(0. 544)
fsize	0. 4623 **	0. 3868 **	0. 1842 ***	− 0. 2221 ***
	(0. 184)	(0. 166)	(0. 046)	(0. 026)
age	0. 0578	− 0. 2460 ***	0. 0937 ***	− 0. 0546 **
	(0. 057)	(0. 044)	(0. 027)	(0. 022)

continued

	(1)	(2)	(3)	(4)
	hma (fe)	ama (fe)	hma (re)	ama (re)
lev	− 2. 5277 *** (0. 725)	− 2. 5889 *** (0. 413)	− 1. 6291 *** (0. 549)	− 1. 2670 *** (0. 300)
dual			− 0. 2752 (0. 226)	0. 1929 (0. 191)
Intercept	− 0. 7395 (4. 093)	− 2. 1524 (3. 850)	− 5. 4234 *** (1. 252)	6. 3429 *** (0. 877)
N	83	83	83	83
r2_w	0. 574	0. 637	0. 506	0. 421
r2_b	0. 115	0. 005	0. 637	0. 727
r2_o	0. 144	0. 000	0. 606	0. 658

Note: This table reports the regression results from both the fixed effects and the random effects models, based on a sub – sample consisting of all observations in the period 2002 – 2004. The dependent variables are defined as the logarithm of (H – or A – shares) market capitalization over total assets. "fe" and "re" in parentheses denote the fixed effect and the random effect models, respectively. $r2\_w$, $r2\_b$, and $r2\_o$ represent within, between, and overall R – squared, respectively. Standard errors (in parentheses) are heteroskedasticity consistent and clustered at the firm level. *** , ** , and * denote significance at the 1% , 5% , and 10% levels, respectively.

Table C8   Corporate Governance and Market Valuation from Different Types of Investors: Full Sample Case (Unbalanced Panel) without Year Effects

	(1)	(2)	(3)	(4)
	hma (fe)	ama (fe)	hma (re)	ama (re)
sh1	− 3. 5919 (5. 734)	− 6. 2938 (5. 204)	− 0. 7404 (2. 523)	− 3. 1910 (2. 466)
sh1_sq	2. 7078 (5. 513)	4. 8520 (5. 491)	0. 3447 (2. 658)	2. 5481 (2. 780)
dual	0. 1775 (0. 126)	0. 1734 (0. 140)	0. 1611 (0. 109)	0. 0875 (0. 127)

continued

	(1)	(2)	(3)	(4)
	hma (fe)	ama (fe)	hma (re)	ama (re)
b_ind	1. 4273 **	- 0. 2833	1. 0932 **	0. 0451
	(0. 627)	(0. 624)	(0. 461)	(0. 580)
cstr2_10	0. 0773	- 0. 0226	0. 1575	0. 0225
	(0. 111)	(0. 116)	(0. 096)	(0. 075)
csw	- 0. 1199 **	- 0. 1271 **	- 0. 1331 ***	- 0. 1307 ***
	(0. 046)	(0. 057)	(0. 037)	(0. 036)
osw	2. 6721 ***	1. 6106 ***	2. 4112 ***	1. 2353 ***
	(0. 359)	(0. 358)	(0. 308)	(0. 284)
fsize	- 0. 2431 **	- 0. 2862 ***	- 0. 1068 **	- 0. 1424 ***
	(0. 114)	(0. 105)	(0. 053)	(0. 048)
age	0. 0063	0. 0690 ***	- 0. 0058	0. 0430 ***
	(0. 020)	(0. 020)	(0. 010)	(0. 011)
lev	- 0. 9676 **	- 0. 8438 **	- 1. 1910 ***	- 1. 0767 ***
	(0. 380)	(0. 382)	(0. 408)	(0. 380)
Intercept	4. 8341 *	7. 6744 ***	1. 5098	3. 8849 ***
	(2. 785)	(2. 403)	(1. 223)	(1. 106)
Year FE	No	No	No	No
N	540	540	540	540
r2_w	0. 348	0. 211	0. 333	0. 190
r2_b	0. 275	0. 465	0. 443	0. 556
r2_o	0. 274	0. 304	0. 401	0. 373

Note: This table reports the regression results from both the fixed effects and the random effects models, based on the full sample consisting of all observations in the period 2002 – 2013. The dependent variables are defined as the logarithm of (H – or A – shares) market capitalization over total assets. "fe" and "re" in parentheses denote the fixed effect and the random effect models, respectively. r2_w, r2_b, and r2_o represent within, between, and overall R – squared, respectively. Standard errors (in parentheses) are heteroskedasticity consistent and clustered at the firm level. *** , ** , and * denote significance at the 1% , 5% , and 10% levels, respectively.

Table C9   Corporate Governance and Market Valuation

from Different Types of Investors: Full Sample Case

(Unbalanced Panel) with Year Effects

	(1)	(2)	(3)	(4)
	hma (fe)	ama (fe)	hma (re)	ama (re)
sh1	− 0. 6127	− 3. 6347	0. 0302	− 2. 8651
	(3. 831)	(3. 941)	(2. 216)	(2. 318)
sh1_sq	0. 0943	2. 8185	− 0. 3483	2. 4623
	(3. 589)	(4. 283)	(2. 227)	(2. 645)
dual	0. 0629	0. 0228	0. 0944	0. 0049
	(0. 091)	(0. 101)	(0. 085)	(0. 095)
b_ind	− 0. 4205	− 0. 4336	− 0. 0541	− 0. 3063
	(0. 595)	(0. 621)	(0. 487)	(0. 575)
cstr2_10	0. 0486	0. 0049	0. 1185	0. 0257
	(0. 079)	(0. 089)	(0. 082)	(0. 072)
csw	− 0. 1017 ***	− 0. 1026 **	− 0. 1080 ***	− 0. 1113 ***
	(0. 032)	(0. 049)	(0. 030)	(0. 040)
osw	2. 0503 ***	0. 8843 ***	1. 8603 ***	0. 7184 ***
	(0. 229)	(0. 287)	(0. 202)	(0. 249)
fsize	− 0. 3175 ***	− 0. 3246 ***	− 0. 1493 **	− 0. 2228 ***
	(0. 100)	(0. 098)	(0. 073)	(0. 066)
age	0. 0729 ***	0. 0601 ***	− 0. 0102	0. 0159
	(0. 018)	(0. 018)	(0. 017)	(0. 013)
lev	− 1. 2235 ***	− 1. 2106 ***	− 1. 3362 ***	− 1. 3053 ***
	(0. 289)	(0. 327)	(0. 321)	(0. 331)
Intercept	5. 4143 **	8. 1511 ***	2. 0446	5. 9011 ***
	(2. 306)	(2. 147)	(1. 601)	(1. 398)
Year FE	Yes	Yes	Yes	Yes
N	540	540	540	540
r2_w	0. 658	0. 602	0. 645	0. 595
r2_b	0. 201	0. 512	0. 378	0. 594
r2_o	0. 268	0. 468	0. 482	0. 569

Note: This table reports the regression results from both the fixed effects and the random effects models, based on the full sample consisting of all observations in the period 2002 – 2013. The dependent variables are defined as the logarithm of (H – or A – shares) market capitalization over total assets. "fe" and "re" in parentheses denote the fixed effect and the random effect models, respectively. r2_w, r2_b, and r2_o represent within, between, and overall R – squared, respectively. Standard errors (in parentheses) are heteroskedasticity consistent and clustered at the firm level. *** , ** , and * denote significance at the 1% , 5% , and 10% levels, respectively.

Table C10   The Effects of Tunneling Activities on Market

Valuation from Different Types of Investors:

Full Sample Case (Unbalanced Panel)

	(1)	(2)	(3)	(4)
	hma	*ama*	*hma*	*ama*
sh1	− 0. 3668	− 2. 7982	0. 0260	− 2. 5767
	(3. 799)	(3. 845)	(2. 244)	(2. 314)
sh1_sq	− 0. 2105	1. 7984	− 0. 4302	2. 0367
	(3. 641)	(4. 210)	(2. 270)	(2. 627)
dual	0. 0116	− 0. 0225	0. 0402	− 0. 0396
	(0. 094)	(0. 108)	(0. 078)	(0. 097)
b_ind	− 0. 3799	− 0. 3622	− 0. 0366	− 0. 2769
	(0. 606)	(0. 638)	(0. 496)	(0. 590)
cstr2_10	0. 0663	0. 0150	0. 1407 *	0. 0387
	(0. 079)	(0. 087)	(0. 081)	(0. 070)
TRPT	0. 0075	− 0. 0019	0. 0089	0. 0002
	(0. 005)	(0. 005)	(0. 006)	(0. 006)
csw	− 0. 0946 ***	− 0. 0973 **	− 0. 1029 ***	− 0. 1077 ***
	(0. 028)	(0. 047)	(0. 027)	(0. 039)
osw	2. 1201 ***	0. 9568 ***	1. 9254 ***	0. 7807 ***
	(0. 224)	(0. 295)	(0. 196)	(0. 246)
fsize	− 0. 2622 **	− 0. 2794 ***	− 0. 1091	− 0. 1941 ***
	(0. 101)	(0. 103)	(0. 068)	(0. 064)
age	0. 0650 ***	0. 0527 **	− 0. 0061	0. 0182
	(0. 020)	(0. 020)	(0. 016)	(0. 013)
lev	− 1. 2425 ***	− 1. 2038 ***	− 1. 3554 ***	− 1. 3105 ***
	(0. 274)	(0. 329)	(0. 309)	(0. 334)
Intercept	4. 1991 *	7. 0138 ***	1. 2023	5. 2375 ***
	(2. 258)	(2. 167)	(1. 500)	(1. 342)
Year FE	Yes	Yes	Yes	Yes
N	527	527	527	527
r2_w	0. 666	0. 601	0. 655	0. 595
r2_b	0. 220	0. 512	0. 405	0. 595
r2_o	0. 300	0. 467	0. 503	0. 561

Note: This table reports the regression results of the effects of total related party transactions on corporate valuation from both the fixed effects and the random effects models with year fixed effects, based on the full sample consisting of all observations in the period 2002 – 2013. The dependent variables are defined as the logarithm of (H – or A – shares) market capitalization over total assets. "fe" and "re" in parentheses denote the fixed effect and the random effect models, respectively. r2_w, r2_b, and r2_o represent within, between, and overall R – squared, respectively. Standard errors (in parentheses) are heteroskedasticity consistent and clustered at the firm level. *** , ** , and * denote significance at the 1% , 5% , and 10% levels, respectively.

Table C11 The Effects of Harmful Related Party Transactions

on Market Valuation from Different Types of Investors:

Full Sample Case (Unbalanced Panel)

	(1)	(2)	(3)	(4)
	hma	ama	hma	ama
sh1	- 0. 3690	- 2. 8049	0. 0224	- 2. 5784
	(3. 799)	(3. 844)	(2. 245)	(2. 315)
sh1_sq	- 0. 2110	1. 8033	- 0. 4282	2. 0368
	(3. 642)	(4. 210)	(2. 272)	(2. 628)
dual	0. 0105	- 0. 0226	0. 0394	- 0. 0399
	(0. 094)	(0. 108)	(0. 078)	(0. 097)
h_ind	- 0. 3803	- 0. 3622	- 0. 0376	- 0. 2777
	(0. 607)	(0. 638)	(0. 497)	(0. 390)
cstr2_10	0. 0674	0. 0156	0. 1420 *	0. 0393
	(0. 079)	(0. 087)	(0. 081)	(0. 070)
HRPT	0. 0044	- 0. 0038	0. 0051	- 0. 0023
	(0. 003)	(0. 003)	(0. 004)	(0. 004)
csw	- 0. 0949 ***	- 0. 0973 **	- 0. 1032 ***	- 0. 1078 ***
	(0. 028)	(0. 047)	(0. 027)	(0. 039)
osw	2. 1216 ***	0. 9564 ***	1. 9257 ***	0. 7802 ***
	(0. 224)	(0. 295)	(0. 196)	(0. 246)
fsize	- 0. 2628 **	- 0. 2794 ***	- 0. 1091	- 0. 1940 ***
	(0. 101)	(0. 104)	(0. 068)	(0. 064)
age	0. 0651 ***	0. 0527 **	- 0. 0061	0. 0182
	(0. 020)	(0. 020)	(0. 016)	(0. 013)
lev	- 1. 2391 ***	- 1. 2035 ***	- 1. 3529 ***	- 1. 3099 ***
	(0. 275)	(0. 330)	(0. 311)	(0. 335)
Intercept	4. 2144 *	7. 0175 ***	1. 2075	5. 2388 ***
	(2. 262)	(2. 169)	(1. 505)	(1. 344)
Year FE	Yes	Yes	Yes	Yes
N	527	527	527	527
r2_w	0. 666	0. 601	0. 655	0. 595
r2_b	0. 220	0. 512	0. 404	0. 594
r2_o	0. 299	0. 467	0. 502	0. 561

Note: This table reports the regression results of the effects of total related party transactions on corporate valuation from both the fixed effects and the random effects models with year fixed effects, based on the full sample consisting of all observations in the period 2002 – 2013. The dependent variables are defined as the logarithm of (H – or A – shares) market capitalization over total assets. "fe" and "re" in parentheses denote the fixed effect and the random effect models, respectively. r2_w, r2_b, and r2_o represent within, between, and overall R – squared, respectively. Standard errors (in parentheses) are heteroskedasticity consistent and clustered at the firm level. *** , ** , and * denote significance at the 1% , 5% , and 10% levels, respectively.

Table C12   **The Effects of Non – tradable Shares Reform**

on Market Valuation from Different Types

of Investors (Unbalanced Panel)

	(1)	(2)	(3)	(4)	(5)	(6)
	hma	hma	hma	ama	ama	ama
sh1	– 2. 4329	– 0. 5213	– 0. 3084	– 3. 4807 *	– 2. 6592	– 2. 7921
	(2. 499)	(2. 724)	(2. 284)	(1. 802)	(2. 079)	(2. 121)
sh1_sq	1. 4138	0. 0303	0. 1549	2. 5237	1. 8638	2. 3988
	(2. 422)	(2. 589)	(2. 368)	(1. 789)	(2. 127)	(2. 390)
dual	0. 0250	0. 1271	0. 1273	0. 3393 **	0. 2697 **	0. 0626
	(0. 222)	(0. 151)	(0. 097)	(0. 141)	(0. 136)	(0. 111)
b_ind	0. 3131	0. 3328	0. 2958	– 1. 0179 **	– 1. 0612 ***	– 0. 9107
	(0. 509)	(0. 430)	(0. 418)	(0. 482)	(0. 395)	(0. 586)
cstr2_10	0. 2444 ***	0. 2088 *	0. 1409	0. 0464	0. 0832	0. 0067
	(0. 088)	(0. 107)	(0. 095)	(0. 069)	(0. 071)	(0. 073)
d_06	0. 3656 ***	0. 3355 ***	0. 6045 ***	0. 7094 ***	0. 5967 ***	0. 6559 ***
	(0. 071)	(0. 085)	(0. 083)	(0. 072)	(0. 074)	(0. 078)
csw	– 0. 0411	– 0. 1102 ***	– 0. 1356 ***	– 0. 1175 ***	– 0. 1126 ***	– 0. 1379 ***
	(0. 028)	(0. 027)	(0. 035)	(0. 028)	(0. 022)	(0. 038)
osw	1. 7698 ***	2. 2928 ***	2. 3820 ***	1. 1213 ***	1. 0338 ***	1. 2190 ***
	(0. 515)	(0. 320)	(0. 261)	(0. 400)	(0. 258)	(0. 230)
fsize	0. 1701 ***	– 0. 0090	– 0. 1883 ***	– 0. 1523 ***	– 0. 1683 ***	– 0. 2283 ***
	(0. 046)	(0. 044)	(0. 055)	(0. 033)	(0. 036)	(0. 051)
age	0. 0184	– 0. 0095	– 0. 0442 ***	– 0. 0418 ***	– 0. 0089	0. 0041
	(0. 017)	(0. 013)	(0. 010)	(0. 015)	(0. 010)	(0. 009)
lev	– 1. 2178 ***	– 0. 9820 ***	– 1. 2657 ***	– 0. 9100 ***	– 0. 8774 ***	– 1. 1475 ***
	(0. 279)	(0. 295)	(0. 343)	(0. 210)	(0. 218)	(0. 319)
Intercept	– 4. 0579 ***	– 0. 5587	3. 5182 ***	5. 1113 ***	5. 0134 ***	6. 0360 ***
	(1. 246)	(1. 243)	(1. 324)	(1. 060)	(1. 015)	(1. 142)
N	190	290	540	190	290	540
r2_w	0. 435	0. 275	0. 434	0. 296	0. 250	0. 294
r2_b	0. 615	0. 583	0. 329	0. 681	0. 654	0. 577
r2_o	0. 546	0. 441	0. 373	0. 484	0. 432	0. 436

Note: This table reports the regression results of the effects of non – tradable shares reform on corporate valuation with a random effects model. The estimates in columns (1), (4) and (7) come from a sub – sample with observations in the period 2002 – 2007; the results in columns (2), (5), and (8) are based on a sub – sample with observations in the period 2002 – 2009; and the estimates in columns (3), (6), and (9) are from the full sample with all observations in the period 2002 – 2013. The dependent variables are defined as the logarithm of (H – or A – shares) market capitalization over total assets. r2_w, r2_b, and r2_o represent within, between, and overall R – squared, respectively. Standard errors (in parentheses) are heteroskedasticity consistent and clustered at the firm level. *** , ** , and * denote significance at the 1% , 5% , and 10% levels, respectively.

Table C13   Corporate Governance and Market Valuation

from Different Types of Investors:

Sub – Sample Case (Balanced Panel)

	(1)	(2)	(3)	(4)
	hma (fe)	ama (fe)	hma (re)	ama (re)
sh1	– 20. 9946 ***	– 9. 9043 ***	0. 6091	– 7. 9253 ***
	(3. 269)	(1. 976)	(4. 222)	(1. 880)
sh1_sq	15. 9901 ***	8. 8338 ***	– 1. 9973	6. 3269 ***
	(2. 809)	(1. 584)	(4. 588)	(2. 084)
b_ind	1. 8089	1. 3542 *	1. 3543 **	0. 3022
	(1. 333)	(0. 761)	(0. 679)	(0. 664)
cstr2_10	1. 9512 ***	0. 2719	0. 5334 ***	0. 1658 *
	(0. 430)	(0. 290)	(0. 150)	(0. 091)
csw	– 0. 0022	0. 0336	– 0. 0760	– 0. 2255 ***
	(0. 131)	(0. 078)	(0. 064)	(0. 047)
osw	0. 8041	0. 8668	2. 1503 **	1. 3462 **
	(1. 275)	(0. 663)	(1. 055)	(0. 561)
fsize	0. 4993 **	0. 4182 **	0. 2027 ***	– 0. 3635 ***
	(0. 219)	(0. 170)	(0. 048)	(0. 053)
age	0. 0576	– 0. 2537 ***	0. 1075 ***	– 0. 0753 ***
	(0. 068)	(0. 046)	(0. 026)	(0. 024)
lev	– 2. 3893 ***	– 2. 6532 ***	– 1. 5857 ***	– 1. 0513 ***
	(0. 734)	(0. 403)	(0. 554)	(0. 402)
dual			– 0. 3198	0. 0612
			(0. 220)	(0. 252)
Intercept	– 1. 8381	– 5. 2067	– 5. 5240 ***	10. 1526 ***
	(4. 779)	(3. 631)	(1. 499)	(1. 154)
N	78	78	78	78
r2_w	0. 579	0. 638	0. 524	0. 436
r2_b	0. 124	0. 166	0. 638	0. 756
r2_o	0. 150	0. 104	0. 598	0. 714

Note: This table reports the regression results from both the fixed effects and the random effects models, based on a sub – sample consisting of all observations in the period 2002 – 2004. The dependent variables are defined as the logarithm of (H – or A – shares) market capitalization over total assets. "fe" and "re" in parentheses denote the fixed effect and the random effect models, respectively. $r2\_w$, $r2\_b$, and $r2\_o$ represent within, between, and overall R – squared, respectively. Standard errors (in parentheses) are heteroskedasticity consistent and clustered at the firm level. ***, **, and * denote significance at the 1%, 5%, and 10% levels, respectively.

Table C14   Corporate Governance and Market Valuation

from Different Types of Investors: Full Sample

Case (Balanced Panel) without Year Effects

	(1)	(2)	(3)	(4)
	hma (fe)	ama (fe)	hma (re)	ama (re)
sh1	− 3. 2320	− 8. 2048	− 2. 9907	− 9. 2749
	(5. 122)	(6. 644)	(4. 689)	(6. 397)
sh1_sq	2. 6657	6. 3102	2. 3603	7. 9681
	(4. 929)	(7. 465)	(4. 619)	(7. 201)
dual	0. 2857 **	0. 4633 ***	0. 2923 ***	0. 4077 ***
	(0. 116)	(0. 133)	(0. 101)	(0. 134)
b_ind	1. 0876	− 1. 3794	1. 2870 **	− 0. 3770
	(0. 733)	(0. 919)	(0. 652)	(1. 306)
cstr2_10	0. 1019	− 0. 0206	0. 1490	0. 0266
	(0. 146)	(0. 171)	(0. 137)	(0. 124)
csw	− 0. 1036 **	− 0. 1445 **	− 0. 1086 ***	− 0. 1292 ***
	(0. 043)	(0. 068)	(0. 029)	(0. 045)
osw	2. 9493 ***	0. 7382	2. 7199 ***	0. 6454
	(0. 441)	(0. 600)	(0. 347)	(0. 456)
fsize	− 0. 2258 **	− 0. 2355 *	− 0. 0988	− 0. 1447 **
	(0. 092)	(0. 134)	(0. 067)	(0. 067)
age	0. 0338 *	0. 1789 ***	0. 0142	0. 1562 ***
	(0. 019)	(0. 031)	(0. 015)	(0. 019)
lev	− 0. 3694	− 0. 8283	− 0. 4803	− 0. 8079
	(0. 335)	(0. 548)	(0. 353)	(0. 526)
Intercept	3. 7710 *	5. 0050	1. 2276	3. 0776 **
	(2. 091)	(3. 013)	(1. 580)	(1. 540)
Year FE	No	No	No	No
N	312	312	312	312
r2_w	0. 342	0. 481	0. 331	0. 475
r2_b	0. 088	0. 331	0. 258	0. 327
r2_o	0. 155	0. 366	0. 289	0. 387

Note: This table reports the regression results from both the fixed effects and the random effects models, based on the full sample consisting of all observations in the period 2002 – 2013. The dependent variables are defined as the logarithm of (H – or A – shares) market capitalization over total assets. "fe" and "re" in parentheses denote the fixed effect and the random effect models, respectively. $r2\_w$, $r2\_b$, and $r2\_o$ represent within, between, and overall R – squared, respectively. Standard errors (in parentheses) are heteroskedasticity consistent and clustered at the firm level. *** , ** , and * denote significance at the 1% , 5% , and 10% levels, respectively.

Table C15   Corporate Governance and Market Valuation

from Different Types of Investors: Full Sample

Case (Balanced Panel) with Year Effects

	(1)	(2)	(3)	(4)
	hma (fe)	ama (fe)	hma (re)	ama (re)
sh1	−0.6387	−7.0331	−0.4148	−6.9577
	(4.009)	(6.754)	(3.869)	(6.238)
sh1_sq	0.2377	5.4600	−0.0715	5.6432
	(3.790)	(7.619)	(3.733)	(7.098)
dual	0.1453	0.2595*	0.1590	0.2618*
	(0.103)	(0.146)	(0.099)	(0.137)
b_ind	−0.6903	−0.4842	−0.4852	−0.3954
	(0.734)	(0.846)	(0.657)	(0.868)
cstr2_10	0.0447	0.0153	0.0700	−0.0217
	(0.114)	(0.151)	(0.119)	(0.138)
csw	−0.0979**	−0.1327**	−0.1050***	−0.1369***
	(0.036)	(0.055)	(0.030)	(0.038)
osw	2.4271***	0.0649	2.2899***	0.2009
	(0.309)	(0.600)	(0.229)	(0.493)
fsize	−0.3018***	−0.2347*	−0.2151***	−0.2733***
	(0.089)	(0.131)	(0.083)	(0.081)
age	0.0871***	0.1309***	−0.1089*	−0.0726
	(0.020)	(0.029)	(0.063)	(0.057)
lev	−0.7108**	−1.2547**	−0.7383***	−1.0780**
	(0.272)	(0.503)	(0.283)	(0.421)
Intercept	4.5279**	5.3273*	4.1489*	7.4487***
	(2.002)	(2.919)	(2.195)	(2.256)
Year FE	Yes	Yes	Yes	Yes
N	312	312	312	312
r2_w	0.625	0.695	0.620	0.693
r2_b	0.039	0.395	0.175	0.574
r2_o	0.170	0.537	0.355	0.647

Note: This table reports the regression results from both the fixed effects and the random effects models, based on the full sample consisting of all observations in the period 2002 – 2013. The dependent variables are defined as the logarithm of (H – or A – shares) market capitalization over total assets. "fe" and "re" in parentheses denote the fixed effect and the random effect models, respectively. r2_w, r2_b, and r2_o represent within, between, and overall R – squared, respectively. Standard errors (in parentheses) are heteroskedasticity consistent and clustered at the firm level. *** , ** , and * denote significance at the 1% , 5% , and 10% levels, respectively.

Table C16   The Effects of Tunneling Activities on Market
Valuation from Different Types of Investors: Full
Sample Case (Balanced Panel)

	(1)	(2)	(3)	(4)
	hma (fe)	ama (fe)	hma (re)	ama (re)
sh1	- 0. 5978	- 5. 2076	- 0. 6456	- 5. 5635
	(4. 027)	(6. 338)	(3. 952)	(6. 049)
sh1_sq	0. 3469	3. 4200	0. 2392	3. 9762
	(3. 858)	(7. 196)	(3. 820)	(6. 873)
dual	0. 1388	0. 2792	0. 1306	0. 2639 *
	(0. 121)	(0. 164)	(0. 108)	(0. 155)
b_ind	- 0. 5163	- 0. 3344	- 0. 2807	- 0. 3270
	(0. 735)	(0. 843)	(0. 647)	(0. 855)
cstr2_10	0. 0446	- 0. 0009	0. 0770	- 0. 0279
	(0. 112)	(0. 147)	(0. 118)	(0. 139)
TRPT	0. 1882 **	0. 0815	0. 1997 **	0. 0468
	(0. 083)	(0. 118)	(0. 084)	(0. 120)
csw	- 0. 0790 **	- 0. 1212 **	- 0. 0856 ***	- 0. 1295 ***
	(0. 030)	(0. 052)	(0. 024)	(0. 039)
osw	2. 3443 ***	0. 0854	2. 2235 ***	0. 2134
	(0. 315)	(0. 600)	(0. 233)	(0. 500)
fsize	- 0. 2238 **	- 0. 1881	- 0. 1456 *	- 0. 2455 **
	(0. 084)	(0. 154)	(0. 075)	(0. 102)
age	0. 0720 ***	0. 1216 ***	- 0. 0765	- 0. 0718
	(0. 021)	(0. 035)	(0. 058)	(0. 064)
lev	- 0. 8755 ***	- 1. 3496 ***	- 0. 8741 ***	- 1. 1612 ***
	(0. 266)	(0. 464)	(0. 244)	(0. 408)
Intercept	2. 8215	3. 8947	2. 3455	6. 5394 **
	(1. 959)	(3. 150)	(1. 988)	(2. 691)
Year FE	Yes	Yes	Yes	Yes
N	301	301	301	301
r2_w	0. 643	0. 690	0. 640	0. 688
r2_b	0. 074	0. 289	0. 243	0. 468
r2_o	0. 244	0. 493	0. 416	0. 605

Note: This table reports the regression results of the effects of total related party transactions on corporate valuation from both the fixed effects and the random effects models with year fixed effects, based on the full sample consisting of all observations in the period 2002 – 2013. The dependent variables are defined as the logarithm of (H – or A – shares) market capitalization over total assets. "fe" and "re" in parentheses denote the fixed effect and the random effect models, respectively. $r2\_w$, $r2\_b$, and $r2\_o$ represent within, between, and overall R – squared, respectively. Standard errors (in parentheses) are heteroskedasticity consistent and clustered at the firm level. *** , ** , and * denote significance at the 1% , 5% , and 10% levels, respectively.

Table C17 The Effects of Harmful Related Party Transactions

on Market Valuation from Different Types of

Investors: Full Sample Case (Balanced Panel)

	(1)	(2)	(3)	(4)
	hma (fe)	ama (fe)	hma (re)	ama (re)
sh1	− 0. 5073	− 5. 1645	− 0. 5055	− 5. 5470
	(4. 120)	(6. 323)	(4. 008)	(6. 070)
sh1_sq	0. 2400	3. 4046	0. 1129	3. 9781
	(3. 934)	(7. 210)	(3. 870)	(6. 913)
dual	0. 1118	0. 2724	0. 1110	0. 2621 *
	(0. 121)	(0. 169)	(0. 109)	(0. 157)
b_ind	− 0. 5302	− 0. 3276	− 0. 2911	− 0. 3249
	(0. 738)	(0. 842)	(0. 650)	(0. 852)
cstr2_10	0. 0530	− 0. 0004	0. 0857	− 0. 0273
	(0. 115)	(0. 146)	(0. 120)	(0. 138)
HRPT	0. 1765	0. 1068	0. 2012 *	0. 0610
	(0. 109)	(0. 155)	(0. 109)	(0. 171)
csw	− 0. 0840 **	− 0. 1223 **	− 0. 0906 ***	− 0. 1301 ***
	(0. 031)	(0. 052)	(0. 025)	(0. 039)
osw	2. 3996 ***	0. 0968	2. 2621 ***	0. 2187
	(0. 308)	(0. 609)	(0. 223)	(0. 505)
fsize2	− 0. 2336 **	− 0. 1898	− 0. 1489 *	− 0. 2461 **
	(0. 088)	(0. 155)	(0. 078)	(0. 102)
age1	0. 0749 ***	0. 1222 ***	− 0. 0753	− 0. 0712
	(0. 022)	(0. 035)	(0. 058)	(0. 064)
lev2w	− 0. 8100 ***	− 1. 3337 ***	− 0. 8209 ***	− 1. 1530 ***
	(0. 259)	(0. 475)	(0. 250)	(0. 416)
Intercept	3. 0206	3. 9079	2. 4026	6. 5401 **
	(1. 994)	(3. 122)	(2. 044)	(2. 677)
Year FE	Yes	Yes	Yes	Yes
N	301	301	301	301
r2_w	0. 636	0. 690	0. 632	0. 688
r2_b	0. 066	0. 290	0. 236	0. 469
r2_o	0. 230	0. 494	0. 409	0. 605

Note: This table reports the regression results of the effects of total related party transactions on corporate valuation from both the fixed effects and the random effects models with year fixed effects, based on the full sample consisting of all observations in the period 2002 – 2013. The dependent variables are defined as the logarithm of (H – or A – shares) market capitalization over total assets. "fe" and "re" in parentheses denote the fixed effect and the random effect models, respectively. $r2\_w$, $r2\_b$, and $r2\_o$ represent within, between, and overall R – squared, respectively. Standard errors (in parentheses) are heteroskedasticity consistent and clustered at the firm level. *** , ** , and * denote significance at the 1% , 5% , and 10% levels, respectively.

Table C18   The Effects of Non – tradable Shares Reform on Market Valuation from Different Types of Investors（Balanced Panel）

Model	(1)	(2)	(3)	(4)	(5)	(6)
	hma	hma	hma	ama	ama	ama
sh1	– 4. 3962 *	– 4. 6824	– 1. 4541	– 10. 1708 ***	– 10. 6144 **	– 7. 4122
	(2. 645)	(3. 465)	(4. 121)	(2. 625)	(4. 620)	(5. 872)
sh1_sq	3. 4420	4. 0342	0. 9712	8. 9882 ***	9. 6697 *	6. 1869
	(2. 361)	(3. 317)	(4. 050)	(2. 767)	(4. 951)	(6. 641)
dual	– 0. 0357	0. 0346	0. 2221 **	0. 3045	0. 3035	0. 3337 ***
	(0. 267)	(0. 184)	(0. 099)	(0. 246)	(0. 230)	(0. 129)
b_ind	– 0. 3757	0. 5521	0. 6596	– 1. 3402 *	– 1. 4384	– 1. 1633
	(0. 602)	(0. 609)	(0. 588)	(0. 748)	(0. 941)	(1. 273)
csu2_10	0. 3782 ***	0. 3331 ***	0. 1315	0. 1137	0. 0336	0, 0010
	(0. 095)	(0. 111)	(0. 127)	(0. 105)	(0. 149)	(0. 128)
d_06	0. 2145 **	0. 2395 **	0. 5259 ***	0. 8547 ***	0. 7334 ***	0. 6198 ***
	(0. 084)	(0. 101)	(0. 074)	(0. 082)	(0. 092)	(0. 082)
csw	– 0. 0223	– 0. 1007 ***	– 0. 1071 ***	– 0. 1670 ***	– 0. 1105 ***	– 0. 1336 ***
	(0. 028)	(0. 028)	(0. 025)	(0. 028)	(0. 021)	(0. 036)
osw	1. 7982 ***	2. 5634 ***	2. 7093 ***	1. 1911 ***	0. 4579	0. 6127
	(0. 609)	(0. 375)	(0. 278)	(0. 349)	(0. 337)	(0. 417)
fsize	0. 2172 ***	0. 0433	– 0. 1476 **	– 0. 2514 ***	– 0. 2093 ***	– 0. 1966 ***
	(0. 042)	(0. 046)	(0. 068)	(0. 044)	(0. 053)	(0. 064)
age	0. 0784 ***	0. 0161	– 0. 0324 **	– 0. 0192	0. 0473 *	0. 1007 ***
	(0. 025)	(0. 024)	(0. 016)	(0. 027)	(0. 028)	(0. 019)
lev	– 0. 9280 ***	– 0. 4074 *	– 0. 6162 **	– 0. 3747	– 0. 6778 *	– 0. 9366 *
	(0. 274)	(0. 231)	(0. 294)	(0. 332)	(0. 371)	(0. 484)
Intercept	– 4. 8000 ***	– 0. 9456	2. 4690	7. 4899 ***	5. 9160 ***	4. 4317 ***
	(1. 144)	(1. 377)	(1. 619)	(1. 041)	(1. 419)	(1. 487)
N	156	208	312	156	208	312
r2_w	0. 503	0. 338	0. 397	0. 403	0. 392	0. 504
r2_b	0. 594	0. 575	0. 230	0. 711	0. 553	0. 394
r2_o	0. 558	0. 466	0. 298	0. 570	0. 468	0. 444

Note: This table reports the regression results of the effects of non – tradable shares reform on corporate valuation with a random effects model. The estimates in columns (1), (4) and (7) come from a sub – sample with observations in the period 2002 – 2007; the results in columns (2), (5), and (8) are based on a sub – sample with observations in the period 2002 – 2009; and the estimates in columns (3), (6), and (9) are from the full sample with all observations in the period 2002 – 2013. The dependent variables are defined as the logarithm of (H – or A – shares) market capitalization over total assets. r2_w, r2_b, and r2_o represent within, between, and overall R – squared, respectively. Standard errors (in parentheses) are heteroskedasticity consistent and clustered at the firm level. *** , ** , and * denote significance at the 1% , 5% , and 10% levels, respectively.

References

[1] Adams, R. B., Hermalin, B. E., Weisbach, M. S., 2010. The role of boards of directors in corporate governance: A conceptual framework and survey. Journal of Economic Literature 48, 58 – 107.

[2] Aggarwal, R., Erel, I., Stulz, R., Williamson, R., 2009. Differences in governance practices between U. S. and foreign firms: Measurement, causes, and consequences. Review of Financial Studies 22, 3131 – 3169.

[3] Agrawal, A., Knoeber, C. R., 2001. Do some outside directors play a political role? Journal of Law and Economics 44, 179 – 198.

[4] Allen, F., Qian, J., Qian, M., 2005. Law, finance, and economic growth in china. Journal of Financial Economics 77, 57 – 116.

[5] Bai, C. E., Liu, Q., Lu, J., Song, F. M., Zhang, J., 2004. Corporate governance and market valuation in China. Journal of Comparative Economics 32, 599 – 616.

[6] Bai, J., Philippon, T., Savov, A., 2014. Have financial markets become more informative? Unpublished Working Paper.

[7] Barber, B. M., Lyon, J. D., 1996. Detecting abnormal operating performance: The empirical power and specification of test statistics. Journal of Financial Economics 41, 359 – 399.

[8] Bebchuk, L., Cohen, A., Ferrell, A., 2009. What matters in corporate governance? Review of Financial Studies 22, 783 – 827.

[9] Bebchuk, L. A., Cremers, K., Peyer, U. C., 2011. The CEO pay slice. Journal of Financial Economics 102, 199 – 221.

[10] Berkman, H., Cole, R. A., Fu, L. J., 2011. Political connections and minority – shareholder protection: Evidence from securities – market regulation in China. Journal of Financial and Quantitative Analysis 45, 1391 – 1417.

[11] Bethel, J. E. , Gillan, S. L. , 2002. The impact of the institutional and regulatory environment on shareholder voting. Financial Management , 29 – 54.

[12] Bhagat, S. , Brickley, J. A. , 1984. Cumulative voting: The value of minority shareholder voting rights. Journal of Law and Economics 27, 339 – 365.

[13] Black, B. S. , Jang, H. , Kim, W. , 2006. Does corporate governance predict firms' market values? evidence from Korea. Journal of Law, Economics, and Organization 22, 366 – 413.

[14] Brick, I. E. , Palmon, O. , Wald, J. K. , 2006. CEO compensation, director compensation, and firm performance: evidence of cronyism? Journal of Corporate Finance 12, 403 – 423.

[15] Brown, L. D. , Caylor, M. L. , 2006. Corporate governance and firm valuation. Journal of Accounting and Public Policy 25, 409 – 434.

[16] Bruno, V. , Claessens, S. , 2010. Corporate governance and regulation: Can there be too much of a good thing? Journal of Financial Intermediation 19, 461 – 482.

[17] Burns, N. , Francis, B. B. , Hasan, I. , 2007. Cross – listing and legal bonding: Evidence from mergers and acquisitions. Journal of Banking & Finance 31, 1003 – 1031. Bricks versus Clicks: The Changing Nature of Banking in the 21st Century Special Issue in Memory of Lawrence Goldberg.

[18] Charitou, A. , Louca, C. , Panayides, S. , 2007. Cross – listing, bonding hypothesis and corporate governance. Journal of Business Finance & Accounting 34, 1281 – 1306.

[19] Chen, G. , Firth, M. , Gao, D. N. , Rui, O. M. , 2006. Ownership structure, corporate governance, and fraud: Evidence from china. Journal of Corporate Finance 12, 424 – 448. Corporate Governance.

[20] Cheung, Y. L. , Jing, L. , Lu, T. , Rau, P. R. , Stouraitis, A. , 2009. Tunneling and propping up: An analysis of related party transactions by Chinese listed companies. Pacific – Basin Finance Journal 17, 372 – 393.

[21] Cheung, Y. L. , Rau, P. R. , Stouraitis, A. , 2006. Tunneling, propping, and expropriation: evidence from connected party transactions in Hong Kong. Journal of Financial Economics 82, 343 – 386.

[22] Chhaochharia, V. , Grinstein, Y. , 2007. Corporate governance and firm value: The impact of the 2002 governance rules. The Journal of Finance 62, 1789 – 1825.

[23] Chhaochharia, V. , Laeven, L. , 2009. Corporate governance norms and practices. Journal of Financial Intermediation 18, 405 – 431.

[24] Claessens, S. , Djankov, S. , Fan, J. P. , Lang, L. H. , 2002. Disentangling the incentive and entrenchment effects of large shareholdings. The Journal of Finance 57, 2741 – 2771.

[25] Coffee Jr, J. C. , 1998. Future as history: The prospects for global convergencein corporate governance and its implications. Northwestern University Law Review 93, 641 – 707.

[26] Coffee Jr, J. C. , 2002. Racing towards the top?: The impact of cross – listings and stock market competition on international corporate governance. Columbia Law Review , 1757 – 1831.

[27] DeAngelo, H. , DeAngelo, L. , 1985. Managerial ownership of voting rights: A study of public corporations with dual classes of common stock. Journal of Financial economics 14, 33 – 69.

[28] Doidge, C. , Karolyi, G. A. , Stulz, R. M. , 2004. Why are foreign firms listed in the US worth more? Journal of Financial Economics 71, 205 – 238.

[29] Elsayed, K. , 2007. Does ceo duality really affect corporate performance? Corporate Governance: An International Review 15, 1203 – 1214.

[30] Fan, G. , Wang, X. , Zhu, H. , 2011. NERI INDEX of Marketization of China's Provinces: 2011 Report (in Chinese) . Economic Science Press, Beijing.

[31] Firth, M. , Lin, C. , Liu, P. , Wong, S. M. , 2009. Inside the black box: Bank credit allocation in china's private sector. Journal of Banking & Finance 33, 1144 – 1155.

[32] Francis, B. , Hasan, I. , Song, L. , 2012. Are firm – and country – specific governance substitutes? evidence from financial contracts in emerging markets. Journal of Financial Research 35, 343 – 374.

[33] Gompers, P. , Ishii, J. , Metrick, A. , 2003. Corporate governance and equity prices. The Quarterly Journal of Economics 118, 107 – 156.

[34] Grossman, S. J., Hart, O. D., 1988. One share – one vote and the market for corporate control. Journal of Financial Economics 20, 175 – 202.

[35] Hallock, K. F., 1997. Reciprocally interlocking boards of directors and executive compensation. Journal of Financial and Quantitative Analysis 32, 331 – 344.

[36] Harris, M., Raviv, A., 1988. Corporate governance: Voting rights and majority rules. Journal of Financial Economics 20, 203 – 235.

[37] Hermalin, B. E., Weisbach, M. S., 1988. The determinants of board composition. The RAND Journal of Economics, 589 – 606.

[38] Hermalin, B. E., Weisbach, M. S., 2003. Boards of directors as an endogenously determined institution: a survey of the economic literature. Economic Policy Review, 7 – 26.

[39] Huson, M. R., Malatesta, P. H., Parrino, R., 2004. Managerial succession and firm performance. Journal of Financial Economics 74, 237 – 275.

[40] Iacus, S. M., King, G., Porro, G., 2011. Multivariate matching methods that are monotonic imbalance bounding. Journal of the American Statistical Association 106, 345 – 361.

[41] Iacus, S. M., King, G., Porro, G., 2012. Causal inference without balance checking: Coarsened exact matching. Political Analysis 20, 1 – 24.

[42] Iliev, P., Lins, K., Miller, D., Roth, L., 2011. Shareholder voting and corporate governance around the world, in: AFA 2012 Chicago Meetings Paper.

[43] Jiang, G., Lee, C. M. C., Yue, H., 2010. Tunneling through intercorporate loans: The China experience. Journal of Financial Economics 98, 1 – 20.

[44] Kang, E., Zardkoohi, A., 2005. Board leadership structure and firm performance. Corporate Governance: An International Review 13, 785 – 799.

[45] Kim, W., Sung, T., Wei, S. J., 2011. Does corporate governance risk at home affect investment choices abroad? Journal of International Economics 85, 25 – 41.

[46] Klapper, L., Laeven, L., Love, I., 2006. Corporate governance provisions and firm ownership: Firmlevel evidence from eastern Europe. Journal of International Money and Finance 25, 429 – 444.

[47] Klapper, L. F., Love, I., 2004. Corporate governance, investor protec-

tion, and performance in emerging markets. Journal of Corporate Finance 10, 703 – 728.

[48] La Porta, R. , Lopez – De – Silanes, F. , Shleifer, A. , Vishny, R. , 2002. Investor protection and corporate valuation. The Journal of Finance 57, 1147 – 1170.

[49] La Porta, R. , de Silanes, F. L. , Shleifer, A. , Vishny. , R. , 1997. Legal determinants of external finance. The Journal of Finance 52, 1131 – 1150.

[50] La Porta, R. , de Silanes, F. L. , Shleifer, A. , Vishny. , R. , 1998. Law and finance. Journal of Political Economy 106, 1113 – 1155.

[51] La Porta, R. , de Silanes, F. L. , Shleifer, A. , Vishny. , R. , 2000. Investor protection and corporate governance. Journal of Financial Economics 58, 3 – 27.

[52] Lel, U. , Miller, D. , D. P. , 2008. International cross – listing, firm performance, and top management turnover: A test of the bonding hypothesis. The Journal of Finance 63, 1897 – 1937.

[53] Li, K. , Yue, H. , Zhao, L. , 2009. Ownership, institutions, and capital structure: Evidence from china. Journal of Comparative Economics 37, 471 – 490.

[54] Lu, Y. , Shi, X. , 2012. Corporate governance reform and state owner-ship: Evidence from China. Asia – Pacific Journal of Financial Studies 41, 665 – 685.

[55] Masulis, R. W. , Wang, C. , Xie, F. , 2012. Globalizing the board-room—the effects of foreign directors on corporate governance and firm performance. Journal of Accounting and Economics 53, 527 – 554.

[56] Ni, Y. , Purda, L. , 2012. Does monitoring by independent directors re-duce firm risk? Available at SSRN 1986289 .

[57] Price, R. , Román, F. J. , Rountree, B. , 2011. The impact of govern-ance reform on performance and transparency. Journal of Financial Economics 99, 76 – 96.

[58] Puhani, P. A. , 2012. The treatment effect, the cross difference, and the interaction term in nonlinear "difference – in – differences" models. Economics Letters 115, 85 – 87.

[59] Qian, J. , Zhao, S. , 2011. Shareholder rights and tunneling: Evidence from a quasi – natural experiment. Unpublished Working Paper.

[60] Rubin, D. B. , 1976. Multivariate matching methods that are equal percent bias reducing, I: Some examples. Biometrics 32, 109 – 120.

[61] Ruigrok, W. , Peck, S. I. , Keller, H. , 2006. Board characteristics and involvement in strategic decision making: Evidence from swiss companies *. Journal of Management Studies 43, 1201 – 1226.

[62] Wang, S. S. , Jiang, L. , 2004. Location of trade, ownership restrictions, and market illiquidity: Examining Chinese A – and H – shares. Journal of Banking & Finance 28, 1273 – 1297.

[63] Yeh, Y. H. , Woidtke, T. , 2005. Commitment or entrenchment? Controlling shareholders and board composition. Journal of Banking & Finance 29, 1857 – 1885.

[64] Zhang, H. , 2008. Corporate governance and dividend policy: A comparison of Chinese firms listed in Hong Kong and in the mainland. China Economic Review 19, 437 – 459.

[65] Zingales, L. , 1994. The value of the voting right: A study of the Milan stock exchange experience. Review of financial Studies 7, 125 – 148.

[66] Zingales, L. , 1995. What determines the value of corporate votes? The Quarterly Journal of Economics 110, 1047 – 1073.

This book is the result of a co-publication agreement between China Financial and Economic Publishing House (China) and Paths International Ltd (UK).

Title: Corporate Governance in China: An Empirical Investigation
Author: Chen Yinghui
ISBN: 978-1-84464-740-8
Ebook ISBN: 978-1-84464-741-5

Paths International Ltd

Published in the United Kingdom
www.pathsinternational.com

Printed in the USA
CPSIA information can be obtained
at www.ICGtesting.com
LVHW080455240524
780636LV00004B/47